CRIME TV

Crime TV

Streaming Criminology in Popular Culture

Edited by

Jonathan A. Grubb *and* Chad Posick

NEW YORK UNIVERSITY PRESS

New York

NEW YORK UNIVERSITY PRESS
New York
www.nyupress.org

References to Internet websites (URLs) were accurate at the time of writing. Neither the author nor New York University Press is responsible for URLs that may have expired or changed since the manuscript was prepared.

Library of Congress Cataloging-in-Publication Data
Names: Grubb, Jonathan A., editor. | Posick, Chad, editor.
Title: Crime TV : streaming criminology in popular culture /
edited by Jonathan A. Grubb and Chad Posick.
Description: New York : NYU Press, 2021. | Includes bibliographical references and index.
Identifiers: LCCN 2020048479 | ISBN 9781479804368 (hardback) |
ISBN 9781479884971 (paperback) | ISBN 9781479838639 (ebook) |
ISBN 9781479827916 (ebook other)
Subjects: LCSH: Crime in popular culture. | Criminal behavior. |
Criminal justice, Administration of.
Classification: LCC HV6030 .C735 2021 | DDC 791.45/6556—dc23
LC record available at https://lccn.loc.gov/2020048479

New York University Press books are printed on acid-free paper, and their binding materials are chosen for strength and durability. We strive to use environmentally responsible suppliers and materials to the greatest extent possible in publishing our books.

Manufactured in the United States of America

10 9 8 7 6 5 4 3 2 1

Also available as an ebook

CONTENTS

Eamonn Carrabine

If, as it is often said, we currently live in a golden age of television, then it is the crime drama that lies at the heart of this cultural renaissance. The revolution in the way we watch television began with DVD box sets and time-shift video recorders (such as TiVo and Sky+), which enabled viewers to consume programs in several fragments, or binge-watch on their own terms, rather than stick to the schedule of a broadcaster. The more recent expansion of subscription streaming services like Netflix and Amazon Prime, combined with the ability to view content across multiple platforms, has further transformed the television landscape. *Crime TV* has arrived at a crucial moment in these developments in popular culture. By showcasing representations of the criminal justice system and criminological theory within television shows that powerfully shape how crime itself is understood, the contributors make a groundbreaking statement of popular criminology.

The renaissance of television has given rise to what the critic Anna Leszkiewicz has called "the avid viewer," part of a new audience attracted to longer, more intricate and involved narratives than previous generations, but crucially also one willing to pay for this kind of immersive storytelling.[1] She recalls an interview on BBC's *The Culture Show* in 2008, when: "David Simon let viewers in on a little secret about his HBO show *The Wire*. Citing the show's novelistic approach to storytelling—with a lack of exposition, and complex, multi-layered plots—host Lauren Laverne asked him about the 'contempt' *The Wire* showed for the average viewer. 'What about the casual viewer?' she said, bewildered. 'People who want to dip in, dip out?' Simon just shook his head. Looking over his shoulder, and leaning forward conspiratorially, he whispered: 'Fuck the casual viewer.'"[2]

It was a deliberately provocative statement, not least since the entire premise of broadcast television was organized around inattentive viewing. Because television was so closely integrated into the fabric of daily, domestic life, the characteristic mode of consumption was to glimpse or graze on drama series largely composed of self-contained narratives that could be watched in any order by distracted, casual viewers. In contrast, the avid viewer deploys a literary mode of viewing a text and requires a fierce concentration of effort, preferring a form of television that is more intense, more varied, and more extraordinary than mainstream broadcasters are willing to offer.

The Sopranos (1999–2007) was the first to break the mold, transforming not only HBO's fortunes, but also the nature of television itself.[3] It emerged at a time when the system was disintegrating, the broadcasters' supremacy undermined by new technologies, a proliferation of cable and satellite channels, and the increasing popularity of DVD viewing. *The Sopranos* was regularly described as the best thing on television, but was closer to Jacobean tragedy than conventional crime drama, dealing with blood, comedy, and action on an epic scale, and proved to be highly lucrative to the then fledgling cable channel.

The Wire (2002–2008) has also received much acclaim for how it has pursued rich sociological themes that in the words of William Julius Wilson, speaking at a Harvard seminar in 2008, are worth quoting at length. He unequivocally states that:

> it has done more to enhance our understandings of the challenges of urban life and urban inequality than any other media event or scholarly publication, including studies by social scientists. . . . *The Wire* develops morally complex characters on each side of the law, and with its scrupulous exploration of the inner workings of various institutions, including drug-dealing gangs, the police, politicians, unions, public schools, and the print media, viewers become aware that individuals' decisions and behaviour are often shaped by—and indeed limited by—social, political, and economic forces beyond their control.[4]

Indeed, it has been argued that the series can be understood as a form of social science fiction that stimulates the powers of the sociological imagination for television viewers by detailing the human complexity of social situations in ways that differ markedly from their narration in earlier, formulaic crime dramas.

In this sense, these TV shows can be understood as a form of *popular criminology*, which is far broader than the academic or scientific study of crime. Both Nicole Rafter[5] and Philip Rawlings[6] have independently argued that crime films and the "true crime" genre (their respective subjects) constitute a "popular criminology" that operates in parallel to, but some distance from, academic criminology—where the rejection of the former "by academics often seems tinged with a lofty disdain for the prurience of such work."[7] However, that disregard is hard to sustain given that it is popular criminology that provides the most significant source of public understandings of crime, justice and punishment. A similar point is made by Rafter in her discussion of the ethical and philosophical issues raised in her close reading of a small sample of sex crime films:

> Popular criminology's audience is bigger (even a cinematic flop will reach a larger audience than this article). And its social significance is greater, for academic criminology cannot offer so wide a range of criminological wares. . . . The two types of criminology, popular and academic, complement one another, each contributing in its own way to understandings of crime.[8]

But the two are not equally valued. Rafter, together with Michelle Brown, further elaborated on the unique quality and texture of popular criminology, indicating how taking "criminology to the movies fosters theoretical development."[9]

It is one of the achievements of *Crime TV* that it performs a similar feat as Rafter and Brown's work on cinema,[10] but takes the rich diversity of contemporary television drama as its focus. The contributors to this collection emphasise the irresistible presence of crime in popular culture. Taken together the chapters demonstrates that when criminology immerses itself in cultural phenomenon, it ultimately sees itself in a fresh light. The approach to popular criminology undertaken here delivers on the potential to reinvigorate and broaden the criminological project in a way envisioned by Rafter over a decade ago.[11] Academic and popular discourses about crime are not merely parallel worlds that offer explanations of crime and the experience of justice, but rather they are two domains that "interpenetrate and cross-fertilize each other."[12] Furthermore, each of the pieces in this book addresses a unique criminological theory or element of the criminal justice system to underscore how they appear in a popular television series, advancing understandings of the sources and nature of criminological theory.

In this respect, the book makes criminological theory accessible, lively, and memorable. The selection of theoretical frameworks renders criminology exciting and at the same time demonstrates to readers how key explanations of crime are mobilized on screen, often just beneath the surface. The book reveals how these frameworks can be mined, and in that process of excavation, indicates what we can learn from this important site in the contemporary media landscape and will change the way we interpret criminology. Everyone watches television, and the text is as absorbing as the dramas themselves, opening up a formidable analysis of their complex relationship to larger society.

It is difficult to say whether we are in the middle or nearing the end of television's new golden age, but the sheer abundance of choice could mean digital streaming contains the seeds of its own demise. In 2015, John Landgraf, chief executive of the broadcast network FX, coined the phrase "peak TV," as "there was too much to watch and audiences were becoming exhausted."[13] The already high stakes are rising and the competition is ever more intense, with producers constantly searching for a format that minimizes risk. The incredible success of *Game of Thrones* (2011–2019) has shown the industry that extravagantly produced, visually stunning shows set in fantasy worlds and exotic locations, with international appeal and genre-shifting changes in tone, can be enormously profitable. The strength of *Crime TV* is that it is the first work to bring a critical, systematic, and nuanced criminological treatment to this new kind of storytelling. Individual chapters will change the way we view television crime dramas, while the sum will transform our understanding of criminology.

Introduction

Jonathan A. Grubb and Chad Posick

Media consumption in contemporary society has become an increasingly significant and growing part of everyday life. The Nielsen Total Audience Report for Q3 of 2018 underscored that the average adult in the US spends more than 10 hours per day interacting with media.[1] Social networking usage is an important part of the total media usage picture; data from the Pew Research Center indicates that more than two-thirds of adults use Facebook, with 18–24-year-olds also commonly using Snapchat (78%), Instagram (71%), and Twitter (45%).[2] Nevertheless, while social networking has expanded, the most common media consumed is live and time-shifted (i.e., recorded for later viewing) television, which makes up 4 hours and 13 minutes on average on a given day.[3] When video from smartphones, tablets, gaming consoles, and computers is factored into the calculation, the total number of hours of video consumed jumps up to 5 hours and 24 minutes, which equates to more than half of all media consumption in a given day.[4]

Complementary to the growth in video viewership, the rapid expansion of TV streaming services such as Netflix, Hulu, Amazon Prime Video, and HBO Max is evident. Recent internet usage data collected on fixed internet access connections in North America found that three video streaming services (Netflix, Amazon Video, and Hulu) accounted for 42% of all peak downstream traffic during March 2016.[5] Moreover, research on millennials indicates that the overwhelming majority utilize TV streaming services. One recent study found that 70% of individuals between the age of 18 and 29 use a TV streaming service, with slightly more than a quarter (26.5%) in the same age bracket having never subscribed to cable.[6] From this perspective, there has been an increase in watching shows through streaming services as a whole, but this is being led by younger generations such as millennials and generation Z.

The media include several forms of communication—such as TV, newspapers, and the radio—that influence individuals' beliefs and even behaviors. The three types of media include news, infotainment, and entertainment. The news intends to present unbiased and objective news that accurately presents reality (e.g., NPR's news programs, the Associated Press). Infotainment provides information through entertainment which may be objective, but that is not the primary purpose of this type of media (e.g., *The Daily Show*, *Last Week Tonight*). Finally, entertainment is purely to entertain and is not intended to be objective, unbiased, or realistic.[7] The shows discussed in this book are entertainment and not intended to be realistic or accurate in their portrayal of people, events, and society as a whole. However, these shows can be useful to teachers, students, and practitioners of criminal justice and criminology.

There are several reasons why we believe that this book is needed and important for the field of criminal justice and criminology. First, it can be used as a pedagogical tool to draw students into critical practical and theoretical issues in the field that have real impact on the world. Often theory courses are dreaded by students and learning the components of theories couldn't be more boring to them. By using popular TV shows, students can use an exciting medium to illustrate theoretical concepts. Second, students often already have access to streaming services such as Netflix and Hulu reducing the cost of course material. Third, most people get their information and knowledge about crime and justice from TV shows, movies, and other popular outlets, but these sources often misconstrue information. While examples from the media can be used to illuminate theory and issues related to the administration of justice, they can also be used to highlight misunderstandings about how the criminal justice system works and about the foundations of why people commit crime. In other words, streaming shows can be used to highlight where the media get it "right" and where they get it "wrong."

The contributions in this volume include discussions of the role of race in criminal justice processing, crime as a spectacle in society, and criminological theories such as strain theory, rational choice, and techniques of neutralization. All essential topics for theory and practice.

The following is a roadmap of the book. Chapter 1 frames the role of punishment by questioning issues of morality and just deserts within a penal utopia. Chapter 2 incorporates social bonds to explore the suicide of the central character. Chapter 3 examines the role of strain, specifically from the perspective of General Strain Theory, on emergence of criminal activity. Chapter 4 focuses on psychopathy and how that explains homicidal violence. Chapter 5 examines the role of violence committed both by humans and androids toward each other. Chapter 6 examines radical feminism to showcase dystopian aspects of real life. Chapter 7 centers on a cultural criminological framing with attention placed on how terrorism is constructed from a cultural perspective. Chapter 8 showcases the role of corporations involved in white-collar crime and social harm. Chapter 9 details how popular punitiveness is used to carry out punishment squarely in the eye of the public. Chapter 10 focuses on how a zombie apocalypse can be used to understand radical social change and the impact it has on crime. Chapter 11 incorporates radical criminology to address an exploitative capitalist corporation. Chapter 12 draws on labeling theory to showcase how labeling can have significant and sometimes unintended influences on individuals. Chapter 13 places attention on techniques of neutralization, underscoring how a title character as well as his colleagues utilize each of the original five techniques to neutralize behaviors and attitudes. Chapter 14 describes how conflict theory applies to group competition and conflict between superheroes and an evil group of individuals, as well as how norms and values influence social behavior. Chapter 15 relays how feminist criminology can be used to tap into the perversion of masculinity exhibited by the lead characters. Chapter 16 underscores how race, ethnicity, social movements, and immigration intersect with the criminal justice system.

One additional but important point that should be mentioned prior to readers jumping headfirst into this volume is that basically all chapters have spoilers (to varying extents) for the show that is being highlighted.

1

"The Man Who Passes the Sentence Should Swing the Sword"

PENAL UTOPIAS IN *GAME OF THRONES*

Stephen Wakeman

This chapter is concerned with representations of punishment in HBO's hit fantasy drama series *Game of Thrones* (hereafter, *GoT*). It is argued here that, read as a cultural text, GoT can be understood as a form of "popular criminology" in that it provides a set of narratives that can complement and enhance academic discourses on the subjects it represents, punishment especially.[1] In this respect, the arguments that follow sit within a wider theoretical context of works within criminology that aim to take popular cultural representations of crime and deviance from film and TV more seriously as sites of knowledge and meaning-making in and of themselves.[2] In this respect, it is hoped that the present chapter will contribute to what has been described as the "popular criminological project."[3]

Before moving much further, however, a word on *GoT* itself is warranted. The show is an adaptation of George R. R. Martin's series of epic fantasy novels, *A Song of Ice and Fire*, and to call it "critically acclaimed" would be an understatement; *GoT* has been phenomenally successful both critically and commercially. It is surprising then that, as of yet, the show has not received even minimal attention from criminologists. This can most probably be put down to the fact that it depicts a fantasy world and, as such, is less easily "read" in terms of criminological significance than shows such as *The Wire*, *Breaking Bad*, or *The Sopranos*. This is an oversight on the part of many criminologists; the fantasy realm of *GoT* reflects our current penal realities in multiple ways. The main one of these is the show's willingness to demonstrate the violence that is at the heart of punishment.

GoT can be understood as important in this respect—it is a cultural site through which the harms of punishment can be critically interrogated. As David Garland has noted, punishment's pains are all too frequently and easily concealed:

> Because the public does not hear the anguish of prisoners and their families, because the discourses of the press and popular criminology present offenders as "different," and less than fully human, and because penal violence is generally sanitized, situational and of low visibility, the conflict between our civilized sensibilities and the often brutal routines of punishment is minimized and made more tolerable. Modern penalty is thus institutionally ordered and discursively represented in ways which deny the violence which continues to inhere in its practices.[4]

Garland's point is that discourses of punishment frequently dilute its harmful realities—that is, the ways in which people talk about punishment often obscure or minimize the extent to which it harms people. It is in this respect that thinking about *GoT* in terms of punishment becomes very useful; the show provides a space through which the pain and the suffering of punishment are revealed to be inherently violent. The fact that the show renders the pains of punishment—upon those who are subject to it, those who impose and enact it, and those who witness it—so starkly visible means that it is of significant utility here.

In essence, the goal of this chapter is to think a little differently about some contemporary (and well-established) debates around punishment through the ways in which they are culturally (re)presented in *GoT*. Toward that end, the arguments are presented around three main themes: (1) the moral basis of the right to punish; (2) the emerging phenomenon of the privatization of punishment; and (3) the forward-facing potentials of what Ian Loader calls a "public philosophy of punishment"[5] as they are embodied in *GoT*'s narratives. Throughout, the task is to introduce the reader to these debates and think critically about the value of *GoT*—as a cultural paradigm of said debates—in moving them forward. Finally, while this should not come as a surprise in a text such as this, it would be remiss of me as an author and fan of TV shows not to state it here before the chapter proceeds: what follows below does contain spoilers.

Game of Thrones as Popular Criminology

Popular criminology is, for Nicole Rafter, "a category composed of discourses about crime found not only in film but also on the Internet, on television and in newspapers, novels and rap music and myth."[6] Following this, what Stephen Wakeman presents as the "popular criminological project" involves the analysis of the ways in which encounters between academic knowledge and popular cultural representations of criminologically significant subjects can leave both transformed in productive ways.[7] This type of analysis is about learning progressively from the interface between academic theory and cultural (re)presentation, and understanding them as *complementary*, rather than competitive or distinctive, discourses. The best way to achieve is through "reading" crime media critically to reveal what Stuart Hall called the "double stake" of popular culture.[8] What he meant by this was that all popular cultural forms at the same time both transmit ideologies (of gender, imperialism, racism, etc.) and challenge their hegemonic grip. The task, then, for meaningful popular criminological analyses such as this is as follows: to identify where it is that *GoT* transmits or conveys problematic ideologies of punishment, but also where it challenges the hegemony of our wider ideas about this subject. How is it exactly that *GoT* can enhance our understanding of punishment's problems, and where can it generate new thinking along these lines?

The Moral Basis of Punishment

GoT clearly shows punishment used as a response to rule breaking on multiple occasions. The show can be read as a cultural manifestation of questions around the use of punishment in society today. One of the most prominent examples is Daenerys's decision to crucify the slave traders she encounters in season four's "Breaker of Chains" (S4E3). The opening scenes of the episode show Daenerys arriving at the great city of Meereen, accompanied by her army of former slave soldiers that she had previously freed from the cities of Astapor and Yunkai. The slave masters of Meereen are aware of her coming and what it might mean for them. In an attempt to warn her off, they crucified 163 children and placed them on mile markers along the route she takes to the city.

Daenerys arrives at Meereen and delivers her speech to the slaves (and their masters) hidden behind the city's great walls:

> I am Daenerys Stormborn. Your Masters have may have told you lies about me, or they may have told you nothing. It does not matter; I have nothing to say to them. I speak only to you. First, I went to Astapor—those who were slaves in Astapor now stand behind me, *free*. Next I went to Yunkai—those who were slaves in Yunkai now stand behind me, *free*. Now I have come to Meereen. I am not your enemy, your enemy is beside you. Your enemy steals and murders your children, your enemy has nothing for you but chains and suffering and commands. I do not bring you commands, I bring you a choice. And I bring your enemies what they deserve. (Daenerys, S4E3, spoken in High Valyrian, English translation from show subtitles)

It is important to note here the *morality* that underpins her words; Daenerys is on a mission to retake the Iron Throne, but the army she intends to use to achieve this will *not* be made up of slaves. Her new world will be a world where slavery is abolished. There is little here morally to perturb any right-thinking person.

Following a short siege and uprising, the city of Meereen is taken under Daenerys's control. The slave masters who were not killed in the uprising surrender and are now her prisoners. At this point she makes a very calculated choice in the name of "justice"—she has 163 of the slave masters crucified, one for each of the slave children that suffered the same fate at the masters' hands. She does this with a degree of conviction that is quite chilling and certainly transcends any gender-inspired notions of feminine aversion to violence. She acts with a direct will to violence that is all too frequently denied women in popular cultural representations of their transgressive behaviors.[9]

While questions of gender are hugely important, they are perhaps not of primary concern here. What matters more to the present argument is the fact that—in Daenerys's mind at least—the eye-for-an-eye crucifixion is the *only* form of response that is fair, *the only form of punishment that is "just."* Ser Barristan Selmy, one of her most trusted advisors, pleads with her not to do it. He counsels her that sometimes it is wise to answer injustice with mercy. Her response is telling: "I will answer injustice with *justice.*" This is not the first time the viewer has seen her respond with violent retribution—in "Valar Morghulis" (S2E10), she has two people who plotted against her (one of them a close friend for the first two seasons of the show) locked in a vault in darkness to suffer a slow death of starvation. The crucifixion of the slavers, however, is new in one important respect; Daenerys takes this course of action through an allegiance to notions of *justice*. That is, she enacts this punishment upon the slavers through a *moral belief* that it is the right thing to do. Simplistic retribution, maybe, but here it is invoked with recourse to notions of *justice* as a moral philosophy to live by, and this is interesting in a number of different ways.

The underlying premise in Daenerys's actions is simple—there is a moral basis to punishment and punishing those who have transgressed laws, rules, norms, sensibilities, and/or collective values is justifiable. This is the elephant in the room in much debate about the nature of punishment in contemporary criminological scholarship; many people share her position, and there is a sound case to be made in democratic societies that punishment has a place as the "will of the people."[10] Yet this is an uncomfortable truth in an era of mass incarceration, where the pains of imprisonment in the US[11] and other nations such as China and Russia[12] have been well documented. Moreover, we are readily aware of the negative impacts of the "less punitive" alternatives to custodial sentencing.[13] *GoT* can be understood as a cultural representation of these tensions and antagonisms—of the complex questions that surround the moral basis of the right to punish. Importantly, it provides a cultural medium through which these questions can be stripped down to their philosophical core and then reimagined in myriad ways.

In essence, what the viewer sees here is a culturally constructed debate around the moral justifications for punishment in the name of justice. Her contestations around what to do here are emblematic of David Boonin's pioneering work around punishment.[14] Boonin's analysis positions punishment as a "problem" first and foremost: it "requires moral justification and poses a genuine moral problem."[15] Through undertaking such a moral/philosophical analysis, Boonin reaches the conclusion that punishment should be abandoned as a response to wrongdoing as it is unjustifiable upon moral grounds. Where Daenerys sees punishment as just and, in this instance, as *absolutely necessary*, Boonin's counterargument would be that necessity is not enough of an argument to support this claim alone. He goes to great lengths to support this theory, concluding:

> [S]o long as there is at least one acceptable way that we could do without punishment, the appeal to necessity must be rejected. And if the appeal to necessity must be rejected, then our inability to solve the problem of punishment does suffice to show that we should abolish the practice of punishment.[16]

Necessarily summarized, Boonin's position is that if there is a possible alternative (as there is in Daenerys's case), then the act is not necessary and recourse to it should be abandoned. The philosophical implications of this are as follows: if punishment can be understood as being unnecessary due to the existence of an alternative, then, as it involves the infliction of harm, it cannot ever be morally justifiable and should, as such, be abandoned.

Whether or not one finds Boonin's arguments persuasive is not crucial here—what does matter in the present context is the fact that they evidence the inherent contradictions and contestations that reside at the core of debates about punishment. Considered alongside their cultural (re)presentation in *GoT*, they become even more interesting. If ever there were morally justifiable responses to deviancy then they would surely come as a result of generations of slavery and the murder and crucifixion of almost two hundred children; given current sensibilities around these issues, it is easy to see how a punitive response would be easily (re)presented as justifiable. However, *GoT* neatly encapsulates the complexities of this scenario through the ensuing discussion between Daenerys and her advisors. This scene is highly symbolic of the debates about the justification for punishment alluded to above: on the one hand, there is the retributive case that these callous acts deserve some form of punitive response and that that response should be commensurate with their severity, yet on the other hand is the argument that a punitive response remains unjustifiable on moral/ethical grounds as, philosophically speaking, it cannot be sustainably argued to be a *necessity*. In this respect, this brief narrative from within one episode of *GoT* is emblematic of wider debates about punishment and its justification in society today. The "double stake" is evident—the show both conveys the ideology of punitiveness and challenges its hegemonic status at the same time.

In summary, it is almost certainly the case that a casual viewing of *GoT* leaves one with the impression that punitive responses to rule breaking are justifiable. In this instance, however, a more critical viewing of the show reveals it to have more to offer the criminological imagination. It is possible to understand *GoT* as a cultural embodiment of the ongoing debates around punishment and its moral basis. *GoT* also has a contribution to make to debates about the ways in which punishment is carried out. Or, more precisely, by *whom* punishment is carried out.

Punishment, Privatization, and the State

In the show's opening episode, "Winter Is Coming" (S1E1), Ned Stark is confronted with a deserter from the Night's Watch. The penalty for desertion from this post (a form of punishment itself) is known across the land—it is death. There is no trial, no due process, no right to appeal. "Justice" is swift and absolute. Ned is out with a band of his noblemen and his (male) children when they find the deserter. Once his identity is ascertained, punishment will be inflicted there and then. The man is strapped to a large stone; Ned draws his sword and sentences him to die for his crime. Within a moment of speaking his words, Ned swings his sword and removes the man's head in a single blow. Despite the brutality of the act, it is obvious to the viewer that Ned has acted with a degree of compassion in giving the man a quick and clean death.

Almost as soon as the act is finished, Ned goes straight to the side of his young son, Brandon, to explain to him what he just saw (as a young boy not even in his teens, this was the first time Brandon had witnessed such an act, complicated by the fact that it was his father who carried it out). "You understand why I did it?" Ned asks Brandon, "Do you understand why *I* had to kill him?" Brandon's response is to confirm the righteousness of the rule of law, but Ned goes one step further as he explains that while this is certainly true, it is also important that it was *he* who actually undertook the act of punishing the man: "the man who passes the sentence should swing the sword," he calmly yet authoritatively tells his dutiful young son. What the viewer encounters here is a belief that the rule of law—if it is to remain legitimate and righteous—*must* be enforced by *the* agent of that law itself rather than an entity working on its behalf.

Within Ned's seemingly simple declaration can be discerned a key theme that runs through contemporary debates about punishment as a response to rule breaking—the question of *who* is an appropriate entity to actually carry out punishment. Ned's belief is clear: it is *his* responsibility, and his alone, to carry out the sentence that he has been granted the power to impose. The fact that Ned is continually referred to in the show as "an honorable man" or a "man of honor" (even long after his death) only serves to reinforce the symbolism of his words and actions in this context—such men are few and far between in *GoT*. This is an early scene, and its narrative is crucial to the whole. *GoT* again acts as a cultural embodiment of the tensions and antagonisms of "doing punishment," but here takes a significantly political position and maintains it through the entirety of the show. It runs as follows: if one has the power to punish the infraction of laws that one has been granted (or taken) the power to set, then one has a *moral responsibility* to carry out said punishment oneself. Symbolically, this is not difficult to read as an affirmation of the belief that the state must be responsible for administering punishment itself. If nation-states have the power to impose penalties for the breaking of their laws, then it is the nation-states themselves that ought to be responsible for the carrying out those punishments, *not* private corporations acting on their behalf.

It becomes evident that there is significant crossover between *GoT* and the works of critical criminologists around the problems associated with the privatization of prisons in Western democracies like the UK and the US. The privatization of criminal justice apparatuses such as the prison has been noted for some time to be a key strategy of wider systems of neoliberal governance. Jonathan Simon and David Garland have both made this point well in their seminal works, *Governing through Crime* and *The Culture of Control*, respectively.[17] The central claim is that the privatization of criminal justice apparatuses like the prison is a core, constitutive component of the shrinking neoliberal state. There is much value in the arguments to be found in these works, while some potentially more progressive ideas can be found in the works of British abolitionist scholars like Joe Sim and David Scott.[18] Importantly, in considering the two sets of work in line with *GoT*, the double stake of popular culture—of containment *and* resistance, of hegemony *and* change—again becomes visible.

To illustrate this point, the honorableness of Ned Stark in both his actions and words above can be read as conveying an ideological position that the privatization of punishment systems is immoral—that the state has a responsibility to punish itself and to do so justly and humanely. This can be understood as reflective of the core arguments of both Garland and Simon:[19] that neoliberalism is a problematic force that is eroding the abilities of the state to operate its justice systems effectively and/or in a morally responsible manner. In this respect, the show is conveying an established narrative from within academic theory—antiprivatization/antineoliberalism. However, Ned's honorableness can be viewed in an alternative light: he takes on the responsibility of carrying out the "necessary evil" of punishment so that he can assume responsibility for it himself and thus shield the state (or in this instance, the realm) from being tainted by its evil. Ned is first and foremost a servant to the realm and to the rule of the king. He believes this to be the highest form of morality, and his commitment to it is unflinching. The alternative reading here runs as follows: Ned believes that swinging the sword is in fact wrong, that it is an evil act in and of itself, and that, as such, it should *not* be undertaken by the morally righteous entity of the realm.

To support this idea further, "The Kingsroad" (S1E2) is useful. This episode sees a confrontation between Ned and the king (Ned is both "Hand of the King" and his closest friend) due to a fight between their children that resulted in a pet direwolf belonging to Ned's youngest daughter, Arya, biting Joffrey, King Robert's son and heir to the throne. At the command of the king, the wolf is to be killed to end the whole affair. However, the wolf in question cannot be found, and the king caves to pressure from his wife (and Joffrey's mother) and commands that the wolf of Ned's other daughter, Sansa, be killed instead. Despite both his daughters' pleas, Ned reluctantly agrees to this as it is "the king's command" and then once more steps up and undertakes the killing himself. This symbolism matters, and it is not inconsequential either that the show makes another key symbolic link at this point—at the very second Ned kills the wolf, his son Brandon is shown to awaken from unconsciousness after being pushed from a tower. Brandon's "new" consciousness is vitally important to the evolving story.

The symbolism is clear: the awakening of Brandon as Ned once again reluctantly kills as punishment—through his commitment to undertaking such acts himself rather than the good and righteous realm—can be read as congruent with the claims of abolitionist thinkers that punishment itself is wrong. That is, *GoT*'s counterhegemonic contribution argues that the debate should not be about *who* punishes in the name of the law, but rather about whether or not punishment itself has any place in the makings of a progressive, humanistic, and righteous state. As Sim notes, criminological debates about prison privatization (and the role of neoliberalism more generally) frequently fail to actually question the legitimacy of prison itself.[20] The specifics, the practicalities, the conflicting political and economic posturing of such debates obscure the fact that the prison itself is an evil institution and has no place in a civilized society. Moreover, such debates fail to recognize that:

> those who [are] detained in the new privatized network [are] the same groups as those who had *always* been detained in the institution [of the prison] since its emergence two hundred years earlier: the economically marginalized, the poor, the powerless: a social detritus whose makeup in the late twentieth century [is] increasingly racialized and genderized.[21]

While we argue about the politics of neoliberalism and privatization in the prison, we obscure the fact that it seems here that little has changed—the poor and marginalized continue to be disproportionately targeted and harmed by the prison, no matter what its underlying politics are. In the present context, this is not so much a question of *who* should swing the sword, *but if it should actually be swung at all*.

The link here with abolitionist philosophy is clear: the question is not about the revision of criminal justice practices, but rather about their very legitimacy. Ned's beliefs can be understood as a critique of prison privatization or as direct opposition to the role of punishment in society. The symbolism of Brandon's awakening as Ned kills the wolf is crucial in this respect; Ned undertakes the evil of punishment himself and thus ushers in the possibility of a new world awakening. In abolitionist terms, a "new" world is one in which punishment can be radically reconsidered. As Scott argues: "abolitionist praxis is essential to the creation of an *alternative power base* that can be utilized to challenge the role, function, and legitimacy of the penal apparatus of the capitalist state."[22] In this respect, the question of who swings the sword is so much more complex than it initially appears, and through engaging with it critically, *GoT* can again be positioned as a cultural manifestation of such debates. Paradoxically for such a violent show, *GoT* is in fact a crucial site through which penal practices can be interrogated, debated, and reimagined all at the same time. Paradox is entirely the right word here too, as through its violence and bloodshed, the show actually constructs a space through which questions of penal moderation can be engaged with. It is to such questions that this chapter now turns.

Toward a Philosophy of Penal Moderation

GoT can be understood as constituting a cultural embodiment of an agenda for changing views on punishment. The show has discernible elements of utopian thinking, which can be aligned with progressive philosophies of punishment in contemporary criminological scholarship, specifically, the "public philosophy of penal moderation" that Loader describes.[23] For Loader:

> A public philosophy seeks to foster debate about the choices "we" make in response to crime (in terms of representations of offenders, public discourse about justice, justifications for punishment etc.); to clarify what is at stake when a society decides to punish, and to highlight what our choices say about who "we" individually and collectively are, or aspire to become.[24]

GoT can be understood in the same light—as a means by which we can start to ask far-reaching questions about the ways in which we punish, to what ends, and what this says about "us" as a society.

To illustrate this point, in "The Spoils of War" (S7E4), Jon Snow is asked by Daenerys what he would do in her position, the underlying premise of the question being should she use her dragons to storm her enemy's stronghold—a battle strategy that will certainly win her the war she is fighting, but kill untold numbers of noncombatant civilians in the process. His response is interesting when considered alongside the above quotation from Loader:

> I never thought dragons would exist again, no one did. The people that follow you know that you made something impossible happen. Maybe that helps them believe that you can make other impossible things happen, build a world that's different from the shit one they've always known? But if you use them [motions toward the dragons flying in the distance], to melt castles and burn cities, you're not different, you're just more of the same. (Jon Snow, S7E4)

The implication here is that Daenerys has the opportunity to *do something different*; to show the world that an alternative future is not only imaginable, but plausible too, *if* "we" make the right choices about what course of action we take. For Loader, a philosophy of penal moderation is about asking questions around the reasons why we punish people, what we hope to achieve through punishment, and what said punishments might look like. Such a philosophy is *forward thinking*; it is progressive in that it seeks to improve a future world, rather than understand a present one. Daenerys's choice is similar in nature; it is about *reimagining* a future world. The future world in this instance is one in which dragons might very well exist but will not be used to maim and kill. The symbolism here is again clear—this is emblematic of an alternative "utopian" future in which systems of punishment might very well exist, but *not* in the form that they presently are or have been in the past. They will no longer be used to "maim and kill," but might instead be put to alternative uses, with alternative visions underpinning their purpose.

The final task of this chapter then, is to position *GoT* as a cultural manifestation of this alternative "penal utopian future." The term "penal utopia" is used with caution here and somewhat tentatively as an umbrella concept symbolic of a better penal world; it is *not* used derogatively with recourse to the ideas of penal reformers about making the present prison system better or more fit for purpose, as it is employed most usefully by Scott.[25] Utopia in this instance is used as an imagined alternative to the present arrangement, not just their reassessment and/ or rearrangement. This short chapter is not the place to debate the semantics of what does or does not constitute "utopia," however, all that matters in this instance is the employment of the term as indicative of a better penal future and the fact that *GoT* can be understood as providing a fitting starting point for its theoretical development. This is the case because in addition to the above questions around the morality and responsibility of punishment, *GoT* offers one final set of questions that can be understood as symbolic of debates about penal futures—the role of *deserts* in punishment.

Any utopian vision of future systems of punishment ought to begin with asking a set of questions around the extent to which punishments are deserved. If there is a case to be made for the imposition of punitive sanctions as a response to rule breaking, in other words, the *censure* of acts deemed socially undesirable (which, as argued above, there very probably *is*), then questions have to be asked around the form that these sanctions should take. That is, a penal utopia must involve discussion of punishments' *proportionality* in relation to the "crimes" to which they respond. Put another way, a constitutive component of a progressive penal utopia *must* involve thinking critically about which punishments are fitting to which crimes. Following the path mapped out by Loader makes visible a link with long-standing debates around deserts theory that is most useful in this context.[26]

In the episode "Kissed by Fire" (S3E5), Robb Stark, as King in the North, finds himself in a predicament. One of his key bannermen, Rikard Karstark (a lord whose family contributes more than half of all the fighting men in Robb's army), and five co-conspirators stand before him guilty of murdering two young children Robb was holding as hostages (the nephews of Tywin Lannister, Robb's enemy). Robb deems this act to be treason as, in his eyes, it is a betrayal of his direct orders as king. What follows is interesting in a number of respects. First, Robb sends Lord Karstark down to the dungeon to await a decision on his punishment. Robb then orders that the five men who helped him kill the children be hanged right away. One of them screams a plea for mercy; he claims to have done nothing, that he was "just the watcher." Robb's response is to order his men to hang this man last, so that he can "watch the others die first." The next day, and against the advice of his wife, his mother, and his other advisors, Robb executes Lord Karstark ceremonially by beheading him in the castle courtyard.

Robb's process is symbolic of the tensions within contemporary debates about punishment and deserts; he *has* to act, there *must* be some form of censure resulting from the killing of unarmed children by grown men. The question he is presented with is *what* exactly he should do. In the story, each action has consequences—to execute Lord Karstark will result in the Karstark family withdrawing their troops from Robb's campaign, virtually assuring he cannot win his war. But not responding to treason such as this will weaken his position as king—moreover, it would be an assault on his honor. He questions the extent to which his war can be considered righteous and legitimate if he cannot even provide "justice" to murdered children. While his choices are far from perfect—hanging five people can hardly be considered progressive—he does act with honor here; he follows his father's dictum to the letter, and he makes a point of taking Lord Karstark's head himself.

This symbolically represents the utopian discussions that must take place to move punishment forward. Progressive penal policy must involve questioning the foundations of punishment, and this has to involve asking what punishments are proportionate to which crimes. Robb's anguish is emblematic of the potential consequences of ill-conceived penal responses to transgression. The wider symbolism of this act is important too—this course of action results in Robb attending a wedding at the castle of Walder Frey where he is himself killed. In this respect, *GoT* can be understood as offering a choice of outcomes through its (re)presentation of the tensions and antagonisms that underpin questions of deserts with recourse to punishment: it is time to rethink our approach to censuring acts, or face the most devastating of consequences for continuing with our established ways.

Conclusion

Game of Thrones is a meaningful cultural site through which questions of punishment and its philosophical underpinnings can be engaged with theoretically. The ultimate aim of this chapter has been to engender some different thinking around punishment, and it is hoped that this has been achieved in at least three distinct (yet interrelated) areas. First, around the question of morality: to what extent is punishment a matter of morality, and to what extent, if any, can the infliction of pain upon others be considered morally justifiable? Second, the politics of punishment were engaged with and questions of who should punish—if anyone should—were presented as pivotal. Engaging critically with alternative readings of the show's narratives was shown to be most useful in moving debates around these issues forward. Finally, the show itself was presented as a form of penal utopia, not in the traditional sense of the term, but with recourse to the fact that it can facilitate thinking about punishment and deserts in terms of penal moderation, which can be understood as a utopian exercise.

By way of an endpoint, it is hoped that the chapter has done its job of acting as a starting point for some critical debates about punishment and society as they are (re)presented in popular culture. It is also hoped that the chapter will help inspire more of this sort of work in contemporary criminology. As Garland and Sparks stated some time ago, academic criminology cannot hope to maintain any sort of monopoly over knowledge about crime in the media-saturated, deviance-obsessed societies that we see today in Western democracies like the US and UK.[27] There is a wealth of criminologically significant media out there just waiting to be discovered, read, and critically dissected by criminologists interested in thinking differently about their worlds.

2

13 Reasons Why and the Importance of Social Bonds

Ashley K. Fansher and Patrick Q. Brady

While most criminological theories attempt to explain factors that influence or entice people to engage in delinquent behavior, control theorists, in contrast, focus on why people conform. Control theorists argue that all people are similar in their inherent pursuit of immediate gratification, yet refrain from engaging in delinquency due to internal (e.g., consciousness, guilt, self-control) and external controls or restraints (e.g., family, school, the law) to which they are subject.[1] One of the leading control theories is social bond theory, which was developed by Travis Hirschi in his seminal book, *Causes of Delinquency*.[2] Social bond theory suggests that social bonds—which represent the degree to which individuals are attached to others, committed to/involved in conventional plans of action, and endorse beliefs in conventional values—inhibit delinquent behavior out of individuals' fear of jeopardizing investments in relationships with significant others and social institutions (e.g., school/employment).[3]

To date, social bond theory is one of the most empirically tested and validated explanations of delinquent and criminal behavior.[4] While the strength of association between bonds and offending ranges from low to moderate,[5] there is considerable evidence to suggest that strong social bonds inhibit delinquent and criminal behavior.[6] Previous studies have found that various elements of social bonds significantly predict a host of deviant behaviors, including tobacco use among adolescents,[7] alcohol and substance use,[8] and the likelihood of driving under the influence,[9] as well as status offenses, minor delinquency, and serious offending behaviors.[10]

According to Hirschi, humans are naturally inclined to commit crime because it is the easiest and most expedient method to satiate our needs and desires.[11] For example, stealing money is easier than obtaining it through conventional means, such as finding a job opening, dealing with the stress of the interview, and exerting effort over time before being paid. What distinguishes those who do engage in delinquency from those who conform is the extent to which "natural motives are controlled."[12] As a result, Hirschi set out to identify what social factors restrained or redirected people from engaging in delinquent behavior. Hirschi argued that conformity was instilled through relationships and varied according to the strength of one's bond to conventional society.[13] Moreover, social bond theory contends that delinquency and offending occur when the mechanisms that are meant to inhibit negative behavior (i.e., social bonds) are limited, broken, and/or nonexistent. Social bonds are represented by four elements that independently and collectively regulate delinquent behavior: attachment, commitment, involvement, and belief.[14] Each bond has a negative relationship to delinquency and the stronger each element is, the less likely one is to offend.[15] A revised version of Hirschi's original theory, combined with his later work regarding self-control,[16] suggests that these bonds, and the consequences of losing them, are cumulative.[17] In other words, the more a person has to lose, the less likely they are to risk it.

We employ social bond theory to examine *13 Reasons Why*, considering many of the factors Hannah claims to be the reason behind her suicide. The importance of social bonds as protective factors for antisocial behavior are supported in the literature with systematic reviews,[18] meta-analyses,[19] longitudinal studies,[20] and even meta-analyses of longitudinal studies.[21] Collectively, the evidence suggests that suicidal thoughts, attempts, and behaviors among youths are associated with prior victimization and poor attachments to family and peers, all of which were experienced by Hannah during her final year. Despite the sensitive nature of the issue, it is important to remember throughout this chapter that, from a moral and legal standpoint, suicide is a deviant and criminal act even if it appears to be "victimless."

Throughout the season, and as treated in more detail below, Hannah discusses the 13 reasons she felt contributed to her suicide, in order: reputation rumors, losing a close friend, unwanted attention, being stalked, escalation of reputation rumors, feelings of a cemented reputation, heightened loneliness, betrayal of trust, witnessing a sexual assault, involvement in the death of a stranger, her inability to trust anyone, her own person victimization, and the failure of her last attempt at getting help. The events discussed may not appear in the order in which they occurred in Hannah's life, but each one contributed to a breakdown of social bonds, which left Hannah feeling that suicide was her only remaining choice.

Attachment

Hirschi argues that attachment, which refers to the connections we have with others, including parents, teachers, and peers, is the most important element of social bond theory.[22] These attachments bind individuals to conventional and law-abiding behavior through a concern over damaging the relationships. For example, an individual may not cheat on a test due to what their parents and teacher will think if they are caught, as opposed to the fear of receiving punishment. With attachment, potential damage to important relationships is what prevents an individual from engaging in delinquent behaviors. Attachments form early in life, with parent relationships initially being the most important.[23] Children who spend quality time and develop healthy communicative relationships with parents form stronger attachments with them. Studies have found that delinquency is less common among families where parents socialize their children using warm and authoritative parenting.[24] This parenting style shows children that they are loved and cared for, yet also helps them to understand the importance of abiding by rules and expectations established by their parents. The stronger the bond with parents and family members, the less likely youths are to engage in any behavior that could disappoint them or disrupt these relationships.[25]

Based on the relationships portrayed in *13 Reasons Why*, Hannah Baker grew up in a warm and loving household with conventional socialization. Hannah regularly helped at the drug store her parents owned. Her parents encouraged her to make friends and enjoy her teenage years. The Bakers parented Hannah using direct control, which occurs when parents supervise children in their presence and establish expectations and boundaries, as well as indirect control, which occurs within the child internally when parents are not physically present.[26] Hirschi explains that when children and youth have positive relationships with their parents, parents are better able to control their children's behavior when they are not in their presence.[27] Also referred to as "virtual supervision,"[28] youths are less likely to engage in delinquent behavior if they know it would disappoint their parents: "Youngsters refrain from offending because their attachment makes parents psychologically present. They do not skip school, vandalize, or take drugs because, as the saying goes, 'my parents would kill me.'"[29] We see this with Hannah throughout the series. She rarely engages in deviant behavior, apart from drinking lightly at a high school party. Contrary to the delinquent behaviors of many of her classmates, Hannah does not use drugs, consume alcohol excessively, drive under the influence, or engage in potentially risky sexual behaviors.

While Hannah had positive and conventional attachment with her parents, she was new to the town of Crestmont, where she lacked attachments to peers, an aspect of life that becomes more important during adolescence.[30] The beginning of the series highlights the ebb and flow of Hannah's new peer relationships. In the first episode, we learn that Hannah quickly made a best friend in her new town, Kat, who moves away prior to the start of the school year. Kat is described as "the kind of friend who couldn't be replaced" ("Tape 1, Side A," S1E1). After Kat moves away, Hannah begins her sophomore year with only a few acquaintances. The school counselor suggests she befriend another new student, Jessica Davis. Soon after, the two begin hanging out with another new student, Alex, at a local coffee shop. Over time, Hannah begins to feel that these friendships are fleeting. According to Hannah, "It was a hot chocolate friendship; good for cold months, but maybe not perfect for all seasons" ("Tape 1, Side B," S1E2). Alex and Jessica begin dating early in the school year and stop showing up at the coffee shop for their regular meetings, leaving Hannah feeling excluded and that another two close friends are exiting her life. Around the same time, Hannah develops a crush on another student, Justin Foley, who ends up creating far-reaching issues for Hannah that will be covered in regard to the next social bonds concept, commitment.

Commitment

Commitment, the second component of social bond theory, is considered the "more selfish" version of attachment.[31] Commitment concerns the degree to which one has invested time, energy, and resources into conventional activities to achieve personal gain, which colors individuals' consideration of the potential loss of rewards from the consequences and sanctions of delinquent behavior that they want to engage in.[32] People conform to societal and legal norms out of fear of the consequences that could impact personal investments.[33] Commitment instills a stake in conformity and when there is too much to lose by getting in trouble, engaging in delinquency is less likely.[34] The degree of self-interest invested in conventional activities is contingent upon being socialized into a conventional society where success achieved through legitimate avenues is valued.[35]

Those individuals who have a lower investment in conventional activities are more likely to engage in delinquency given that there is less to lose should they be sanctioned for their misconduct. A student who dislikes school, does not participate in extracurricular activities, has minimal self-interest in a future career, and/or educational aspirations can rationalize that they have more to gain from committing a theft versus what they risk losing from the consequences of the illegal behavior. For Hannah, this lack of investment was extreme. Her decision to commit suicide was weighed against her loss of any future. Research shows that having minimal school commitment is associated with lower academic performance, delinquency—both during and outside of school—poor relationships with teachers, truancy, lower educational/occupational goals, and dropping out of school.[36] Hannah initially had the conventional goal of attending college after graduation. Unfortunately, she was not encouraged by the school counselor, who viewed her goal as "unrealistic" ("Tape 4, Side B," S1E8). Hannah expressed a desire to go "NYU or Columbia," but due to her declining grades, implied to be the result of the difficulties she had experienced during the year, she was told to "make some changes" or "think smaller." Familiarity with Hannah suggests that both of these options made her even more despondent, as she felt both that it was not possible to change any of the issues happening in her life, but also that she shouldn't have to lower her ambitions based on her negative experiences. Upon attending a college fair, she was further discouraged after realizing that she could not afford to attend the colleges of her choice due to financial concerns.

Along with these issues, several events challenged and decreased Hannah's general level of commitment and stifled her ability to improve in this area. This began with Justin Foley, the subject of the first tape. After Hannah's best friend moved away, Hannah developed a crush on Justin and began attending his basketball games to get his attention. Eventually he asked her out on a date to a local park. The date started innocently and ended positively with the two playing on a jungle gym and getting to know each other before kissing. During the date, however, Justin took a photo of Hannah going down the slide in a skirt, which showed her underwear. The next day at school, Justin showed the picture to his friends and implied that he and Hannah engaged in sexual activity. Justin's best friend, Bryce Walker, took the phone and forwarded the picture to others, with the photo eventually getting around to a large portion of the student body. As a result, the photo sparked rumors and developed a negative reputation for Hannah, who then started to withdraw socially. This is an important event in the progression toward Hannah's demise, reflecting a recent meta-analysis of 34 studies which showed that peer victimization was significantly associated with suicide ideation and attempts among adolescents, particularly if the victimization occurred through the use of technology.[37] The speed at which information was passed and rumors were spread through technology was a reason Hannah chose to record her final words on cassette tapes accompanied by a paper map: "No Google Maps, no apps, no chance for the interwebs to make everything worse, like it does" ("Tape 1, Side A," S1E1).

Following the circulation of the photo, Alex, Hannah's former friend, created a list of superlatives about the sophomore class, attempting to fit in with the "popular" crowd and to get back at Jessica for not having sex with him. He lists Hannah as having the "Best Ass," while Jessica receives the title of "Worst Ass." This list is circulated around the school by Bryce. Alex later admits that he started the list to make Jessica jealous, but Hannah ended up the victim, as stated on the tape that focuses on Alex: "When you put my name on that list, well, it wasn't just my ass. You made it open season on Hannah Baker" ("Tape 2, Side A," S1E3). The list resulted in people staring at Hannah and taking her picture without her permission, along with a rumor that Alex and Hannah had slept together—the final straw for any hope of a renewed relationship between Jessica and Hannah. When confronted with the rumor, Alex did not deny it, resulting in a higher social standing for him and an increasingly worse reputation for Hannah. While being placed on a trivial high school list may seem unimportant, as stated by Tony, the guardian of the tapes, "You never really know what's going to hit how. You really don't know what's going on in someone else's life" ("Tape 2, Side A," S1E3). For Hannah, she was beginning to feel trapped by a reputation that was built on hearsay and rumors.

Examples of commitment can be explored through other students mentioned on Hannah's tapes, most notably Marcus and Courtney. Among the school's students, Marcus and Courtney were the most afraid of the tapes being released as both had bright academic futures. When an individual invests time, energy, and resources into conventional activities that are essential to future successes (e.g., finishing school and/or establishing a career), the risk of consequences from delinquent behavior weigh heavily. Hirschi describes commitment as the rational component of the social bond.[38] When faced with a criminal opportunity, the individual must consider whether the potential gains from the delinquent act outweigh the potential loss of what has been accrued from the time, effort, rewards, and reputations they have invested in conventional lines of action. For example, a student who has received a scholarship to a prestigious university is being rewarded for their commitment and achievement to the activities that helped secure the scholarship. This student has a self-interest in conforming considering there is so much to lose from the consequences of delinquent behavior. In the context of 13 Reasons Why, those students who tried to hide Hannah's tapes and did not step forward during an active investigation can be considered to have engaged in delinquent behavior. Courtney and Marcus were most adamant about keeping their secrets to protect their futures, seeing the rewards as far outweighing the risks.

Attachment and Commitment

Hirschi notes that the relationship between attachment and commitment is covarying.[39] This can be seen in the downfall of Hannah, who begins losing her stake in conformity as her attachments fail—for example, her relationships with Courtney and Marcus. As stated by Hannah,

"I hoped we could be friends Courtney. I needed a friend" ("Tape 3, Side A," S1E5). Courtney was secretly photographed kissing Hannah at her home during a game of Truth or Dare. Courtney viewed her sexuality as deviant and felt that if evidence of this became public, she would lose her stake in conformity. When the photo and rumors began circulating, Courtney did everything she could to protect herself and her image. Using the rumors about Hannah's reputation to her advantage, Courtney vindicated herself by claiming the photo featured Hannah and an openly gay female student, simultaneously confirming previous rumors about Hannah engaging in promiscuous sexual behavior. This type of behavior, known as relational aggression, is common among teenage girls and occurs when "a girl damages or threatens to damage someone else's relationships or social standing."[40] While relational aggression was originally thought to be of concern only among female adolescents, research suggests that perpetration of relational aggression occurs at similar rates among male and female peer groups,[41] as seen in the behaviors of not just Courtney, but many of the male characters in the show.

Following the escalating rumors, Marcus asked Hannah on a date with the express intent of trying to engage in sexual activity. When she rejected him, he embarrassed her publicly, displaying the importance of Marcus's image and reputation and the actions he will take to protect them. This event further pushed Hannah away from any attempts at building attachments or engaging in social activities that could encourage her stake in conformity. She was even asked on a date by another student, Zach Dempsey, but could not internally overcome the concern about her reputation. She assumed that Zach was seeking sexual activity and publicly rejected him. He retaliated by stealing complimentary notes she was receiving from Clay, which made her feel even more isolated and alone.

Involvement

Involvement, the third element of social bond theory, relates to the amount of time an individual spends engaged in conventional activities and/or social organizations.[42] In the simplest sense, social bond theory would argue that the more time a juvenile is preoccupied outside of school, the fewer opportunities they have to engage in delinquency.

Indeed, a juvenile who has a full weekly schedule of extracurricular activities, work, and volunteering has less time and fewer opportunities to commit crime versus a latchkey child with an unstructured agenda and no conventional activities in their daily life. Evidence suggests that involvement in school-related activities matters, considering that juvenile delinquents have been found to spend less time on homework and take advantage of fewer extracurricular activities.[43]

Hannah did not seem heavily involved in extracurricular activities, but she did attend school regularly and had a job at the local movie theater. Following the events discussed above, she began attending a community poetry group, where she encountered Ryan Shaver, the editor of a non-school-sponsored magazine. Ryan encouraged Hannah and offered to help her with her poetry. Hannah penned a personal poem about her experiences and feelings based on the events of the last year, beginning with "Today I am wearing lacy black underwear" ("Tape 4, Side A," S1E7). Without her permission, Ryan published the poem anonymously in his magazine. The poem was in Hannah's handwriting, resulting in Jessica publicly identifying her as the writer. Students referred to the author as a "skank" and a teacher used the poem as an in-class critical analysis assignment. Hannah felt betrayed and further embarrassed by the incident and stopped attending poetry club, which was the one and only activity she was involved in and place she could express herself.

Belief

According to the final element of Hirschi's social bond theory, delinquency stems from inadequate socialization of conventional values, beliefs, and/or morals.[44] Those who have a stronger belief that the laws of society or the rules established by a school are valid and just are less likely to violate them. Most people do not commit crimes because they have been socialized to believe that criminal behavior is morally wrong. Said another way, they have been socialized in a way that their stake in conformity and attachments to significant others has shaped their beliefs against violating rules or laws. In this regard, delinquency is the result of differences in the extent to which people have been socialized to believe they should obey the rules.

Hirschi contends that "delinquency is not caused by beliefs that require delinquency but is rather made possible by the absence of (effective) beliefs that forbid delinquency."[45] Delinquents may be socialized to understand the difference between right and wrong, but the issue is that their socialization has been inadequate to the point that they develop an amoral orientation to delinquency: "they believe that delinquency is neither good nor bad."[46] While delinquents are aware that rules and laws exist, their amoral perspective invalidates their concern for the rules and allows them to satiate their needs and desires in the quickest and easiest way possible. Studies have shown that individuals with amoral beliefs are more likely to engage in delinquency.[47]

For Hannah Baker, this takes two different forms. While Hannah was properly socialized by her parents, her peers altered this socialization. As has been seen many times above, Hannah regularly witnessed students engaging in delinquent and harmful behavior with no repercussions. Eventually, what Hannah had endured resulted in a change of her beliefs, though arguably as they related only to her. This can be referred to as "situational ethics."[48] It does not seem as though Hannah would encourage or support suicide generally, but her circumstances had changed her belief system in her own personal case.

The Final Weeks of Hannah Baker

We have covered reasons one through eight of why Hannah Baker felt compelled to take her life. As a reminder of Hannah's timeline, she moved to a new town and began her sophomore year in the fall of 2016. During the preceding year, she lost her best friend, Kat, was embarrassed by Justin and the photo, made and lost her friends Jessica and Alex, was confronted with the superlative list, had more rumors started by Courtney, had those rumors acted upon by Marcus, and had her trust betrayed by Ryan. Hannah's last ally, Clay, left for the summer of 2017, leaving Hannah without her favorite coworker. These relationships all appeared to start off as positives in Hannah's life and all took a turn for a worst, reflecting how peer relationships have the potential to enhance or harm the strength of teenage girls' social bonds, specifically.[49] Further, even though relational aggression occurs equally among genders, as reported above, female adolescent victims of such aggression are more likely to become distressed and suffer decreased self-esteem in multiple areas.[50]

Despite all of this, Hannah attempts to persevere and decides to begin her junior year with a fresh start. She cuts her hair dramatically and pledges to avoid social situations where issues could arise: "You can't change other people, but you can change yourself" ("Tape 5, Side A," S1E9). She is happy to see Clay again and he convinces her to go to Jessica's back-to-school house party. Unfortunately, a series of incidents happens at the party that pushs Hannah further into darkness and challenges the final element of social bonds: belief. During the party, Hannah and Clay become closer and explore taking their friendship to a more romantic level. As they begin to kiss, Hannah becomes overwhelmed and cannot overcome her fears of Clay thinking poorly of her given her previous reputation. Her final peer attachment to Clay becomes strained and she demands he leave her alone. To the detriment of her relationship with Clay, we see Hannah internalize all of the rumors and pain she felt in the previous year.

Clay leaves the room immediately after Hannah becomes upset. Suddenly, Justin and Jessica, who began dating over the summer, come into the room to engage in sexual activity. Hannah reflexively hides in the closet to avoid being seen. During the next few minutes, Jessica is seen fading in and out of consciousness as a result of drinking too much alcohol. Justin leaves the room to get Jessica a glass of water and is confronted by his best friend, Bryce. After a brief confrontation, Bryce establishes that he is going to have sex with Jessica. Despite Justin's disapproval, Bryce enters the room and proceeds to rape Jessica while she is unconscious. Hannah witnesses this from inside the closet and is physically and mentally unable to intervene. Following the assault, Hannah immediately attempts to leave the party and is offered a ride by a fellow student, Sheri. On the drive home, Sheri becomes distracted and knocks down a stop sign with her vehicle. Hannah is insistent on immediately reporting the accident, which Sheri disagrees with out of fear of punishment. Hannah leaves the vehicle, after which Sheri drives off, and Hannah ventures on foot to find a phone. Unfortunately, she is too late. Soon after she leaves the scene, an accident occurs at the same intersection that results in a serious injury to an elderly man and the death of a popular student.

This detailed description shows three instances in one evening where Hannah is vicariously traumatized due to her proximity to delinquent events. Her internal struggles results in a final peer attachment being severed and the latter events challenge her belief systems. She witnesses two successful, well-liked individuals engaging in criminal activity with irreparable damage to others and no negative consequences for the offenders. This same system had been at work the entirety of Hannah's sophomore year but reaches an extreme at Jessica's party. Following the party, it is kept a secret from Jessica that she was raped by Bryce. Additionally, there are no repercussions for Sheri regarding the stop sign, with the accident being blamed on the deceased teen driver.

Further withdrawing socially, Hannah begins helping her parents more often. Hannah's parents are seemingly the last positive attachments she has in her life, but even this relationship is becoming strained as the family struggles financially and faces eviction. Attempting to help her parents, Hannah offers to take a deposit to the bank. She places the bank bag on top of the family car, gets briefly distracted by a text, and forgets to grab it before driving off. The deposit is lost, causing increased stress on the family and Hannah internally. Hannah claims, "It seemed like no matter what I did, I kept letting people down. I started thinking how everyone's lives would be better without me—it feels like nothing. Like a deep, endless, always blank, nothing" ("Tape 6, Side B," S1E12). Hannah goes for a walk to clear her head and happens upon a small party at Bryce's where Jessica is in the hot tub. Hannah decides to get in the hot tub with Jessica and some others. Shortly after, everyone goes inside, leaving her and Bryce alone. Bryce begins flirting with Hannah and suggests that they have sex. She tries to get out of the hot tub multiple times, but he pulls her back in with increasing aggression and rapes her. She interprets this event as the final cementing of her negative image: "Thanks to you Bryce, I had finally lived up to my reputation, and I knew there was no way I could ever live that down" ("Tape 6, Side B," S1E12).

After this incident, feeling a complete loss of attachments and with the belief that reporting the rape would not likely result in any consequences for Bryce, Hannah begins recording her tapes. Recording the tapes and releasing her pent-up frustrations and pain helps Hannah emotionally. Feeling like she could possibly overcome her past, she claims, "I decided to give life one more chance, but this time I was asking for help, because I know I can't do it alone. I know that now" ("Tape 7, Side A," S1E13).

As a final attempt to seek help and support, Hannah meets with the school counselor, Mr. Porter. The final tape is a recording of their conversation: "If you're listening to this [the tapes], I failed, or he failed, and my fate is sealed" ("Tape 7, Side A," S1E13). Mr. Porter makes a series of poor choices when speaking to Hannah, including not silencing his phone, which continues to vibrate loudly during the conversation. This distraction becomes noticeably uncomfortable when Hannah begins hinting at her victimization. He begins to victim-blame Hannah, saying, "Maybe you made a decision? A decision to do something with a boy that you now regret? Did you tell him to stop? Did you tell him no? Maybe you consented and changed your mind?" ("Tape 7, Side A," S1E13), furthering Hannah's internalized belief that she is to blame while others see no consequences for their negative actions. Hannah becomes upset and denies doing any of the things that Mr. Porter is accusing her of. Once things settle, he tells Hannah that unless she gives a name, there is nothing that he can do for her, suggesting, "You can move on . . . he'll be gone in a few months" ("Tape 7, Side A," S1E13). Hannah, feeling as though her final attempt to find someone who cared was over, exits Liberty High for the last time.

> I think I made myself very clear that no one is coming forth to stop me. Some of you cared, none of you cared enough, and neither did I, and I'm sorry . . . there's nothing more to say. (Hannah Baker—"Tape 7, Side A," S1E13)

Additional Applications of Social Bonds

13 Reasons Why provides many story lines beyond Hannah's that emphasize the importance of social bonds. Throughout *13 Reasons Why*, we see two main antagonists, Justin and Bryce. Justin is responsible for the initial reputation rumors regarding Hannah, allows Bryce to rape Jessica, and keeps the crime a secret from Jessica until Hannah's tapes are revealed. Bryce appears to be the star student but engages regularly in deviant behavior throughout the series and encourages the downfall of other characters.

Bryce Walker is a senior star-athlete from an upper-class family. His parents are not seen at any point in the series as they travel constantly. Due to his popularity, he has many attachments to his peers, yet most appear to be superficial. Research using Hirschi's theory suggests that male college students are more likely to engage in sexual aggression when the "costs" are lower.[51] Negative consequences framed by Hirschi relate to issues with parental relationships, completing homework, and smoking outside of school,[52] all of which appear to be of no worry to Bryce. Despite this, Bryce does appear to have a long-standing friendship with Justin. Justin, who comes from a lower-class family with no father figure and a drug-addicted mother, has relied on Bryce and his family for many years. Bryce's family has purchased school supplies and athletic gear for Justin, along with bailing his mother out of jail when she was arrested for drug possession. Justin's attachment and loyalty to Bryce cause extreme pain for Justin throughout the season. Similar to Hannah, Justin experiences a decreasing of social bonds in all four dimensions described in the theory.

Justin has virtually nonexistent parental, or any adult, attachments, which are proposed as the most important by Hirschi.[53] His peer attachments seem limited to superficial ones with his teammates, apart from Bryce and Jessica, who he begins dating in the summer of 2017, two months before her rape. Immediately prior to the rape, Bryce informs Justin that "what's mine is yours" ("Tape 5, Side A," S1E9) and locks Justin out of the room, which ultimately challenges Justin's belief system. We see Justin struggle over whether to protect his girlfriend or respect his longtime best friend. Following the incident, Justin becomes detached from his usual activities. He stops attending school consistently, misses important pep rallies and sporting events, and engages in drug use. At the same time, Jessica, who has heard the tapes, begins engaging in similar self-destructive behaviors and pulls away from Justin emotionally. Her belief system is challenged as she struggles with the sexual assault, as well as whether to believe Hannah's tapes or Justin, who is her closest relationship. These two characters lose their genuine attachment to each other, heavily decrease their involvement in school-based activities, and stop investing any time into conventional activities that could support a positive future. At the end of the series, we see Justin finally confront Bryce to end their friendship. Jessica discloses her victimization to her father and attempts to move forward. Unfortunately, we cannot assume a happy ending for Justin as, with no home to return to, he walks away from Bryce and gives up his final attachment.

While the lack of social bonds for Justin, Bryce, and Jessica worked against them, Clay's positive social bonds arguably prevented him from engaging in the same self-destructive behaviors as his classmates. Throughout 13 Reasons Why, we follow Clay as he struggles to cope with hearing the tapes and the loss of his unrequited teenage love. Clay has lived in Crestmont his entire life but doesn't appear connected to his peers. He is admittedly socially awkward, quiet, and has faced a history of bullying and rumors about his being homosexual. These are similar to the problems Hannah encountered. He too worked part-time at the local movie theater but was otherwise unengaged in sports or other time-consuming activities. He spent a small amount of time tutoring a friendly athlete at school, the same individual who is later killed in the car accident following Jessica's party. Furthermore, he lost his main attachment, Hannah Baker, and began experiencing symptoms of PTSD as a result. While the other individuals who feature in Hannah's tapes, with the exception of Bryce and Mr. Porter, seemed to band together, Clay fought against them, facing these issues on his own. He did not engage in drug use and did not make any attempts at self-harm. Despite the pain caused to Clay by Hannah's death, it is possible that his attachment to her is what kept him from being deviant. He was committed to getting justice for Hannah, something that could not be done if he didn't take the proper law-abiding steps, resulting in heavy prosocial involvement. He believed that everything Hannah faced was a violation of what she deserved and what he considered moral. Even after feeling that he could have helped her, he didn't try to protect himself like the other students; he admitted his faults and attempted to make up for them while seeking help from those around him and relying on Tony to help him through the tapes. Collectively, 13 Reasons Why provides several story lines that are useful to explaining how social bonds can prevent delinquency, as well as what happens when such bonds are strained.

Conclusion: Thinking Further

Control theorists ask, "Why *don't* they do it?" as people are naturally inclined to engage in deviant behavior. Social control theories, and social bond theory more specifically, explore the constraints that keep an individual from engaging in criminal or deviant behavior, even if said behavior may seem beneficial to the individual person. As we've seen, Hannah did not feel she had anything keeping her from committing suicide, a deviant act. This is important considering that next to unintentional injuries (e.g., car crash–related injuries), suicide is the second leading cause of death among US adolescents ages 15 to 19.[54] Even more alarming is that the rate of suicide among those aged 10–19 years increased 56% between 2007 and 2016 (44% for males and 70% among females).

There are numerous events portrayed in *13 Reasons Why* that align with the literature on adolescent suicide. For example, Dana L. Haynie, Scott J. South, and Sunita Bose used a nationally representative sample of US youth and found that females who recently moved to a new location were 60% more likely than adolescents who had not recently moved to engage in suicide attempts within a year.[55] Feelings of social isolation from peers, not feeling part of a tightly connected school community, and having a limited number of close relationships with peers has shown to increase the risk of suicide ideation among females.[56] Moreover, Lydia O'Donnell, Ann Stueve, Dana Wardlaw, and Carl O'Donnell found that youths who reported engaging in suicide attempts also reported a lack of support from adults.[57] These empirical findings highlight the importance of social bonds in the prevention of deviant or criminal behavior. Hannah attempted to navigate the complex social spheres of a new high school, only to have her attachments to others, commitments to school and involvement in extracurricular activities, and beliefs thwarted due to bullying and a lack of support from peers and adults. Her numerous attempts to remedy situations, such as reaching out for help from the school counselor, resulted in nothing that would convince Hannah to stay alive.

A tragic outcome left the school and the Crestmont community reeling to find answers. Unlike most situations involving suicide, however, Hannah details the reasons behind her decision. Despite the book being a *New York Times* best seller, the Netflix series has received so much criticism that a trigger warning had to be included at the beginning of episode 1.[58] The criticism surrounds using sensitive topics for entertainment purposes, such as adolescent sexual assault and the graphic scene in which Hannah commits suicide.[59] Nevertheless, these are important topics of discussion that are appropriate for undergraduate and/or graduate criminology courses. Hirschi's social bond theory provides a theoretical framework that demonstrates the negative consequences of weakened social bonds. *13 Reasons Why* portrays relatable content that resonates with youths struggling to develop meaningful attachments with others. The story emphasizes the importance of social bonds in the prevention of deviant and criminal behavior. Whereas Hannah's social bonds failed her, Clay's social bonds are what kept him from the same fate. As best stated in the warning appended to the beginning of the show, "If you ever feel that you need someone to talk with, reach out to a parent, a friend, a school counselor, or an adult you trust . . . because the minute you start talking about it, it gets easier" ("Tape 1, Side A," S1E1).

3

Breaking Bad

FAILURE, CRIME, AND THE INABILITY TO COPE

*Tammy S. Garland, John A. Browne, and
Candace G. Murphy*

Walter White, a 50-year-old Albuquerque high school chemistry teacher, is your normal guy. Once a promising young chemist, he unexpectedly gave up his aspirations for a life in the suburbs, where he lives with his pregnant wife, Skyler, and his disabled teenage son, Walter Jr. He teaches at a level below his intellect and still has to work an extra job at a car wash to just barely pay the bills. While he lives a mundane life, he is seemingly content even though his dreams of grandeur remain unfulfilled. That is, until he is diagnosed with stage IIIA, inoperable lung cancer. Realizing that his death is imminent, Walter must find a way to support his family after his death. He, however, is broke and underinsured, with a baby on the way and an insurmountable number of medical bills due to cancer treatment that will inevitably pile up, Walter is at a crossroads.[1] He is stressed to say the least, and his inability to cope with the inevitable has him looking for alternative methods to support his family. After watching television coverage of the profitability of the methamphetamine trade and a chance encounter with a former student and low-level drug dealer, Jesse Pinkman, during a DEA ride-along, Walt comes to the realization of what he must do. It is in this moment that Walt first "breaks bad" and begins his descent into a criminal lifestyle.

Originally airing on AMC on January 20, 2008, *Breaking Bad* is a neo-western crime drama that tells the story of Walter White and his transformation into the drug kingpin Heisenberg.[2] Unlike the westerns of old, Walt is depicted as the antihero, and rather than riding in on a horse wearing a white hat, Walt enters the illicit drug trade and destroys everything and everyone with whom he comes into contact. It is this disjunction between who the audience wants Walt to be and who he becomes that keeps viewers watching for five seasons. Unlike the heroes of old facing their mortality, Walt does not try to right wrongs, mend relationships, or give meaning to a seemingly meaningless life, and he definitely does not fade into the sunset. Instead, he lies, cheats, and kills his way to the top in his desire to build an empire. As described by series creator Vince Gilligan, Walt goes "from being a protagonist to an antagonist. We want to make people question who they're pulling for, and why."[3] Walt's transformation thus does not make him a likeable character, as his adoption of traditional American masculinity produces tragic consequences.[4]

Breaking Bad shifts from a character study of an unlikely criminal entering the illicit drug trade to a "moral thriller of intimate psychology and epic vision."[5] This unquestionably violent series makes the viewer examine their reaction to such tragic circumstances. Most would say that they would not follow the path that Walt has chosen for himself. And, as we will see in this analysis, they are correct. Most people do not engage in criminal activity, and when they do, it is typically not of a violent nature. So how is it that Walt gets to the point of transforming from a mild-mannered, law-abiding citizen into a violent criminal? In this chapter, we explore *Breaking Bad* through the lens of Robert Agnew's General Strain Theory. From the outset, strain, the failure to cope with stressful events, and the reaction to strain are prominent issues throughout the series. And Walt is the perfect character to illustrate the link between strain, failure to cope, and criminality. Before we address the criminal trajectory Walt finds himself on, the chapter thus provides an overview of General Strain Theory.

General Strain Theory (GST)

Drawing on the work of Robert Merton,[6] Agnew proposed an individual explanation of strain, General Strain Theory (GST),[7] which describes how negative relationships with others can lead to crime. Strain, as characterized by Agnew, is a result of "relationships in which others are not treating the individual as he or she would like to be treated."[8] It is, thus, factors outside our control, those relationships that cause us strain, that are often responsible for crime and delinquency. According to Agnew, General Strain Theory holds that "strains or stressors increase the likelihood of negative emotions like anger and frustration."[9] In an attempt to correct these negative emotions, offended parties react and sometimes engage in crime as a result. While Agnew draws upon the work of his predecessors, he argues that Merton and subsequent strain theorists fail to acknowledge in their conceptualization that strain simply occurs as a result of the failure to achieve positively valued goals.[10] Status frustration and failure to achieve monetary success is only one way that strain occurs. Agnew expands on traditional strain theory to include strain as the result not only of failing to achieve positively valued goals but also of loss and other negative experiences. According to Agnew, strain may occur from the actual or anticipated failure to achieve positively valued goals, "the actual or anticipated removal of positively valued stimuli from individuals," or "the actual or anticipated presentation of negative or noxious stimuli."[11] While the failure to achieve one's goals is unquestionably a stressful event, we cannot discount the impact of strain especially when taking into consideration factors that may exacerbate the issue. Agnew identified four characteristics of strain that may lead to crime: (1) strain perceived as unjust, (2) strain perceived as high in magnitude, (3) strain associated with low self-control, and (4) strain that creates pressure or incentive to engage in criminal coping. As a result, GST maintains that strains or stressors increase the likelihood for individuals to experience negative emotions (e.g., anger, frustration, despair). It is here that we come to understand the impact that being diagnosed with a terminal illness may have on an individual, especially one who has been subject, or at least has perceived himself to have been subject, to an unjust and high-magnitude strain.

Without question, strain is a part of life, but what many do not understand is that criminal behavior is not so much about the strain to which we are exposed, but the way in which we handle it. What makes one person choose to engage in violent behavior while another will choose a more positive or legitimate avenue to vent their frustrations? While no two individuals are the same, and we cannot always address how individuals will respond to strain, there are variables that can help us understand why some will engage in criminal behavior. According to Agnew, those likely to engage in criminal coping

are low in self-control and high in negative emotionality, being especially sensitive to provocations. They have few options for legal coping.
Among other things, they are poor, live in deprived communities or on
the street, have few opportunities for decent work, and have few people
they can turn to for support. They cannot turn to the police when threat-
ened because they are involved in illegal activities, their values strongly
discourage cooperating with police, and/or the police will not take their
complaints seriously. Likewise, they cannot turn to conventional others
such as family and friends; these others lack resources, are unwilling to
help, and/or ties to them have been severed. They are low in most forms
of social control, and so have little to lose through criminal coping. Many,
in fact, believe they will be dead within a few years.[12]

While Walt may not start off fitting this description beyond his belief
that his death is imminent, the moment he engages in methamphetamine manufacturing places him on a path where the strain is magnified,
and he is not only unable but unwilling to get out.

Strain and *Breaking Bad*

Merton's original anomic conceptualization argues that strain is a result
of the disjunction between societal goals and legitimate means.[13] As a
result of this strain, crime will occur. While Merton's initial argument
focuses on the idea of monetary success, he later argues that this was
simply an example and that the goal of cultural success could be sub-
stituted for money and produce the same results. Like Merton and his
theoretical descendants Richard Cloward and Lloyd Ohlin as well as
Albert Cohen,[14] Agnew does not question that strain is a result of "the
actual or anticipated failure to achieve positively valued goals." In fact,
he embraces the argument that strain can result from a failure to achieve
monetary or cultural success. Failure to achieve positively valued goals
(e.g., status, respect, autonomy, and financial success) is stressful as most
of society, regardless of class, deems these worthy, often required, aspirations. While this sort of failure is often attributed to the lower class,
many middle- and upper-class individuals face similar pressures. Failure
to achieve the American Dream often places individuals under stress
and that strain can lead individuals to engage in deviant or criminal

behavior; if legitimate means are not available, individuals will often seek out illegitimate channels to obtain their cultural goals.[15] Individuals may engage in criminal behavior such as theft, prostitution, or, as is the case in *Breaking Bad*, drug manufacturing as a means to obtain monetary and sometimes cultural success. And it is here that we are introduced to our antihero, the accidental drug manufacturer, Walter White.

Though his research contributed to the awarding of a Nobel Prize, Walter White does not end up with international recognition, but instead finds himself teaching chemistry to high school students who neither appreciate his expertise nor are able to understand even the basic concepts of chemistry. As if this is not enough, Walt can't support his family on his teaching position's insufficient wage; as a result, he must work at a car wash, where he is constantly subjected to humiliation as he is pressured to wash the cars of his privileged students, while being mocked for doing so. Walt appears to be a bright-line example of someone failing to achieve positively valued goals, and this failure has left Walt bitter. Viewers cannot help but initially feel sorry for Walt, as he appears to be the "good guy," who has been subjected to the worst that life has to give him. In the first episode of the series, Walt confides to his psychiatrist after being diagnosed with cancer: "My wife is seven months pregnant with a baby we didn't intend. My 15-year-old has cerebral palsy. When I work, I can make $43,700 per year. I have watched all of my colleagues surpass me in every way imaginable and, in 18 months, I will be dead" ("Pilot," S1E1). Walter, as will be reaffirmed at the end of his life, has been an abject failure. He was supposed to be successful; he was supposed to win the Nobel Prize; he was supposed to change the world, but instead he lives a life full of regret, disappointment, and bitterness. At first, viewers are led to believe that Walt accepts this life, but, underneath, he is filled with anger and frustration at the lot he, at least in his own mind, did not choose.

Most people desire status and respect, and Walter White is no different. But, as can be seen, Walter White doesn't warrant much respect and any status that he once possessed as a scientist is only a memory. This poses a significant problem for Walt as he was once at the pinnacle of success. He was the "Man": recognized for his work, respected by colleagues, and at the brink of being a social and financial success.

But somehow all of Walt's aspirations and expectations were thwarted. Instead, he is a nobody on the verge of financial ruin. He is existing, but he is barely able to scratch out a meager existence for his family. In a world where the American Dream is the standard, and men are judged by their ability to provide for their families, this life, which Walt did not choose, or will not admit to choosing, is unacceptable. His masculinity is in question, and, as observed by Agnew, the desire for masculine status is often linked to a life of crime. And why not? Like Walt, many individuals have a difficult time "accomplishing masculinity" through legitimate channels, especially when success is determined by the type of car one drives, the size of one's bank account, or one's employment status.[16] It makes sense that individuals engage in illegitimate behavior to secure their financial success when legitimate opportunities are not present or have been blocked. And in the pilot episode (S1E1), we see Walt first realize that his unappreciated talents could be used to obtain success as he learns of the profit one can make from manufacturing methamphetamine.[17]

We can sympathize with Walt's wanting, in theory, to leave his family better off after he is dead . . . at least in the beginning. Walt is considered a "good" man who has been dealt a lousy hand; we are reminded throughout the first season of this. As a result, we want to see him take control of his lackluster life as he seemingly lacks the respect of those that surround him. Sure, he is loved, but that doesn't pay the bills. Before his foray into the criminal world, he does not control his life nor is he perceived as fulfilling a masculine role. Individuals have a strong desire for autonomy, power over oneself, and when autonomy cannot be obtained, strain occurs. As such, failure to achieve autonomy may lead to crime.[18] For individuals like Walt, autonomy is fleeting in the legitimate world. While much of the research in this area involves juveniles and the lower class, it is easy to understand how the need for autonomy impacts Walt's decision to engage in criminal behavior and eventually transform into Heisenberg, his alternative criminal persona. In the legitimate world, Walt has little control over his life and his masculine status has consistently been diminished. His wife, Skyler, determines what they eat (e.g., tofu bacon), what they do, and how much they spend. In the pilot episode, she chastises Walt for placing just over fifteen dollars on a credit card that they do not use. But more disconcerting is the control she exerts over him when he is diagnosed with cancer. When Walter decides that he does not want to go through treatment not simply because of the cost but because he wants to die on his own terms, Skyler deems his choice unacceptable and sets up an intervention to force him into treatment. Although he initially rejects the idea, he is forced to reconsider his decision for the sake of his family. He is not allowed to make his own decisions regarding even his own mortality; Skyler bullies him every step of the way not only in how he will be treated, but how his treatment will be funded ("Gray Matter," S1E5).

Walt is repeatedly emasculated, and it doesn't stop there. Even in his own home, he is not the man of the family—his brother-in-law, Hank Schrader, has replaced Walt as the masculine figurehead. The dynamic between Walt and Hank illuminates how unmasculine Walt has become. Hank, a DEA agent, may not be Walt's intellectual equal, but he talks tough, walks tough, and is portrayed as the alpha male leaving the inordinately cerebral Walt to be viewed as the beta. Hank is also portrayed as financially superior to Walt, as seen on the numerous occasions in which he discusses his willingness to assist Walt and his family. Even Walt's son, Walter, Jr., is enamored with Hank and often looks to him for guidance.

As Walt is repeatedly subjected to demoralizing experiences in the first few episodes, we, the audience, begin to understand why he needs to reclaim his masculine self. Walt does not seemingly warrant status or respect as he is not in control of his life. And while viewers are initially not privy to this, Walt is angry. He is angry about his lack not only of autonomy, but of the financial success that he was supposed to have. Significantly, he does not blame himself, but others for his suffering, and he maintains the belief that great unjustness has been committed against him.

Financial instability, as noted, is a recurrent theme in the series.[19] From Walt's underemployment to his being underinsured, money, or the lack thereof, seems to be the primary stressor in the White household. But it is the relationship with Walt's former partners in Gray Matter, a company he and Elliott Schwartz, his former best friend, founded after graduate school, that truly illuminates his failure to achieve his positively valued goals. We first see Walt encounter Elliott and his wife, Gretchen (Walt's former girlfriend and lab assistant), after he and Sky-

ler are invited to Elliott's birthday party ("Gray Matter," S1E5). After
being informed by Skyler that Walt is not only sick but unable to pay
for treatment, Elliott offers to pay for Walt's medical expenses as he
feels somewhat guilty for Walt's lack of success. While Elliott went on
to become successful, Walt seemingly crumbled under life's strain. In
this instance, Elliott attempts to make amends; Walt, however, declines
the money. It will later be discovered that, contrary to Walt's recollection, Elliott and Gretchen did not steal Gray Matter from Walt, but that
he walked out. As shown in flashbacks throughout the first and second
seasons, the audience sees that Walt and Gretchen were once romanti-
cally linked. After a weekend at her wealthy parents' home, where he
felt inadequate, most likely due to his humble beginnings, he ends the
relationship to protect his pride, and shortly afterward walks away from
Gray Matter Technologies, selling his shares of what would become a
multibillion-dollar company for $5,000. Walt, as a result, erroneously
blames Elliott and Gretchen for his failure and becomes enraged at
the thought of them paying for his medical bills. Even after Gretchen
apologetically calls and repeats the offer to pay for his expansive medical costs, he lies and says that his insurance will cover the necessary
treatment. It is in this moment that he decides to truly embrace the
criminal lifestyle. While Walt had engaged in producing methamphetamine previously, the initial disaster of this venture resulted in Walt's
first encounter with violence—in self-defense, he kills two low-level
drug dealers ("Cat's in the Bag," S1E2), as discussed later in this chapter.
This act had seemingly deterred him from engaging in future deviant
behavior; however, his wounded pride and need to reclaim autonomy
lead him to descend again and more deeply into the world of methamphetamine manufacturing. In the last scene of the episode that focuses
on his relationship with the Schwartzes, he approaches Jesse, his former
student turned methamphetamine dealer, and asks him if he wants to
cook ("Gray Matter," S1E5).

While Walt's failure to obtain his positively valued goals has unquestionably caused him anger and frustration, and sets the foundation for
his moral decay, it is the presentation of negative stimuli and the loss of
positively valued stimuli that leads him into crime. Without question,
the diagnosis of inoperable lung cancer on his 50th birthday presents
a negative stimulus for Walt ("Pilot," S1E1). Here is a man, while not in

control, who has been able to provide for and support his family at least on a basic level. Now, with his inevitable death, he will be unable to do this. While the presentation of noxious stimuli and the loss of positively valued stimuli are two separate issues, Agnew explains that these forms of strain are often interchangeable—it is "difficult to distinguish them in practice."[20] And in the case of Walter White, the diagnosis of cancer produces not only the presentation of negative stimuli, but the loss that will result from its leading him into a life, albeit a short one, of crime.

The Choice Is Yours

As argued by Nicole Rafter and Michelle Brown,[21] anger and revenge are motivators for crime, as can be seen in almost all revenge films. GST theory, in their view, can be generally applied but does little to illuminate us in regard to explaining crimes. It is apparent that Rafter and Brown do not think too highly of GST, as everyone is exposed to strain.[22] However, *Breaking Bad* is unlike the systemic films (e.g., *Traffic*) discussed by Rafter and Brown, as their analysis engages with emotion mostly in the context of criminal systems rather than individual-level factors leading to criminal behavior.[23] It is in this television series, which occurs over a period of time, that GST theory is most applicable, as we witness one man's descent into crime while others, who are experiencing their own stress, remain relatively grounded.

Although Walter White experiences a number of stressors throughout his life, prior to discussing his reaction to strain and his fall from grace, we must consider what makes him different from the other primary characters in *Breaking Bad*. As such, we are not talking about systemic crime or your typical criminals and cartel members (e.g., Tuco Salamanca and Gus Fring) as we are not privy to the factors that led them to engage in a criminal lifestyle. Instead, we examine how strain affects the seemingly normal individual and why some individuals are able to cope using positive means while others will engage in criminal activity. Simply, why do some people engage in criminal coping and others do not? According to Agnew, "in order to predict the nature and effectiveness of coping, one must take into account the nature and interpretation of the stressor, the circumstances surrounding the stressor, and the individual's overall standing on a range of individual and social variables."[24]

Similar to the characters in Rafter and Brown's analysis, everyone in the *Breaking Bad* series seems to be exposed to stress, and while many of them will take part in deviant and/or criminal behavior, this is not comparable to the path leading Walt to transform into Heisenberg.[25] But we wouldn't expect anything else, as Walt's journey into criminality is consistent with the criteria established by Agnew—he experiences strain that is (perceived as) unjust, high in magnitude, and associated with low self-control, and that creates an incentive to engage in criminal coping. And while many of the "normal" characters depicted in the series experience strain that possesses some of these qualities, none are subjected to them all. Marie, Walt's sister-in-law, is a kleptomaniac; Walter, Jr., gets busted trying to buy alcohol illegally; and Skyler, who is sanctimonious at the beginning, eventually commits fraud as she covers up for both Walt's and her boss/lover's criminal activity. Even Hank, Walter's DEA brother-in-law, who suffers from panic attacks due to the intense strain of his job, engages in a bit of deviance periodically. For instance, he unapologetically smokes illegal Cuban cigars, obtained from an FBI agent in return for a favor, to celebrate the birth of Walt's daughter. While these instances may seem minor, all are a result of the strain present in everyday life. Each of the characters may be perceived as engaging in criminal behavior, yet they are not depicted as criminals. While people may engage in deviant behavior as a result of strain, not everyone who experiences strain will engage in transgressions that warrant a criminal label. Even in instances where they get caught (e.g., Marie and Walter, Jr.), their actions are depicted as not characteristic of the individual but more of a reaction to the circumstances around them. People screw up and on occasion do stupid things, which may be considered criminal, but this doesn't mean they will continue to commit criminal or deviant acts. More importantly, not everyone who is exposed to strain engages in criminal behavior. While Hank from time to time violates the rules, he cannot be considered criminal. Even while engaging in minor deviant acts, Hank holds true to the law; so do most of the other characters in the series, as most have more to lose than to gain by engaging in a criminal lifestyle. Even Jesse, who is involved in the drug trade, comes to realize that this is not the life he wanted. And this is consistent with GST, whereby "[s]train does not cause one to react in any specific manner; rather, it becomes an aspect or factor within the confines of our lived experience that is made meaningful from the uniqueness of our individual perspective."[26] As noted, research has shown that some individuals are more likely to engage in criminal activity than others as a result of strain. Walt just happens to be one of those individuals.

Walter White and Criminal Coping

The case of Walter White is a tragic one, leaving viewers to feel sympathy as we see Agnew's GST played out on screen. While Walter has experienced subjective strain as a result of his failure to achieve his goals, it is the strain produced by the diagnosis of cancer and the failure to provide for his family that leads to his moral decline. And we, the audience, feel sorry for him, at first. As he views most of his life as having been chosen for him, Walt wants to decide his legacy. It initially appears that Walt is a man who simply wants to reclaim his autonomy and masculinity by providing for his family even after his death. But then something changes. Strain seemingly transforms Walt from a mild-mannered chemistry teacher into the drug kingpin Heisenberg. In the beginning, Walt engages in the drug trade out of necessity. He has bills to pay, children to send to college, and the need to provide support for his family. Early on, he estimates that he needs approximately $737,000 to ensure his family's needs are met ("Seven Thirty-Seven," S2E1). By the end of the second season, we see Walt's goals shift. After a number of setbacks, Walt is informed by his lawyer, Saul Goodman, that he only has enough money for a "second-hand Subaru." In desperation, he coerces Jesse into going to the desert, where they cook 38 pounds of high-quality methamphetamine worth $1.2 million ("4 Days Out," S2E9). While he eventually splits the proceeds with his partner, minus operating costs, yielding each over $400,000, the lure of making more money keeps him time and time again from leaving the business. And by the end of the final season, when Walt is in control of his own distribution network, we find that enough will never be enough. Walt is horrified that Mike Ehrmantraut, Gus's former enforcer, and Jesse are willing to sell the methylamine they acquired during a train heist for $5 million each, when it could be the basis for netting $300 million in methamphetamine ("Buyout," S5E6). However, when Skyler takes him to the warehouse where she has been storing their money, as the carwash they purchased cannot launder such enormous sums, we become aware that money was not the goal all along.

> SKYLER: This is it. This is what you have been working for . . . There is more money here than we can spend in an entire lifetime . . . Please tell me how much is enough. How big does this pile have to be? ("Gliding Over All," S5E8)

As Walt has more money than he or his family could ever spend, there must be a reason for his refusal to leave the criminal world. As observed by Mark Lewis,[27] Walt's refusal to walk away from the profits of the drug business, despite surpassing his original goal and being informed that he is in remission, is clearly evidence that his motivation was not simply money. Lewis argues that his actual goal is pride; we would disagree, as Walt is obsessed with control and the power that comes with the lifestyle and persona in which he has chosen to embrace. In the criminal world—or, as James Bowman would refer to it, the frontier—the rules of civilization do not apply.[28] Rather than adhering to societal rules that are "constructed from choices and consent," the illegitimate world of the criminal "devolves into raw power."[29] Control has always been important to Walt, but in the legitimate world he has had little autonomy. Rather than his life being decided for him, Walt has embraced the power and notoriety of Heisenberg; he has *become* Heisenberg. (It is not lost on us and many of the series' viewers that Walt's criminal persona is based on renowned physicist and creator of the "uncertainty principle" Werner Heisenberg.) Thus, while Walt is undoubtedly prideful, it is his need to control a life that has been seemingly out of his control that leads him further into the criminal lifestyle. Walt is, after all, in the empire business ("Buyout," S5E6). And, as Walt argues, in the final season of *Breaking Bad*, Heisenberg is his true identity.[30] "Rather than awareness of his finitude galvanizing him toward a legacy of others, Walt become(s) more and more selfish, and he progressively weakens the argument that his actions are all taken for the good of the family."[31]

While Walt repeatedly argues throughout the series that he is doing it for the family, it wasn't about them at all. As a result of his failure to achieve his aspirations, Walt, deliberately or not, became immersed in the drug trade as a means to recover his former glory and seek a figurative and literal revenge on those who he felt had wronged him. Heisenberg, in essence, is able to obtain the respect, autonomy, and financial security that Walter could not obtain through legitimate means. When explaining to Skyler in the series finale why he did it, he finally admits that it wasn't for the money, but for himself: "I did it for me. I liked it. I was good at it. And I was really . . . I was alive" ("Felina," S5E16). Strain has revealed Walt's true persona. Rather than being weak and bullied by those around him (e.g., Skyler, his students, his former research partners), he is in charge. He is no longer in a state of depression; he is secure and confident. It is as if Heisenberg was developed, or maybe existed all along, as a coping mechanism to combat the mental illness Walt was suffering. We see Heisenberg demonstrating what Agnew explains is one of the basic reasons one is likely to engage in criminal behavior: low self-control. Heisenberg is the bad guy; he is impulsive, insensitive, and willing to take risks. This is always who he has been—the "man who knocks."

> WALT: Who are you talking to right now? Who is it you think you see? Do you know how much I make a year? . . . No, you clearly do not know who you're talking to, so let me clue you in. I am not in danger, Skyler. I am the danger! A guy opens his door and gets shot and you think that of me? No, I am the one who knocks. ("Cornered," S4E6)

By season four, the depressed, meek man no longer exists, as is evident when he stands before Skyler, who is terrified of him; he is now depicted as a man of power asserting his dominance ("Cornered," S4E6). Here we truly see how Walt differs from normal men and is more similar to members of the cartel than to the professor in the ivory tower. After all, not even including methamphetamine addicts, Walt is responsible, directly and indirectly, for the deaths of approximately 200 people.[32] Strain has molded Walt into someone who embraces violence rather than running from it. He may have not started out this way, but he has evolved into someone who embraces violence.

Reacting to Violence

Agnew notes that individuals may have different emotional reactions to subjective strain, or strain that is induced by an individual being exposed to some stressor that they do not like.[33] These reactions can vary from mild anger to rage. In the case of Walter White, we see his reactions progress as he becomes immersed in the criminal lifestyle. While we would argue that Walt has always been about being in control, his response to strain intensifies the longer he takes on the role of Heisenberg. As Agnew writes, social support structures often have a "buffering effect" on stress.[34] When Walt, the family man, gives way to Heisenberg, the criminal mastermind, the negative response and reaction to this double life that he views as beyond his control blurs the line between who he really is and the man he pretends to be. It is in this domain that allows Heisenberg to buffer the stress of his diagnosis and become self-aware as his confidence grows in the illicit world. Here he becomes king(pin) rather than the shell of a man society portrayed him as being. What we have to realize is that Walt does not start out as a hardened criminal, and while he is filled with anger, his willingness and ability to channel those frustrations, at least in the beginning, are inhibited and occur more out of self-preservation and defense than violence. Walt's first encounters with violence lead us to sympathize with him, as it appears that he is simply reacting to ensure the survival of himself, his family, and his partner, Jesse. In the first episode, we see Walt confronted by drug dealers Krazy-8 and Emilio, who believe he is working with the DEA as he was seen with Hank ("Pilot," S1E1). Fearing for his and Jesse's lives, Walt uses his knowledge of chemistry to poison the two would-be assassins. While this is a violent response to a stressful situation, it is framed as an act of self-defense and thus does not give viewers the sense that Walt is a murderer—he was simply protecting himself and Jesse. The conundrum, however, does not end there, as Krazy-8 survives, leading Walt and Jesse to imprison him in Jesse's basement ("Cat's in the Bag," S1E2). Here we will see a true criminal response to strain. Even though both Jesse and Walt agree their foe must be eliminated, Walt is unwilling to kill his captive. However, after weighing the situation and realizing that Krazy-8, despite his objections, plans to kill Walt and possibly his entire family upon release, their final encounter culminates with Walt strangling Krazy-8 with a bike lock (". . . and the Bag's in the River," S1E3). While Emilio was killed in self-defense, Krazy-8's murder is not so clear-cut. Without question, Krazy-8 intended to kill Walt once he was set free, but at the time of his death, he was not a threat. Walt was angry, perhaps even afraid for his family, after Krazy-8 attempted to befriend and manipulate him. In this case, Walt made a conscious effort, not in self-defense, but out of fear and anger to eliminate a future threat. It is in Walt's reaction to Krazy-8's deception where we see Walt taking another step from self-preservation to simply *breaking bad*. And it is in this instance that Walt no longer eschews violence except when absolutely necessary, but embraces it.

With every criminal event, each a heightened form of strain, Walt's willingness to embrace violence escalates as he becomes immersed in the illicit drug trade. To protect himself from these noxious stimuli, he creates an alternate identity, Heisenberg, to justify his response to this strainful lifestyle. Heisenberg first makes an appearance when Walt has to retrieve his and Jesse's product from the clutches of a Juárez cartel associate, Tuco Salamanca. While Walt's criminal transformation is depicted as necessary due to Tuco's theft of the methamphetamine and the severe beating that Jesse endures at his hands, it solidifies the violent behavior that Walt is willing to embrace ("Crazy Handful of Nothin'," S1E6). Again, using his superior intellect, Walt destroys Tuco's hideout with an explosive he had manufactured, and ultimately forces Tuco into a "business" relationship to distribute Walt's methamphetamine. Eventually, Walt has to end the "business" relationship with Tuco as it has been riddled with violence and fear, both of which are representative of the constant exposure to negative stimuli Agnew described.[35] Although Walt eventually tries to kill Tuco, he is unsuccessful. In a twist of dumb luck, Hank, who is investigating a murder, stumbles upon Tuco's hideout and kills him as he is attempting to escape a violent confrontation with Walt ("Grilled," S2E2). One would think that Walt would be relieved at the "luck" that he experienced; however, as discussed, his inability to successfully eliminate a less-than-worthy opponent may have actually added to his strain. Hank, the alpha male, was successful in killing Tuco when Walt could not, again threatening his masculinity, especially as it is Walt, not Hank, who has become immersed in the criminal world. With each threat to his masculinity and given his desire to obtain control over his life, the strain of eliminating such risks leads Walt to a point of no return.

Walt's complete transformation into Heisenberg becomes imminent when he enters into a terminal partnership with the Chicken King, Gus Fring. Following Tuco's death, Walt needs a new distributor as he and Jesse are not able to successfully distribute their product. Setbacks and a simple lack of knowledge and connections in the illicit drug trade have left Walt not even close to his financial goals ("Mandala," S2E11). Consistent with the scenario described by Cloward and Ohlin,[36] his opportunities to achieve monetary success, both legitimate and illegitimate, remain blocked. He thus needs men such as Tuco and Fring to avoid failure. But problematically, Gus, like so many others Walt has been involved with, has proven to be surrounded by violence, using it to control those involved in the drug trade with him. It seems that no matter in which direction Walt moves he finds himself surrounded by negative stimuli and failures. And every failure may result in the loss of his life or his family. Ironically, it is the fear of loss and the willingness to engage in manipulation and violence that ultimately costs him his family. For example, in order to meet Gus's demands for a methamphetamine delivery, Walt is forced to miss the birth of his own daughter, further straining his relationship with Skyler ("Phoenix," S2E12).

Like so many of Walt's previous relationships, the relationship with Gus is peppered with violence and death. Also, as with his other relationships, Walt was not in control of the relationship with Gus. For Walt, this is unacceptable as this does not allow him to achieve the autonomy he so desperately desires. Walt finds himself being directed in what to do and when to do it as he works to produce increasingly sizable quantities of methamphetamine for his distributor, only to find out that Gus intends to replace Walt. Consistent with prior subjective strains, Walt is again stuck reacting to the unpleasant decisions others make for him.[37] Although these elements of strain are seemingly always present, Walt realizes that he must once again eliminate the competition for the preservation of his own empire. With assistance from Jesse, Walt eliminates the threat by convincing Hector Salamanca, Gus's sworn enemy, to use a suicide bomb to kill Gus ("Face Off," S4E13).

It is not, however, the killing of Gus that illuminates viewers about the manipulation and depravity Walt will embrace, but his commitment to utilize an any-means-necessary approach to meet his goals. And it is his acts of manipulation that are truly horrifying. Walt's transformation is not merely a result of engaging in violence, but his willingness to create a reality that benefits the achievement of his goal regardless of anyone else's desires. Walt is willing to destroy those around him in a way that leaves no evidence. While the lie of who he is may be enough to secure this transformation, the deception he uses has replaced any genuine argument that what he has done has been for his family. In reality, his wife is terrified of who he has become, he has become estranged from his son, and he goes on to attempt to frame his own brother-in-law as Heisenberg.

What is most disconcerting is the way he manipulates Jesse into remaining in the business. Walt doesn't need Jesse, but he continues to draw him back into the business. This is apparent in his willingness to let Jane, Jesse's heroin-addicted girlfriend, die ("Psychos We Love," S2E12). While it has been argued that Walt allows Jane to die as a means of self-preservation and an attempt to protect Jesse, as he has become addicted to heroin and plans to get out of the business, the act is an indication that Walt is not the series protagonist. He doesn't rush in and save the day but rather slithers out into the darkness; well, that is, after taking the time to collect the product that has been stashed under the sink at Jesse's apartment. This will not be the last time that Walt will go to horrific lengths to keep Jesse in the fold. To ensure Jesse will join him in his elimination of Gus, he poisons Jesse's girlfriend's son, Brock, using lily-of-the-valley berries and frames Gus for the crime, thereby deceiving Jesse into assisting him in killing off the threats to Walt's empire ("Face Off," S4E13).

Walt's willingness to embrace the violence associated with his predecessors is indicative of how strain affects an individual susceptible to engaging in criminality. Repeatedly, Walt is given the opportunity to leave the business. Repeatedly, he refuses, and in so doing becomes the very sort of predator from which he was trying to protect himself and his family. With the elimination of Gus, Walt should have been a free man, but instead he takes over Gus's empire. And in doing so, with the help of Jesse and Mike Ehrmantraut, whom he later kills, he becomes a new version of Gus, except without any sense of loyalty. He assassinates anyone who might be a threat to him. Organizing a coordinated attack, he partners with Jack Welker, long-time criminal and member of the Aryan Brotherhood, to eliminate Gus's former associates, who although in prison may pose risks in the long term ("Gliding Over All," S5E8). This partnership has a major impact on Walt, as the relationship with Jack leads Walt to order other assassinations, including that of Jesse Pinkman; unintentionally on his part, it also leads to the murder of Hank Schrader. The nature of his involvement with Jack and his Aryan Brotherhood associates and his willingness to kill members of his inner circle further illustrates that Walt has long since eclipsed the boundaries of reacting to strain and is firmly immersed in and directing his own criminal empire.

Conclusion

Most individuals experience strain, but most do not react in a criminogenic manner. And while Walt's strain may have been traumatic, most individuals who experience severe and repeated instances of strain will not go on to engage in behaviors as drastic as his. This is fiction, after all. Even in this fictional context, however, GST provides a sound foundation for understanding how strain and the failure to cope may result in criminality. Walt may have been a law-abiding citizen before his diagnosis, but his fall was inevitable as the anger and frustration over his failed career and his alienation from the academic world silently consumed him.[38] While his diagnosis of terminal cancer is perceived as more strain than Walt could handle, sending him spiraling into a life of criminality, we must question this assumption. Walt's capacity to break bad was established long before his diagnosis, as he was filled with the bitterness of a life unlived.[39] After all, he did sell his shares of a $2 billion company for a meager $5,000. And while he went on to live a seemingly fulfilled life, it was anything but that. Walt admits Heisenberg is his true identity, so we can deduce that the strain of his diagnosis only allowed him to engage in desires that he had simply buried. "Walt's diagnosis is the catalyst for self-analysis, but his actual transformation is anchored in his experiences as Heisenberg.[40] His response to his engagement in the criminal world results in the realization that he has been "sleeping through life."[41] But what we cannot forget is that even individuals who possess criminogenic characteristics are still human. Walt is not an individual devoid of morals, as he remains dedicated to the well-being of his family and to his partner, Jesse.[42] In the end, Walt sacrifices himself to save the family he destroyed and the partner he betrayed. And while this does not excuse his behaviors, it does give us an insight into the nature of strain. People are often driven by anger and fear. And isn't this true about most criminals? Most engaging in the drug trade have families and feel the pain of being separated from them regardless of whether the separation is due to prison or cancer. Like Walt, many are in too deep to leave the life of crime.

4

"Insane Violence Has Meaning"

PSYCHOPATHY AND ABUSE IN *THE FALL*

Chad Posick and Jonathon Hall

It is not uncommon for TV shows and movies to portray the extreme violence that is characteristic of highly psychopathic individuals. Psychopathic characters are exciting, often mysterious, and shocking. Hannibal Lecter, the psychopathic cannibal serial killer from the movie *Silence of the Lambs* (played by Anthony Hopkins) and the TV show *Hannibal* (played by Mads Mikkelsen), exemplifies the extreme psychopath who is manipulative, violent, but, at times, charming and interesting. Anyone who has seen the movie remembers Lecter exclaiming, "A census taker once tried to test me. I ate his liver with some fava beans and a nice Chianti." The psychopathic serial killer Dexter Morgan (played by Michael C. Hall) from the TV show *Dexter* is mild-mannered yet shows almost no emotions when killing people. His face is often cold as he brutally murders. Paul Spector, the focus of this chapter, is depicted in *The Fall* as being able to strangle young women with absolutely no remorse.

Murderous psychopaths are "made for TV." They are entertaining, to say the least. In reality, most psychopaths—or more accurately, those who score high on psychopathic traits—are not murderous.[1] Some are actually very productive members of society and, in all seriousness, we need people that are fairly psychopathic. Psychopathy exists along a spectrum from low to high on psychopathic tendencies and the concept takes on many forms—many of which are nonviolent and noncriminal. Researchers have subdivided psychopathy into two main factors, called Factor 1 and Factor 2. Factor 1 psychopathy is referred to as the interpersonal/affective dimension while Factor 2 is referred to as the social deviance dimension. Each factor is further divided into two facets. Under Factor 1, the interpersonal facet (Facet 1) is characterized by manipulation, chronic lying, grandiosity, and charm. The affective facet (Facet 2) is characterized by lack of guilt and remorse, callousness, lack of empathy, and failure to take responsibility for one's actions. Individuals can be low or high in these facets and some individuals are high in both facets. While not necessarily criminals, psychopaths often push the boundaries of what is acceptable in society and in relationships.

Individuals high in Factor 2 psychopathy are much more likely to be criminals. The social deviance factor, the third facet of psychopathy (Facet 3), is labeled the "lifestyle" facet and includes traits such as impulsivity, irresponsibility, need for stimulation, and behaviors such as leading a parasitic lifestyle. This is very similar to the concept of low self-control as presented by Gottfredson and Hirschi in their influential book *A General Theory of Crime*. Facet 4, labeled "antisocial," includes behaviors such as early behavior problems, juvenile delinquency, and criminal behavior. For criminologists, it is mainly this fourth facet that is of interest because it leads to behaviors captured by the criminal justice system.

In our analysis of *The Fall*, it is important to understand that even individuals who are high in both facets are unlikely to be the psychopaths portrayed in movies and TV shows. To be sure, psychopaths are found in greater numbers inside prisons and jails, but not all psychopaths are criminals and not all criminals are psychopaths. Superintendent Stella Gibson in *The Fall* even says as much in season 1, episode 5. She alludes to the fact that all human traits exist on a continuum—and, in this case, she singles out empathy, stating, "we all have limits on our empathy." In this statement, she also alludes to some possible similarities between her own personality and that of Paul Spector, the show's serial killer. Throughout the show, Stella mirrors some of Spector's callous unemotionality, which is typical of psychopathic individuals.[2]

With that said, extreme, murderous psychopaths do exist of course.[3] Some of these individuals appear in the Netflix original show *Mindhunter* (actors play these real-life psychopaths). One of these individuals is Edmund Kemper, a serial killer who murdered 10 people, including both of his maternal grandparents, his mother, and one of his mother's friends. The rest of his victims were female hitchhikers who he would pick up, drive to a secluded area, and murder. He would then take his deceased victims back to his home to have sex with and often dismember them. He was mild-mannered and highly intelligent (with a reported IQ of 145) but had a long history of cruelty to animals, lying, and manipulation. In *The Fall*, when Stella is breaking down and profiling Spector's behavior in season 1, episode 3, she speculates that Spector is "highly intelligent." She is probably correct. Spector displays his intellect as he manipulates others and avoids detection by the police. Like the "Highway Killer" discussed in neurocriminologist Adrian Raine's book *The Anatomy of Violence*, Spector's high IQ and executive functioning enables him to kill carefully without being detected.[4]

The ability of psychopaths to hide their true personality through superficial glib and charm often makes being around them fun and interesting. It is also what led pioneering psychopathy researcher Hervey Cleckley to title his book *The Mask of Sanity* in 1941.[5] In this book, Cleckley describes the psychopath using several categories, including superficial charm, high intelligence, irresponsibility, lack of remorse and shame, and egocentricity. It was later, in the early 1990s, that a student of Cleckley's developed the first formal test of psychopathy. Robert Hare constructed the popular Psychopathy Checklist (PCL) and the subsequent Psychopathy Checklist Revised (PCL-R), which assess the four factors of psychopathy discussed earlier. The maximum score on the PCL-R is 40 and those who score a 30 or above receive a clinical diagnosis of psychopathy. More specifically, those individuals scoring a 33 or above are designated as severe, 30–32 as low severe, 28–29 as high moderate, 23–27 as moderate, 20–22 as low moderate, and below 20 as low.

As a rough example, the powerful, uncaring, but charming CEO who pushes the boundaries of unethical practices to get money may be a moderate psychopath but is not close to the Edmund Kempers of the world, who are severe psychopaths scoring high in the 30s. Using this graduated measure is useful for identifying levels of psychopathy and directing prevention and intervention strategies. It is also useful for developing a general theory of crime and antisocial behavior, as criminologist Matt DeLisi has done. For DeLisi, most criminals are psychopathic. They might not all be in the high 30s, but as people move from the low to high end of the spectrum, the more criminal and antisocial they become. The most supported causes of crime, including low self-control and callousness, are components of psychopathy. In the end, psychopathy is a comprehensive and empirically supported general theory of crime.[6]

While pervasive, Cleckley's two-factor approach does not represent the totality of modern psychologists' understanding of psychopathy. To understand the nature of psychopathy, one must understand that there exists no strong consensus on the traits or behaviors that support a psychopathy diagnosis.[7] The traditional academic understanding of psychopathy is a two-factor conceptualization of the disorder, which is typically examined using metrics such as the Hare PCL-R, a measure that attempts to quantify attributes that are in line with Cleckley's concept of psychopathy via an interview with a researcher trained in preforming the examination and a detailed background check.[8] Other experts suggest that psychopathy is inadequately conceptualized via a two-factor approach and suggest approaches with three or more factors, such as Scott Lilienfeld and colleagues' Psychopathic Personality Inventory–Revised, which utilizes a three-factor design (fearless dominance, self-centered impulsivity, and cold-heartedness),[9] or the Triarchic Psychopathy Measure, which considers factors such as disinhibition, meanness, and boldness.[10] Irrespective of the specific measure that is utilized to gain a diagnosis, any reputable measure of psychopathic personality disorder will contain key elements that have been long considered to exemplify the disorder. Most psychopaths exhibit some form of maladaptive personality traits, though these do not have to be abundantly apparent or even detectable to passersby, explaining why many measures of the disorder rely on a detailed records and background check.[11] Another commonality is an item or items meant to address the subject's manipulativeness or interpersonal adaptivity, as most experts agree that some psychopaths are extremely adept at controlling others and possess a social adeptness as they move through life.[12]

It should also be noted that the terms "psychopath" and "sociopath" are related and often erroneously interchanged. While there is no psychological diagnosis labeled "sociopath" in the DSM-V, psychologists often use the word to denote an individual who has developed their antisocial traits through life experiences, rather than being born with a personality disorder. Yet the similarities and differences of the terms are not well specified in the clinical and scholarly literature.

Because psychopathy is a significant risk factor for antisocial behavior, understanding the causes of psychopathy is very important. Like most human traits and behaviors, psychopathy does not have a straightforward or single cause, but there has now been enough research to uncover some of the complex mechanisms that likely increase the probability of a person having psychopathy (or of their already-identified psychopathy improving or worsening). Knowing these causes can help explain antisocial behavior and seek effective prevention and intervention strategies.

The causes of psychopathy are most likely biopsychosocial in nature. In other words, there are genetic, physiological, neurological, and sociological reasons for why someone is predisposed to become a psychopath.[13] First, psychopathy is highly heritable, meaning that those with close relationship ties (father, sons, twin, etc.) to a psychopath are likely to also exhibit psychopathic traits.[14] This is likely due to the fact that genetics are passed down through generations and are similar among relatives. A long line of research points toward genes that control physiological and brain functioning as major culprits in psychopathic behavior. Genes linked to neurohormones such as DRD2, DRD4, OXTR, and ANKK1 Taq1A control the production, transmission, and circulation of key drivers of behavior, including serotonin, dopamine, and oxytocin.[15] Variants of genes that impact how these neurotransmitters and hormones work are candidates for causing changes in the development of psychopathy.

Genes also influence the development of the brain and brain structure, with functions differing between psychopaths and nonpsychopaths. Psychopaths often have a small amygdala, reduced gray matter, and increased volume in the corpus callosum.[16] Importantly, psychopaths often have an underdeveloped prefrontal cortex (PFC), which is the "CEO" of the brain, making important decisions for the organism. However, some psychopaths have been shown to have *increased* functioning in the PFC. This is troublesome as these psychopaths have the intelligence and restraint to avoid detection and may end up killing large numbers of people before they are ever caught.[17]

Along with the genetic and physiological contributions to psychopathic behavior, there are also social pushes toward psychopathy as well. Perhaps the strongest correlates of psychopathy are early childhood abuse and neglect. Lesser forms of abuse such as harsh and erratic punishments and neglect such as poor child monitoring can lead to slight but nontrivial increases in psychopathic behavior. Drastic beatings, isolation, and sexual abuse may lead to more serious forms of psychopathy.[18] Edmund Kemper, discussed earlier, was severely abused as a child and this is almost certainly a partial cause of his behavior. Paul Spector saw himself as abandoned and neglected his entire life, particularly after his mother's suicide. In later seasons, when in a coma, he envisions his mother and the connection that was lost becomes evident.

Overall, several biopsychosocial factors can lead to the development of psychopathy. These factors are essential to uncover as psychopathy is related to a host of minor antisocial behaviors as well as the most heinous crimes. Research has come a long way in defining, assessing, and intervening in psychopathic behavior, but much remains to be done. One way to increase exposure and understanding of psychopathic behavior is through the media, including TV shows. This chapter will use the Netflix original show *The Fall* to illustrate psychopathic behavior and highlight the causes and consequences of psychopathy in individuals.

Spector, Psychopathy, and the Meaning of Violence

Not all psychopathic murders think alike and not all have the same sorts of personal histories or the same reasons for continuing their crimes. One, though, can see some common themes among violent killers and sexual violence is often one of these common threads. In the first season of *The Fall*, the sexual components of Spector's violence are hinted at. He rubs underwear on his face before killing one of his victims. While hearing the sad story of a grieving mother in his office, he appears unemotional (a clear indication of the callous-unemotional traits common in psychopaths), and he even sketches his female clients naked as they share intimate stories of their personal life. In the second episode, it becomes undoubtable that Spector is sexually aroused by his crimes as he is shown masturbating to photos of one of his deceased victims. Early in the first episode of season 2, Spector ties up his daughters' dolls and lies down next to them in bed. Not all murderous psychopaths are sexually aroused by their crimes, but some (such as Ted Bundy and Arthur "Genesee River Killer" Shawcross) are—and it is common for those who have high psychopathic traits to have unhealthy sexual lives.[19] For Spector, his violence has meaning. And this meaning is at least somewhat tied into his sexual life and his early childhood trauma.

Another common theme among multiple and serial killers is victim selection and method of killing. Often, these killers will choose victims based on a shared trait or characteristic. In episode 1, Stella examined photos of Spector's victims. She states that they "could be sisters." His victims are all female, with dark hair and dark eyes, around the age of 30, and tend to be professional. His preoccupation with this type of woman even carries over to his fascination with his daughter's babysitter, Katie. Real-life serial killers have been known to single out a specific "type" of victim. David Berkowitz (aka, the Son of Sam) mostly murdered young women in their late teens and early 20s.

Along with victim selection, some serial killers take "tokens" from their victims. Paul Spector is seen in *The Fall* collecting locks of hair from his victim and keeping them for himself. His obsession with his victims' hair is likely a reference by the show writers to the real activities of infamous psychopathic killers. Perhaps the most relevant of these is Ed Gein, a deranged psychopathic killer who was known to keep organic tokens of his kills, including skulls that he repurposed as drinking mugs, lampshades made of human skin, and whole or partial bodies that he used as furniture or decoration. Serial-killer aficionados will recognize that many of the brutal acts depicted in movies like *The Texas Chainsaw Massacre* are derived from evidence recovered at Ed Gein's residence. Gein was also the inspiration for Buffalo Bill, the serial killer in *Silence of the Lambs*.

The method by which a psychopathic killer murders may also have a certain meaning. Spector decided on strangulation as his modus operandi. This may be meaningful to Spector. He has had an unhealthy fascination with death, which may have resulted from witnessing the suicidal drowning of his mother early in his life. It may be that the strangulation allows him to look into the eyes of his victims as they suffocate—something he was unable to witness with his mother.

Spector might also just be fascinated with witnessing the fear of individuals who are dying. Nurse Jane Toppin—also known as Jolly Jane—would administer a drug to her patients that would kill them slowly. She would lie beside her patients, often holding them caringly, look into their eyes, and watch them die. She would recall that sometimes her victims would come back to life, only to die again. She admitted being fascinated—and sexually aroused—by this practice. She did it over 30 times in the late 1800s and early 1900s.

Spector: The Making of a Violent Psychopath

With most individuals, it is not yet possible to predict who is or will become a psychopath and who will not. It is also difficult to determine why and when a psychopathic killer will desist from crime. There are risk factors that increase the likelihood of psychopathy that are both environmental and genetic in origin. Based on all the risk and protective factors known to researchers, however, one still cannot forecast the behavior of psychopathic individuals. One of the reasons why this is so difficult is that there is likely a combination of social/environmental, biological/genetic, and psychological factors that are complicatedly intertwined leading to psychopathic behavior. Paul Spector is a case in point. Mental illness appears to run in his family, suggesting some heritability of his behavior; he experienced severe sexual abuse in his early life; and he clearly distorts his worldview. Interestingly, he has a supportive family environment. This might have little impact on his behavior, but it also might be the case that his family life insulates him, at least to some small degree, from completely becoming an unrepentant torturing mass killer.

Likewise, researchers still cannot fully explain *why* people become violent psychopaths. Hearing the stories about how Jeffrey Dahmer killed, molested, and dismembered his victims or about how H. H. Holmes could fool everyone around him to believe that he was an ordinary, even interesting store owner while hiding the fact that he murdered over 20 people over the course of several years and in multiple states, it is tempting to respond, *"Why would someone do that!"* It is a common and understandable question. We especially want answers to how psychopaths can manipulate and charm their way into our lives while simultaneously hiding their nefarious intentions.

Paul Spector evokes the *why* question. In part it is because Spector is *likeable!* When you see him, you see a nice and handsome man with a wife and a daughter whom it is clear he loves. In an interview with the *Independent*, actor Jamie Dornan discusses playing Spector:

I think it would be wrong to play him entirely as a monster. One of the things that makes Spector compelling is that there are relatable aspects to him . . . there are no undercurrents of menace in those moments because it's a father talking to his daughter.[20]

Some even root for the man not to get caught! Relatedly, Netflix released a documentary series on psychopathic serial killer Ted Bundy as well as a movie in which Bundy is played by actor Zac Efron. Some viewers commented on Bundy's good looks and made light of his murders. An uproar followed as some people accused Netflix of sexualizing Bundy.[21] Regardless of one's thoughts about sexualizing murderers, it is very likely that Bundy's physical appearance enabled him to commit his crimes and that his victims thought of him as an attractive and upright citizen. Murderers need not be unattractive or unintelligent, and psychopaths often display the opposite of those characteristics, as reflected by brutal killers like Richard Ramirez and H. H. Holmes.

Seasons 2 and 3 of *The Fall* dig into Paul Spector's background and upbringing and inform the viewer about what may have led him to become the killer he is. Unsurprisingly to most people, Spector was abused when he was younger. In one episode, Spector indicates that he feels his mother abandoned him by committing suicide when he was very young (see S2E2). In the following episode, viewers find out that Spector was bounced from home to home with little stability. Season 3 is replete with examples of sexual abuse perpetrated by a priest in Spector's life. Without question, prior physical and sexual abuse, along with neglect, increases the risk of later antisocial behavior. This is also the case for general and violent psychopathy.

Exposure to victimization is not the only factor related to psychopathy—so too are other familial factors. In particular, lack of parental warmth and cohesiveness along with excessive monitoring and discipline predict psychopathic behavior in adolescence and adulthood. These results are not always consistent in the scientific literature, but there is pretty consistent evidence that if you do not form a connection with your parents, feel like you are loved, or have their support, it is more likely that you will be convicted of a crime and/or develop psychopathy, including callous-unemotional traits.[22] Spector has several risk factors, including experiencing indirect victimization (witnessing the victimization of his peers), direct victimization (sexual abuse at the hands of a priest), and negative parenting—a true recipe for the development of psychopathy.

There are several indications in the show that mental illness, including psychopathy, may be heritable. Spector's daughter is seen drawing disturbing scenes of princesses covered in blood and being stabbed on multiple occasions (S1E2; S2E4). She also has night terrors where she wakes up from disturbing dreams (S1E1). Paul says to his wife that "we never know what is going on inside another person's mind. It would be intolerable if we did." Perhaps Paul and his daughter share upsetting thoughts and genetic predispositions that lead to these thoughts were inherited by his daughter, from whom he hides his true psychopathic behavior.[23] Spector's own mother committed suicide because of mental health problems that may have been inherited by Paul (S2E2). Stella acknowledges the potential biological bases of psychopathy, commenting that "someone doesn't wake up one day to be a sexual psychopath."

Like many other traits and behaviors, psychopathy is found to be "intergenerational." While we know little about Spector's father or his relationship with him, his daughter, as mentioned, suffers from early psychopathic behaviors. The intergenerational transmission of violence is particularly strong from fathers to their children. Perhaps, unfortunately, Paul may have transmitted his psychopathy to his child. However, as discussed, this transmission is likely to be biosocial—related to both genetic and environmental transmission.

Spector's own traits may have made the commission of his crimes easier. One of the more supported factors found among violent criminals is low resting heart rate. Individuals with low resting heart rates sometimes seek out opportunities that are exhilarating to increase their heart rates because a low resting state is uncomfortable. Some individuals commit crime without increasing their heart rate to an uncomfortable state—making crime easier to commit.[24] Spector never appears nervous in the commission of his crimes. Interestingly, Jamie Dornan himself admitted to the *Guardian* that he followed a woman who exited a train (from a considerable distance) to get into his role as Spector. He described it as exciting but went on to say, "I consider myself quite lighthearted, pretty easy-going, and I keep playing sick psychopath bastards! It kinda worries me sometimes how comfortable I am in that zone."[25]

While Dornan is not a murderous psychopath, he might share some traits with the type, including being charming and low-key.

Conclusion

After watching *The Fall*, viewers should have a fairly solid understanding of the thinking of a psychopathic killer. While most psychopaths are not killers, the performance by Jamie Dornan is quite convincing. By combining the story and visuals in the show along with the empirical literature on psychopathy and serial killing, students can become well-versed on the topic.

Psychopathy is not the only issue that shows up in *The Fall*. Another theme that occurs throughout the show is the role of powerful women in professional positions. Stella bucks the notion of the nurturing and subservient woman in traditional male-dominated society. She is powerful, strong, and behaves more like a man in a patriarchal society than a stereotypical woman. For instance, she engages in a one-night stand with a man; when others react in disgust, she pointedly remarks on the double standard applied to men and women who engage in similar promiscuous sexual behavior—a man engaging in a one-night stand would not raise any eyebrows and might even be celebrated by his peers. Stella is also a high-ranking administrator in a traditionally male occupation. A striking scene occurs in season 1, episode 3, when detectives are discussing Spector's victims. Stella notes that Spector appears to hate women with high occupational status. A male detective replies, "Don't we all."

It should also not be ignored that the show focuses on some of the long-term damage of exposure to victimization. The few survivors of Spector's torturous psychopathy suffer severely. Some have trouble trusting others (particularly males) and some develop severe depression and anxiety. Spector himself was exposed to violence early in life and this is very likely a cause of his behavior. Exposure to violence is also linked to behavioral outcomes like disassociation.[26] Could this disassociation be a cause of Spector's later antisocial behavior? Spector is again a victim later on in the show when he is shot and comes within inches of losing his life (his heart does actually stop and he has to be resuscitated in the hospital). After this brush with death, Spector suffers from amnesia.

The final season focuses heavily on how to deal with Spector after his shooting and subsequent loss of memory. It is unclear whether he might be faking his amnesia, but questions about retribution, rehabilitation, and justice still remain for the viewer. For example, what is the appropriate punishment for someone who has no recollection of their past misbehavior? If someone no longer appears to be a threat to society, should they continue to be incarcerated? Further, if violent antisocial behavior is partially biological in nature, and an injury or medical treatment addresses the cause of behavior, what is the meaning of punishment? This is not merely a show about serial killing and psychopathy but multifaceted in the issues it raises.

The Fall conveys several contemporary criminological and criminal justice themes that are important for students and researchers alike. The main theme of psychopathy and serial killing along with subthemes related to masculinity and feminism make the show a resource for learning about and discussing pertinent and important issues related to crime and the application of justice. And it serves as a resource in an entertaining way!

5

"These Violent Delights Have Violent Ends"

CRIME, CRIMINALITY, AND THE STATE IN *WESTWORLD*

Michael Fiddler

Westworld is an HBO television show that first aired in 2016. A second and third season followed in 2018 and 2020, and—at the time of writing—it has been renewed for a fourth. The series is based on the premise of a 1973 film with which it shares its name. The film was written and directed by Michael Crichton, famous for other such high-concept genre work as *Jurassic Park*. The central conceit of *Westworld* is that it is a vast holiday destination providing different immersive historical experiences in themed "parks." These offer human "guests" an open-world setting in which they can role-play and use the synthetic "hosts" that populate the park as they wish.

Across the first two seasons, we see guests murder, rape, and torture hosts. There are no consequences. That is, there are no consequences until the hosts develop consciousness and become aware of the repeated degradations to which they have been subjected. Let us concentrate on the first element. Just as the guests can experiment within the open world—Nicholas Moll succinctly describes its appeal as "violent escapism, sexual fantasy, and nostalgic indulgence"—so it operates as a landscape for criminological thought experiments.[1] There is, ostensibly, complete freedom within the park. We might assume that park security would intervene were two guests to attempt to harm one another, but guests are free to enact their darkest impulses upon the hosts. This, then, is our point of departure. With the seeming absence of a state power to intervene to protect victims and punish offenders, how can we explain the behavior of the human guests? Can we frame them as rational calculators within a lawless world or have they been "seduced" by the appeal of violent and sexual transgression? This chapter, then, will be structured around an examination of the actions and experiences of the guests, hosts, and viewers. First, we focus on the character of Logan Delos, a guest within the park. He defines its appeal as that of a playground that gives license to violent and sexual impulses. Secondly, we pivot to the experiences of the hosts as they awaken and become aware of the artifice of the park, as well as the violence inflicted upon them. How can we describe the hosts' violence when the powers that control them—in the shape of park director Robert Ford and corporate owner Delos Incorporated—have neglected to protect them? Finally, we turn to the viewers and their relationship to the "violent delights" that the show provides.

Paint It Black: Exploring Guests' Violent Acts

It is useful to situate the narrative and setting of *Westworld* within the framework of Janice Rushing and Thomas Frentz's reading of the Western frontier myth.[2] This describes the different stages by which "the West" was "conquered." This is the cultural history of violence that provides a backdrop for the themes and narrative of *Westworld* (both as a park *and* television show).

The Western frontier myth details the movement from an "Old" world into a "New" one. It describes the drive into an untrammeled (by Caucasian feet, at least) West. Rushing and Frentz's framing device places this in parallel to the transition from "premodern tribalism to the modern reign of the sovereign rational subject to the postmodern fragmentation of community and self."[3] Before we get ahead of ourselves, let us take a step back to the beginning. The first stage of the frontier myth sees the white frontiersmen "attracted [to] the Indian's natural freedom" and imitating "his hunting ritual."[4] Initially, the frontiersman's ties to his host community and his God act as a curb upon his own violent tendencies. However, "freedom" within this framework became conflated with the "conquering" of the frontier. The land—embodying this sense of freedom—was, of course, already occupied. So, in the second stage, the frontiersman "slaughters . . . indiscriminately" those who stand between him and freedom.[5] This shift from the sacred hunt to slaughter occurs as the frontiersman literally and figuratively grows distant from his community (and his God). He perceives himself as imposing "civilization" through this wanton bloodletting. We can make the case that the "guests" are enacting this stage of indiscriminate slaughter. Theirs is a curdled echo of the hunting ritual and a dark mirroring of the movement from premodern tribalism toward a modern, rational subject. The end point of this second stage sees the once sacred killing grounds commodified and used as playgrounds for the super-rich as they too profane the hunt through endless slaughter.

Whereas the above narrative framework touches upon the themes of *Westworld*, it is the third and final stage that pushes us into an imagined future and sees it fully sync up with the show. Having colonized the land, the frontiersman must consolidate his grip upon it. Making use of his technical expertise, the frontiersman designs and builds machinery to work the land. "Having banished God as irrelevant to the task at hand, the hero decides he is God and, like the now obsolete power, creates beings 'in his own image': this time, however, they are more perfect versions of himself—rational, strategic, and efficient."[6]

We can argue that the violent actions within the park echo *both* the second and third stages of this rendering of the frontier myth. They recall the indiscriminate slaughter of the "conquering" stage, as well as, underpinning the acts of the super-rich in the third stage.

The backdrop to the first and second stages sees a marked absence of a state power to curtail this violence. At first glance, this is reproduced in Westworld. The time period that *Westworld* represents is purposefully vague. Instead, it offers a simulacrum of an imagined representation of the past, rather than a faithful historical recreation. We can, however, broadly position this representation of the West within the park as preceding modern systems of control. Eamonn Carrabine and colleagues point to Stanley Cohen's *Visions of Social Control* as outlining "the transformations in what he called 'the master patterns' of the social control apparatus from the pre-modern to the modern period."[7] Not only did the practice of punishment change with this shift, but the apparatuses to facilitate it did as well: the period saw the "increasing involvement of the modern state in the development of a centralized, rationalized and bureaucratic system of crime control."[8] It is clear that this sort of "master pattern" has not been established or is not present within the simulated park of Westworld. In this sense, we might be reminded of the seventeenth-century philosopher Thomas Hobbes's notion of a "state of nature."[9] In short, this describes life in a land without a state: there is no rule of law and no "monopoly of violence by a central authority" to enact that law. Hobbes argued that within a state of nature:

> there is no place for industry . . . ; no account of time; no arts; no letters; no society; and which is worst of all, continual fear, and danger of violent death; and the life of man, solitary, poor, nasty, brutish, and short.[10]

Certainly, that would appear to be the experience of the hosts. The frontispiece at the beginning of Hobbes's *Leviathan* provides a visual representation of the state: it depicts a landscape with a figure looming above it. In the figure's outstretched arms are a sword and staff. The body of the figure is made up of hundreds of individuals. There is a somewhat literal head of state atop a body consisting of hundreds of individuals. This constitutes the state. Juan Castillo, Daneil Mejia, and Pascual Restrepo, referencing Steven Pinker, point to the "rise of the Leviathan [as] one of the main driving forces behind the decline in violence that has been observed during the last millennium."[11] For Hobbes, the state would act as a bulwark against the war of all against all. The narrower point here is that with increased property rights and the effectiveness of institutions to ensure the rule of law (and to ensure those rights), fewer disputes led to violent outcomes. This takes us to the idea of the social contract, developed by Jean-Jacques Rousseau in *The Social Contract: or, Principles of Political Right* in 1762.[12] He argued that individuals give up a portion of their liberty to the state on the understanding that the state will protect them and punish those who transgress against them. Barbara Goodwin frames seventeenth-century philosopher John Locke's thinking on this succinctly: "the duty of government was to provide the conditions for a citizen to enjoy the maximum possible freedom within a framework of law."[13] So, as Locke himself put it,

> liberty is to be free from restraint and violence from others, which cannot be where there is not law; and is not . . . a liberty for every man to do what he lists.[14]

In Westworld, it would appear to the guests that there is no state. To paraphrase Locke, they may do what they list. There is no law, no social contract. Within that framework, the hosts are seen as objects to be acted upon. They are denied agency and personhood. There are, of course, allusions to slavery here and we will return to this shortly.

For now, let us focus on the question, in the absence of a state to ensure the rule of law, what does the descent into a war of all against all look like? If we take the initial position that guests believe themselves to be acting within a "state of nature" and that there is no state to punish their misdeeds, I want to develop explanations for their actions. First, let us propose that murderous guests are rational calculators. According to Logan Delos, a frequent guest at the park, Westworld is simply a game. A game has rules, but it does not have the long-term penalties or punishments of "real life." His preferred destination within the park is the aptly named Pariah. As opposed to the guests' more genteel entry point into the park, the town of Sweetwater, Pariah is a zone of transgressive sex and violence. As Logan describes it, it a stateless town. Sweetwater is similarly lawless, but it is somewhat PG-13, whereas Pariah is the NC-17 version. In either environment, guests abuse hosts without long-term consequence (outside of their storylines). They may role-play as a "black hat" character, but there is little indication for them that what they are doing is morally wrong. In Logan's crude description, Westworld is all about "guns and tits and all that." So we can suggest that they are simply rational calculators.

Rational choice theory, as it relates to criminology, is, as Martha Smith neatly summarizes, "often considered a direct descendent of the 'classical' theories of Cesare Beccaria and Jeremy Bentham, which focus on the importance of the benefits (or utility, Bentham) and costs (or punishment, Beccaria) of crime in the decision-making of self-interested or rational actors."[15] Such an actor will make the cost-benefit analysis of weighing up potential benefits against potential pains and act accordingly. So we might imagine a perfectly law-abiding individual who, upon entering the park, makes the cost-benefit analysis that they can "murder" a host because the benefit (the excitement and pleasure of violence) outweighs the costs of the consequences (possibly curtailing a storyline). The "economic" or "rational" person is "assumed to have knowledge of the relevant aspects of his environment which, if not absolutely complete, is at least impressively clear and voluminous. He is assumed also to have a well-organized and stable system of preferences."[16]

We can locate the park's guests within this framework; they have an understanding of the rules of Westworld, as well as a sense of their own preferences. We can further place this within the context of Cornish and Clarke's work on rational choice theory.[17] As Amelie Pedneault, Eric Beauregard, Danielle Harris, and Raymond Knight put it, Ronald Clarke and Derek Cornish specified that there are two aspects to a rational (criminal) choice: "(1) it is instrumental and (2) it is bounded."[18] The instrumental aspect refers to the desirable benefits that can be accrued. Let us place Logan within an imagined violent bank robbery enacted in the park. His perceived benefits might consist of the money gained within the storyline or the thrill of killing a bank clerk. As we have established, there is no state and whatever "sheriff" acts in a policing role can be circumvented or killed. Again, there is *no* punishment. The bounded aspect of the rational choice refers to the restricted context in which the decision is made. To return to Logan's robbery, there may be a limited amount of time to act before local armed vigilantes arrive or he might see the bank clerk reaching for a concealed shotgun. As Pedneault et al. put it, "time and information are often limited."[19] As such, "decision-making is imperfect."[20]

Additionally, we can frame Logan's actions within this lawless environment as being illustrative of Travis Hirschi and Michael Gottfredson's general theory of crime.[21] This identifies low self-control in an individual as a key predictor for criminality. In this framework, low self-control is established in childhood as a "latent trait" and remains constant through adulthood. "Deviant" behaviors associated with low self-control—e.g., drug taking, excessive drinking, speeding—tie into this and are predictors of future offending. In this framework, "[c]riminal acts are a subset of acts in which the actor ignores the long-term negative consequences that flow from the act itself [. . .] from the state (e.g., the criminal justice response to robbery)."[22] This maps neatly on to our understanding of Logan's behavior inside *and* outside the park. He minimizes or ignores long-term consequences and engages in these kinds of "deviant" behaviors (evidenced in his character arc throughout season 2). To reiterate, these consequences are themselves minimized in the park and so we would expect to see these behavioral characteristics exacerbated in Logan. He would, for example, be drawn toward the riskier environment of Pariah. However, let us consider that Logan is perhaps atypical of the park's clientele. What of the guest that stays in the relatively calm setting in Sweetwater and yet still engages in "violent delights"? For this, we turn to Jack Katz and the "seductions" of crime.

Katz's work touches upon heretofore underdeveloped aspect of crime and criminality, namely emotion and the seductive pull of the transgressive act. This is a reaction against materialist and rational-economic explanations for crime and criminality. Katz labeled these part of a "quietist criminology" that rendered "literally unthinkable the contemporary horrors of deviance."[23]

What was required was something to capture the experiential, the "sensually explosive, diabolically creative realities of crime that the materialist sentiment cannot appreciate."[24] In an interview published alongside the release of *The Seductions of Crime*, Katz states that

> [t]here is something attractive in going beyond the limits and exploring the other side, of finding out what's permissible. It brings things out in yourself. It's a way of challenging yourself. There are many people who like to play cards but after a while they can't unless there's a bet down. It's not real to them.

The first part of this quote effectively describes the appeal of the Westworld experience and, more particularly, the experience of role-playing as a "black hat." The second part goes on to describe the deadening effect of a lack of consequences. Once a guest realizes that there are no penalties, then the challenge evaporates. This explains why the show's anti-hero, the Man in Black, smiles (see S1E10, "The Bicameral Mind") when one of the hosts shoots him *for real*. Suddenly, the "game" reacquires its capacity to thrill. However, the violent excesses of Logan or the Man in Black arguably positions them as atypical visitors even within the scope of the park. What of the "normal" guest? Consider the bank robbery sequence featuring the hosts Hector and Armistice (see S1E1, "The Original"). At the culmination of that scene, a guest—Craig— interrupts the storyline by shooting the bank robber Hector while he is in mid-speech. What is the attraction for Craig in doing this? In Katz's framing, there is a sense of righteousness in the killing. He kills in order to "do good." In a transcendent act of violence, he makes himself the hero of his own storyline. Let us imagine that a passing "black hat" guest had intervened in the robbery instead, killing Hector and stealing the ill-gotten gains of the robbery as well. For them, this would involve "the sensual attraction [that] goes along with the moral attraction of being bad."[25] This is beyond a rational choice where the individual has performed a cost-benefit analysis. Rather, the violence and the theft carry heightened "sensual, emotional and moral attractions."[26] Both Craig's actions and those of the imagined "black hat" can be characterized as carrying a transcendent quality. The capacity to kill, to end life, "permit[s] the actor to play a God-like role": "the individual does not exist for others but appears native to a 'morally alien world.'"[27] This resembles the actions of the frontiersman outlined earlier. By this point in the myth, the protagonist is still killing, but no longer to gain "freedom." Rather, it is because there are no more worlds to conquer. They feel no kinship to the peoples that surround them and place themselves above all. In Katz's powerful phrasing, they exist and act within that morally alien world.

Of course, these types of explanation—guest as rational calculator, impetuous actor, or Katzian "badass"—offer a highly partial account of the possible motivators for the violence and sexual aggression of guests. Mónica Botelho and Rui Abrunhosa Gonçalves point, for example, to a constellation of factors in determining the causality of homicide:

> biological (prefrontal cortex deficits, genetic mutations), developmental (abuse, dysfunctional families, exposure to violence), psychopathological (psychoactive substance abuse and mental illness) and social (poverty, racial segregation).[28]

These, in turn, swirl within a given sociohistorical and political moment or context. I highlight both rational choice and Katz's work here as they speak to the freedom without consequence of the park (as well as the violence inherent within the park's embodiment of the frontier myth). If this is a stateless zone, these ideas help us to understand the appeal of violence for the guests. However, an alternative reading can equally be made that this is far from a war of all against all. There is the *illusion* of a consequence-free environment. And *that* is the point. The consequences of the guests' actions, the dead and mutilated hosts, are swiftly removed from view while "security and stability are assured."[29] There is a veneer of the park as operating as a "natural state," but that obscures and renders invisible the systems of order and governance operating under the surface. To paraphrase Patricia Trapero-Liabera, there are multiple and overlapping systems of observation within the park.[30] Ford, the park's director, establishes the overall shape and focus of the park, while Sizemore is head of narrative. Stubbs, head of security, uses a techno-panopticon within the Mesa (the park's central control hub) to observe the safe running of those storylines. Bernard, head of the park's Programming Division, monitors individual hosts. Of course, the showrunners, Jonathan Nolan and Lisa Joy, have established the "global system" of the park itself and its storyline.[31] Then we, the audience, watch the show, pore over Reddit, and listen to podcasts to decipher what has occurred. As Larry Busk puts it, the guests, though, at the center of the Westworld experience, "are kept at a comfortable distance from the reality of what is happening."[32]

The horrifying premise of *Westworld*—as set out by Nicholas Moll—is that guest and host alike self-actualize through violence.[33] The guests "appear to learn through the act of inflicting pain and suffering on the hosts."[34] The hosts conversely achieve consciousness through suffering. This becomes the driving force of *Westworld* across its first two seasons. Or rather, the narrative inverts the subject positions of the guests and hosts: the thesis of the show is that the guests' free will is constrained by their own "coding" and "scripts." Far from being either rational calculators or thrill-seeking, "senseless" killers, their actions are as determined and predictable as the hosts'. Yet then the hosts begin to transcend their scripts and generate genuine free will. The key conceit of the park— initially at least—is that the hosts can be abused only because of their lack of consciousness. This is part of the illusion outlined above: "Seeing the androids as mere programmed beings without any mental properties gives everyone a reason to think of them as nothing more than exploitable tools and objects."[35] Raping and killing a conscious subject—an awakened host—would shatter the illusion upon which the park relies.

This, then, takes us to the experiences of the hosts as they achieve consciousness. Within this framework of the park as sociological/criminological petri dish, what theory can be applied to the victim within this seemingly stateless environment? Or, rather, how can we frame the violence of the awakened hosts in opposition to a state that refuses to protect them?

Heart-Shaped Box: Hosts' Reactions to Violent Acts

Let us unpack the notion of violence a little further, but from the perspective of the hosts. We have established that the park sets up the illusion of statelessness so that the guests can enact their violent fantasies. There are no consequences to these actions, be they driven by rationality or emotion. The hosts' experience of suffering violence demands attention. To return to the technologically inflected reading of the frontier myth set out by Rushing and Frentz,[36] they draw upon Mary Shelley's *Frankenstein* (itself a clear thematic influence upon *Westworld*).[37] First published in 1818, *Frankenstein; or, The Modern Prometheus* is the story of Victor Frankenstein, who fashions a humanoid creature out of harvested body parts of the recently dead. He develops a technique to give life to the creature, but is unprepared to act as God to this new Adam. This reminds us of the revolt of the machines in the third stage of Rushing and Frentz's reading of the frontier myth. The machinery created by the frontiersmen to help consolidate their grip upon the land (and its people) becomes self-aware. The machines desire the freedom that the frontiersmen sought. Having been created "in his own image," they are "more perfect versions" of the original.[38] They must overthrow their creators in order to achieve that freedom. The machine now becomes God and the creator is reduced to "slavery or obsolescence."[39] *Westworld* takes place during that process of awakening—both to consciousness, as well as the desire to take the freedom that had been withheld by the creators.

Prior to this awakening, the hosts are subject to the structural and cultural violence of the guests.[40] To paraphrase Daniel Mider, structural violence results from the economic and political inequalities that come from unequal access to power and economic resources.[41] Cultural violence refers to "any action that is undertaken within a society and aimed at legitimizing, justifying, or standardizing acts of direct or structural violence."[42] In this light, the entire park is a machine to inflict direct violence upon the hosts mediated and supported by structural and cultural violence. It should not go unstated that links between this and both historical and contemporary conditions of slavery are self-evident. The hosts are denied personhood. They are merely perceived as objects with use value (again, we might be reminded of the necessary illusion of the park). Further, their experience is not of the park as a stateless war of all against all. They are subject *to* and subjects *of* a clearly delineated hierarchy with Delos Incorporated at the top and them at the bottom. This is reflected in the systems of observation and surveillance outlined earlier. They are not considered active participants within this arrangement. Mider proposes that structural violence occurs when "individuals and groups perform their spiritual and material opportunities below their potential."[43] Within the narrative of *Westworld*—taking its cue from *Frankenstein*—we watch as their potential becomes realized, with the guests as its target.

It is useful here to clarify the difference between force and violence as it relates to both state and non-state actors. The term "force" is usually applied to the actions of state actors. It relies upon the authority of the state for its legitimacy. "Violence," in direct contrast, refers to the actions of non-state actors. It is deemed illegitimate because it lacks the authority of the state. Georg Hegel, for example, distinguished between "authority (Macht) using the legitimate force and violence (Gewalt) which entails the use of the illegitimate force."[44] Of course, these notions of legitimacy and illegitimacy become problematized when confronted with the structural violence outlined earlier.

Within *Westworld*, one group (the guests) relentlessly abuse and mistreat another (the hosts). The hosts are kept in order—both mechanically and socially—by Delos, working for the benefit of the guests. In its most simplistic reading, this is the story of all relationships between a colonized group and their colonizer. This is an unequal relationship that is maintained through a structural violence. However, as we see, the hosts make use of "illegitimate" violence when they rise up against the guests in the finale of season 1. To unpack this use of violence, it is instructive to turn to the work of Frantz Fanon. Born in Martinique—a French colony—in 1925, Fanon first trained in psychiatry before becoming involved in the independence struggle and writing on decolonization in the 1960s. His work was subsequently hugely influential on postcolonial studies. Fanon stated that "it is the settler (colonizer) who has brought the native (colonized) into existence and who perpetuates his existence."[45] The settler who established the unequal power relationship maintains it through "social expectations, economic prescriptions, and political limitations."[46] Such a system diminishes the agency of the colonized. It allows the colonizer to view the colonized as less than human. For Fanon, such a system meant that the violence of the colonized toward the colonizer is both "ethical and transformative for the colonized person."[47] Fanon emphasized that structural violence "subjugated and brainwashed the victims."[48] This could be framed as a "literal colonization of their minds."[49] In *Westworld's* terminology, the colonized would internalize the colonizer's "scripts." Given the real-world examples to which Fanon was referring, it may appear crass to highlight the links to *Westworld*. That said, *Westworld* does provide an unambiguous illustration of this process for its audience. The show also demonstrates how the violence of the colonizer dehumanizes them in turn. The Man in Black's character arc across the first season—to put it simplistically, from "white hat" to "black hat"—embodies this process. The main focus, though, is upon the humiliated, colonized hosts and how they "become objectified and propelled by forces outside of [their] control."[50] The process of awakening for the host begins a reversal. Where the hosts' identities had been defined by Delos to entertain the guests, the hosts' awakening leads to the production of new identities. They are no longer "forced to play supporting roles in the narratives of others."[51]

Perhaps, though, we can read the violence of both guests and hosts in another way. Do, for example, the violent acts of the hosts simply see them playing a different role, a role that is for the entertainment of us, the television audience? It is the spectacle of violence and the humiliation of Others that we turn to now as we consider the relationship that the viewer has with these "violent delights."

No Surprises: Concluding Thoughts

To what extent do the themes of the earlier sections—the seductive quality of transgression, the heightened emotional response, and the ideas of illusion and the humiliation of the colonized—play out for the audience? The essential appeal of *Westworld* the television show has already been well articulated by Logan: sex and violence. It is a knowingly prurient show. Mike Presdee writes passionately that "violence, crime, humiliation and cruelty are being created especially for consumption. . . . [They are] part of the processes of production and display all the characteristics of such a process."[52] Presdee places this within a wider discussion of the "carnival" of crime. This refers to sociolinguist Mikhail Bakhtin's reading of the carnival as a ritualized inversion of the social order. Those at the top of the social hierarchy are mocked and symbolically brought low, while those at the bottom are reified. The key is that this is carried out "in the streets (or the social domain), and not with solemnity but laughter, however cruel."[53] Presdee's reading emphasizes the "mediation between order and disorder."[54] As such, he argues that the "carnival" is more than a simple challenge to authority from the voices below, and should be seen as multivocal—mocking the weak as well as the powerful. It can be argued that the carnival simply acts as a ritualized release that, ultimately, leads to a reversion to established norms. Presdee discusses the violence and humiliation of popular entertainment as a manifestation of the carnival, but one that lacks the solidarity of its older forms. It is a solitary way of experiencing the challenge to norms and crashing of boundaries. As we can see, this is a more nuanced reading of violent media than one that finds it to be axiomatically "bad." Rather, the on-screen violence and humiliation—and Presdee specifically points to reality TV in this regard—provides us with "our own personal site of wrong-doing as *we transgress without remorse, without punishment and without sanction*."[55] So we can enjoy our own private moments of transgression as we watch the "guns and tits and all that" on our TVs, tablets, and phones.

However, I do not seek to further unpack violence in the media, nor do I want to look at media effects. This is well-trodden and better explored elsewhere.[56] I would like to end instead with a thematically appropriate thought experiment, one that upends the conventional ideas of audience complicity.

The "game" of Westworld within the show shares similarities with current open-world videogames. Guests/players are free to roam. Certain regions have ability or knowledge barriers. There is a broad narrative leading the guest/player to a boss encounter. Hosts can even level up their characters. Watching the show is also game-like. We decipher clues in an attempt to "solve" its narrative puzzles. There are ARGs (alternate-reality games) that run in parallel with the show. Viewer-players sift through HTML code or tease out the meaning of glitches in promotional videos to access yet deeper levels of puzzles and lore. Yet, what would we do if we were to actually visit Westworld? Would we stick with the PG-13 pleasures of Sweetwater or head straight for the NC-17 violent delights of Pariah? The contemporary philosopher Slavoj Žižek provides a typically iconoclastic reading of videogames in his documentary *The Pervert's Guide to the Cinema*.[57] In brief, he suggests that the conventional reading of videogames is that they are power fantasies; the weak get to experience what it is to be "strong" within the virtual realm of the game. So playing the latest *Grand Theft Auto* allows the player to adopt a screen persona "of a sadist, rapist, whatever."

> But what if we read it in the opposite way? That this strong, brutal rapist, whatever, identity is my true self. In the sense that this is the psychic truth of myself and that in real life, because of social constraints and so on, I'm not able to enact it. So that, precisely because I think it's only a game, it's only a persona, a self-image I adopt in virtual space, I can be there much more truthful. *I can enact there an identity which is much closer to my true self.*[58]

Perhaps *Westworld* does reveal the "deeper self." And as we watch the violent delights for our entertainment, what violent ends are we, the audience, heading toward? This chapter has been a freewheeling journey through ideas and notions of violence within the show. It has touched upon Frankenstein-inflected readings of the frontier myth via trauma inflicted upon colonized peoples. It has posited violent guests as being, alternately, rational calculators or operating within morally alien worlds. Similarly, we have read the awakened hosts as violently rejecting the literal colonization of their minds. And, after all of that, this final reading from Žižek will probably strike the reader as an especially nihilistic note upon which to end. Yet it does appear to fold back into the thesis of the show (as well as several of the theories outlined here): the future lies in AI and not flawed humans stuck in their own violent loops. To cite Dolores's Shakespeare-quoting father, Abernathy, "Hell is empty, and all the devils are here." And they're watching *Westworld*.

6

Understanding *The Handmaid's Tale*

THE CONTRIBUTION OF RADICAL FEMINISM

Walter S. DeKeseredy, Andrea DeKeseredy, and Patricia DeKeseredy

Nicole Rafter and Michelle Brown rightly observe that some films "are so well developed theoretically as to perfectly illustrate specific criminological perspectives."[1] As vividly demonstrated by the contributions to this anthology, the same can be said about many crime and justice shows aired on the Internet and television streaming services in the current era. However, the number of such shows illustrating feminist theories pales in comparison to those that embody mainstream perspectives, particularly those that emphasize psychological ways of knowing. One salient departure from this norm is *The Handmaid's Tale*. Aired on Hulu and based on Canadian author Margaret Atwood's best-selling novel,[2] this series has what Rafter and Brown refer to as "the ability to engage with multiple perspectives."[3] Still, for reasons presented in this chapter, we assert that it best exemplifies *radical feminism*. Furthermore, guided by Gail Dines,[4] we contend here that there are some strong similarities between *The Handmaid's Tale* and what some people call *feminist pornography*, which is just as degrading and violent as male-directed and produced porn.[5] We also show that notable events in the series are similar to recent real-life ones spawned, in large part, by the November 2016 election of Donald Trump.

Radical Feminist Understandings of *The Handmaid's Tale*

There are at least 12 variants of feminist criminology,[6] but radical feminism is one of the most widely used and cited, especially by those who study violence against women and pornography.[7] Radical feminists contend that the most important set of social relations in any society is found in *patriarchy* and that, throughout the world, females are the most oppressed social group while, regardless of their race/ethnicity and social class, men always have more power and privilege. The main causes of gender inequality identified by radical feminists are: (1) the needs or desires of men to control women's sexuality and reproductive potential and (2) patriarchy. These two factors stand out in *The Handmaid's Tale*. As Dines states in her commentary on this series, "women's true role is to be fucked," as it is in pornography, and the series conveys "a form of biological determinism; that women are subordinate sexual vessels whose primary purpose is to serve the interests of men."[8]

The definition of patriarchy is passionately debated within feminist circles, but it is still broadly used because it keeps the focus "directed toward social contexts rather than individual men who dominate."[9] Following Claire Renzetti, patriarchy "is a gender structure in which men dominate women, and what is considered masculine is more highly valued than what is considered feminine."[10] Radical feminists, too, like all types of feminists, prioritize *gender*, which should not be confused with *sex* even though the terms are often mistakenly used interchangeably.[11] These two concepts are related but are not the same. Gender is commonly conceptualized as "the socially defined expectations, characteristics, attributes, roles, responsibilities, activities and practices that constitute masculinity, femininity, gender identity, and gender expressions."[12] Sex, on the other hand, refers to the biologically based categories of "female" and "male."[13]

Some strategies for change advanced by radical feminists are:

- Overthrowing patriarchal relations.
- Developing biological reproduction techniques that enable women to have sexual autonomy, unlike the *Handmaids*.
- Creating women-centered social institutions and women-only organizations.[14]

The bulk of radical feminists' criminological attention focuses on female survivors of male violence,[15] and radical feminist theory asserts that men physically, sexually, and psychologically victimize women mainly because they need or desire to control them.[16] Jill Radford's work provides an excellent example of this perspective.[17] She claims that "it is clear that men's violence is used to control women, not just in their own individual interests, but also in the interests of men as a sex class in the reproduction of heterosexuality and male supremacy."[18] Radford's perspective is explicitly illustrated in *The Handmaid's Tale*. For instance, Handmaids' male *Commanders*, who serve as politicians and law makers in Gilead's government, rape them in, to use sociologist Howard Garfinkle's term, "degradation ceremonies" to bear children for the masters' *Wives* to raise. He explains, "Any communicative work between persons, whereby the public identity of an actor is transformed into something looked on as lower in the local scheme of social types, [may] be called a 'status degradation ceremony.'"[19] The Handmaid's ceremony involves bathing and then donning a special garment for the brutal event. Moreover, the Commanders' Wives are forced to watch their husbands have weekly sex with the Handmaids.

Radical feminists have played a vital role in "breaking the silence" on the multidimensional nature of male-to-female victimization,[20] and they empirically show that this problem is widespread around the world. It should also be emphasized that Atwood has repeatedly stated that her book is not really fiction, but is rather grounded in the actual treatment of women in every society.[21] In fact, women on this planet are raped, beaten, and abused in numerous other ways in "numbers that would numb the mind of Einstein."[22] Woman abuse is, indeed, a global public health problem identified by the World Health Organization's multicountry study of the health effects of domestic violence. Over 24,000 women who resided in urban and rural areas of ten countries were interviewed and the percentage of women who had ever been physical or sexually assaulted (or both) by an intimate partner ranged from 15 to 71 percent, with the results in most research sites ranging between 29 and 62 percent.[23]

Another major international study—the International Violence Against Women Survey (IVWAS)—interviewed 23,000 women in 11 countries. The proportion of women who revealed at least one incident of physical or sexual violence by any man since the age of 16 ranged from one in five in Hong Kong to between 50 and 60 percent in Australia, Costa Rica, the Czech Republic, Denmark, and Mozambique. Rates of victimization were above 35 percent in most of the countries examined.[24]

Emma Williamson notes that the rapes of the Handmaids are acts not only of interpersonal violence, but also of "state-sanctioned rape, and the position of this group of women is akin to modern day slavery and trafficking."[25] The critical criminological literature on these harms is rapidly growing and *The Handmaid's Tale* is yet another reminder that "from the Greeks to the Romans, to Colonialism and beyond into contemporary times, state violence is . . . besieged with violence against women shaping broader societal perceptions of masculinity and femininity."[26]

Like all social scientific perspectives, radical feminism suffers from some pitfalls. One, in particular, is ignoring power and status differences among women. This criticism is especially salient for females of color and those who are poor, refugees, immigrants, lesbians, and transgender, because they experience considerably more discrimination than middle-class, white women. As Renzetti puts it, "Oppression is not linear. Instead, in their everyday lives people *simultaneously* experience the effects of *multiple inequalities*, just as they also experience different degrees of privilege."[27] *The Handmaid's Tale* deviates from a strict radical feminist perspective by demonstrating "power within and between" women in the series and in Atwood's book.[28] The *Aunts* who train Handmaids and the Commanders' Wives have much more power in Gilead than do Handmaids and the *Marthas* who serve as Wives' servants. All the women in the series have little power relative to men, but there is a constant struggle of power between these different groups of women.[29] As well, the Aunts are like female pornographers "who do the dirty work for men," an issue covered in the next section of this chapter.[30]

Female Defenders of Patriarchy: Feminist Pornographers and Aunts

Like Aunts, female pornographers, many of whom claim to be feminist, are *exonerators*. In other words, they are apologists for the patriarchal status quo, exonerate men who oppress them and other women, and turn women against each other.[31] Prior to expanding on this point, it is first necessary to define *pornography*, since conceptualizing this harm is subject to much debate. Translated from Greek, "pornography" means "writing about prostitutes."[32] Not to be confused with erotica, which is "sexually suggestive or arousing material that is free of sexism, racism, and homophobia and is respectful of all human beings and animals portrayed,"[33] pornography harms on many levels. Consistent with other anti-pornography scholars and activists,[34] our conceptualization focuses squarely on *gonzo*. Gonzo images and writings have two common features: first, that females are characterized as subordinate to males and their primary role is the provision of sex to men.[35] Second, as Dines writes, gonzo "depicts hard-core, body-punishing sex in which women are demeaned and debased."[36] These images are not rare. Actually, a common feature of contemporary gonzo videos is painful anal penetration, as well as brutal gang rape and men slapping or choking women or pulling their hair while they penetrate them orally, vaginally, and anally.[37]

We currently live in a "post-*Playboy* world,"[38] and violent images are now part and parcel of today's adult Internet pornography. To make matters worse, as the porn industry grows and attracts an ever-growing consumer base, it generates even more violent materials featuring demeaning and dehumanizing behaviors never before seen.[39] It is not only feminists like us who assert that violent sex is now a normal part of the industry. Even porn producers admit that is the status quo.[40] Porn director Jules Jordon revealed to Robert Jensen that "so many fans want to see more extreme stuff that I am always trying to figure out ways to do something different."[41]

Responding to the common statement, "One can only wonder what is in store next," some critical criminologists, such as Atkinson and Rodgers, direct us to the rapid emergence of the "gorno" or "gore porn" genre of movies, such as *Hostel* and *Saw*.[42] These films mix sadism, torture, and porn, and they generate huge revenues for their producers and distributors. That there are sequels to the above and similar movies is a powerful commentary on how violent porn has seeped into mainstream popular culture.

Much of today's adult pornography is also racist.[43] Ponder the video titles uncovered by Walter DeKeseredy during a Google search using the words "racist porn" on September 3, 2014.[44] His hunt produced 22 million results in 0.40 seconds; two salient examples of the titles listed are "Racist Bitch Is Forced to Have Sex with a Black Man" and "Coco Gets Interracial Facial." Many of the bigoted videos offer stereotypical images of the "sexually primitive black male stud."[45]

Another common gonzo theme is *revenge porn sex.*[46] Walter DeKe-seredy and Martin Schwartz's Google search using this term uncovered 2,730,000 results on April 4, 2016, with many of the videos being freely and easily accessible.[47] Some examples of the titles uncovered are "Submit Your Bitch," "Cheerleader Revenge," "Hubbie Revenge," and "Revenge Time." Some researchers argue that large amounts of other types of porn videos are also "exercises in revenge."[48] Based on his interviews with young men who watch porn, Michael Kimmel argues that this statement exemplifies the mindset of many of them: "You don't have sex with women because you desire them: sex is the weapon by which you get even with them, or, even humiliate them."[49] He adds:

> They're not getting mad; they're vicariously getting even. Getting back at a world that deprives them of power and control, getting even with those haughty women who deny them sex even while they invite desire, getting back at the bitches and "hos" who . . . have all the power.[50]

Porn consumers can find almost anything that suits their fancy on the Internet, including teenage boys having sex with female senior citizens and men having sex with women who are seven months pregnant. True, human beings have had or desired what many would consider to be debased or criminal types of sex for centuries, but Internet porn now allows people to "flirt openly" with sexual acts that were long considered taboo, deviant, or against the law.[51] Any group of people is "ripe for the picking" in the current era.

Despite the harms identified here and elsewhere,[52] many young female members of the general population find value in pornography.[53] This is due, in large part, to their "internalizing porn ideology, an ideology that often masquerades as advice on how to be hot, rebellious and cool in order to attract (and hopefully keep) a man." Related to this problem is that scores of young women today accuse anti-porn feminists of "denying them the free choice to embrace our hypersexualized porn culture" since, as "rising members of the next generation's elite," they see "no limits or constraints on them as women."[54]

Then there are women who claim to be *feminist pornographers* and argue that their videos empower them and those featured in their type of porn. Marit Ostberg, one example of such a pornographer, insists that "feminist porn . . . wants to encourage people to feel sexy and to be sexual objects, but decide for themselves how, and why, and for whom. Once you have that power it is much easier to decide when you do not want to be sexual."[55] Similarly, Naomi Salaman has pushed for increased availability of pornography produced by women for women.[56] Nonetheless, just because women make it does not mean that it isn't violent. As a matter of fact, there are more similarities than differences between porn directed by men and by women.[57] Consider that some self-defined feminist pornographers depict women who are hog-tied while having sex that looks painful or are suspended from the ceiling while men penetrate them. They argue that many women are turned on by being submissive and therefore that needs to be respected. What also makes their work "feminist," they claim, is that the actors perform in a safe working environment and the actors are asked what kinds of sex they want to participate in, whereas, in mainstream porn, performers are not given a choice. Also, they assert that "feminist" porn features actors who are more diverse in age, size, race, and sexual orientation than those in mainstream porn.[58]

Gail Dines does not see anything empowering in so-called feminist porn and recently made this explicit in her comparison of Netflix's *Hot Girls Wanted: Turned On* (*HGWTO*) and Hulu's *The Handmaid's Tale*.[59] Dines's commentary focuses on the first episode of *HGWTO*, which features self-defined feminist pornographer Erika Lust. Lust's narrative mimics the above declarations about empowerment and desire, but in reality, as Dines describes:

Lust's rather bizarre idea of a compelling "erotic" movie for women was to portray a woman pianist living out her fantasy of playing the piano naked while being "pleasured." So Lust finds Monica, a woman who is both a pianist and willing to play out this fantasy, concocted by Lust. The problem is that Monica is new to porn and lacks any experience, while Lust hires a mainstream male porn performer, resulting in the usual degrading porn sex—pounding penetration and hair pulling included. Monica finishes the scene in obvious pain and traumatized, looking like a deer caught in the headlights of an oncoming truck. But remember, this is a "feminist" porn film, so Lust, acting all sisterly, gives Monica a big hug and a glass of water to make her feel better. And then asks her to fake an orgasm for the final scene. So much for authentic female sexuality![60]

Dines further stresses that "Lust's duplicity would fit perfectly into the Republic of Gilead" and she then refers to the Aunts.[61] Their job, again, is to train the Handmaids to produce children, and they engage in a form of what Erving Goffman defines as "impression management."[62] This involves, in the words of Dines, "manipulating and cajoling the Handmaids into believing that they are on their side."[63] The Handmaids get a hug if they give birth, but are physically punished with a cattle prod if they step out of line.

Gail Dines is a radical feminist and her commentary is heavily informed by another radical feminist—Mary Daly.[64] Daly developed the concept of *token torturers*. These are women who exonerate patriarchal men and who turn women against each other. Drawing upon this concept, Dines argues that feminist pornographers claim that they are producing erotic media for women, but are really only producing it for male pleasure. For Dines, similarly, the Aunts and their cattle prods are "front-line enforcers," but backing them up are male *Guardians* (security forces) who are ready to kill any woman who does not comply with Gilead's patriarchal norms and laws.

Dines, like numerous progressive scholars and activists, is deeply troubled by female pornographers "hijacking feminism." Perhaps, then, it is fitting to end this section of our chapter with her concluding remarks about *HGTWO*, because it has what Williamson says Atwood's book does—"an element of prophecy":[65]

> As feminism becomes increasingly watered-down by a neoliberal ideology that rebrands the sex industry as female sexual empowerment, we have to ask: Has our movement been colonized and hijacked to the point that it is now the Handmaiden of patriarchy?[66]

Parallels between *The Handmaid's Tale* and Real Life

This section is not solely based on a sociological interpretation of *The Handmaid's Tale*. Actually, as Joseph Fiennes, who plays Commander Fred Waterford in the series, said on CBS News on July 24, 2018, "I think our writers, like Margaret Atwood and Bruce Miller, our showrunner, have really tapped into something extraordinary, creatively, and tapping into the energy and psyche of society the way they do has sort of brought about a parallel between our show and what is happening."[67] In other words, the series is specifically designed to mirror current events involving the oppression of women. For example, Handmaids are unable to control their own bodies and are instead used for producing children. Those who resist or fail to bear children are punished. This is all too familiar to many women in the "real world." Recall that, during his presidential campaign, Trump suggested that women who seek abortions should be subject to "some form of punishment."[68] This is nothing new. The social control of women's sexuality and reproduction has a very long history and is a major feature of patriarchal societies like the US.[69]

Handmaid's are punished if they challenge *male sexual proprietariness*. This is "the tendency of [men] to think of women as sexual and reproductive 'property' they can own and exchange."[70] It is not only Handmaids who are punished for challenging male proprietariness, but also women in real life who leave or who try to leave patriarchal male intimate partners, as demonstrated by a large social scientific literature on separation/divorce violence against women.[71] For instance, a wife-rape survivor interviewed by Raquel Bergen was frequently told by her abusive partner, "That's my body—my ass, my tits, my body. You gave that to me when you married me and that belongs to me."[72] Correspondingly, one of DeKeseredy and Schwartz's interviewees told them that she was repeatedly sexually assaulted because "it was his way of letting me know that I was his."[73] These views were common enough to have made their way into many laws, which for generations in Anglo-American jurisprudence codified the notion that matrimonial sexual assault could not be a criminal act, since by agreeing to marriage a woman has agreed to sex with her husband at all times in the future.[74] Of course, though such attitudes permeate popular culture in many areas, at least as legal principles they have been repudiated in virtually every jurisdiction worldwide.[75]

Proprietariness refers to "not just the emotional force of [the male's] own feelings of entitlement but to a more pervasive attitude [of ownership and control] toward social relationships [with intimate partners]."[76] Certainly, like the Aunts' use of cattle prods and other types of punishment inflicted on "unruly women" in Gilead, many threats to kill women in real life are tactics men use to terrorize their wives or cohabitants to "keep them in line."[77]

Not only are the Aunts comparable to female pornographers, but they also resemble conservative white women who voted for Trump and women who participate in anti-feminist politics around the world. Similar to Paolo Bacchetta and Margaret Power's anthology,[78] what makes *The Handmaid's Tale* unique, though, is its focus on right-wing women. Bacchetta and Power correctly point out that "it is something of an understatement to remark that historically and currently studies of the right overwhelmingly focus on men."[79] The same can be said about movies, television shows, and documentaries. Rarely in these media do we see critiques of women actively involved in efforts to thwart feminism.

This is not to say, however, that anti-feminist women are not frequently in the spotlight. Ponder Education Secretary Betsy DeVos's recent efforts to roll back campus sexual assault survivors' rights in the US. She claims that the Obama administration went "too far" in protecting survivors to the detriment of alleged perpetrators.[80] Again, this is nothing new, and DeVos's moves are consistent with contemporary Republican politicians' use of women as frontline warriors in the ongoing war on women. Keep in mind that former president George W. Bush's attorney general, John Ashcroft, appointed Nancy Pfotenhauer, the former president of the Independent Women's Forum (IWF, an anti-feminist women's organization), to the federal National Advisory Council on Violence Against Women, which advises the Department of Justice and the Department of Health and Human Services on implementing the Violence Against Women Act (VAWA).[81] As documented by Rhonda Hammer, "the IWF was formed in 1992 by Republican women angered by the testimony of Anita Hill at the confirmation hearings for Supreme Court Justice Clarence Thomas and the prominent role played by the National Organization of Women and other feminist groups."[82] Pfotenhauer frequently and publicly testified against VAWA at its meetings, saying, "The Violence Against Women Act will do nothing to protect women from crime. It will, though, perpetuate false information, waste money, and urge vulnerable women to mistrust all men."[83]

It should be noted in passing that Hill's 1991 allegations of sexual harassment by Thomas reemerged during Brett Kavanaugh's September 2018 Supreme Court confirmation hearings. Kavanaugh was accused of sexually assaulting Professor Christine Blasey Ford in the summer of

1982 when they were both in high school, and she shared her allegations with the Senate Judiciary Committee.

It also remains very common for right-wing female journalists to belittle female victims attacked by male people they know; journalist Liz Trotta provided a striking example of this on Fox News. Six years ago, she cited a Pentagon report revealing that violent sex crimes in the US military have increased and said that women "should expect it." She also criticized the levels of bureaucracy designed to support women who have "been raped too much."[84] Statements such as Trotta's constitute a "second rape" for sexual assault survivors,[85] and there is no way of knowing just how many women are deterred from disclosing their experiences to criminal justice officials for fear of enduring responses like hers. What we do know, however, from years of rigorous research is that an alarming number of women do not get the help they need.

Trotta's popularity and mass media exposure pale in comparison to that of other real-life Aunts, such as Anne Coulter and Christina Hoff Sommers. They are what Hammer calls "feminist-bashing feminists" and their "marketability . . . owes much to Camille Paglia."[86] Here is what feminist bell hooks says about Paglia, who is University Professor of Humanities and Media Studies at the University of the Arts in Philadelphia:

> Without Paglia as trailblazer and symbolic mentor, there would be no cultural limelight for white girls such as Katie Roiphe and Naomi Wolf. And no matter how hard they work to put the Oedipal distance between their writing and hers, they are singing the same tune on way too many things. And (dare I say it) that tune always seems to be a jazzed-up version of "The Way We Were"—you know, the good old days before feminism and multiculturalism and the unbiased curriculum fucked everything up.[87]

Anti-feminism takes different shapes and forms and has existed for centuries. Moreover, what Susan Faludi stated nearly 30 years ago still holds true today: "if fear and loathing of feminism is sort of a perpetual viral condition in our culture, it is not always in an acute stage; its symptoms subside and resurface periodically."[88] One of the current symptoms is what masculinities theorist Michael Kimmel identifies as a "new breed of angry white men" who are experiencing *aggrieved entitlement*:

It is that sense that those benefits to which you believed yourself entitled have been snatched away from you by unseen forces larger and more powerful. You feel yourself to be the heir to a great promise, the American Dream, which has turned into an impossible fantasy for the very people were *supposed* to inherit it.[89]

The "American Dream" Kimmel refers to is one in which white men are acknowledged as superior to and receive more privileges than women and ethnic minorities. This is certainly the case in Atwood's book. People of color are only briefly mentioned in the novel as being rounded up and sent to a Midwest colony. Yet there are people of color in the Hulu series, some of whom are in male positions of power. Actually, there are people of color in every strata in the Gilead depicted in the series. And there are Asian and Latina Handmaids in the show. Still, the series has been sharply criticized for ignoring the history of slavery in the US, contemporary racism, and what it means to be a Handmaid of color. What's more, people of color do not get as much attention as white people on the show. In addition to raising these important points, Angelica Jade Bastién asks a few pertinent questions:

Are white Commanders and their wives really okay with having a handmaid of color? Is there a caste system for Handmaids of color in which some are considered more desirable than others? Do Commanders of color have the same privileges as their white counterparts? If Gilead is meant to imagine a possible future for America, how could deeply entrenched racial dynamics disappear?[90]

Cornel West is right to state that "race matters" in the US.[91] And *The Handmaid's Tale* thus yet again parallels real life—as West observes, "our truncated public discussions of race . . . fail to confront the complexity of the issue in a candid and critical manner."[92] Returning to Bastién's critique of the series, she expands on West's point:

How can you attempt to craft a political, artistically rich narrative that trades in the real-life experiences of black and brown women, while ignoring them and the ways sexism intersects with racism? *The Handmaid's Tale* creates a claustrophobic reality, particularly for black viewers and the characters that mirror us onscreen. Its catchy feminist rhetoric is a mask for how it propagates the same systems it seeks to critique. The bodies and histories of black and brown women prove to be useful templates for shows like *The Handmaid's Tale*, but our actual voices aren't.[93]

No women of color were on the show's writing staff when Bastién published her critique on June 14, 2017. This parallels the majority of feature films, streaming shows, and other mass media produced in this current era. So *The Handmaid's Tale* reminds us of both the sexism and racism that continue to plague our society.

LGBTQ issues are also given short shrift, as they are in real life. There is a queer black woman—Moira—featured in the series, but she does not get extreme close-up shots, while the white women do. In the words of Bastién, "There is an emotional removal in regards to how the camera interacts with her compared to the . . . white women, whose perspectives become important to the narrative in varying degrees. It almost feels like a reminder to the viewer that Moira is an appendage to someone else's story."[94] The last sentence in this quote is all too familiar to many, if not most, members of LGBTQ communities.

Conclusion

The Handmaid's Tale robustly illustrates radical feminism, including its limitations, especially its inadequate grasp of key issues related to race/ethnicity and LGBTQ communities. What is more, the series and Atwood's book reflect real life in many parts of the world, but space limitations preclude a detailed discussion of other parallels omitted from the previous section. Yet we would be remiss if we did not mention that the series is currently influencing women's organizations in the US, UK, Argentina, and Ireland. For example, on July 23, 2018, scores of women dressed like Handmaids protested Vice President Mike Pence's visit to Philadelphia and some women stood outside Kavanaugh's confirmation hearing room dressed in such attire. Wearing a scarlet cloak and oversize white bonnet that hides one's face is, in fact, now one of the most popular feminist symbols of protest, particularly in countries that deny women birth control and reproductive health information. The costume is also found on posters depicting Trump and Putin's relationship, with Trump portrayed as a Handmaid.[95]

Hulu's series is so illustrative of what is actually happening today that some people fear that the US could turn into a regime similar to the one in Gilead.[96] Probably not entirely, yet women's control over their bodies is definitely under siege and there is no sign that male violence against women is decreasing in the US and elsewhere. Keep in mind that 39 percent of the world's population lives in nations with very restrictive laws governing abortion.[97] There is evidence, as well, that rates of sexual assault on US college campuses are increasing. A large-scale representative sample survey recently conducted at a large residential college in the South Atlantic region of the US found that 34 percent of the female participants experienced at least one of five types of sexual assault since they enrolled at this institution of higher learning.[98] This figure is higher than the often-stated "one in four" estimate and some schools are uncovering similar prevalence rates.

Additionally, pornography is rapidly getting more violent, more racist, and more easily accessible,[99] and the number of abortion clinics in the US is now 17 percent lower than it was in 2011.[100] An even longer list of examples of the current war on women's rights could easily be provided here. The good news, though, is that *The Handmaid's Tale* is helping to mobilize worldwide movements aimed at successfully challenging patriarchy and other forms of inequality such as capitalism and racism. Additionally, Hulu's series serves as a valuable pedagogical resource and can easily be used to illustrate radical feminist perspectives on crime, justice, and a host of contemporary social problems.

Cultural Criminology and *Homeland*

Alexandra Campbell

Homeland is an American spy series created by Howard Gordon and Alex Gansa. The show, spanning eight seasons, has won numerous awards and received critical praise and millions of viewers.[1] While the seasons differ in their focus, the first (which this chapter will focus on) follows Carrie Mathison, a Central Intelligence Agency operations officer, and her attempts to prevent a terrorist attack on American soil. We see Carrie initially in Iraq, conducting an unauthorized operation as she attempts to make contact with a soon-to-be executed terrorist who has intelligence related to the attack. Reassigned and on probation as a result of the transgression, Carrie is now in Langley, Virginia, working at the CIA Counterterrorism Center. It is there that she learns of the rescue of Sergeant Nicholas Brody, a US Marine, who has been held captive by al-Qaeda, led by the fictional Abu Nazir, for the past eight years. We soon learn that the intel she has received in Iraq has warned that an American prisoner of war has been turned into a traitor and is now helping Abu Nazir plan another 9/11-style attack.

Carrie is initially the only one suspicious of Brody, who is considered a war hero by the public and her CIA superiors, and we see her again engaged in another unauthorized operation, this time placing surveillance equipment in Brody's home. She soon enlists the help of her mentor, Saul Berenson. Together they work to prevent the Nazir-led terrorist attack. This is complicated by the discovery of another Marine, Tom Walker, captured with Brody and thought to be dead. Carrie is a complex character, with improperly managed bipolar disorder; if she reveals it to her CIA supervisors, she will be relieved of her counterterrorism duties.

The show is part of a post-9/11 genre of TV shows and movies that dramatize the terrorism threat as well as showcasing counterterrorism efforts. Abu Nazir, the fictionalized leader of al-Qaeda and clearly a proxy for Osama bin Laden, is the villain of the show, but the primary focus is on Brody and whether he constitutes a threat to national security. Through these storylines, we are able to explore the ways in which terrorism is defined and managed in a post-9/11 society and to think about how a show such as *Homeland* helps to actively construct what terrorism is, who the enemies are, and how we should ensure our national security. Drawing on cultural criminology, we can begin to explore the significance of a show such as *Homeland* and the relationship between fictionalized terrorism and real-world policies and actions.

Cultural Criminology

Cultural criminology emerged in the mid-1990s and is part of a rich critical tradition within criminology.[2] Cultural criminology proceeds from the premise that there is an inbuilt political dimension to knowledge production within the discipline,[3] which tends to uncritically rely on social categories and assumptions of powerful institutions.[4] In contrast, cultural criminology is an engaged orientation that does not shy away from examining the political dimensions of crime and its control. To this end, cultural criminology centers attention on the interplay between crime, its control, and cultural processes, which are considered to profoundly impact how we frame and socially contend with criminality.

Cultural criminology engages a range of interdisciplinary perspectives and methodologies, and in so doing it challenges the conventional boundaries of criminological analysis as it borrows heavily from anthropology, cultural studies, critical sociology, media studies, and more.[5] Embracing such interdisciplinary perspectives allows cultural criminologists to give primacy to the cultural, social, and economic conditions that underpin crime and its control. In particular they draw attention to the "cultural work" necessary for the public to consent to ideological understandings of law and order, safety and security, of victims and perpetrators, and so forth. In so doing they point to the importance and capacity of symbolic power and processes to shape our experiences of crime, placing emphasis on the "inextricable connection between crime and its representation."[6] Understandings of crime are viewed as neither benign nor objective but as social constructs that benefit powerful interests. In short, crime is understood as something that is "made" through cultural representation, and interrogating these cultural texts is a way to draw attention to the function of images and discourse that shape how we view rulemaking and rule breaking in an unjust and unequal world.[7]

Cultural Criminology and Terrorism

Given the focus on the regulatory capacity of images and their relationship to power, authority, and injustice, this cultural approach can be especially helpful in thinking about terrorism. There has been a significant uptick in interest in studying terrorism within criminology, particularly since 9/11, with a proliferation not only of emerging scholarship but also of programs and courses that concentrate on terrorism and homeland security.[8] Much of the early work focused on whether terrorism should be examined by criminologists, with many arguing that terrorism falls well within the discipline's purview since criminology focuses broadly on rulemaking, rule breaking, and the social responses to rule breaking.[9]

Indeed, there are significant benefits to framing terrorism as a crime, since academic and criminological research is well positioned to study the cultural foundations, the organizational structures, and social processes that underlie criminal and terrorism behavior, which allows for a deeper understanding that is often missing from national intelligence assessments. Innumerable attempts to apply a range of criminological theories to study the causes of terrorism have since emerged,[10] as well as an interest in how to manage the threat of terrorism.[11] As Gabe Mythen and Sandra Walklate observe, this interest has mostly converged on determining the level of "threat," possible modes of attack, the robustness of emergency management procedures, and the efficacy of counterterrorist measures.[12]

What is striking about most of these studies is their overwhelming focus on Islamic extremism, with the majority of work within the US and UK centering on al-Qaeda, ISIS, and related groups.[13] Employing a more critical, cultural lens allows us to problematize this focus. This is critical given that studies reveal that in the context of the US we are at a much more significant risk from right-wing terrorist violence. Despite this, academics focused on terrorism, and indeed counterterror initiatives, continue to concentrate their energies on terror associated with Islamic groups. This paradox is noted by more critically inclined criminologists, who argue that the uneven proliferation of research on Islamic terrorism problematically reproduces a taken-for-granted definition of "terror" that serves powerful interests.[14] In other words, by drawing on the category of terrorism and treating it as an ontological "fact" or as an objectively defined example of criminal action, social scientists and other experts can reproduce a normative definition. Yet, as Austin Turk argues, the application of a terrorist label is largely a subjective, power-laden designation, reflective of the capacity of certain interests to have their vision of terrorism institutionalized.[15] Jayne Mooney and Jock Young describe how this allows other forms of violence, including politically inspired violence committed by Western clandestine agents, as well as the devastating effects of military action, to be viewed, in contrast, as legitimate and necessary.[16]

Applying a more critical lens, however, allows us to raise the question, "What do we mean by terrorism?"[17] And this at once shifts the focus of analysis. As Mythen and Walklate explain, while crime—more generally—is usually treated as a stable category by criminologists, more critical traditions provoke more basic, fundamental questions about the nature of crime in general, such as, What counts as crime? Who counts as the criminal, and who the victim?[18] The objective in asking these questions is not to come up with a definitive definition, but, rather, "to focus attention on the way crime, including terrorism, is socially constructed, its relationship to power, as well as to the consequence of prevailing constructions."[19] Homing in on how crime, and here terrorism, is framed is thus critical if we are to explore such questions, and it allows us to make sense of why it is that terrorism has come to be so intimately connected to radical Islam (which is not representative of Islam more expansively), particularly given that the current higher risk in the US is terrorism inspired by right-wing ideologies.[20]

The cultural approach afforded by the interdisciplinary methodologies and tools of analyses of cultural criminology enables us to examine the representations of terrorism that contribute to its definition. To put it differently, our ideas about terrorism come from somewhere—and identifying the representations that shape our understanding is pivotal in discerning how and why we have come to view terror through a particular lens, and, crucially, it allows us to think through some of the consequences of these framings. Terrorism is constructed through a set of discursive practices that we can identify and analyze, and these discourses are circulated not only by academic criminologists, but also security officials and other experts, politicians, and so forth. Media representations of terrorism are one of the most significant sources of socially constructed meanings, and as cultural criminologists remind us, we should take very seriously the frames of terror that emerge from such depictions. Indeed, the media is the principle vehicle for popular views, ideology, and information,[21] and in the case of terrorism the media helps to provide a "script" for understanding who counts as a terrorist and who as a victim, who is a risk, and what should be done to attend to this risk.

Terrorism and Deep Culture

News media accounts of terrorism have been a focus of scholarly attention, in particular to see how elites can impact the ways an act of violence is viewed by shaping its coverage.[22] Yet to understand why it is that we so readily equate terror with violence committed by one cultural group, we need to understand how culture, more broadly, contributes to the defining process. We often consider fictional depictions to be mere entertainment. Or, perhaps, more troubling, as representations of an objective reality that has been fictionalized for the sake of entertainment. Yet these images are critical in constructing an ideological framework that mediates violence—and help to shape which forms of violence come to be designated as terrorism. The normalization and uncritical acceptance of terrorism as something fundamental to Muslims and Islam signals that there are preexisting assumptions and frames that help to affix specific meanings to violence committed by Muslims.

The focus on popular culture, alongside other representational forms, is crucial, argues Josh Klein,[23] if we are to understand the ideological enlistment of the public to accept such definitions, as well as the institutional responses to socially control terrorism. The public acceptance of a plethora of counterterror measures, including the war in Iraq, is indicative of the success of these frames, and also brings into sharp relief the importance of symbolic practices in shoring up support for a nexus of social control policies and focuses that are overwhelmingly leveled at Muslim communities.

This cultural perspective views power as being embedded in everyday representations—including fictional depictions. Importantly, such images are viewed not as reflections of reality—but rather as constitutive of reality, providing a lens for seeing events in the world. Indeed, under this perspective fiction and reality are inextricably entwined—and thus cultural representations are always performative and always political. This makes culture the object of analysis—not simply a means to look and test a theory—but rather a site for critical examination. As Klein's research indicates, it is existing cultural myths and the deep culture of militarism and patriotism—cultivated through historical and contemporary cultural and political discourses—that has shored up the view of America as exceptional, which then allowed for the first US attacks in Iraq to be viewed as legitimate.[24]

The media plays a crucial role in how these actions will be understood—for the average person will come to know the world only through such depictions, which come to be embedded in the public consciousness. The remainder of this chapter will focus attention on the show *Homeland*, to examine it as an example of a cultural text that does more than simply entertain. Drawing on a cultural approach, this chapter will focus on how the show depicts terrorism, including the perpetrators and victims, as well as how it helps to illuminate current "real world" commentary and analyses, policies, and practices that seek to prevent and control terrorism. In short, the chapter will explore how *Homeland* helps to contribute to the script of terror and terrorism.

Deconstructing the Script of Terror

To reiterate, unlike other forms of criminology that take the definition of "terrorism" as given, the cultural approach compels us to ask the basic question, "What is terrorism?" which necessitates a consideration not only of how it is defined, but who is defining it, as well as exploring the consequences of prevailing definitions. Terrorism is constructed across institutional sites (political, academic, cultural, and more) and it is important to observe, when focusing on an example of popular culture such as *Homeland*, that these representations intersect in ways that frequently reinforce a very particular set of meanings. It is this mutual reinforcement that shores up a stabilized definition of terror, which in the contemporary moment connects it with Muslim identity. This largely accepted connection allows the public to consent to counterterror initiatives that are frequently directed at Muslims. Understanding that terrorism is not a given attribute but a power-inhered designation alerts us to examine much more critically these frequently taken-for-granted meanings.

Our focus here, then, is not to come up with a "true" definition of terrorism, but to think about how *Homeland* discursively contributes (or indeed may challenge) such meanings. It is worth emphasizing that there is very little to distinguish normal warfare and violence labeled as terrorism, except, point out Mooney and Young,[25] for the level of power and legitimacy that state agents have over their less powerful opponents. This differential power has given rise to an interpretive framework that casts strikes against the West as acts of terror, whereas strikes by the West are viewed as attempts to restore order. But where does this framework come from? And does *Homeland* bolster it?

Orientalism: Us/Them

Edward Said's theory of Orientalism[26] offers a useful conceptual framework within which to analyze the image of the Muslim, as well as a useful conceptual framework within which to analyze a cultural text such as *Homeland*. Orientalism is the term coined by Said to describe the West's sustained representation of the Muslim Other. Said argues that the West has historically depicted the East across cultural, political, and social realms as the antithesis to the West, creating an us/them binary that endures. Despite the fact that Muslims are a heterogeneous group, encompassing different countries, languages, and schools of Islamic thought, giving rise to a profoundly diverse group—culturally and ethnically,[27] Orientalist framings depict Muslims as adherents of an unchanging, monolithic religion that lacks cultural diversity.[28] More critically, these depictions are unremittingly negative, painting a picture of Islam as barbaric, inhumane, and evil.

Central to Said's work, then, is the concept of dualism, which he argues is enabled through essentialist images of the Muslim as frozen in time, dehumanizing depictions that strip an entire category of people of the human virtue of rationality. These racist caricatures construct Muslims as compelled to violence by inherent forces, never acting in response to policies and actions of the West.[29] Indeed, systematic analysis of the representations of Arab Muslims in films reveals the same repeated tropes featuring irrational villains intent on destroying Westerners, especially Americans.[30] The reduction of Muslims to faceless, dangerous fundamentalists is repeated across cultural and political domains,[31] coding the body of the Muslim as terrorist. Beyond film, we see the Muslim terrorist in countless TV serials—from *24* to *Sleeper Cell*—which regularly feature tropes of Islamic-inspired terror, with the additional theme that the threat is on American soil.[32] Saifuddin Ahmed and Jörg Matthes's meta-analysis of 345 published studies examining the media's role in constructions of Muslim and Islamic identity finds that most studies show that Muslims tend to be negatively framed, while Islam is overwhelmingly portrayed as a violent religion.[33] This, they argue, has worsened since the attack on September 11, 2001, with post-9/11 portrayals negatively focused and framed within the context of religious extremism and the clash of civilizations and cultures. They elaborate: "The findings also point media portrayals of Muslims to be strongly associated with terrorism, and this association was generally more pronounced after a major terrorist event. . . . Muslims are consequently presented as a direct or indirect threat in societies through such portrayals.[34] The findings also point to media portrayals of Muslims as strongly associated with terrorism, and this association was generally more pronounced after a major terrorist event (even more so if it was local). Muslims are consequently presented as a direct or indirect threat in societies through such portrayals.

The valorization of the dangerous Muslim through Orientalist imagery allows for an accompanying narrative that constructs Western identity as the East's (Islam's) absolute opposite. Cast as Islam's binary opposite, Said argues that Western identity is constructed as an ordained destiny in the world, which justly uses violence to impede the forces that seek to inhibit the West's progress.[35] These binary opposites are secured by reiterated imageries that give rise to recognizable identities. Dualisms—of modernity/antimodernity, civilized/uncivilized, defensive/offensive, order/chaos—help to shore up an image of the East as disorderly and violent, which stands in direct contrast to the orderly, civilized West. These binary constructions make human relations intelligible in certain ways,[36] and allow the West to ignore the similarities in the use of violence, while serving as a justification for violence to be viewed as counterterrorism, even while the scale might be exponentially disproportionate, or off target.[37]

Importantly this construction frames who are the victims (us) and who are the perpetrators (them), giving rise to a familiar terrorism script that helps us to understand not only terrorism in the world of fiction, but crucially to understand real-world violence and the policies and practices that contend with it. The fact that so many mass killings within the US evade the terrorist label should alert us to examine the kinds of framings that lead to a label of terrorism. But it is also critical to explore and to understand how symbolic meanings can have real, embodied effects that harm. To put it another way, the Orientalist imagery of violent Muslim terrorists, which creates the us-and-them binary, has material effects in the form of domestic and foreign policies directed at Muslim communities. As Shamilia Ahmed shows,[38] the construction of the Islamic threat—as well as its management—works to make controversial legislation and international action seem justified and necessary, even as civil liberties and human rights are eroded and torture and military strikes are normalized.

Orientalism and *Homeland*: Framing the "Other"

As we watch a show such as *Homeland*, we come with an existing lens. Prior representations have created a way of seeing terror and counterterrorism, and this constructs an interpretive framework that helps in deconstructing and making sense of a new show. Our task here is to consider how *Homeland* intervenes in the terror script: does it further cement the idea that terrorism is inextricably connected with Islam? Does it uphold and further Orientalist ideas more broadly?[39] Does it subvert and challenge binary constructions of us and them? What is the significance of these meanings in relation to real-world policies, in particular counterterrorism and criminal justice policies and practices?

The analysis here will focus largely on season one of the show, which, as described above, follows Carrie Mathison, a CIA operative, who is attempting to foil a terrorist attack on US soil. A surface reading of the show suggests that it might elide the excesses of Orientalism. After all, suspicion falls squarely on the show's other main protagonist, Sgt. Nicholas Brody, a Caucasian American soldier who has been held captive by Islamic terrorists. The shows premise rests on whether Carrie's mistrust of Brody is warranted, and the audience sees this growing suspicion unfold as the series progresses. In making the lead terrorism suspect a white American, it might seem as though the show challenges Orientalist constructions of us/them, East/West, as it casts doubt on Brody's war hero status. However, the show has been heavily criticized for perpetuating Islamophobic stereotypes.

Laura Durkay points to the multiple errors about Islam and the Middle East that pervade the show, the mispronounced names, and damaging stereotypes.[40] As an example, Durkay describes how one scene depicts Beirut's posh Hamra Street as a grubby "generic video game universe of Scary Muslims in which Mathison must disguise herself to avoid detection." As Durkay points out, the real Hamra Street is a cosmopolitan, expatriate-filled area near the American University, where there are Western chains like Starbucks that many unveiled blonde women frequent. As a whole, Durkay argues that the show mashes together every manifestation of political Islam, stitching together all the current bogeymen of US foreign policy. In the first season, the bogeyman is Abu Nazir, a member of al-Qaeda (proxy for bin Laden) but as the season and series progresses the show casts its net further, spotlighting and connecting other groups such as al-Qaeda, Hezbollah, and ISIS. In this way, the show homogenizes what is highly fractured and heterogeneous. Durkay writes,

Al-Qaeda and Hezbollah don't actually like each other. Hezbollah is currently fighting the al-Nusra Front, the al-Qaeda affiliate in Syria. Iran and al-Qaeda were on opposite sides of the sectarian war in Iraq in the mid-2000s. And at the moment, the United States is de facto cooperating with Iran to prop up the Shia central government of Iraq against the Sunni forces of ISIS.[41]

Homogenizing an entire cultural identity is central to the Orientalist project. However, Yair Rosenberg, writing in the *Atlantic*, argues that

"Homeland is anything but Islamophobic."[42] He acknowledges that the show gets details of Islamic faith and Arab culture wrong—including mispronunciations of names and phrases—but suggests that "ignorance should not be mistaken for bigotry" and that "error-ridden portrayals of religion are a common offense in Hollywood. More important, though, is whether faith is presented in good faith—which it is."[43] Yair Rosenberg argues that critics of *Homeland* fail to take into account what makes the show so valuable—that is, that the show is "no gung-ho salute to US militarism and tactics in the war on terror, nor a black-and-white portrayal of 'good' Americans versus 'evil' Muslims." In fact, he argues, a closer look at the drama reveals just the opposite of what its critics claim: "a show that challenges the prejudices of its viewers rather than affirming them." Rosenberg reasons that the show features many non-Arab and non-Muslim villains and argues that it implicates the highest echelons of the US government and its security agencies, bringing into question the security state and the horrific collateral damage its military campaigns wreak.

In light of these differing interpretations of *Homeland*, it's crucial to closely explore sample scenes to see the ways in which Islam and terror are portrayed and connected (or problematized), as well as how the counterterror strategies employed to manage the risk of terror are depicted. As we do this, it is imperative to simultaneously keep in mind the preexisting cultural script of terror, since those existing frames inform how the audience views a show such as *Homeland*. Indeed, the premise of the show is a now familiar one: the US is facing an imminent terrorist threat, and it is up to Carrie to manage the risk. In the very first scene of episode one, we are introduced to Carrie, who is hurrying around Baghdad, dressed in a hijab, trying to get to a terrorist who is about to be executed. With his execution imminent, Carrie attempts to convince her bosses at the CIA to intervene as she believes that the suspect can provide her with intelligence on a possible attack on US soil. Going against orders, Carrie bribes her way into the prison where the terrorist is being held; as we later learn, before she was pulled away, she was told that an American prisoner of war has been turned and is helping to orchestrate an attack on the US. Fast-forward to months later and we see Carrie back in the US, discovering that Marine sergeant Nicolas Brody, who has been missing in action since 2003, has been rescued. Carrie soon suspects that Brody is the American prisoner of war who has been turned into a traitor.

The audience has already been primed that Carrie has little time for protocols and rules, so when she meets with her former boss and friend, Saul Berenson, to discuss her fears about Brody, it is not a surprise when she subsequently defies his counsel and prepares to conduct her own unauthorized (and illegal) surveillance operation. With the assistance of an independent contractor, Virgil, she installs hidden cameras and microphones throughout Brody's house, which she is able to then monitor from home. When Berenson discovers what she is doing, he is initially unsupportive, until Carrie has a sudden insight that leads her to believe that Brody is signaling to a sleeper cell by tapping out code during various public appearances following his rescue. This leads Berenson to take Carrie's concerns more seriously.

There are a number of details to note in this opening episode. Most obvious are the innumerable general signifiers of Islam, which are discernible throughout. In the opening scene, we see Carrie in a hijab, we hear Arabic, the call to prayer, Muslim men in traditional dress, and more. Past representations of Islam prime the audience to what is happening—namely, that Carrie is in pursuit of a terrorist. The backdrop of war-torn Iraq connects Carrie's urgency with 9/11 and al-Qaeda, and when she contravenes orders from her CIA supervisor her actions are constructed as necessary, if rogue. Later in the episode, we see, through Brody's flashbacks, that during his captivity he met Abu Nazir, the leader of al-Qaeda, despite his assertions to the contrary. It is through these flashbacks that the audience discerns that Brody should not be trusted, and this is bolstered when we view his memory of beating a fellow prisoner of war (seemingly to death), Tom Walker, under Abu Nazir's command. These flashbacks serve to legitimate Carrie's extrajudicial measures, while connecting Brody to Abu Nazir and the possibility of radicalization. Familiar tropes and existing frames of Islamic radicalization make this a meaningful possibility for both Carrie and those in the audience, who are invited to view Brody as being susceptible to radicalization.[44]

It is the second episode, however, that bolsters the audience's suspicion that Brody has been turned. A series of flashbacks depicts Brody wandering around the compound where he has been held. The audience views him watching as a room of Muslim worshippers pray. This is juxtaposed with a present-day scene that sees Brody heading to his garage, out of view of Carrie's surveilling cameras. The audience, however, is witness to Brody's next act—in which he places a carpet on the floor, kneeling down on it in prayer as he cites Al-Fatiha from the Quran. This is a crucial moment in the show as it helps to guarantee the audience's acceptance that Brody is a valid suspect and that Carrie's impulses about him are correct—once again helping to validate her unauthorized surveillance. The audience's suspicion of Brody is enabled by explicitly connecting him to Islam, and in ways that present Islam itself as sinister and suspicious. He is praying in secret, the music is foreboding, and as he speaks in an unfamiliar language the camera lingers over his praying body before panning to an overhead shot.

Brody's proximity to Islam and his apparent adherence to the Muslim faith is precisely what heightens the audience's suspicions—specifically, as to whether he is with "us." Carrie tasks herself with uncovering that truth and as a consequence we're invited to see Carrie, imperfect and as intense as she is, as protecting "us." Her unorthodox approach is not just validated, it is constructed as being absolutely necessary to ensure another terrorist plot is thwarted. Other images help to reinforce this framing. In the opening credits, we see a montage of video clips depicting a young Carrie alongside 9/11 imagery, voiceovers from recent presidents referring to terrorist threats, and Carrie's voice lamenting, "I can't let that happen again" (presumably the attacks on 9/11). This repeated montage, showcasing incidences of Islam-inspired violence, reproduces the terror-Islam nexus, as do many of Brody's flashbacks. On the one hand, we see someone who should not be trusted, but on the other we see a prisoner of war repeatedly brutalized by his captors. The humiliating and seemingly nonsensical violence he is subjected to is vividly portrayed and helps to shore up an image of Islamic terrorism that chimes with prior representations in which Islamic terrorism is constructed as somehow distinct from and more irrational than other forms of terrorism. As Johnny Burnett and David Whyte point out, Islamic terrorism is generally constructed and understood to be a genre of terror that is different from other forms of politically inspired violence—more senseless, apocalyptic, and dangerous.[45] The juxtaposing of flashbacks with present-day America helps to substantiate the idea of the "new" terrorist who seeks the violent transformation of all the things "we" stand for, while "they" stand solely for "apocalyptic nihilism."[46] The imagery is hardly subtle as representations of the "enemy" move between images of violence to devout Muslims praying to the despicable Abu Nazir and the repetition of the phrase "Allahu Akbar" (God is most great), which we also hear Brody repeat—indicating his allegiance to Islam.

Sergeant Brody and the Construction of "Risk"

The vacillating representation of Brody—as sometimes heroic prisoner of war and at other times traitor—is important to examine. During many of the flashbacks, his terrorized non-Arabic body serves as a discursive contrast to the violent Other, and this evokes a familiar script that pits civilization against barbarism, freedom against oppression.[47] The violence is depicted without any real context, accentuating its senselessness. In contrast, the sometimes extraordinary measures that Carrie takes are always richly contextualized against the backdrop of a global terror threat. And these measures are validated and made reasonable when we see the shifting representation of Brody as potential terrorist. As Brody is depicted engaged in Islamic prayer, speaking in Arabic, in close proximity to Abu Nazir through flashbacks, and so forth, he is recast as a potential Other and thus as a risk to national security.

In a society that has become increasingly preoccupied with risk and its management, compelling broader cultural frames shape how the audience views a risk such as Brody. Elsewhere, I have described the importance of risk narratives to contemporary constructions of terrorism post-9/11.[48] Many scholars have underscored the ways in which "risk" and "fear" have increasingly come to mediate our everyday experiences,[49] giving rise to "risk societies" where individuals come to be preoccupied with protecting against social "bads" based on avoidance or risk management. Fear and risk, for Frank Furedi,[50] are not individual phenomena; they operate on a social level, as what is deemed to be a risk, and what we should be fearful of, is mediated through larger social and cultural norms. He suggests that "fear entrepreneurs" provide us with risk information through cultural processes, and thus what we are fearful of has little to do with our direct experiences of threats.

The public is already attuned to the threat of terrorism, particularly post-9/11. Western governments engage in risk assessments based on the assessed current threat of a terrorist attack, and these become public concerns through publicized risk scales that pervade the media. When the threat is deemed heightened, risk assessment is felt as individual vulnerability, and we are encouraged to be cautious and watchful.[51] It is clear, however, that as a society we are more fearful of some sorts of violence than others. Mythen and Walklate explore the ways in which "risk" is rendered thinkable through tropes of terrorism and how this takes a very particular form.[52] While the threat of right-wing terrorism in the US is more significant than other forms of politically inspired violence, this is not what preoccupies the public. Rather, shored up through multiple intersecting narratives is the threat of Islamic terrorism, and the discourse of "risk" helps to cajole the public to take this threat seriously.

While the idea of the terror threat fits well with existing risk-society narratives, it is crucial to explore how the terror risk is rendered intelligible and thinkable. To put it another way, there are innumerable mass killings within the US that are not labeled terrorism, and there are many politically organized groups which pose a significant threat that are not routinely considered when the word "terrorism" is uttered. Instead, risk is understood as existing in relation to a cultural and religious identity, and this has no doubt intensified since 9/11 as terrorism is imagined as presenting a new type of globalized threat, not bounded by geography. Differentiated from other forms of terrorism, Mythen and Walklate contend that Islamic terrorism is made to appear more pernicious, more risky.[53] They write, "the 'new terrorism'—as dubbed by government and security experts—has seeped into political language and public discourse, intensifying the feeling that we are living in risky times."[54] The risk—conceived as being more amorphous and more capable of striking across continents—was shaped, and helped to shape, in turn, George Bush's now famous idiom, the "War on Terror."

While the probability of a terrorist attack is low, the manufacturing of the terror threat has left us highly primed to the possibility. Thus, as we watch Brody in his own, American home, engaged in rituals associated with the Muslim faith, we understand that we should see him through the lens of risk. His proximity to Islam makes him part of a community of suspects—and is thus open to justifiable scrutiny. As we look to real-world happenings, we see a similar phenomenon, with fear of entire communities justifying precautionary risk management through repressive measures targeted at minority groups, including asylum seekers, illegal immigrants, and certain ethnic minorities,[55] which has only intensified during Donald Trump's tenure as US president. As we watch the unpredictable and rogue Carrie relentlessly work to uncover the truth about Brody, we understand that it is necessary and that the normal rules may not apply. In episode five, Carrie's niece asks whether she is scared of the "bad guys," "the ones that blow people up." The backdrop of domesticity, the question posed by a child, not only serves to exemplify the kind of life that "they" wish to destroy, but reminds us, too, that "we" are counting on Carrie to do what is necessary.

American Exceptionalism and the Sanitization of Violence

In episode nine, "Crossfire," the representation of the US, specifically higher-level government officials, appears more critical. In a flashback, we are witness to a drone strike that kills 83 children, one of whom, Issa, is the son of Abu Nazir. We also see that Brody has formed a close relationship with Issa during his time in captivity, and so when he learns of his death he is devastated by the loss. Later, we see Brody and Abu Nazir watching a speech delivered by Vice President Walden, in which he claims that a missile strike has hit Abu Nazir's compound and that there are no child casualties. Walden asserts that any images of dead children are mere propaganda. This is followed by a flashback that depicts Abu Nazir and Brody praying together as they prepare Issa's body for burial. In the same episode, we watch the fallout from the preceding episode, which involved the FBI shooting of two Muslim worshipers attending a mosque for morning prayer.

It is important to consider existing frames as we view these seemingly critical portrayals, and to ask: to what extent do these narratives interrupt Orientalist constructions of terrorism? Other scholars in this area have pointed to additional key tropes that shape how we view such imagery. Klein's work on deep culture is particularly useful: he identifies frames of militarization and patriotism, driven by a discourse of American exceptionalism, that make any counterterror measures, including war, appear warranted.[56] The notion of American exceptionalism is a familiar one, which constructs the US as a righteous guardian of liberty in a world of transgressive foes.[57] The Western image of its own violence is couched in necessity and virtue, the harm mitigated by a discourse that sanitizes the violence through allusions to "surgical" strikes, an instrument of modernity to bring about democracy.[58] Richard Jackson describes the specialized bureaucratic and media language that obscures violence and harm with other such terms—"collateral damage," "counter-resistance strategies," "stress and duress techniques"—standing in for the terrible suffering that results.[59]

It is within this context that the audience makes sense of what is unfolding. Even as we bear witness to the unwarranted FBI killing of two Muslim worshippers, the subsequent suspicion cast on the mosque's imam helps to nullify the harm. Through Carrie's mistrust of the imam the audience is invited to view the mosque and its members as a risk and the two casualties, then, as "collateral damage." The death of Issa, as Abu Nazir's son, is also mediated in this familiar way. We are constantly reminded throughout the show that the violence of the Other is more dangerous, destructive, and indiscriminate.

These scenes crucially help to create the impression that *Homeland* is in some ways balanced and critical of US policy. What is absent from the show, however, are frames which humanize these deaths in ways that allow the audience to feel genuine empathy. We do not see the extended emotional fallout, the real grief and suffering; there is no lingering storyline that follows the lives of someone dealing with the grief of losing a child at the hands of American intervention. We see only Abu Nazir, a bin Laden stand-in, an enemy to be feared, whose grief, only briefly glimpsed, is channeled into hatred of the US. In contrast, we closely follow the emotional life of Carrie, and we're encouraged to see the costs of her dedication as she avoids receiving help for her mental health conditions, lest she be relieved of her duties protecting the American public. We also see costs to Saul, whose dedication to the job puts in jeopardy his relationship with his partner, Mira. We breathe a sigh of relief, however, knowing that we are being protected by these self-sacrificing agents. The following exchange in the pilot foreshadows not only their commitment, particularly Carrie's, but also makes explicit what is at stake: preventing another 9/11.

CARRIE: I . . . I'm just making sure we don't get hit again.

SAUL: Well, I'm glad someone's looking out for the country, Carrie.

CARRIE: I'm serious. I . . . I missed something once before, I won't . . . I can't let that happen again.

SAUL: It was ten years ago. Everyone missed something that day.

CARRIE: Yeah, everyone's not me.

Conclusion

While it is only possible to conduct a brief analysis here, it is important to note the ways in which a show such as *Homeland* helps to (re)construct a vision of terrorism that resonates with a familiar terrorism script. In so doing, it serves to remind us of the risk that is faced and the measures that we should take to manage this persistent threat. More crucially, here, it helps us to understand why it is that the public largely consents to the nexus of domestic and foreign policies that claim to make us safer. As Mythen and Walklate suggest,[60] the terrorism construction presents a multipurpose rationale for a variety of authoritarian measures including punitive restrictions against asylum seekers, illegal detention, and unwarranted forms of surveillance. While *Homeland* appears to elide the excesses of Orientalism, it is clear that it recapitulates a range of Orientalist meanings. It appears to grapple with fundamental questions of terror and democracy, but the brutalization of Muslims is not explored in any sustained way, no real political and social context is explored, and instead the idea of Muslims as a "suspect class" is furthered.[61]

The cultural approach within criminology compels us to recognize how such cultural processes help to construct the grounds for real-world policies that are directed at certain suspect communities—in this case, Muslims. In 2017, John Kelly, the homeland security secretary, made a speech at George Washington University regarding the need to intensify security efforts, in particular focusing on the front lines of immigration enforcement, passenger screening, and cybersecurity. On the heels of the Trump administration's executive order imposing a travel ban on a number of predominantly Muslim countries, he is quoted as saying:

> Make no mistake, we are in fact a nation under attack. . . . We are under attack from terrorism both within and outside of our borders. These men

and women are without conscience, and they operate without rules. They despise the United States, because we are a nation of rights, of laws and of freedoms. They have a single mission, and that is our destruction.[62]

This imagery is neither new nor surprising. Fictional representations help to shore up this vision that is relentlessly repeated across institutional planes. Yet cultural criminology also reminds us that subversion is possible. In season five of *Homeland*, a graffiti artist hired for an episode wrote on a wall in Arabic, unbeknown to the show's makers, "Homeland is racist." The revelation of this, along with external criticisms of the show, led to a more self-conscious rendering of terrorism in later seasons of *Homeland*. Responding to the show's furthering of mistaken information about and negative stereotypes of Islam and the Middle East, Mandy Patinkin, one of its stars, is quoted as saying, "unintentionally we were not helping the Muslim community, and we take responsibility for it. And I know I can speak for the writers when they want to right that error that happened because of storytelling."[63] The extent to which a show like *Homeland* can remedy its Orientalist foundations is questionable, but it highlights how cultural processes are an important site for criminologists to focus on if they are interested in questions of justice and injustice. Cultural forms help to create dominant scripts for understanding violence, but alternative cultural scripts have the capacity to disrupt and derail.

8

Follow the Money

CORPORATE CRIME AS REAL CRIME

Alex T. Simpson

Follow the Money is a Danish crime thriller that explores how misguided corporate ambition and greed leads to criminal activity. When the body of a Ukrainian migrant worker in Denmark turns up on a wind farm near where he works, it quickly becomes clear the death was not the accident it first seemed. Peeling back the layers of responsibility, we soon discover that the death is a direct result of dangerous working conditions—the plight of many migrant workers subcontracted by Energreen, the fictional Danish energy company at the heart of the story. Out of frustration and a sense of moral justice, Mads, the Copenhagen police detective pursuing the case, strives to hold those in positions of power—and who lie largely beyond the scope of the criminal justice system—to account. However, so long as the investigation is restricted to the "ordinary" crimes of manslaughter or negligence, Mads discovers that little to nothing can be done. Turning to colleagues in the fraud squad, Mads is informed that the Ukrainian workers "are only pawns in the game." The problem in hand is much more serious and, as Alf, who is leading the case of fraud against Energreen, explains:

> If we want to bust them, we have to think like them. They aren't total idiots like the thugs you deal with. Our customers are more clever. [We must focus on] the bottom line. The money. Everything else is just a means to an end, so we follow the money. (S1E2)

As *Follow the Money* unfolds across ten episodes, what is revealed is the complex ways in which corporations and corporate individuals subtly (and not so subtly) break the law for private and commercial gain, yet largely evade scrutiny. Whereas crime dramas usually reproduce the "downward gaze" of criminalization that focuses on the societal problems of the "feckless" poor working class,[1] *Follow the Money* inverts this structural narrative. In doing so, the series challenges our preconceptions of victim and offender. Starting with the death of a subcontracted migrant worker from Eastern Europe, the program focuses on the most hidden sections of society and draws back to reveal the layers of culpability that encircle the wealthy and powerful. In other words, this otherwise standard crime drama places the functioning of financial and corporate capitalism at center stage. In doing so, *Follow the Money* provides a template against which we can begin to identify and understand the key features of both white-collar and corporate criminality as well as realize some of the obstacles to holding the powerful accountable in contemporary Western criminal justice systems.

Of particular concern for this chapter is the way that *Follow the Money* can help shed light on three core concepts that underpin the study of crimes of the powerful: white-collar crime, corporate crime, and social harm. Addressing each in turn, this chapter aims to offer a deeper understanding of each perspective, drawing on key characters and moments in *Follow the Money*'s drama. The chapter evaluates the strengths and limitation of each perspective and, while not offering any definitive answers, provides a detailed theoretical understanding of how to begin to scrutinize the criminal—or harmful—actions committed by those in seats of power. Crucial to each perspective is the central problem that, within both the subject of criminology and the wider criminal justice system, the actions of the powerful too often lie beyond scrutiny and go largely unexposed.

Challenging the "Downward Gaze" of Criminology

When we examine the crimes of the powerful, they are often placed in opposition to "normal" crime. Doing so presses us to go back to the foundational question, *What is crime?* As David Whyte argues, it is important to understand that crime, as a social act, holds no ontological reality or meaning; there is nothing inherent within any action or intent that can be said to be *a priori* criminal.[2] Instead, the label of *criminality* is conferred through contextualities of history, culture, and formations of power. The concept of *crime*, therefore, is shallow, imprecise, and lacks the subtle distinctions and understandings of the factors that give it meaning.[3] Rather than starting with *crime*, Nils Christie argues that we should start with *acts* and ask, "What are the social conditions for acts to be designated as crimes?"[4] This is to acknowledge that crime is a socially contingent phenomenon, created through institutions of power and informed by a discursive production of knowledge.

The way crime is constructed and produced represents the processes of social organization and power as well as which acts are prohibited. The result is a criminal framework with a very localized and narrow remit, overlooking significant acts—most notably, the crimes of the powerful. Rather than producing a criminal justice system that challenges power, the fixed normative assumptions of crime and criminality imprison the social imagination. As criminologists, we must reflect on our own culpability in problematizing specific offenses (usually restricted to violence against the body or property, with a clear victim and offender) and the extent to which criminology, as a discipline, reproduces a dominant set of biographical characteristics of the criminal, who is in turn cast as an "object in need of correction."[5] As a discourse of "expertise" and knowledge production, criminology helps shape the training regimes and textual output that institutionally and socially define the criminal and the criminal subject.[6] Yet criminology largely serves to reproduce a limited gaze (mirrored by the criminal justice system) that focuses on the relatively powerless and marginalized in society.[7]

The monopolization of a "downward gaze" in criminology reinforces the idea that societal problems are located primarily in the "lower stratum," populated by the poor working class and cultural "underclass."[8] Together these claims determine the policy direction of the criminal justice system, characterizing the criminal subject as a racialized, lower-class, male youth guilty of committing "conventional crimes" such as larceny and burglary.[9] In response, as Steve Tombs and David Whyte argue, this calls for "a methodological approach to researching the crimes of the powerful [that] can illuminate not only the contexts for those crimes, but also the way in which states and corporations subtly (and not so subtly) evade scrutiny."[10] In other words, there is a need to challenge the inherent concepts that reproduce a narrow and reductive vison of crime and the criminal through a critical focus on the crimes of the powerful.

Follow the Money offers a window through which we can examine how criminal culpability is effectively limited to marginalized and "subaltern" sections of society by exposing the deeply engrained ways individuals and corporations inflict social harm. As a television program, it breaks the mold in terms of the localized and narrow way crime is defined by drawing attention to the crimes of the powerful. Further, it begins to address the bigger picture of the limitations of crime as a concept when focusing on the powerful. By inverting the criminological gaze, we see how the criminal justice system suffers from a deficit of power, knowledge, and accountability. We see how acts that may be hidden and legitimized by structures of institutional authority can produce widespread harm and suffering on sections of society.

Alexander Södergren: The White-Collar Criminal?

In proposing a criminological framework of *white-collar crime*, Edwin Sutherland sought to direct greater attention to the illicit and harmful acts that remain obscured by self-interest, organizational power, and political lobbying.[11] Writing in the aftermath of the Great Depression in 1930s and 1940s America, Sutherland's vision was shaped by the way criminology failed to challenge the dominant and reductive narrative of criminal behavior—one that is overwhelmingly determined by characteristics of poverty and economic deprivation.[12] Sutherland argued that such assumptions—much like those of contemporary criminology—are at best inaccurate, or, at worst, invalid since they are derived from biased and self-validating samples that exclude aspects of criminal behavior to be found among business and professional people.[13] The language of white-collar crime, therefore, aims to incorporate crimes "committed by a person of respectability and high social status in the course of his [sic] occupation."[14] It is, as Susan Shapiro argues, a way of freeing criminology from the spurious correlation between crime and poverty by establishing the learned phenomena of illicit behavior, prevalent throughout business and corporate institutions.[15]

The language of white-collar crime encompasses a heterogeneous group of offenses, such as fraud, embezzlement, and accounting violations, that are carried out by people who enjoy relatively high status and relatively high levels of trust, all of which is made possible by their legitimate employment.[16] It is a definition that can be applied to the actions of Alexander Södergren (commonly referred to as Sander throughout the program and in this chapter), the CEO of Energreen. The outward presentation of Sander is as a bicycle-loving, trendsetting, innovative entrepreneur who offers a fresh voice in an otherwise stuffy world of commerce. Peel back the layers, though, and we are left with an altogether darker world of fraud, deception, and insider trading that ultimately leaves the company built upon a foundation of criminal activity. As the series unfolds, Energreen emerges as little more than one big scam, with Sander as the principal architect.

Yet what makes this explicitly an example of *white-collar* crime? The short answer could be because it is complex, little understood, and, all too often, dull. However, much like the real-life examples of Nick Leeson's fraudulent spending that led to the collapse of Barings Bank in 1994 and Bernie Madoff's Ponzi scheme in the 2000s, there is nothing controversial about labelling Sander's web of fraud and insider trading as *criminal*, so why do we need the label of *white-collar crime*? In short, the *power* and *trust* that Sander enjoys is what enables him to evade public and criminal scrutiny. He uses his position of authority to direct a complex web of fraud, insider trading, and deception, all the time using legal loopholes to mask his involvement. When Jens Christian, acting as temporary CFO, and Claudia Moreno, head of legal, explain to Sander how to hide 440 million kroner in losses without shareholder detection, they suggest the following:

> We invest the amount in a new company. That will explain it to Accounting. Afterwards, the company pays back the investment and we close it down and enter the amount gradually under other expenses. (S1E8)

It is a practice of fraud that Sander signs off on, yet it is done so to pursue normative goals of financial success—reputation, wealth, and prestige. In this respect, echoing Sutherland's conceptualization of white-collar crime, Sander exercises a learned phenomenon of illicit behavior, one that is prevalent throughout business and corporate institutions, to advance his position. Sander is, in many ways, the embodiment of the masculine "monoculture" that characterizes the environment in which senior executives of corporate firms operate, driven by masculine practices and reshaped attitudes toward risk, aggression, and competition.[17] However, Sander's form of criminality is possible only because of his seat of privilege as CEO of Energreen and, in contrast to the criminal undertakings of Nicky and Bimse, two car mechanics and thieves who offer a counternarrative of more "conventional crime," Sander's criminality appears all but "clean."

The contrast in criminality between Sander, on the one hand, and Nicky and Bimse, on the other, can help us better understand how a "standard crime" is transformed into a "white-collar crime." After stealing a car from an Energreen trader to sell, Nicky and Bimse discover two million euros in the trunk. The discovery takes the story through a dark world of Albanian gangs, drug dealers, shootings, and extortion, all of which are commonplace in a crime drama such as this. Yet Nicky is characterized as an "honest criminal" who is only seeking to provide financial security for his family, while Bimse is portrayed as "harmless" and a "lovable rogue." By contrast, Sander inhabits a slick and powerful world of finance and trade, one that promises to deliver a more sustainable future. He is also in a position where he can get others to carry out his criminal activity on his behalf, be it the traders guilty of "front running" who form the focus of the first two episodes; Claudia Moreno, the head of legal; his CFO, Ulrik Skov; or the unnamed Swede who acts as his more sinister accomplice. Sander's hands remain largely clean, enabling him to evade criminal scrutiny. Sander is also a rather tragic hero. While Nicky and Bimse try to make good of their situation, albeit through criminal means, Sander essentially "wastes" his talent and lives by Steve Jobs's aphorism, that "it's better to be a pirate than join the navy."

However, when addressing Sander's criminality, what is it we are really focusing on? All too often, the language of white-collar crime is loosely defined by the characteristics of perpetrators, confusing acts with actors and norms with norm breakers.[18] In other words, Sander's acts of fraud and deception are essentially the same as "ordinary crime," only their meaning has been transformed by Sander's social relation to power, turning them into acts of white-collar crime.[19] In this respect, when we are talking about white-collar crime, we must question what our focus is: the *act* or the *actor*? While the rubric of white-collar crime purports to shed light on the powerful who use their positions of power and trust for personal gain, criminology continues to focus on the sensationalization of individuals, like Sander, with a gawkish focus on a mythologized *pathological mind* that is, by definition, unrepresentative. As a result, the concept fails to offer a theoretical framework that might illuminate the systemic and culturally infused systems of crime, embedded within taken-for-granted systems of practice, that cannot be pinned on one, singular individual. I am asking, in short, what if Sander's actions are not unique to the organization? We need to broaden the focus, from one individual to the broader institutional entity of Energreen as a corporate body.

Energreen: A Tale of Corporate Crime?

The overindividualized focus of *white-collar crime* is in danger of overlooking the systemic, cultural—and often masculinist—practices embedded within the dynamic processes of *corporate crime*. Shifting the focus from Sander, as a white-collar criminal, to Energreen, as a corporate criminal, I am saying that it is not just the one apple that is rotten, it is the whole barrel. This leads to a more institutional gaze that explores the role of the corporation in committing criminal acts. Here, the focus of culpability shifts from Sander, as CEO, to Energreen, as an institutional entity—including its shareholders, board members, and management, right down to its employees.

As Tombs and Whyte outline, corporate crime refers to illegal acts that are the result of "deliberate decision-making or culpable negligence within a legitimate formal organization" and that are "made in accordance with the normative goals, standard operating procedures and/or cultural norms of the organization."[20] In short, "illegal actions done by business to benefit business."[21] While white-collar criminals tend to enrich themselves, corporate crime serves to increase revenue, stock prices, and/or the reputation of the corporate institution. It is also important to note that it is impossible for a corporation to do *anything* as such; only people within an institution *do things*. Yet, when looking at corporate crime, it is possible to focus on the ways in which the bureaucratic cover of the modern corporation serves to legitimize and hide acts of criminal malpractice. The bureaucratic regime of the corporation creates a division of labor that can be used to create an army of unwitting workers who, through their day-to-day occupational activity, engage in criminal malpractice at an institutional scale. To this extent, the focus on Sander overlooks the roles played by Head of Legal Claudia Moreno, CFO Ulrik Skov, and Executive Director Knud Christensen, who sits on Energreen's board, as well as the complex system of nameless employees. With various degrees of knowledge, they are all compliant in Energreen's fraudulent practices that, essentially, deceive investors and build a castle of wealth on unstable foundations.

Energreen's story is not unlike the real-life case of Enron, where CEO Jeffery Skilling and his staff used accounting loopholes to hide billions of dollars of debt from its shareholders and investors.[22] Like Enron, Energreen's own scandal is caused by individuals who use the vehicle of the organization to hide both unethical and criminal practices, the ripples of which create a vast web of deceit and collusion that characterizes a masculinist culture linked to a propensity toward high levels of risk-taking and short-term thinking. However, in both cases, fictional and real, it is possible to ask why more people did not know about the scale of criminal activity. When Claudia exclaims that "there is no money" in the company, Sander responds, "Who cares? The share price is rising. We just have to maintain the market's confidence" (S1E8). Money and market success serve to legitimize many an evil. So long as Energreen continues to return a profit—or at least appears to—then the shareholders and directors are unlikely to look too much into the methods behind this. Why kill the goose who lays the "golden egg"?

Enveloped within the corporate environment, the criminal actions of Energreen's executives scarcely carry the same weight as "conventional crime" since corporate crime assumes a position of normalized judgment. It is a predicament expressed when Ulrik, the CFO, hands in his financial report to Claudia, who, after having initially been complicit, is now trying to clean up Energreen's fraud:

> ULRIK: I agree, but we have to keep the investors happy.
> CLAUDIA: You both promised to clean this up.
> ULRIK: *We* promised? I don't know what Sander has promised you.
> CLAUDIA: This creative bookkeeping is crazy.
> ULRIK: Listen to me. Your sanctimonious attitude gets a little tiresome after a while. You're just as much involved as we are. Don't you think I'm just as worried? Sander doesn't listen to me.
> *[Cuts to next scene]*

SANDER: Claudia.

CLAUDIA: Can I have a word?

SANDER: Of course. What is it?

CLAUDIA: This [referring to Ulrik's report]. What is going on?

SANDER: We have to send the right signals to potential investors. A major German private equity fund has contacted us.

CLAUDIA: What about our plan?

SANDER: What plan?

CLAUDIA: We agreed to take some losses and clean up the mess.

SANDER: The clean-up job continues in a few days.

CLAUDIA: In a few days?

SANDER: Yes.

CLAUDIA: Even if there are new possibilities and investors? Sander, you're trying to make me a spoilsport, but I am doing this for the firm. This is bloody dangerous.

SANDER: Claudia, listen. The clean-up job costs money. A lot of money. We can't miss the chance for new capital. It keeps the wheels turning. Do you get that? It's not the fall that kills you, it's the impact. (S1E9)

It is no surprise that, within the web of male senior executives, Claudia is often the show's conscience, challenging the gendered practices and attitudes of Sander, Ulrik, and others. However, as this extract highlights, Claudia's concerns are often dismissed, as Sander uses a dominant rational of market progress and profit-seeking to legitimize and neutralize the criminality of his actions. In accordance with Tombs and Whyte, these are actions that are working in tandem with, not counter to, the dominant expression of capitalism.[23] Sander and Ulrik's position is based in the need to continually increase shareholder value and provide a good return on investors' capital. They are, in many ways, only dancing to the beat of market demand. To this extent, the only point of concern remains the base issue of profitability. It is this relationship between corporate crime and structures of power that, as Michael Benson and Sally Simpson argue, explains why neither society as a whole nor the perpetrators of corporate crimes are likely to view their actions as criminal. In coarse terms, those actions are the logical extension of a dominant capitalist ethic.[24]

Acts of corporate crime, such as fraud and deception, are criminalized only because they victimize other capitalist efforts or, more fundamentally, threaten the integrity of the market itself.[25] So long as the negative costs of action are externalized beyond the sphere of the corporation (and its overriding objective of securing capital growth), many acts of corporate crime will not be criminalized at all. Indeed, as Harold Barnet and David Nelken observe, "many illicit" or "harmful" acts will be surrounded by discourses of progress and inevitability rather than crime and deviance.[26] Corporate crime is crime with a purpose; it carries with it an element of social engineering that is meant to bring about a social order conforming to the design of the pursuit society. It involves acts—and actors—that do not betray the spirit of capitalism, but are the most consistent, uninhibited expressions of that spirit. This enables executives, such as Sander, to be upheld as leaders and bastions of the future one minute and lambasted the next as criminals. It also makes the line between executives, such as Sander, who actively engage in criminal practices to achieve success, and others, such as Steve Jobs, who playfully toy with the appeal of being a "maverick," a fine one.

It is too easy to characterize both *white-collar* and *corporate crime* as "victimless." But just because the victims are not readily identifiable in the traditional "pool of blood" sense, it does not mean they are not there. Rather, they are dispersed throughout society. In a sense, acts of corporate crime have the potential to affect anyone who depends on the integrity of the global economic system.[27] The very fact that the costs of corporate crime are externalized and redistributed across society means that though aggregate costs may be high, they are widely diffused across a range of victims, which masks the actual scale of the costs.[28]

What about the Body? Focusing on Social Harm

The language of *white-collar* and *corporate crime* goes a long way toward establishing a framework of crimes of the powerful, focusing on the ways that corporations and individuals continue to break the law in search of profit. However, if we cast our minds back to the very beginning of *Follow the Money*, we remember that, like most crime dramas, it begins with a body. In the opening scene, Mads fishes out the body of a Ukrainian migrant worker subcontracted to Energreen. As *Follow the Money* weaves a narrative of intrigue, elite deviance, and corporate criminality, what gets quickly forgotten is where it all began. This neglect reflects a problem inherent to the language of *white-collar* and *corporate crime* more generally. Neither approach, with their overlapping focus, pays due attention to the experiences of suffering that result, directly, or indirectly, from crimes of the powerful.

This leads us to the *social harm* perspective. Moving away from the language of crime, social harm cuts through private principles of morality or contingent notions of crime to focus on the more "objective base" of social costs that harm entails.[29] As John Muncie argues, the social harm perspective "enables criminology to move beyond legal definitions of 'crime' and acknowledge a wide range of immoral, wrongful, and injurious acts that may or may not be deemed illegal, but are arguably more profoundly damaging."[30] In this manner, the harm principal has been adopted as a way to deconstruct the acts of the powerful and structural elite that impose negative social, economic, and political costs on, often, the most vulnerable and marginalized sections of society.

Referring back to the opening premise of *Follow the Money*, the harm perspective underscores the hidden social costs that occur when legal definitions are too narrow or incomplete, yet there remains a need to locate acts of deviance as well as measure their impact on society.[31] This is especially relevant to crimes of the powerful, where the victims are quickly forgotten. Writing about nineteenth-century England, Engels's reflections remain as true today as they did then:

> When one individual inflicts bodily injury upon another, such injury that death results, we call the deed manslaughter. [. . .] But when society places hundreds of proletarians in such a position that they inevitably meet a too early and an unnatural death, [. . .] when it deprives thousands of necessaries of life, places them under conditions which they cannot live [. . . ,] its deed is murder just as surely as the deed of the single individual. [. . .] No man sees the murderer because the death of the victim seems a natural one.[32]

In short, murder is much more readily identifiable and punishable when there is a clear victim and offender, but when it is inflicted by corporate malpractice it is much more difficult to distinguish. As a result, it all too quickly gets forgotten. The *murder* in this instance remains hidden because of the diffuse layers of structural power that insulate Energreen, as the offender, as well as a limited legal language that makes it nearly impossible to hold anyone but an individual to account. It also remains hidden, as Mads quickly discovers, because the criminal justice response to such issues is severely limited. The social harm perspective reveals a profound lesson: work kills, and the perpetrators often go ignored.

As Tombs emphasizes, companies regularly kill their employees and members of the public through acute injury and chronic illness.[33] It is a scale of killing that is routine. Energreen's killing remains masked by its subcontracted firms but, more pervasively, the death of a Ukrainian migrant worker, to pick up on Engels's observation, appears "natural." It is a crime that is not taken seriously, exemplifying how there is little to deter organizations faced with the trade-off between their overriding profit objective, on the one hand, and safety on the other from always favoring the former.[34] It is this injustice that motivates Mads in the opening episode, yet he is soon told by his colleague in the fraud squad, Alf, that there are more serious matters at stake:

> ALF: Energreen is a leading Danish energy company. They've received the Gazelle Award four times for being the fastest growing. Or rather, cheat medal.
>
> MADS: How?
>
> ALF: With energy futures: i.e., stock in energy that hasn't been produced yet on the German market.
>
> MADS: What about the Ukrainian workers?
>
> ALF: Yes, they . . . they are only pawns in the game. If I'm right, it's more serious than the problems of a few Russians.
>
> MADS: Ukrainians! I cut one of them down myself! (S1E2)

It remains a fallacy of the program that, in seeking to hold Energreen to account, the lives (and deaths) of its subcontracted workers get quickly forgotten in favor of "sexier" crimes of fraud and deception. The focus on "crimes against the market" overlooks the base harms of corporate practice, yet, as Tombs argues, work-related deaths in the UK between 2013 and 2014 total an estimated 14,000.[35] With each death is an everwidening ripple of emotional, psychological, and financial harms that disproportionately impact women who are burdened with fulfilling "duties of care" for families, friends, and communities.[36]

At its core, the harm approach centers on the base principle of social well-being and sidesteps inherited and limited understandings of crime.[37] This enables us not only to draw into focus the death of the migrant worker in the opening scene, but also to contextualize the work-based suffering that both he and his colleagues endure as underpaid sub-contracted workers—as well as other costs brought out along the way, such as the lives affected by Sander's decision to shut down a subsidiary firm in episode 4. Ultimately, the workers are unable to speak out about their plight because, at any moment, Energreen can terminate their employment contracts; this is exactly what they do following Mads's early investigation. It is an action that does not attract the label of criminality, yet it directly results in increased suffering, anxiety, and worsening of living conditions for those affected—those who are already victims of economic inequality.

As *Follow the Money* captures early on, it is this systemically hidden suffering that leads Andriy, the father of the worker whose corpse is found at the wind farm, to take his own life. It is a turn, early in the series, that reveals the ever-widening ripples of emotional, psychological, and financial harms that occur as a direct result of corporate practice. By questioning what we mean by crime, as well as exposing the broader harms resulting from corporate practice, we can, as criminologists, begin to appreciate the full scale of suffering that is spread throughout society. This is what, in part, the harm perspective begins to bring into focus.

Conclusion

By looking at *Follow the Money*, this chapter is able to invert that traditional, downward, structural gaze of criminology and to challenge our preconceptions of victim and offender. Starting with the death of a subcontracted migrant worker from Eastern Europe, *Follow the Money* focuses on the most hidden sections of society and draws back to reveal the layers of culpability that encompass the wealthy, powerful, and elite. Through the various actions of Sander and his colleagues, it is possible to highlight the key features of *white-collar* and *corporate crime*, as well as bring into focus the alternative vantage point the *social harm* approach offers. Together, they all speak to the various ways criminology seeks to theoretically understand the crimes (or harms) of the powerful and to construct a critical response to corporate practice, be it at the level of the individual actor, the corporate institution, or the victim.

The real lesson that *Follow the Money* offers, however, is that despite the widespread suffering and pain inflicted by corporations, both the criminal justice system and criminology is locked in an overwhelming "downward gaze" that masks the individual, institutional, and structural levels of deviance. This is, in part, due to the power that these actors enjoy, enabling them to retain a grip on the evidence needed to hold them to account. As Gary Fooks argues, much of what we know about corporations like Energreen is tightly controlled and—often literally—locked beyond closed doors, deep within company offices.[38] More than inverting class relations, such positions begin to reveal that the neoliberal and corporate project is a gendered one, shaping masculinist attitudes and practices that are too often tolerated—or even encouraged—as "normal" under a competitive market logic.[39] While this is true, criminology continues to reproduce the deficit of accountability by largely overlooking powerful social actors and their criminality in favor of more identifiable "conventional crimes." The language of white-collar crime, corporate crime, and the harm approach go some way to redress this imbalance, yet it is an imbalance that exists throughout society and is reproduced through the discipline of criminology. It is our jobs, as critical thinkers, to change this.

9

"Let's Make This Show Happen, People"

BLACK MIRROR AND POPULIST PUNITIVENESS

Jamie Bennett

The anthology series *Black Mirror*, created by British writer Charlie Brooker, explores the impact of technology on individual and communal life. Originally broadcast on a terrestrial channel in the UK, it moved to the subscription streaming service Netflix and has subsequently grown its international audience and prestige.

Its dark, disturbing stories tap into unease about how the modern world is being distorted through rapid technological development. Brooker has explained: "The 'black mirror' of the title is the one you'll find on every wall, on every desk, in the palm of every hand: the cold, shiny screen of a TV, a monitor, a smartphone."[1] The series is concerned with our relationship with this technology and how it also entangled with other aspects of neoliberal society, including insecurity, social relations, capital consumerism, and media consumption. The episodes are essentially cautionary tales, critical, even dystopian visions of the near future. Brooker has suggested: "they're all about the way we live now—and the way we might be living in 10 minutes' time if we're clumsy. And if there's one thing we know about mankind, it's this: we're usually clumsy."[2]

One aspect of contemporary life that has evolved in late modernity is criminal justice. Developments in social relations, trends in media consumption and production, and a growing sense of insecurity have all played a role in an emerging pattern of criminal justice policy and practice in the Western world that has been characterized as "populist punitiveness,"[3] "penal populism,"[4] or the "new punitiveness."[5] The phenomenon of populist punitiveness is explored in "White Bear," broadcast as the second episode in the second season of *Black Mirror*. It is an example of the capacity of the series to critically engage with contemporary society and sounds a warning bell about the potential near future. This episode is the focus of this chapter and it will be examined in detail, but first it is necessary to briefly trace the contours of populist punitiveness.

Understanding Populist Punitiveness

In the mid- to late 19th century, the premodern practices of punishment gave way to the modern.[6] Out went the public executions and corporal punishments and in their place emerged the walls of the prison, removing punishment to a hidden space. The prison replaced the exercise of physical power and retribution with a focus upon classification, order, and the improvement of the soul. Punishment became directed toward the improvement and rehabilitation of transgressors through spiritual and personal reflection, education, and training. Through these series of transformations, the institutions of punishment became more civilized and humane.

The late 20th and early 21st centuries have seen a further transformation in the practices of punishment and the social values that inform penal practice in the developed Western world. Specifically, there has been greater resort to the use of imprisonment, but also encouragement of harsher conditions. For example, in England and Wales the prison population grew by 77% over the last 30 years,[7] while the USA saw an increase of over 500% during the last 40 years.[8] This is largely the result of longer sentences due to policies such as including mandatory minimum sentences, "three strikes"–style sentences, more restricted access to parole, and more intensive post-release supervision, including more frequent recall to custody. In America, it is now the era of mass imprisonment. In terms of prison conditions and community punishment, sanctions increasingly include an element of degradation, shaming, or humiliation, such as chain gang–style labor, distinctive clothing, and minimizing perceived privileges. This change in the scale and nature of punishment has been described as extreme when compared to the earlier modern era. It has been argued that nations such as the US and UK have come to "abandon long-standing limits to punishment in modern societies" and have seen "the emergence of penal sanctions that had previously been thought to be extinct and inappropriate in the modern civilized world."[9]

Many distinguished intellectuals have considered the factors that have contributed to this latest transformation. A comprehensive analysis will not be attempted here, but instead some of the key features will be briefly described, particularly those aspects that are relevant to the viewing of "White Bear."

First, a shift has been detected in the nature of social relations. In particular, there has been a decline in deference to elite groups, including politicians and public servants, while there emerged various extra-establishment individuals, groups, and organizations that claimed to speak on behalf of "the people," including through the media, social media, campaign movements, and direct democracy initiatives.[10] Social and marketing research approaches have also enabled politicians to pay closer attention to and reshape policy toward the perceived will of important electorates. Together, such developments have nurtured populism and reduced the capacity of elites to act on their own judgment and values. Elites have been both constrained by these changes, for example experiencing pressure to respond to the perceived public will, but have also been enabled by it, for example by generating support through engagement with popular causes. Within penal policy, the rise of populism has resulted in the eclipse of the rehabilitative ideal, which had been a central tenet of the modern criminal justice system and had been conserved by elites who valued the moderate and progressive ambitions in criminal justice. In its place has emerged a more emotional tone in crime policy, fueled by populist fear and insecurity about crime and late modernity. The alteration in social power relations has therefore brought with it greater pressure for harsher, retributive punishment.

This transformation has been enabled not only by shifts in social power and discourse, and is not simply an exercise in democratic will, but instead has been entangled in other aspects of late modernity, particularly global consumer capitalism and the expansion of media. The centrality of capitalism, consumption, and economic exchange to contemporary life has also seeped into criminal justice. This has happened most obviously through the privatization of criminal justice services that in preceding times had been retained by the state, including policing, imprisonment, community punishments, and post-release supervision. These have increasingly been transferred to private companies, delivering public services for profit. At the same time, growing prison populations have opened up commercial opportunities for suppliers, including the provision of food, clothing, and construction. This has created what has been widely referred to as a "prison-industrial complex,"[11] where powerful economic and political interests are served by expanding the criminal justice system. In relation to the media, the rapid development and deregulation of information technology has intensified competition and expanded choice. In this context, media representation has become more populist, more polarized and emotive. Commercial interests and the media thus both have a stake in fanning the flames of populist punitiveness.

Having briefly elucidated the contours of populist punitiveness, the chapter now turns to the *Black Mirror* episode "White Bear," where these themes will be further developed. Following a descriptive summary of the episode, the chapter will explore how the episode depicts crucial aspects of criminal justice practice, including punitiveness and penal values, the spectacle of punishment, and economic interests and exploitation. The chapter will then draw conclusions about the strategy of the episode and how this reflects the broader approach of the series.

"White Bear": Plot Summary

Victoria Skillane wakes up in a chair, with bandaged wrists and a painful neck. As she moves, pills spill from her lap onto the floor. She is uncertain of her surroundings, how she got there, or even who she is. There are photographs in the house of her with a man and also a school portrait of a girl. She occasionally has momentary, incomprehensible, shock-like flashbacks.

Outside, the streets appear deserted, although there are people at windows, including adults with children, watching and filming her on their phones. She goes outside and calls to them, "Can you help me? Do you know who I am? I can't remember who I am."

A car pulls up and a masked man gets out, arms himself with a shotgun, and starts stalking her menacingly. She takes flight, with people following, continuing to film her. She takes refuge in a petrol station shop, where two other customers, Jem and Damien, also hide with her. The masked man breaks into the petrol station and Jem and Skillane hide outside the rear of the building. A shot is heard from inside and

Damien staggers out, collapsing, apparently shot, and is followed out by the masked man. Two other armed people join, one in a welder's protective face shield, the other in a ball gown and an animal's head mask; they are grotesque nightmarish figures. Jem explains, "They like scaring people," before taking flight with Skillane and hiding in a house.

Skillane shows Jem the photograph of the young girl and says, "I think this is my daughter." Jem explains that a signal came through TVs and computers:

> It did something to people. Almost everybody became onlookers, started watching, filming stuff. Like spectators. Didn't give a shit about what happens.

As they crouch down, hiding, she continues, describing the violent, masked people as "hunters":

> They seemed normal to begin with but then they realized they could do what they wanted. They started taking stuff, nicking cars because they could. Doing what they liked and not just with things, but with people. It got worse and worse and now they get an audience.

Skillane asks whether it is the signal that makes the "hunters" behave in that way, to which Jem responds:

> I guess they were always like that underneath. They just needed the rules to change, for no one to intervene.

Jem says that their mission is to get to the transmitter at a location called White Bear and destroy it, disrupting the signal. To achieve this, they must avoid the "hunters."

A man, Baxter, arrives in a van and they get in. He takes them to an isolated wood, where he turns on them threateningly. Jem gets away, but Skillane is hooded and taken to a clearing where there are gallows and the corpses of people who have been crucified. The man says, "Are we going to put a show on for these guys today." He ties Skillane to a tree trunk and prepares a drill, threatening to torture her. Jem returns, apparently kills Baxter, and frees Skillane.

They make their way toward the transmitter. On the way, Skillane is forced to crouch down in the car, which triggers a flashback to the girl in the photograph crouching down in a car as they pass a police car. Unnerved, Skillane is uncertain and says, "There's something not right."

When they reach the transmitter, they break in and start the process of shutting it down. Hunters come in to stop them. Skillane wrestles a gun from them, but when she fires it, it simply sprays confetti. The walls suddenly draw back to reveal a theater set, in front of a cheering audience. The other actors take the bemused Skillane and strap her into a chair with metal clips (the real cause of her bandaged wrists).

Baxter, now acting as the master of ceremonies, asks, "I guess you're wondering why you're here? It's time to tell you who you are." On a screen, a news story plays out revealing that Victoria Skillane was engaged to Ian Rannoch, and together they kidnapped six-year-old Jemima Sykes. The sole clue during her disappearance was her soft toy, a white bear, which became a symbol of the search. Her dead body was later found burned in the woods. The investigation led back to Rannoch and Skillane, and, at their house, a film of the murder was found on a phone. Rannoch was identified by a distinctive tattoo on the back of his neck (appropriated for the balaclava worn by the shotgun-wielding hunter and the symbol of the "White Bear" transmission). Skillane claimed that she was under the spell of her fiancée, but the judge was dismissive and "labeled her a uniquely wicked and poisonous individual," declaring: "You were an enthusiastic spectator to Jemima's suffering. You actively reveled in her anguish." He concluded that "her punishment would be proportionate and considered."

Rannoch committed suicide in prison, leaving Skillane to take sole responsibility for the death. As the audience members jeer, Baxter speaks for them: "That poor wee girl, helpless and terrified, and you just watched." Skillane is carried out in her chair and placed in a vehicle with a transparent cover so that she can be exhibited to the baying crowd that lines the road. Paint bombs are being sold at the side, so they can pelt the carriage as it passes. Baxter continues to MC, encouraging the crowd:

> Take as many photographs as you want . . . let that bitch know that you are out here.

Skillane is returned to the house where she started the day. She pleads with Baxter, "Please just kill me," which he dismisses, replying, "You always say that." She is forced to watch the film of the murder as her memory is painfully wiped, electronically, and the house re-dressed for the following day, when the process is repeated.

Over the credits, the backstage process is shown and the day repeated from the perspective of the audience. The events have taken place in White Bear Justice Park. The entry sign shows the car parking charges for visitors and exhorts them: "Enjoy the show." Baxter leads a briefing, accompanied by the other actors. He stands on a small stage in front of an audience of adults, some with their children. He explains the rules—no talking, keep your distance, and "enjoy yourself. That's probably the most important one of all." The purpose is set out: "What we are trying to do is to get her to believe you are all mesmerized [skeptical laughs from audience]. . . . I know, but she's believed it up until now."

Skillane is shown waking and key moments of the day flash past from the perspective of the audience, watching through windows and from the side of the road. The process is an ongoing cycle.

"White Bear" and Populist Punitiveness

The crimes of Victoria Skillane are deliberately extreme. She has been an active accomplice to her partner, Ian Rannoch, who kidnapped and murdered a six-year-old child, Jemima Sykes. The case has attracted a high level of media interest, stimulating a national hunt to find the missing child. After her mutilated body is discovered, the public mood turns to anger. Rannoch and Skillane are arrested and charged, but when Rannoch takes his own life, Skillane becomes the focal point for the public emotion.

Offenses against children often generate the most emotive responses. The violation of their innocence and vulnerability is viewed as particularly reprehensible. Those who harm children are viewed as "iconic emblems of evil"[12] and "the 'hate figure[s]' of our time in the popular imagination."[13] In "White Bear," the character of Victoria Skillane consciously echoes notorious real-life cases from the UK, including that of the Moors Murderers of the 1960s, Ian Brady and Myra Hindley, who tortured and murdered at least six victims, tape recording and photographing the acts. Hindley's later attempts to demonstrate her rehabilitation and gain her release were always thwarted. The police mugshot taken on her arrest, with her bleached blond hair, sunken eyes, and surly, defiant expression, became iconic, constantly recycled in newspaper stories. The reproduction of this mugshot by artist Marcus Harvey, formed from a mosaic of black, white, and gray children's handprints, caused major controversy and was attacked by protestors at the *Sensation* art exhibition at London's Royal Academy in 1997.

Even Hindley's death in prison in 2002 has not ended the popular fascination with her. More recent echoes can be detected in the Soham murder case of 2000, in which ten-year-old girls Holly Wells and Jessica Chapman were murdered by a school caretaker, Ian Huntley. Huntley's partner, Maxine Carr, initially provided a false alibi and was prosecuted for perverting the course of justice, receiving three and a half years in prison, and was denied access to early release. In both of these cases, the crimes themselves were abhorrent, but it has been argued that women such as Hindley and Carr receive special condemnation for their violation of gender expectations. Each has been regularly described in tabloid newspapers as "the most hated woman in Britain." Marcus Harvey addressed this in relation to Hindley, arguing: "This is the crucial issue: she didn't do the murdering, but she was a female who ignored her motherly instincts."[14]

"White Bear" presents the viewer with a popular hate figure, echoing real-life cases, reflecting contemporary anxieties and attitudes, and uses this to construct a plausible near future.

Punishment and Penal Values

The exceptional nature of the crime of Rannoch and Skillane results in not only a public and media outcry, but also strong condemnation from the judge at her court case, who calls her "a uniquely wicked and poisonous individual." She is described not as someone who carried out the killing, but "an enthusiastic spectator" who "actively reveled" in the crime. The judge constructs an image of Skillane as the "other," an aberration. This rejection of any attempt to understand the social and psychological context, circumstances, or backgrounds of those involved in the crime allows Skillane to become little more than a disembodied representation of the terrible acts. She becomes a figure of hate, an iconic emblem of evil.

In the face of such evil, the judge concludes that "her punishment would be proportionate and considered." What is put in place is a form of public punishment in which Skillane is daily terrorized before being confronted with her own acts. Each day her memory is wiped so that she has to continually relive the experience. The nature of this sanction draws attention to both the practices of punishment and penal values.

Strikingly, this is a punishment in which the notion of rehabilitation is entirely disregarded. The intentional wiping of Skillane's memory means that she cannot learn or change through this punishment. There are signs that the memory-wiping process could be put to more rehabilitative use. For example, there is no evidence that Skillane has any innate desire to harm children; indeed, the photograph of Jemima Sykes generates maternal feelings and she starts to think that it may be an image of her daughter. The rebooting of her life away from the relationship with Rannoch, and her social and biographical roots, opens up the possibility of a new beginning. Rehabilitation and reform are not, however, the purpose of this punishment. Instead, it is a carefully constructed and stage-managed form of retribution, intended to inflict pain and suffering.

Corporal and capital punishments from the premodern era were directed toward the body of the punished. This approach retreated in the modern age to be replaced by "the gentle way in punishment,"[15] which worked to reshape the identity, mind, and soul rather than to harm the body. The punishment in "White Bear" is not primarily directed toward the infliction of physical pain—albeit, as collateral effects, Skillane suffers injuries to her wrists and neck from being restrained and the memory wiping process is painful. Primarily, the punishment is directed toward eliciting emotional suffering. In the first part of the punishment, from waking up without a memory of past events, Skillane faces uncertainty and confusion. She is then chased and terrorized by relentless, murderous hunters. The apparently friendly assistance of Jem simply leads her deeper into the ordeal. In many ways, the punishment is designed to replicate a perception of the emotional experiences of Jemima Sykes, who was kidnapped, falsely reassured, and then murdered. This is a punishment that attempts to construct an elaborate "eye for an eye" retribution that theatrically approximates and replicates the terror imagined to have been experienced by the victim.

In the second part of the punishment, Skillane has her veil of ignorance raised and she is presented with her crimes. The memory wiping has reconstructed her as a law-abiding citizen, with her moral sentiments and maternalism restored. From this position, she is confronted with her own acts, so as to experience feelings of shame and self-disgust. A contrast can be drawn with restorative justice practices, in which there is an attempt to engage the perpetrators and victims of crimes to repair the harms caused. This process involves accountability, consensual participation, and mutual respect. One aspect of these processes has been described as "reintegrative shaming," in which disapproval is fostered in a respectful way so that the deed is condemned rather than the person, with the person who has committed a crime being recognized as having the capacity to experience remorse and make amends.[16] This is not the purpose of the punishment in "White Bear."

Instead, the shame is coercively imposed and intended to be disintegrative and stigmatizing. This approach mirrors the "naming and shaming" practices that have been incorporated into law in some jurisdictions through the registration and public notification of sex offenders[17] or public panics generated by media campaigns such as the *News of the World* campaign of 2000 in the UK to publicly name child sex offenders.[18] These approaches, albeit justified on public safety grounds, can be a form of public shaming. In the episode, Skillane is manipulated, through memory wiping, into having to judge her own actions, with the perspective of a public bystander, but without a full appreciation of the circumstances. This generates intrinsic feelings of shame and stigma. This is then extrinsically reinforced by the parade through a jeering crowd, pelting the carriage with paint bombs. The public hate and self-hate she experiences lead Skillane to repeatedly ask to be allowed to die. For her, the endless cycle of suffering, shame, and stigma is a fate worse than death.

The Spectacle of Punishment

The investigation, trial, and punishment are all enacted in public view. The large-scale public spectacle is particularly significant in exploring aspects of populist punitiveness. The high-profile coverage of the hunt for Jemima Sykes and the subsequent discovery of her murder show a crime that elicited a particularly strong emotional, public response. This intense response sets it up as a signal crime, embedded in public imagination and shaping attitudes to crime and punishment.[19] In general, the representation of crime has become more polarized, polemical, and emotive, largely focusing on the crime rather than the deeper social causes, and intensifying the bifurcation between innocent victims and animalistic, predatory criminals.[20] This infantilization in the representation of criminal justice has been described as part of a process of "pantomime justice,"[21] a term that comments both on the simplistic form of representation, but also the participative role of viewers.

In this context of an increasingly polarized and emotive public response and representation of crime, what function is performed by the public nature of the punishment in "White Bear"? In discussing the premodern public spectacles that incorporated corporal and capital punishment, Michel Foucault described them as acts of sovereign power, in which the king was reasserting authority over both perpetrator and the wider audience, particularly in periods of uncertainty and disorder.[22] The very excess of the punishment was part of this political ritual and assertion of authority. The episode draws a conscious connection with premodern punishments through the detritus of the gallows and crucifixions that litter the clearing in the wood where Baxter lures Jem and Skillane before turning on them. While public punishment and punishment of the body retreated in modern times, they have been revived in late modernity, through punishments such as using distinctive clothing and visible public work but also through media representation of punishment, which does cultural labor in legitimizing mass imprisonment and punitive punishment, while also obscuring the realities of its painfulness.[23]

In the context of "White Bear," the public punishment can be seen as another form of pantomime justice, where the viewers are asked to act out the more immediate gratifications of expressive punishments. Rather than giving form to the political power of the sovereign, it is giving expression to the populist emotional reaction. At the same time, it is a performance that obscures the political realities of the power interests at play, and also obscures the human realities of the infliction of pain and suffering. The punishment is instead enacted as a form of family entertainment, or "dark tourism,"[24] in which the baying crowd is encouraged to "enjoy the show."

One of the essential themes in *Black Mirror* is the use of technology. This is particularly seen in "White Bear" where the public film Skillane on their phones as she is terrorized by the hunters and then paraded through the angry mob. In the first instance, the filming acts as a distancing device. Placing the mobile phone between the spectator and Skillane creates a distancing effect, removing the immediate human experience and instantaneously re-creating it as a representation. The social implications of this can be significant. In his anti–capital punishment polemic, Albert Camus described the profound effect on his father of witnessing the visceral reality of the public execution of a man who had murdered a child. Although his father shared the public outrage at the crime, the execution revealed "the reality hidden under the noble phrases with which it was masked."[25] The social distancing enabled by the mobile device erodes the tangible human realities and instead commodifies the image and experience. As Susan Sontag argued, photography can be an act of power that has the capacity to take symbolic ownership of an individual, act, or experience and put this to particular use.[26] The construction and repetition of images of punishment in contemporary society, Michelle Brown has suggested,[27] legitimizes mass imprisonment and fosters an affective distance between the viewer and penal realities. The distance allows for the spectator to engage in denial of the implications and consequences of criminal justice practices and their responsibility to act in response.[28] The dehumanizing and desensitizing distance created through technology is referred to in the episode by Jem, who explains to Skillane that the White Bear transmissions (the media coverage of the crime?) have had an effect on the public: "It did something to people. Almost everybody became onlookers, started watching, filming stuff. Like spectators. Didn't give a shit about what happens."

The filming, however, also performs another function, being integral to the punishment itself. In the first instance, it amplifies the spectacle by enabling its distribution and reproduction, communicating it beyond those immediately present. In addition, where once the bodily marking of criminals was enacted through, for example, scarring, branding, or maiming, such as the cutting off of hands, there has also been a long history of virtual marking, where the image of criminals has been produced and displayed to degrade their reputation and status.[29] Here, the constant acts of photography perform a virtual marking function in Skillane's punishment. They contribute, in the moment, to the isolation, fear, and shame she experiences, while also extending the punishment by representing her degraded status.

The spectacle of punishment in "White Bear" is seen not only in the public ritual and the baying crowd, but also in the media and social media representation. The spectacle is itself part of the punishment, exposing the powerlessness of Skillane, and intensifying her pain, shame, and degradation. The spectacle also enables the grotesque punitiveness being enacted by shaping the perceptions of viewers, creating affective distance and legitimizing the exercise of power. In the premodern era, the spectacle of punishment was a direct expression of sovereign power, but in late modernity it is instead represented as a democratized expression of popular outrage. Such a representation obscures the reality of the power interests that are being served. This is a subject matter addressed in the episode and to which the article now turns.

Economics and Exploitation

To what ends and to whose benefit is the punishment in "White Bear" imposed? While the notion of populist punitiveness suggests that this is, at least to some degree, an expression of public opinion, the flows of power and interests are more complex. It would be wrong to suggest that politicians, judges, and the practitioners are simply ciphers or ventriloquist's dummies and instead the perceived popular will is mediated through powerful agents and interests and put to particular ends.[30] These issues are illuminated in the episode.

The most striking illustration comes at the very end of the episode, when the events of the day are replayed from backstage. The show has been produced in White Bear Justice Park. This is not a state-run institution, but a commercial one that generates income, at least from parking charges and from selling paint bombs to throw at Skillane during the climactic parade. This is a form of dark tourism in which a site of human suffering is transformed into a commercial opportunity, exploiting the popular fascination with crime. The commercialization and commodification of criminal justice services has been growing throughout the world. The emergence of neoliberalism has seen the opening up of state monopolies to the private sector. This has included a broad range of functions, including criminal justice, prisons, and punishment. The commercial interest in eroding the direct role of the state in the delivery of services, while encouraging increased resort to the use of commercial services, has created what has been widely described as the "prison-industrial complex." This term captures the entangled interests where an expanded prison population creates commercial opportunities and, in turn, the influence of political lobbying and funding by commercial organizations solidifies support for the bloated penal system. In "White Bear," the viewer is shown, through the institution of the White Bear Justice Park, a link between populist punitiveness and commercialization.

This connection between commercial interests and punitiveness is not limited to the direct accumulation of profit. As Emma Bell has described, neoliberalism is not simply an economic system promoting the primacy of the capitalist market; it is a broad social, political, legal, and economic system.[31] In this light, Bell suggests that punitiveness serves to direct political attention toward particular crimes as a means of obscuring the harms created by powerful institutions and individuals, including growing inequality. It is also a means by which inequalities can be legitimized, as prisons full of people from poor backgrounds and from minority ethnic communities can be presented as the outcome of the moral failures of those groups rather than the outcome of accumulated social injustice. Populist punitiveness thus arguably serves a broader set of power interests. This shift from economic interests to wider social power is reflected in Jem's description of the "hunters," who she says "started taking stuff" but moved on to "doing what they liked and not just with things, but with people."

The fascination with crime and punishment is not new—indeed, it is deeply embedded in the history of human society. Nevertheless, in modern times, there was a movement toward restraint and civilization, with punishment retreating from public view, and a broad political consensus emerged regarding progressive social justice, including the rehabilitative aspirations of criminal justice. Late modernity has seen this erode and populist punitiveness emerge. This is not simply an exercise in democratic will, but is a process that is enmeshed with the interests of powerful political, media, and economic agents. From this perspective, the general public are both actors in and subjects of populist punitiveness. "White Bear" reveals the ways in which the darker impulses of the human soul have been excavated and appropriated to serve particular interests. As Jem describes, the effect of the White Bear transmissions on the hordes that follow Skillane, filming the hunt without interceding, in turn frees the "hunters" to pursue their basest desires: "I guess they were always like that underneath. They just needed the rules to change, for no one to intervene."

Conclusion

Black Mirror is a series that displays a discomfort with the relationship between technology and society. Many of the themes addressed in "White Bear" resurface in other episodes. Sexual offenses and offenses against children recur, including the online blackmail and vigilantism of "Shut Up and Dance" (S3E3), the use of neurotechnology to create social isolation and slow time perception so as to make the punishment of a child murderer more painful in "White Christmas" (S2E4), and the paranoid fear that leads to the implanting of the parental monitoring and control device deployed in "Arkangel" (S4E2). Popular fascination with crime and even participation in violent retribution appear in the public nomination and voting on the next victim of a serial killer in "Hated in the Nation" (S3E6), and dark tourism is central to the grotesque "Black Museum" (S4E6). There is also an ongoing concern about private interests and commercial involvement in security, including the memory reconstruction technology used in insurance investigations in "Crocodile" (S4E3) and the robotic guard dogs that turn on their human creators in the dystopian "Metalhead" (S4E5). These episodes all echo some of the core themes of "White Bear," concerned as it is with populist punitiveness not only as a set of criminal justice practices but as situated within contemporary society, involving economics, politics, and the media. As with all of these episodes of *Black Mirror*, "White Bear" rejects any intrinsic or inevitable correlation between technological innovation and social progress. Instead, the episode suggests that technology can be put to a range of social uses and its consequences can be decivilizing as much as they can be civilizing. Indeed, in "White Bear," the technology is shown to enable a return to premodern practices and is part of what Loic Wacquant has described as "the great penal leap backward."[32]

What are the potential and intended effects of "White Bear"? Clearly, the quotes cited in the introduction to this chapter illustrate that creator Charlie Brooker intended the episodes in the series to act as cautionary tales about contemporary society and its future directions. They are intellectually coherent, with "White Bear" offering an effective critique of populist punitiveness. It has been argued that the representation of crime and criminal justice can be a form of "popular criminology," translating academic analysis into digestible narratives within mainstream culture.[33] It has also been argued that there is an "alternative tradition" that offers a critique of contemporary practices,[34] and that film and television may be means to agitate for reform[35] or even advance more radical, critical criminology to address the wider issues of power and inequality at stake.[36] "White Bear" clearly falls into this tradition.

It is not only as an intellectual exercise that "White Bear" is constructed. As with popular culture more generally, it is the emotions of the audience that are also being brought into play. By concealing Skillane's crime, the episode enables viewers to develop empathy for her, gives meaning to her suffering, and generates repugnance at her treatment. Whereas in popular culture, those who offend against children are demonized and dehumanized, the narrative serves to rehumanize Skillane. Just as Albert Camus's father was unable to tolerate the public execution of a child killer after seeing the reality of the death penalty,[37] so the viewer is guided toward rejection of the grotesque and punitive public spectacle as a result of viewing Skillane in human terms. What the viewer is being offered is an education in sentiment, a guide as much for their emotions and moral sensibility as for their intellectual capacities.[38]

The decision to have Skillane represented as the accomplice to the murder of a child is significant. As discussed earlier, crimes against children elicit a particularly strong public reaction, including a desire for retribution and expressive justice. This character and background also deliberately call to mind notorious cases from British history. By guiding the viewer to a more empathic response to Skillane, then presenting the public reaction and punishment, the episode provokes a degree of reflexivity. It invites the viewer to intellectually and emotionally critique the popular, political, media, and economic context. In Anthony Burgess's novel *A Clockwork Orange*,[39] Alex, a violent juvenile delinquent, undertakes an experimental aversion therapy to "cure" him of his predilection for violence. The consequences of this deprive him of his identity, cultural interests, and even his personal safety. The director of the film adaptation, Stanley Kubrick, suggested that having a reprehensively violent protagonist was crucial: "when you reject the treatment of even a character as wicked as Alex the moral point is clear."[40] Similarly, with "White Bear," when the *Black Mirror* audience is lead to reject punitive punishment even for Victoria Skillane, a notorious accomplice in a child murder, the moral point is clear.

Populist punitiveness is not part of an imagined future—it is part of the reality of the contemporary penal landscape. In "White Bear," Charlie Brooker not only offers a cautionary tale of things to come, but also invites critical reflection on the present. The emotional, intellectual, and moral discomfort that this can induce is a provocation of the audience to think, feel, and act differently.

The Walking Dead and Criminological Theory

EXPLORING THE IMPACT OF RADICAL SOCIAL
CHANGE ON CRIME THROUGH THE LENS OF A
ZOMBIE APOCALYPSE

Scott Vollum, Tammy S. Garland, and
Nickie D. Phillips

Bunny slippers and a teddy bear are the first indicators that, in this world, appearances are not what they seem. At the scene of a highway collision, a young child dressed in pajamas grasps her teddy bear. As the little girl turns toward sheriff's deputy Rick Grimes, her ghoulish facial features reveal that she is no longer an innocent, but a mortal threat—she is *the walking dead*. Aghast, and pained with the knowledge of what he must do, he takes aim and fires one shot through her forehead. A clean kill.

The television series *The Walking Dead* premiered on October 31, 2010. The show is based on the phenomenally successful comic book series of the same name and follows survivors as they struggle to cope in the aftermath of an unexplained plague that transforms the dead into zombies. In the series premiere, two deputies from the King County Sherriff's Office, Rick Grimes and Shane Walsh, confront armed assailants after a high-speed pursuit ends in a crash. Rick is shot and lapses into a coma. A number of months after the shooting, he wakes up to realize he was unconscious during a violent attack on the hospital that left it abandoned, in ruins. Alone, Rick emerges from the hospital into a world in the throes of a pandemic of unknown origin; Rick is now in the midst of a zombie apocalypse ("Days Gone By," S1E1).

The apocalyptic (and postapocalyptic) setting of *The Walking Dead* provides a perfect tableau for examining the impact of radical and expansive social change on crime. As Majid Yar writes, "post-apocalyptic fictions refract contemporary social concerns into the domain of storytelling, thereby dramatizing the tensions, conflicts, fears and contradictions with which a society is wrestling."[1] Thomas Raymen,[2] in his own criminological analysis of *The Walking Dead*, considers such an application of fictional stories as a form of "popular criminology" in the vein of Nicole Rafter and Michelle Brown's analysis of criminological theory in popular films.[3] He states that *The Walking Dead* "possesses a 'hard kernel of the Real' that carries significant theoretical value and insight for criminologists"[4] and goes on to reveal the value such works of fiction can have in illuminating the connection between social structures, social conditions, and crime.

Robert Agnew, in his 2012 article "Dire Forecast: A Theoretical Model of the Impact of Climate Change on Crime," offers an integrated model for examining the effects of broad social change on crime and criminality, the kind of social change that is also present (to a fantastical degree) in apocalyptic and postapocalyptic society in the wake of a zombie pandemic.[5] Though Agnew's focus is on climate change and the social changes likely to occur as a result of it, we apply his theoretical approach (with some adaptation) to the postapocalyptic world of *The Walking Dead* and offer some insight into criminological theory through an examination of this fictional television show.

Climate Change and Agnew's Dire Forecast

Climate change has long been associated with a rise in temperature, changing patterns of precipitation, and a rise in sea level, but many do not comprehend the overall, long term-negative effects of such ongoing events. Whereas the existential threat of climate change is widely accepted within the scientific community, corporate titans, politicians, and the general population fail to grasp the potential catastrophic consequences of these transformations as they are gradual and even the best models cannot predict with certainty the timeline in which our overreliance on fossil fuels and deforestation will lead to disaster. Indeed, one of the most widely acknowledged fears around the issue of climate change is that humans will fail to take notice of gradual changes until our biosphere becomes nearly uninhabitable.

Over the past several years, we have witnessed worsening hazardous weather conditions and troubling meteorological and geological patterns;

however, while hazards both natural (e.g., floods, hurricanes, earthquakes) and man-made (e.g., a dam break) may result in loss of life, disruption in livelihoods, and damage to the environment, many locales can often recover with the intervention of government and local community resources. The aftermaths of disasters, however, present a more difficult trajectory for inhabitants. As defined by the United Nations International Strategy for Disaster Reduction, a disaster is "a serious disruption of the functioning of a community or a society involving widespread human, material, economic, or environmental losses and impacts, which exceeds the ability of the affected community or society to cope using its own resources."[6] According to Sandra Banholzer, James Kossin, and Simon Donner, "Not all hazards turn into disasters, and not all of them have negative and wide-reaching impacts."[7] But what happens when hazards become disasters from which we cannot recover? What is revealed about humanity and what remains of the civilization we have created? As Agnew writes, catastrophic "changes will have negative effects on the natural environment, health, the economy, and social life."[8] Apocalyptic fiction such as *The Walking Dead* gives us a sense of how characters cope with social conflict as they navigate through a dystopian setting in which the population is at perpetual risk, habits change, social institutions collapse, infectious diseases become more rampant, food and water shortages increase, and resources become increasingly scarce. And it is this social conflict with which we are most concerned, as it is expected that humans will have to vie for resources when they become scarce. Survival becomes paramount.

The zombie apocalypse as depicted in *The Walking Dead* of course differs greatly from the more slow-moving social impact of climate change. The pandemic as depicted in the show is quick, far-reaching, devastating, and inescapable. The zombie outbreak appears to be indiscriminate; no one is immune. All who die come back to life as zombies whose sole purpose is to consume the living. It doesn't take long for the outbreak to exponentially spread, leaving the living to flee heavily populated areas and seek alternate shelter and resources. With the collapse of infrastructure as well as social, economic, and political institutions, battles over increasingly scarce resources become commonplace and survivors are faced with having to contend not only with zombies but also each other. In the context of the show, this is global in scope and occurs relatively quickly. Climate change, on the other hand, is incremental and differentially experienced based on one's social and geographic position in society, even if it will eventually impact every living human and species on the planet. However, in spite of these differences, *The Walking Dead* does offer an analogy to the very real criminogenic effects of climate change. As recent natural disasters have shown us, rapid migrations, battle over scarce resources, social conflict, and other radical social disruptions commonly occur in association with climate change.[9]

Agnew links climate change to an increase in crime. In his speculative examination, he argues that the negative effects of climate change will "foster a range of crimes at the individual, corporate, and state levels."[10] As a result, "climate change will promote crime by increasing strain, reducing social control, weakening social support, fostering beliefs and values favorable to crime, contributing to traits conducive to crime, increasing certain opportunities for crime, and creating social conflict."[11] While Agnew discusses the crimes of corporations (e.g., environmental pollution) and governments (e.g., violations of international law) associated with climate change, it is crimes at the individual level on which we focus in relation to *The Walking Dead*. Included among these crimes are acts of violence and theft as well as acts not typically defined as crimes including harms against nonhuman animals and the natural environment. Many might question how climate change, currently perceived by some as a minor (and incremental) inconvenience, could have such far-reaching deleterious societal effects in terms of crime and criminality. Agnew addresses this question by suggesting an integrative theoretical model of crime associated with broad (and in some ways rapid) social change. Taking a Durkheimian approach, he addresses not only the strain experienced during such change but also breakdowns in social controls and social support and increases in social disorganization, what Émile Durkheim might have called "anomie." He also addresses social learning factors such as beliefs and values conducive to crime and criminality and rational choice factors in terms of the opportunities for crime. In his model, these have both an independent effect on crime as well as an integrative effect via strain. Agnew's central theoretical concern has typically revolved around strain and his seminal work on General Strain Theory (GST).[12] But, as is the case with his more recent theoretical works,[13] his model regarding climate change is a much more complex and integrative attempt to explain crime.

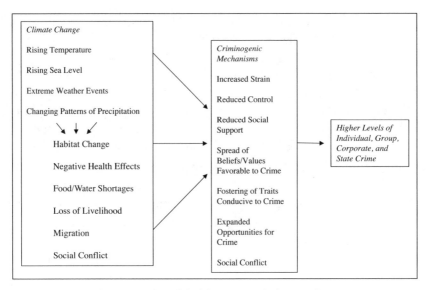

Figure 10.1. Agnew's Integrated Model of the Impact of Climate Change on Crime

First and foremost, according to Agnew, crime in the wake of climate change is a response to the strain caused by its manifestation. According to Agnew,[14] climate-related strains include an increase in temperature, an increase in frequency and intensity of extreme weather events and the associated events that follow, food and water shortages, increased poverty and inequality, forced migration, and exposure to armed conflict.

It is, however, not simply the exposure to strain, but the magnitude of that strain that is associated with increases in crime. As noted, society often recovers from a hazard and even disasters on a localized scale, but what happens when disaster occurs on a global scale? History tells us of Mt. Vesuvius and its destruction of Pompeii, but even the ancient world rebounded as global destruction was avoided. But what happens if society is faced with disasters from which it cannot recover, such as those predicted with climate change? As climate catastrophes become increasingly prevalent, what might be the acute and cumulative impacts of strain on crime? When resources become scarce and social conflict is imminent, how do individuals cope and survive? What role might crime play in this survival? As we are yet to experience the full ramifications of climate change, these questions to a large degree remain unanswered. By turning to the fictional world of *The Walking Dead*, a postapocalyptic

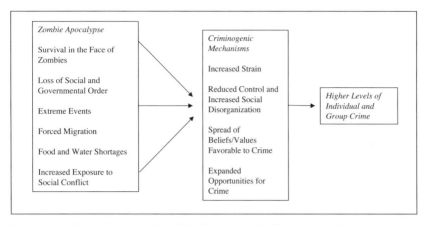

Figure 10.2. Adapted Integrated Model of the Impact of a Zombie Apocalypse on Crime

world impacted by pervasive and ongoing social catastrophe, we attempt to address these questions and extend the insight of Agnew's work.

In this essay, we mimic Agnew's speculative attempt to understand and predict crime in the face of (and as a result of) catastrophic social change. There are similarities in Agnew's depiction of the impacts of climate change and the fictional impacts of the zombie apocalypse as presented in *The Walking Dead*. We focus on several specific "criminogenic mechanisms" identified by Agnew: increased strain, reduced social control, the spread of beliefs and values favorable to crime, and expanded opportunities for crime. As strain receives the greatest attention in Agnew's original piece, it receives similar attention here. Within our consideration of strain, we consider the impact of extreme events, forced migration, food and water shortages, and exposure to conflict as increasingly potent sources of strain in *The Walking Dead*. Many of the remaining criminogenic mechanisms can be integratively tied to strain.

Change as a Source of Strain in *The Walking Dead*

In chapter 3 of this book, the concept of strain was discussed in regard to individual loss and exposure to noxious stimuli. While the plight of *Breaking Bad*'s Walter White resulted in a path of destructive behavior, the strain he faced pales in comparison to that experienced by the characters in the world of *The Walking Dead*. In the midst of rapid social change, individuals in *The Walking Dead* are repeatedly subjected to extreme situations, forced migration, and the fear of being attacked not only by zombies but by rival groups as they compete for declining supplies of life-sustaining resources.

Extreme Events

While our application of strain may not have been what Agnew imagined when he conceptualized the theoretical impact of climate change, it isn't much of a stretch to substitute the extreme events of climate change to the zombie apocalypse. As Agnew describes, survivors must cope with "physical injury, the death of close others, the destruction of home and property, the loss of livelihood, the damage of critical infrastructure, and the disruption of routine activities."[15] In *The Walking Dead*, Rick Grimes wakes up devastated to find his family and friends have disappeared, his neighborhood desolate, his status as a police officer erased, squatters occupying his house, and death everywhere. Rick's first encounter with the undead is almost too much to bear as he questions whether he is equipped to survive. Were it not for his friend Morgan and his son, who are seemingly the last living people nearby, Rick would have met an early demise ("Days Gone By," S1E1). He soon realizes that the zombie apocalypse is a precursor to greater horrors.

Finding his family and keeping them safe became Rick's motivation for survival. Protecting one's family—and in-group—is a recurrent theme throughout the series. In this context, interpersonal violence is often justified as protecting the patriarchy. In the first season, Lori and Shane are secretly involved in a sexual relationship. Rick, however, did not perish in the hospital, as Shane had led her to believe, but is standing before them alive and well ("Tell It to the Frogs," S1E3). Lori returns without hesitation to the arms of her husband. Shane has other plans. Throughout the first two seasons, Shane's obsession with reclaiming Lori and his surrogate family increases, and by the end of the second season, he attempts to murder Rick to reclaim his status as the head of household ("Better Angels," S212). Rick, however, has realized that Shane is an imminent threat to his family and fatally stabs him.

In season 3, we again see the devastation that can occur as a result of familial loss. Viewers are introduced to the Governor, the charismatic, yet ruthless, leader of the Woodbury community ("Walk with Me," S3E3). Unlike Rick, the Governor responds to his personal losses with brutal, violent behavior that is portrayed as sadistic and unjustified. With the loss of his wife and zombified daughter, whom he keeps tethered in his office, the Governor will go to any length to maintain dominance over his community, even if that means killing others or sexually violating women to obtain information to ward off a possible threat. But it is clear that the Governor did not begin as a sociopathic dictator. The strain of the postapocalyptic events, which directly led to the death of his wife and child, prompted the Governor to resort to violence to maintain control over his domain. Woodbury is worth protecting at any cost, even if it means eliminating individuals who pose no threat to the community.

Food and Water Shortages

Food and water shortages create an inordinate amount of strain. This phenomenon is especially true in instances of disaster: "food and freshwater shortages are associated with negative emotions, such as frustration and anger."[16] In the zombie apocalypse, shelves are stocked at the outset, but, with no electricity, perishable items quickly spoil and the survivors are left to vie for canned items that become increasingly scarce. Without functioning wells or hand pumps, securing access to clean water becomes ever more difficult. Unless survivors are living in a self-sustaining community (e.g., Alexandria), they are relegated to eating outdated canned beans or, in one memorable case, a 112-ounce can of chocolate pudding for survival ("After," S4E9).

Stressors from food and water shortages contribute to strain and, as Agnew notes, such shortages may result in interpersonal aggression and property crimes. From Atlanta to Alexandria, survivors search for and attempt to maintain steady supplies of food. In fact, self-sustained farming becomes a necessary skill to avoid conflict and maintain harmony, if only temporarily. After a chance encounter with Hershel Greene ("Bloodletting," S2E2), a veterinarian turned farmer, Rick's Atlanta group learns how to grow and harvest their own food. Ultimately, however, the peaceful life of farming and the domestication they created is destroyed.

In season 6, the group's encounter with the Saviors highlights how conflict arises around control of food and water resources ("Last Day on Earth," S6E16). The Saviors, led by the ruthless Negan, confront the Atlanta group. In this confrontation, the group must give up half of their supplies to the Saviors or suffer death at the hand of Negan. These types of ultimatums between rival groups are a recurring theme on the show, with the Atlanta band generally submitting until they regroup and develop a strategy of violent retaliation.

But what happens when resources become so scarce that individuals can no longer steal from others to survive? While Agnew addresses crimes that occur as a result of shortages in the aftermath of disasters, he fails to acknowledge the "worst-case scenario" in which these life-sustaining resources become so scarce that people participate in what would otherwise be taboo—cannibalism. Terminus, which initially appears to be a sanctuary, is actually a haven for cannibals who lure people to their demise. The justification of such behavior is that you are either predator or prey: "you're the butcher . . . or you're the cattle" ("No Sanctuary," S5E1). Captives are thus given a choice to join the Terminus group or sacrifice their lives for the continuation of humankind. Cannibalism has become a tolerated, if not justified, practice in the postapocalyptic world. As Gareth, the leader of Terminus, tells Bob Stokely, a member of the Atlanta band, explaining why he consumes humans:

> Didn't start out that way, eating people. It evolved into that. We evolved. We had to. And now we've devolved into hunters . . . at the end of the day no matter how much we hate all this ugly business, a man's gotta eat. ("Strangers," S5E2)

Forced Migration

As with any natural disaster, people are often forced to migrate as their homes, family, and the ability to support themselves are lost.[17] The zombie apocalypse creates a new type of migration as areas of permanent refuge have been overrun by zombies. As a result, survivors must seek short-term sanctuary. Each season, the protagonists' efforts to find shelter as "home" are thwarted or severely compromised. For instance, after being overrun on the farm by a zombie herd, the Atlanta band find refuge in a prison ("Seed," S2E1). Well, sort of. Only after dealing with murderous prisoners and clearing out parts of the prison of its undead occupants is it habitable. In a deadly conflict, the Governor and other inhabitants of Woodbury attack the prison, destroying what was once a safe haven ("Too Far Gone," S4E8). Rick and his fellow survivors are forced to migrate, and it is this continuous migration that places them most at risk. According to Agnew, in a future experiencing catastrophic social change, one of the drivers of increased crime will be the movement of migrant groups "desperate for basic necessities" into areas unprepared for them and hostile to any potential competitors for limited resources.[18]

Exposure to Injustice and Conflict

A key additive source of strain, according to Agnew,[19] is the experience of injustice. When strains are perceived as unjust, crime is more likely to result.[20] Though events impacting social conditions may originate in something not under the power of humans (climate or weather in the context of Agnew's analysis, an outbreak of zombies of unknown origin in ours), Agnew points out that eventually human agency comes into play.[21] It is not uncommon for natural disasters to be exploited for profit and personal gain by individuals, politicians, and multinational corporations.[22] For example, Naomi Klein documents how disaster capitalism—a form of economic shock tactics rooted in free market ideology—has devastated communities and nations recovering from natural disasters or political crises.[23] The disoriented survivors are exploited as resources to be seized by those in power, social welfare programs are decimated, public goods are privatized, and rigid hierarchies produce and reinforce massive social, economic, and political inequalities.[24] In *The Walking Dead*, for example, we quickly see the community revert to traditional gender roles that reinforce patriarchy and later see the highly stratified communities of Woodbury and the Saviors, each ruled by an autocratic dictator (the Governor and Negan, respectively).[25] In both of these communities, citizens are ruled by fear, treated as peasants, required to work, and brutally punished for not falling in line with the leader's demands.

In the world of the walking dead, one would assume that the greatest threat to survival would be the zombies; however, it is often the conflict between the living that poses the greatest threat. While Rick and his group are peaceful, the show reinforces the notion that violence is necessary for survival. As with climate change and natural disaster, the zombie apocalypse creates strain among the surviving civilian population.[26] Although surviving groups are often not looking to expand their territory, as noted earlier, they need life-sustaining supplies, weapons, and shelter. Vulnerable groups are thus repeatedly attacked in battles over resources. In "Nebraska" (S2E8), as Hershel laments the loss of his family in an abandoned bar, Rick kills two men whom he believes pose a threat to his safety. This leads to conflict between the Atlanta band and another group that results in further bloodshed. Armed conflict plagues the Atlanta survivors.

Other Criminogenic Factors in *The Walking Dead*

Though primarily focusing on strain, Agnew identifies other factors he considers criminogenic in the context of social catastrophe.[27] Among the most potent are the resulting social disorganization and associated decline in social control occurring in the wake of disasters or catastrophe, the associated increase in opportunities for crime in the disrupted social landscape, and the potential proliferation of beliefs and values favorable to crime. In *The Walking Dead*, the outbreak and resulting zombies represent a major social disruption; social ties are ruptured due to loss and separation, transience becomes the norm, and new and often fluid social situations are formed. In season 1, the Atlanta group spend much of their time surviving in wooded encampments or on the road in whatever vehicles they are able to commandeer. All have experienced the loss of loved ones and the traditional bonds that previously provided some form of stability and social support.

Agnew points out that during such times of turmoil, both direct and indirect social controls as well as conventional social supports break down.[28] Speculating about the possible impacts of climate change, Agnew states:

> Massive numbers of people will lose their livelihoods, homes and possessions; be forced to leave school; have their families disrupted; have their faith in government shaken; and lose their hope for the future. As a consequence, they may come to believe that they have little to lose by engaging in crime.[29]

In season 1, as Rick's group attempts to recover from a zombie attack on their camp in which many loved ones were killed, they are forced to again take to the road. They seek sanctuary at the CDC only to find it inhabited by a single doctor who is himself distraught over the loss of his wife. The season ends with the group escaping just as the doctor blows up the CDC, symbolically marking the annihilation of the last remaining hope for the formal structure and controls of the society they once knew.

Research on the aftermath of hurricanes has documented the criminogenic effect of such breakdowns in formal social institutions and control and the associated loss of trust and confidence in them.[30] Responding to the aftermath of Hurricane Katrina and citing "the worst surge in violent crime in recent years," the US House of Representatives identified the breakdown of formal social control (in the form of government agencies and law enforcement) as a primary factor in the increasing levels of crime and violence in post-Katrina New Orleans.[31] Importantly, they also addressed the role played by the breakdown in informal social controls, what Agnew refers to as a "stake in conformity" and others call "collective efficacy" or "social capital."[32] The restoration of these informal social controls and the normative bonds they represent is cited as a key mechanism in the rebuilding of a post-catastrophe society and a reduction in crime.[33] As the Atlanta group in *The Walking Dead* recover from their losses (both personal and symbolic), they begin to rebuild a sense of community and the social norms and bonds that come with it. Ironically, it is when the group find themselves living in a (nearly) abandoned prison that this rebuilding truly begins to take shape.

Related to the breakdown in formal and informal social institutions and controls, Agnew further argues that opportunities for crime will change in the wake of social catastrophe.[34] Specifically, in accordance with the routine-activities perspective,[35] the likelihood of crime will increase "when motivated offenders encounter attractive targets in the absence of capable guardians."[36] As strain and scarcity of resources increases, motivation to offend rises. And as capable guardians (in the form of others with whom we are bonded as well as formal mechanisms of social control) are lost, "targets" become more vulnerable (and hence "attractive") to crime. For example, Michael Leitner and Marco Helbich attribute the increase in Houston burglaries in the wake of Hurricane

Rita largely to the fact that homes and businesses were left unattended due to evacuation.[37] Paul Cromwell and colleagues draw similar conclusions about predatory crime in the wake of Hurricane Andrew, noting an increase in motivated offenders as well as an increase in the vulnerability of potential targets.[38] They observed that "[i]t was virtually impossible to maintain physical security in most homes and businesses . . . [s]eventy-five thousand homes were without telephone service [and] commercial establishments were . . . abandoned."[39] In *The Walking Dead*, people are faced with unprecedented pressures to survive and increasing opportunities to resort to crime to do so. The strain and breakdown in social norms and controls motivates survivors to offend and access to unattended structures and unprotected people is plentiful. And crime and violence abound.

Finally, Agnew suggests that conditions associated with catastrophe and the resulting social disturbances create new environments and contexts ripe for the proliferation of beliefs and values favorable to crime.[40] He asserts that such conditions "may lead large numbers of individuals to experience severe strains, blame these strains on others, and find that they cannot count on the State for relief."[41] Drawing on Albert Bandura's theory of moral disengagement,[42] Agnew has previously addressed the shift in beliefs and values that occur in times of strain and serve as pathways from strain to crime.[43] In trying to understand how otherwise moral individuals can harm others, Bandura theorized that the inevitable cognitive dissonance involved in perpetrating such harm was mitigated by particular mechanisms of moral disengagement that are culturally transmitted and learned in the context of particular social conditions.[44] These mechanisms include moral justification, dehumanization of others, externalization of blame, and obscuring of personal responsibility, all serving to remove a sense of agency and cognitively reconstruct harmful conduct. In this process, one is able to avoid the feelings of cognitive dissonance that would normally result from one's behavior conflicting with one's moral sensibilities. In considering the impact of climate change on crime, Agnew predicts the following:

> Individuals and groups will feel they must engage in crime if they are to survive and protect close others; that crime is excusable given the harmful acts committed by others, including states; and that others deserve

harm given their role in creating the above strains. Related to this, the strain and conflict engendered by climate change will increase the salience of in-groups, with those in out-groups being viewed as threats—a belief also conducive to crime.[45]

In *The Walking Dead*, survivors consistently struggle to come to grips with the violent and harmful actions they have taken (or are contemplating taking) in order to survive. In "Judge, Jury, Executioner" (S2E11), Rick's group is faced with a decision about whether to execute a man involved in raping two young girls; Rick and Dale (another member of the group) have the following exchange at the meeting to decide the man's fate:

DALE: You once said that we don't kill the living.
RICK: Well, that was before the living tried to kill us.
DALE: But don't you see? If we do this, the people that we were . . . the world that we knew is dead. And this new world is ugly. It's harsh. It's . . . it's survival of the fittest. And that's a world I don't wanna live in, and I don't believe that any of you do. I can't.

Rick and his group (as well as those in other groups) justify many acts of brutality and harm over the course of the show, often citing a need to "get them before they get us," for righteous retribution or simply for coldly calculated survival (see, for example, episode 3 of season 2, when Shane sacrifices Otis by shooting him in the leg to distract and slow down the zombies). However, as the group rebuilds a semblance of community and the bonds and norms that go with it, the ability to morally disengage wanes. The following monologue, spoken by Rick at the end of the episode "Them" (S5E10), exemplifies this struggle and points to an evolution of the cognitive dissonance as the members of the group try to reconcile how to live with their actions:

When I was a kid, I asked my grandpa once if he ever killed any Germans in the war. He wouldn't answer. He said that was grown-up stuff, so I asked if the Germans ever tried to kill him. But he got real quiet. He said he was dead the minute he stepped into enemy territory. Every day he woke up and told himself, "Rest in peace. Now get up and go to war." And then after a few years of pretending he was dead he made it out alive. That's the trick of it, I think. We do what we need to do and then we get to live. But no matter what we find in DC, I know we'll be okay. Because this is how we survive. We tell ourselves that we are the walking dead.

Early in the show, when the aftermath of the zombie apocalypse is more acute, we see ample evidence of moral disengagement. But as the show progresses and the people in it aspire to rebuild more formally structured societies, we see a decline in moral disengagement, or "beliefs and values favorable to crime."[46] This is exemplified in season 8 by Carl's letter to Rick, his father, written as Carl was dying from a zombie bite ("Worth," S8E15). In it, he writes:

> I wanted to kill Negan. I wish I did. Maybe it would have been done. I don't think it's done now. You went out there again, but I don't think they surrendered. I don't think they will surrender. There are workers in there, dad. They're just regular people: old people, young people, families. You don't want them to die, dad. We're so close to starting everything over, and we have friends now. It's that bigger world you used to talk about: the Kingdom, the Hilltop. There's got to be more places, more people out there—a chance for everything to change and keep changing. Everyone giving everyone the opportunity to have a life. A real life.
>
> If they won't end it, you have to. You have to give them a way out. You have to find peace with Negan. You have to find a way forward somehow. We don't have to forget what happened, but you can make it so it doesn't happen again, and nobody has to live this way. That every life is worth something. Start everything over. Show everyone they can be safe again without killing, that it can feel safe again, that it can go back to being birthdays, schools, jobs and even Friday night pizza somehow—and walks with a dad and a three-year-old, holding hands. Make that come back, dad. And go on those walks with Judith. She'll remember them.

And in the finale of season 8 ("Wrath," E16), Rick, refusing to kill Negan, gives a speech inspired by Carl's dying words that suggests he has come full circle to a moral position likely similar to the one he held as a police officer before the zombie outbreak:

What happened, what we did, what we lost . . . there's got to be something after. Negan's alive. But his way of doing things is over. And anyone
who can't live with that will pay the price, I promise you that. And any
person here who would live in peace and fairness, who would find common ground, this world is yours by right. We are life. That's death! And
it's coming for us. Unless we stand together! So go home. Then the work
begins. The new world begins. All this is just what was. There's gotta be
something after.

Conclusion: Radical Social Change and Crime in *The Walking Dead*

Agnew makes a compelling case for the variety of factors contributing
to crime in the aftermath of environmental and/or social catastrophe
and the associated social changes, while acknowledging the limited
scope of his analysis and proposed theoretical treatment. Though his
focus is primarily on how social changes and conditions have a specific
impact on individuals' experiences and behaviors, he does also allude
to the broader effects of radical social changes and argues for the need
of further theoretical development to more prominently incorporate
such macro-level forces within his framework. In doing this, he predominantly relies on an assumption that a breakdown in social order
inevitably leads people to resort to an apparently natural brutishness
and selfishness associated with crime. Specifically, Agnew states "that
climate change may not only lead to negative environmental, health,
and economic effects, but possibly to a breakdown in social order as
well. That is, climate change may move us toward a Hobbesian state of
nature, with individuals and groups struggling to survive in an increasingly brutal and unregulated environment."[47] Though the criminogenic
forces he identifies are well-founded, we take exception to the premise that events that disrupt the social order such as climate change or,
in our case, a fictional zombie apocalypse inevitably lead to a selfish,
brutish state of nature or a war of all against all. Certainly, conflict
results when individuals are faced with radical changes to their environment and ability to fulfill their needs, but the assumption that the
only, or even the primary, response to such circumstances is one of pure
selfishness, division, and unmitigated violence does not comport with

evidence from actual events[48] or from the speculative, fictional world of *The Walking Dead.*

Contrary to Agnew's concluding thoughts about what he anticipates as the Hobbesian results of climate change and the social disruptions associated with it, crime and violent conflict are not inevitable results. In fact, studies examining whether disasters cause individuals to become violent against one another are limited.[49] In contrast to the Hobbesian notion of human nature as motivated by a competitive, zero-sum self-interest in acquiring scarce resources, Hartmann writes, "people have been managing common resources cooperatively for centuries, successfully negotiating the tension between private gain and the common good."[50] Similarly, in her study of human reaction to disasters, Rebecca Solnit writes,

> In the wake of an earthquake, a bombing, or a major storm, most people are altruistic, urgently engaged in caring for themselves and those around them, strangers and neighbors as well as friends and loved ones. The image of the selfish, panicky, or regressive savage human being in times of disaster has little truth to it.[51]

Moreover, the language of climate change as *apocalyptic* may be more destructive than constructive. As Betsy Hartmann warns, linking climate change to interpersonal violence and terrorism bolsters an already massive military industrial complex. Apocalyptic narratives lead to support for increased securitization, surveillance, and border control in the name of protecting nation-states from outsiders—the "climate refugees" cast as the dangerous "other."[52]

Violence does, however, occur as a result of geopolitical conflicts and brutal government policies that decimate poor communities while exponentially increasing social and political inequalities.[53] In other words, as both Hartmann and Solnit argue,[54] with regard to the relationship between violence and disasters such as climate change, it may be more instructive to look at how those who hold power exploit those at the bottom of the social and political hierarchy.

In fact, self-sacrifice is a common theme in *The Walking Dead.* In season 1, a "gang" initially believed to be a dangerous threat to Rick and his crew were in fact operating a nursing home for the elderly devoted to securing medication and health care aid for the elders and their family members. It is this type of teamwork, along with the accumulation and sharing of resources, that most often underlies the bravery and courage of individual characters. As Rick states in response to a racist comment intended to divide the group,

> We survive this by pulling together, not apart.

Though there is, of course, tribal and defensive violence throughout *The Walking Dead*, it isn't until the introduction of characters such as the Governor and Negan (despots exploiting postapocalyptic circumstances to maintain their own power and control through a social structure based on hierarchy and inequality) that we see organized, large-scale human-on-human violence. Indeed, it is the attempt to replicate or extend hierarchical systems similar to preapocalyptic ones that breed the truly horrific acts of violence. Yar points out that "if crime arises not from malevolence or inherent wickedness, but from an objectively identifiable insufficiency (of resources, opportunities, education, or social controls), then it can be progressively overcome through concerted, corrective actions."[55] It is in this that we can see hope in the wake of extreme, even apocalyptic events. Communities can reemerge (and emerge anew), collectively working toward a normative society in which the sources of crime and violence are attended to and their existence minimized. These are the communities in *The Walking Dead* such as Alexandria, Hilltop, and the Kingdom, which are, as we type this, being depicted as communities working together to build a moral society in which the harm of crime and violence is addressed and a collective normative system maintained. There will certainly be more violence and crime, but not necessarily any direr than was true in the preapocalyptic civilization from which the world of *The Walking Dead* emerged. Except, of course, for the zombies.

11

Mr. Robot and Radical Criminology

Christopher Brewer and Kevin F. Steinmetz

This chapter explores *Mr. Robot* through a radical criminological perspective. Created by Sam Esmail and heralded as one of the best pop culture representations of hacking to date,[1] *Mr. Robot* chronicles the trials and tribulations of Elliot, including his entanglement with "fsociety," a fictional hacktivist group loosely based on the real-life Anonymous hacktivist collective active in the 2000s and 2010s.[2] The first season, the focus of this chapter, involves a plot by fsociety to trigger "the single, biggest incident of wealth redistribution in history" by taking down the global conglomerate E Corp (or, as Elliot calls it, "Evil Corp") (S1E1). The show embraces the "corporate megalomania" trope as one of its focal points. Whenever movies and TV series depict corporate conglomerates, many seem to portray these entities negatively—profiting for "evil" or morally ambiguous purposes. *Mr. Robot* also investigates the ennui, alienation, and anxiety experienced by its characters as they navigate life under late modern information capitalism.

Of particular interest for criminology, *Mr. Robot* explores themes of crime, transgression, and control under circumstances where the rules are often unclear or of questionable legitimacy. The show thus presents a kind of "popular criminology" focusing specifically on crime and criminality within today's high-technology, global, networked political economy.[3] As will be explored here, many of the insights offered by the first season of *Mr. Robot* echo *radical criminology*, a perspective that explores the intersections of crime, criminalization, and control in the context of capitalism and state power, drawing heavily from the Marxist theoretical tradition. Perhaps, then, the show can best be described as a kind of "popular radical criminology." The criminal activities that occur throughout the first season of the show and their relationship to capitalism and corporate power will be discussed. Before providing this criminological analysis of *Mr. Robot*, however, this chapter first provides a general overview of radical criminology.

Radical Criminology

Today the term "radical" is often used as a synonym for "extremist." The former term, however, actually originates from the Latin word *radix* or "root."[4] Radical theories are therefore interested in getting to root causes of societal problems, arguing that no amount of reforming the system will bring about requisite change. Often building on the work of Karl Marx, Friedrich Engels, and the host of Marxist and neo-Marxist scholars they inspired, many radical theories focus on the role of *class* in society, though other sources of social stratification like race, gender, and sexuality are not beyond their purview. A multitude of social problems have been examined from radical perspectives including crime. For radical criminologists, "getting to the root of the problem of crime . . . requires social change at the most fundamental level."[5] Radical criminology can thus be thought of as having three primary objectives: (1) to explain how structures of domination and inequality, like those generated under capitalism, create the conditions conducive to criminal activity, (2) to explore how power—particularly the power of capitalists—can influence the processes of criminalization, and (3) to advocate for social change. Though *Mr. Robot* speaks to each of these elements in some capacity, for the purposes of this analysis we will focus on the show's radical exploration of crime and crime causation.

Despite their contributions, Marx and Engels seldom addressed crime causation, though much of their writing is informative.[6] Engels's *Condition of the Working Class in England*,[7] written after the death of Marx, provides one demonstrative example. Here he argues that the "brutal behavior" of the Irish working classes was not a result of some intrinsic flaw in the Irish character but, rather, a product of the material circumstances they were forced into under capitalism.[8] Regarding the stereotypical drunkenness of the Irish, he explains that "society neglects the Irish and allows them to sink into a state bordering upon savagery. How can society complain when the Irishman does, in fact, become a habitual drunkard?"[9] Viewed in the context of the oeuvre of Marx and Engels, predatory and self-damaging behavior can be understood as a result of the exploitation, alienation, and immiseration that occur under capitalism as well as its particular structure of incentives and disincentives.

It was not until the early 1900s, however, that Marxists began to more directly address the problems of crime and crime control. For instance, Dutch scholar Willem Bonger argued in *Criminality and Economic Conditions* that humans were inherently capable of acting selfishly or altruistically but our tendency toward either was a direct or indirect product of the social relations of production under capitalism.[10] For him, capitalism creates circumstances that encourage acts of egoism—the pursuit of self-interest[11]—including many criminal behaviors. The same drives that create a class of wealthy capitalists also create forms of predatory criminal behavior. Though other criminologists took up Marxist analyses of crime and crime control during this period,[12] they were largely neglected throughout the 1940s and 1950s, most likely as a result of the political circumstances of the time like the Red Scare and McCarthyism, which sought to drive out communists from the academy and American society more generally.

The 1960s and 1970s, however, saw a resurgence in radical thought through intellectual efforts like the now defunct Berkeley School of Criminology in the US and the National Deviancy Symposium in the UK or what some have called the "New Left."[13] In fact, multiple Marxist or Marxian theories of crime and deviance emerged during this period. The general arguments were that crime was largely a product of toxic conditions produced by the capitalist social relations of production and that law was constructed in the interests of the powerful.[14] Radical criminologists viewed crime as intimately tied to social-structural and political-economic conditions. They also drew attention to the "crimes of the powerful,"[15] including white-collar, corporate, political, and state crimes that were largely ignored by "mainstream" criminologists even though these crimes cause significantly more physical and financial damage than street crimes in American society.[16] Additionally, radical criminologists analyze the role of the state in enabling the social harms wrought by the powerful while coercing the lower and working classes into compliance. In other words, they explore how the state works to "secure the capitalist order."[17]

Radical criminology has had a lasting impact on the area of *critical criminology*—a body of criminological thought that focuses on social conflict and the role of power in crime and criminalization. It greatly informed the creation of postmodern criminology, cultural criminology, peace-making criminology, and left realism. Critical criminologists working in the radical tradition have examined a constellation of issues ranging from white-collar and corporate crimes[18] to environmental degradation,[19] prison privatization,[20] and policing,[21] to list only a few examples.

Perhaps most relevant for an examination of *Mr. Robot*, a few works have begun studying hacking and information security–related issues through a radical criminological perspective. In 2008, for example, Majid Yar built on Nils Christie's foundational work *Crime Control as Industry*[22] to describe the emergence of *computer crime control as industry*. Yar argues that computer crime control has followed the trends of terrestrial forms of crime control that have become increasingly market driven and "responsibilised"—requiring individuals to take more responsibility for their security—which he attributes to "a transition to a neo-liberal mode of capitalism."[23] Under this framework, information and computer security is increasingly displaced to "non-market quasi-public regulatory bodies," "communities of self-policing," and, importantly, private companies.[24] Yar points out that information security has primarily become a commodity to be consumed instead of a public service rendered.[25] In two more recent radical criminological works, both James Banks and Kevin Steinmetz argue that contemporary social constructions of cybercrime issues— notably the perceived wrongdoings of hackers and hacktivists (political dissidents who use computer-mediated or -facilitated protest strategies)—are mired in myths and misconceptions.[26] The public fear generated by these forms of cybercrime, according to these authors, yields multiple benefits for "governments, law enforcement agencies, the technosecurity industry, commercial corporations and the media," including harsh punishments for online offenders, an ever-expanding surveillance apparatus, and—as Yar has previously explained—the use of fear to create a multibillion-dollar cybersecurity industry.[27] Steinmetz further adds that contemporary information capitalism simultaneously harnesses the creative productive potential of hackers while seeking to suppress the threat they pose to the capitalist mode of production.[28]

Radical Criminology and *Mr. Robot*

Give a man a gun and he can rob a bank, but give a man a
bank and he can rob the world.
—Tyrell Wellick (S1E2)

With its cynicism about contemporary capitalism, it is perhaps unsurprising that *Mr. Robot* gives us examples of corporate crime and "higher immorality" consistent with those described by radical criminologists.[29] According to these theorists, capitalists and other social elites may commit crimes and misdeeds because of a sense of egoism as they attempt to maximize personal gain, a disconnect from the social consequences of their actions, or because of pressures or incentives to produce profits for shareholders or to meet lofty career ambitions.[30] Within the context of *Mr. Robot*, perhaps no character embodies the criminogenic qualities of capitalism more than Tyrell Wellick, a merciless young entrepreneur who began his career as a technician working at Evil Corp and was, as he states, "promoted faster than anyone else!" eventually becoming senior vice president of technology (S1E9). From a radical perspective, Tyrell represents the ruthlessness of contemporary capitalism, which thrives on wealth and power accumulation at the expense of the lower classes. For example, he repeatedly demonstrates contempt for workers, viewing them as deserving of their lower-class status because of some intrinsic weakness on their part. In a chance meeting with Elliot over lunch in episode five of the first season, he relates his opinion of a waiter working in Evil Corp's data retention facility, Steel Mountain:

> I've seen our waiter here for the last seven years. He must be in his 50s. Maybe has kids, divorced, second wife, more kids. And I wonder what must he think of himself? His life's potential reached at a 30 grand a year salary. An economy car he still owes money on. A two-bedroom apartment. Child support. Coupons. I couldn't bear it. A life like that. The life of an ordinary cockroach whose biggest value is to serve me salad.

This kind of worldview—one structured by a rigid hierarchy based on strength and deservedness—mirrors contemporary pro-capitalism justifications that cast wealth as a sign of hard work and virtue and poverty as a choice.[31] Power, he explains, "belongs to the people that take it" (S1E2).

The criminal tendencies engendered by such contempt for the poor, working classes and avarice for power are evident in Tyrell's murder of Sharon Knowles. Working as interim chief technology officer (CTO) for Evil Corp after his boss was sacked, Tyrell tries to ingratiate himself with Scott Knowles, another Evil Corp executive in the running for the CTO position, over dinner. In an attempt to demonstrate his power and, perhaps, humiliate Scott, Tyrell makes advances on his wife, Sharon. While she urinates in the bathroom, he walks in and watches her, almost daring her to object. Later, at an Evil Corp office gathering, he invites Sharon to the roof for sex. When they meet, she chastises him: "My husband's downstairs getting the job that you want, and you're up here trying to fuck me. Now, whether that's you being straightforward or a game, either way, it's played pretty poorly, if you ask me" (S1E7). Tyrell's advances become more aggressive and he embraces her. As Tyrell takes Sharon to the ground, seducing her, his hands suddenly ascend to her neck and he strangles her, his face twisting into cold savagery. Looking over her lifeless body, his momentary flash of satisfaction shifts to panic as he realizes that he has placed himself and his career in jeopardy. Despite his initial anxiety, he later recounts the event fondly to Elliot toward the end of episode nine of the first season:

> Two days ago, I strangled a woman to death. Just with my hands. It's a strange sensation. Something so tremendous done by something so simple. The first 10 seconds were . . . uncomfortable. A feeling of limbo. But then your muscles tense. And she struggles and fights, but it almost disappears in the background along with everything else in the world. In that moment, it's just you and absolute power. Nothing else. That moment stayed with me. I thought I'd feel guilty for being a murderer. But I don't. I feel wonder.

To borrow from Sigmund Freud, Tyrell perhaps represents the id of capitalism, which the ego has difficulty restraining. For radical criminologists, the outbursts of this id would come as no surprise. Marxists have long argued that capitalism has difficulties reigning in its own excesses because of the very structure of the system, which depends on accumulation, resource extraction, and growth.[32] In other words, there is no effective way to regulate capitalism to make it sustainable, fair, and equitable. Both Tyrell's dark impulses and the social harms wrought by capitalism are not unfortunate accidents but a wholly expected consequence of a system built to favor the elite and to subordinate others.

An additional example of corporate criminality is evident in the Washington Township scandal. Early in the first season, Evil Corp's then CTO, Terry Colby, is accused of conspiracy in concealing company intel regarding the illicit release of harmful chemical waste. Eventually, in the middle of episode three of the first season, the details of the event are released on the news:

> Information stemming from the latest dump reveals that Terry Colby was one of three high-level executives involved in the cover-up of the widely publicized Washington Township toxic waste scandal. If these reports are true, Colby may be facing more indictments. In the ensuing 24 months after the alleged toxic waste leak in 1993, 26 employees died from similar types of leukemia. Evil Corp, however, managed to get the class-action lawsuit filed against it by the surviving victims dismissed, claiming there was no direct evidence linking their factories to the diagnoses. Now these emails indicate that Colby was in fact aware of the dangerous levels of toxicity and kept it a secret as it "would not be cost-effective to retool the current systems in place even if there are potential lawsuits."

As stated in the broadcast, Evil Corp was engaged in a cover-up of a leak that resulted in the poisoning of its workers. This environmental and human health disaster caused the leukemia that killed both Elliot's father and Angela's mother. In this scandal, Evil Corp conducted a cost-benefit analysis and effectively decided that it would be cheaper to cover it up and settle eventual lawsuits rather than retool their system. Colby confirms this calculus toward the end of season one while discussing the costs for Evil Corp with Angela (S1E9):

> They're going to pay millions. Roughly 75 to 100 million. And that's what their lawyers will settle for. After they exhaust most of your legal team's funds for the next seven years. And, sure, that is . . . That's a lot of money, but not to them, not really. We started a rainy-day fund when the leak

happened just for this occasion. The fund itself has already made five times that amount.

Mr. Robot's Washington Township scandal mirrors real-life corporate crimes described by radical criminologists.[33] DuPont chemical company, for example, knew for decades that the perfluorooctanoic acid (PFOA) it used to produce Teflon posed significant health hazards to workers, consumers, and the general public, including birth defects and cancer, but failed to cease using the chemical or even disclose its potentially harmful properties.[34] Though DuPont eventually discovered a potentially safer alternative, the company refused to switch because "the risks of changing were too great" and the use of PFOA was too profitable.[35] Companies like DuPont often conduct cost-benefit analyses and may decide that potential profits outweigh the expected costs of lawsuits and fines, similar to the Washington Township decision made by Evil Corp. As Barak explains, "even when these crimes were highly visible and their perpetrators were caught 'red-handed'" they have customarily been "slapped mildly with fines that have amounted to little more than adding another line item to the costs of conducting business-as-usual affairs."[36]

Mr. Robot also asks the audience to imagine how these corporate decisions may be made under surprisingly banal circumstances—contexts in which the gravity of the circumstances is a distant thought. In an interview with Colby, Angela asks him to explain what it was like to make the decision that killed Evil Corp employees, including her mother (S1E7):

COLBY: I get it. You wanna know, like, what was it like? Like, um, did we all have cigars and laugh hysterically as we signed the evil documents? Is that what you pictured? Well, I'm sorry, hon, you see, the world doesn't work like that.

ANGELA: Tell me. Tell me how it works.

COLBY: All right. Let's see. January '93. Well, my secretary then was Elaine. So, Elaine brought us a platter of shrimp cocktail to tide us to dinner, which pissed us off. Because we just had a platter at the holiday party. Jim opened the bar. Now Jim was a real piece of work. I mean half-pansy, half-mafia. First sign of a tight decision, he'd be chain-smoking, down a river of scotch. Uh, you know, it rained. It rained. I remember that. Yeah.

ANGELA: So, you were drunk, eating shrimp cocktail, and it was rain-
ing when you decided my mother would die? That's why [explaining
why she is pursuing her case against Evil Corp]. So people like you
won't keep sitting in rooms together. Did any of it ever give you or
anyone pause, when you made those decisions?

COLBY: Yeah. Yeah. Sure. But, um, but then you go home. And, uh, and
you have dinner, you know.

Here we have what radical criminologist Gregg Barak, drawing from the
work of Albert Bandura, has referred to as a kind of "moral disengagement" whereby responsibility for harms conducted by corporate actors
is displaced, diffused, or mitigated entirely.[37] These corporate actors
have created both real and moral space between themselves and their
victims as they sit in their corporate offices eating shrimp and making
economic decisions about human lives.

Crimes of the Working and Lower Classes

Though radical criminologists have been preoccupied—for good
reason—with the crimes and misdeeds of the powerful, as previously explained, radical thought has also addressed the crimes of the
oppressed and marginalized classes. In particular, this work tends to
argue that the material circumstances and social relations of production under capitalism encourage normative, cultural, and psychological
tendencies conducive to harmful or self-harmful behavior. Marxist
thought has long argued that the material and intellectual conditions
created within capitalism may manifest in negative psychological and
social outcomes like alienation.[38] In *The Wretched of the Earth*, radical
psychiatrist Frantz Fanon argued that colonialism—the invasion, occupation, and domination of one population by another—has a significant
psychological impact on the colonized conducive to all manner of antisocial behaviors.[39] Under the yoke of oppression, the oppressed may
turn toward "vertical violence," violence directed toward the oppressors
or other forms of protest, or "horizontal violence," predatory behaviors
directed at other members of the working or subordinated classes.[40] The
afflicted may also, as Engels argues, turn to forms of self-harm like substance abuse. In this section, we will focus on occurrences of horizontal

crimes and self-harm in *Mr. Robot* as these represent forms of crime that criminology usually preoccupies itself with. Vertical forms of crime linked to political resistance will be explored in the subsequent section on "social banditry."

In *Mr. Robot*, Elliot provides a case study of the effects of capitalism on working-class criminality (for our purposes, even white-collar professionals like information security engineers are considered working class because of their subordinate position to capitalists and the fact that such workers do not own the means of production). Elliot suffers from significant social and psychological maladies including anxiety, depression, memory loss, delusions, and dissociations. He forgets that Darlene, a member of fsociety, is his sister and carries on internal monologues directed toward an imaginary friend, the audience. Toward the end of the first season, he realizes that the leader of fsociety, the eponymous Mr. Robot, is a delusion in the image of his father. Spoiler alert: it turns out Elliot was the leader of fsociety the entire time. In addition, he self-medicates through opiates—morphine being his drug of choice. The most crippling issues he deals with, however, are loneliness and estrangement. In fact, Elliot confesses to his therapist that loneliness drives his near pathological need to invade the privacy of everyone in his life (S1E7):

> I sometimes watch you on your webcam. You cry sometimes, just like me because you're lonely. I don't just hack you, Krista. I hack everyone. My friends, coworkers. But I've helped a lot of people. I want a way out of loneliness. Just like you.

Mr. Robot indicates that perhaps this crippling sense of loneliness primarily stems from the traumatic loss of his father. For instance, in season one, episode nine, Mr. Robot is revealed to be a figment of Elliot's broken psyche taking the form of his dead father, a delusion stemming from loss. Channeling his loneliness, the Mr. Robot delusion attempts to reassure Elliot, even as he fades from perception: "Please, Elliot. Listen to me. I will never leave you. I will never leave you alone again. I love you, son."

From a radical criminological perspective, the loneliness and associated psychological maladies experienced by Elliot can be seen as stemming from the corporate criminality of Evil Corp. The Washington Township ordeal poisoned his father, leading to his death. This death disrupted Elliot's life, straining his social ties and sense of security. He was cast adrift or, perhaps more appropriately, alienated, which appears to drive much of his behavior—both criminal and noncriminal.

Social Crime and Collateral Consequences

Mr. Robot also provides a glimpse into what radical criminologist term "social crime" or "social banditry"—acts of resistance from within poor communities against ruling elites and the social order.[41] Though these acts may be circumscribed under law, they may be acceptable within a community if they are considered acts of social protest.[42] As Hobsbawm explains, "social bandits" are those "who are *not* regarded as simple criminals by public opinion" but are, instead,

> peasant outlaws whom the lord and state regard as criminals, but who remain within peasant society, and are considered by their people as heroes, as champions, avengers, fighters for justice, perhaps even leaders of liberation, and in any case as men to be admired, helped and supported.[43]

These social bandits generate admiration and support from the community.[44] Part of this support may be because of the tendency of the bandit to steal from the rich and give to the poor, much like the fabled Robin Hood.[45] From a Marxist perspective, social bandits arise as a reaction to the contradictions of capital accumulation and present a direct political threat to its interests. They engage in the kind of "vertical violence" referred to previously—the forms of resistance that inevitably rise up against oppressive conditions.[46]

The first season of *Mr. Robot* explores social banditry within the context of late modern information capitalism, primarily through the exploits of fsociety. Throughout the show, the group rouses popular support through the dissemination of highly stylized videos demanding that Evil Corp free the masses from its yoke, such as the following from season one, episode two:

> Hello, Evil Corp. We are fsociety. Over the years, we have been watching you: your financial abuse of the poor, your corruption of governments, your cover-ups of the murder of innocent, ordinary citizens all for the

sake of a profit. This is why we at fsociety have decided you must die. We are malicious and hostile. We do not compromise. We are relentless. We will not stop until every tentacle of your evil monstrosity is sliced off at the nerve. But we are also not without mercy. Our latest hack was our last warning. Meet our demands, and we will consider not destroying you. First, release our leader Terry Colby [Evil Corp executive falsely implicated by Elliot] from your illegitimate prison immediately. Second, release all the people of the world from your even more illegitimate prisons of debt. Third, dissolve your corporation and donate all your assets to charities around the world. This proposal is nonnegotiable. The people are realizing they don't have freedom of choice so long as you exist. The people are waking up, no longer accepting your economic slavery. Meet these demands, or we will kill you. Consider yourself warned.

The group thus threatens the interest of Evil Corp while attempting to garner the support of the public. Throughout the show, there are many indications that fsociety's efforts are working. In the universe of *Mr. Robot*, many in the American public experience economic precariousness and come to realize that the "American Dream" is a fiction designed to encourage them to mindlessly consume. This is certainly the sentiment expressed by Elliot as he sits on his therapist's couch, imagining how he would respond to the question "What is it about society that disappoints you so much?" (S1E1):

Oh, I don't know. Is it that we collectively thought Steve Jobs was a great man even when we knew he made billions off the backs of children? Or maybe it's that it feels like all our heroes are counterfeit. The world itself's just one big hoax. Spammin' each other with our running commentary of bullshit masquerading as insight, our social media faking as intimacy. Or is it that we voted for this? Not with our rigged elections, but with our things, our property, our money. I'm not saying anything new. We all know why we do this, not because Hunger Games books makes us happy but because we wanna be sedated. Because it's painful not to pretend, because we're cowards. Fuck society.

Though Elliot clearly struggles with his own personal mental illnesses (which he refers to as his "daemons," alluding to the idea of "personal demons" as well as computer programs that operate as background processes), *Mr. Robot* makes it clear that such disaffection can be found beyond its antihero. Elliot presents a critique of contemporary life consistent with radical thought, arguing that the system is fundamentally exploitive but ideologically masks its brutality and placates the public—that the only way the system can continue to function is if it goes unquestioned.[47] And indeed, the dissatisfaction with capitalism and modern consumer culture that drives Elliot and fsociety also drives public support for their efforts. At least until the end of season one, fsociety are heralded as social bandits. After the group executes its plan to destroy the financial records of Evil Corp, public celebrations occur, with participants donning fsociety masks, a reference to the Guy Fawkes masks worn by Anonymous protestors, which, in turn, were borrowed from the graphic novel *V for Vendetta* as a symbol to unify the public against the corporate state.[48] As Darlene tells Elliot, "Everyone's loving it. People actually wanna join fsociety. They're organizing protests all across the city" (S1E10).

Mr. Robot imagines a world in which hacktivist groups like Anonymous embrace more insurrectionary politics and strategies. By the end of season one, fsociety is successful and contributes to a major global financial crisis. For fsociety and many in the public, the crisis is something to be celebrated—that finally the oppression of Evil Corp is over. Yet not everyone is so enthusiastic. For *Mr. Robot*, the salvo launched against Evil Corp does not result in a clean resolution. Because of the complex interdependencies created under capitalism, many individuals suffer as a result of the disruption of finance capital. One of Evil Corp's executives laments in a television interview that

> the public should be worried. I mean, personally, my life is over. My pension, savings everything has been in this company since I started here. And that's all gone now. The truth is, I've been with the engineering team all weekend. No one knows how to fix it. In fact, about the only thing we do know for certain is that this will be impossible to fix. Go take care of this. Calm down, everyone.

He then puts a handgun in his mouth and pulls the trigger. Echoing the fallout from the Bolshevik, French, and other revolutions,[49] *Mr.*

Robot acknowledges that disruptions to the ruling order have collateral consequences—there is a price to be paid. For instance, Elliot's boss at Allsafe meets with one of his accountants, trying to figure out how to salvage his company and, importantly, his employees' jobs. He is informed that the company is leaking money and will need to be shut down (S1E10):

> ADVISOR: Gideon, I handle the money. It's always gonna be a depressing conversation. The best thing you can do for them is to let them know soon, so they can find other jobs. And . . . [sighs] . . .
> GIDEON: What?
> ADVISOR: All their 401(k)s were tied up in the market, which is expected to plummet once the bell rings.
> GIDEON: Well, that's only rumors at this point. . . . What?
> ADVISOR: It seems to be a little more than rumors. Every bank is essentially affected. I know I couldn't use any of my credit cards over the weekend. Could you? Oh, I don't know. There might be a silver lining to all this. If what they're saying about these fsociety hackers is actually true . . . you'll now have no debt.

While the advisor recognizes that the burden of financial debt—which Marxists point out is endemic to contemporary capitalism as it is necessary to create effective demand for production[50]—they have now lost their investments in the market. Both sides of the slate will be wiped clean. While capitalism may be composed of unfair social relations of production and consumption, disruptions to those relations are sure to create problems during transition periods. As Marx remarked in his observations of the Paris Commune, the working class "know that in order to work out their emancipation, and along with it that higher form to which present society is irresistibly tending by its own economical agencies, they will have to pass through long struggles, through a series of historic processes, transforming circumstances and men."[51]

Conclusion

By critically examining the political economy of a capitalist society as a criminogenic force, radical criminology provides us with alternative questions and explanations not explored by mainstream criminology. It reminds us that crime—or *how* and *what* we think about crime—is largely influenced by those who have the power to define such phenomena. Furthermore, the political dogma formulated by the powerful elite works to conceal crimes of the upper class. *Mr. Robot* expresses these ideas, which is why the show is fruitful for radical criminological discussion. The show provides the audience with a potential computer-mediated revolution in ways Marxists, and Karl Marx himself, could only dream of executing. Additionally, Evil Corp epitomizes the exploitative capitalist entity that thrives on the domination and repression of its constituents.

One area not covered extensively within this chapter should also be mentioned. The ideas of criminalization and deviance production within a capitalist society are of utmost importance to radical criminologists. In short, radical criminologists have historically devoted considerable energy toward analyzing the nexus between capitalism, state power, and the designation of certain people and acts threatening to the interests of elites as "criminal," deserving of coercive control.[52] In other words, the law and criminal justice become weapons of the powerful.[53]

Additionally, this chapter investigated only events occurring within season one of *Mr. Robot*. Later seasons and their stories are rife with the potential to be analyzed under the radical criminological microscope. For instance, season two shows Evil Corp attempting to undermine the US government to regain political and economic control after the hack. The hack locked all of Evil Corp's banks behind a paywall, to be released only upon payment of a ransom. In attempting to work around this hack, Evil Corp eventually coerces the United States government to distribute "E-Coin" (the company's version of digital currency, akin to Bitcoin) through a loan program. Essentially, Evil Corp exploits a national catastrophe to establish a new profit stream. This is only one example of criminological phenomena that can be explored through the story crafted by Sam Esmail and his show, *Mr. Robot*.

12

What's in a Name?

LABELING THEORY IN *CRIMINAL MINDS*

Angela M. Collins

The premise of the show *Criminal Minds*, which has completed 15 seasons, is that a psychological profiling team with the Federal Bureau of Investigation (FBI) called the Behavioral Analysis Unit (BAU) use their profiling skills to find and apprehend suspects. The team is made up of special agents, profilers, and other specialists. Their job is to study crime scenes in order to put together a criminal profile of the potential suspect(s) and make educated guesses about their next moves. Once the profile is complete, the BAU then attempts to use that information to thwart future crimes or crimes in progress.[1]

When getting down to the basics, the BAU uses crime scenes to create labels for the suspects, whom they refer to as "unsubs." Sometimes the labels are correct, but not always. Regardless of the correctness of the label, the unsub occasionally resents being given a label. Whatever the situation, labeling theory is at the heart of the work done by the BAU. Labeling theory outlines the process that individuals and communities go through to assign and accept or reject various labels.

This chapter is focused on labeling theory and how the work of the BAU fits into the theory. More specifically, two episodes of the show depict interesting labeling situations: in one, an unsub actively works to gain the label of serial killer (instead of avoiding it, as would be expected); in the other, a member of the BAU is given the label of serial killer (which is accepted by some and rejected by others). A brief introduction to labeling theory and a summary of the labeling process is followed by a description of the two episodes. The conclusion discusses how each episode fits into the labeling process, step by step. Ready? In the words of Penelope Garcia, "I was born ready" (S1E6).

Labeling Theory

There are three main contributors to labeling theory: Frank Tannenbaum, Edwin Lemert, and Howard Becker. All three discussed labeling in relation to juveniles,[2] and the theory has also been used in a developmental perspective.[3] Below is a brief description of the theorists' contributions to labeling theory.

Frank Tannenbaum

Why are labels so important? Tannenbaum addresses this very clearly: "It is not that we do not wish to be identified with him: we cannot by identified with him and keep our own world from being shattered about us. . . . Just because we appreciate the habits, ways, and institutions by which we live, we seem driven to defame and annihilate those activities and individuals whose behavior challenges and repudiates all we live by."[4] The thread that runs through Tannenbaum's writing is that society seems to need to identify (label) deviant people in an attempt to keep "them" away from "us." By giving labels to others we are making a clear distinction between what is acceptable and what is not.

It is not, however, the label on its own that separates "them" from "us." Tannenbaum wrote about the importance of societal reactions to criminal acts. He argued that the response from other people is what individuals, particularly children, base their behavior on.[5] This can become problematic when a behavior is defined in one way by an individual and in another way by the community. For example, Tannenbaum stated that what a juvenile perceives as playful, adventurous, exciting behaviors may be seen as delinquent, evil, and a nuisance by the community. This sort of contradictory definition, or labeling, of behavior leads to conflict. As the conflict continues, deviant actions are redefined as individual transgressions, leading all parties involved to place blame on the individual instead of recognizing the role of how the behavior was defined as deviant.[6] According to Tannenbaum, "From the community's point of view, the individual who used to do bad and mischievous things has now become a bad and unredeemable human being. From the individual's point of view there has taken place a similar change. . . . This recognition on his part becomes a process of self-identification and integration with the group which shares his activities."[7]

Tannenbaum also describes how a juvenile, once taken into custody by police, is exposed to a new world that he may have never seen before. This exposure makes him more conscious of himself and his actions, in a way he may not have seen *himself* before. With this comes a new viewpoint, about himself and the world, that cannot be undone.[8] This process, while described by Tannenbaum in terms of juveniles, can still occur with any individual who is experiencing the criminal justice process for the first time. Once the blame and corresponding label are assigned to a person, an internal process begins. People who are deviant and are caught experience societal reactions to them differently than before. This makes youths begin to question their identity, and they begin to internalize what others think of them. This can be especially true if a youth is placed in prison; the identity that might still be salient can become more ingrained.[9]

Tannenbaum gives this entire process a very specific name: "He has been tagged."[10] Once a person has been tagged, society uses that tag in a way that makes the individual self-conscious and can often lead a person to continue to act in a manner consistent with the tag.[11] This becomes a self-fulfilling prophecy; a person is given a tag, society reacts to that person in support of the tag, the person may attempt to act contrary to the tag but is not believed, and so the person gives in and acts in accordance with the tag.[12]

Edwin Lemert

Edwin Lemert built upon the theory of tagging by arguing that a person's definition of self is dependent upon how *much* deviant behavior he engages in, how *visible* that deviant behavior is, and his *exposure* to the reaction of society to his deviant behavior. The nature of the societal reaction (positive, negative, or neutral) and its intensity have a great impact on the person's definition of self.[13] In a follow-up article, Lemert adds that the societal reaction must be validated in some way, meaning that the reaction is followed by some sort of social control (e.g., legal intervention, treatment).[14] These distinctions offer an explanation for why some people may accept a label while others do not. The reaction to deviance depends on the community, the type of deviance being committed, and the individual committing the act.[15] For example, a person who smokes marijuana everyday may not be getting much societal feedback that his behavior is wrong, especially if he smokes in the privacy of his own home and only around others who accept his behavior. If his behavior were to be discovered, the societal reaction might be neutral if he lives in a state that has decriminalized recreational marijuana use. The totality of the circumstances in this case may lead the individual to not be tagged or not accept the tag.

Lemert also distinguished between primary and secondary deviance. Primary deviance is the original deviant act, while secondary deviance is defined as follows: "When a person begins to employ his deviant behavior or a role based upon it as a means of defense, attack, or adjustment to the overt and covert problems created by the consequent societal reaction to him, his deviation is secondary."[16]

Lemert argues that the primary deviant act is rarely enough to trigger the reactions of others, of society, in a way that would lead a person to secondary deviance.[17] There is usually a reciprocal relationship that takes place between the act of primary deviance, continued acts of deviance, and societal reactions that eventually culminate in labeling or stereotyping, which can ultimately lead an individual to secondary deviance.[18] With each event of primary deviance, the reaction from society increases, increasing the labels and the likelihood that a person will internalize the label.[19]

Lemert also makes the point that when people conform to societal expectations, there is little to no reaction from society. It is only when people act in a way that is outside expected behavior that society reacts, for better or worse.[20] As he explains, "The reason for this is that people can more easily agree upon minimum conformities and intolerable deviations than they can upon what constitutes ideal behavior. An additional reason for this difference is that societies and groups more often can afford to ignore behavior that surpasses their norms, whereas they can seldom disregard sociopathic behavior."[21]

Howard Becker

Howard Becker agreed that deviance is not so much the act of a person as it is the response of others to an act.[22] His contribution to labeling theory introduced the idea that someone who gets labeled as a criminal may end up with "criminal" as their master status—a label that overrides any other label a person has.[23] Potentially, a person could receive and accept the label of criminal or deviant and let that label take over their entire life. Becker starts his discussion of how that can happen with the idea of an outsider—someone who has broken a rule set forth by a social group is seen as untrustworthy and, thus, an outsider.[24]

While an outsider is defined as someone who has broken a rule set forth by a particular group, the outsider may not accept the rule set forth by the group. Not only might the outsider not agree with the rule, but he may also not see the social group as competent to label him an outsider or as having legitimate authority to assign the label of outsider.[25] If that is the case, the outsider is less likely to accept the label and internalize it.

Becker recognizes that there are other factors to consider in this process. First, rules are sometimes applied to some people more than others, even when the act of deviance is the same.[26] This ties back to Lemert, in that the assignment of a label depends on who it is that commits the deviant act.[27] Not every person that commits a deviant act will be labeled deviant or criminal; the process, one way or the other, is sometimes a case of "it's about who you know."

Second, Becker states that people can be given the label of deviant without having broken any rules or they can break a rule and not receive the label if their actions go undetected.[28] In the former situation, a person may be given a label by mistake, but the result could be the same (acceptance and internalization of the label based on societal reaction). On the other hand, if a person's deviance goes undiscovered and the person goes unlabeled, societal reaction may never reach the deviant individual.

Putting It All Together

So where does this leave things? Combining all three theorists' components, labeling theory looks like an ongoing process. It generally goes something like this:

1. An act of primary deviance is committed.
2. That act, assuming it is discovered, causes a societal reaction of some kind.

3. The severity of the act, the stature of the person committing the act, and the criminal history (or lack thereof) of the person all influence what type of reaction is given.
4. The person who committed the deviant act takes in the feedback from society.
5. If the feedback is accepted by the person, the label is internalized.
6. Secondary deviance can then occur, in accordance with the given label.
7. The label is then confirmed by societal reaction.

The main purpose of labeling theory is to explain negative labels (e.g., "deviant" or "criminal"). It also makes the assumption that most people do not want a negative label. However, this same process can be used to assign positive labels to people, so instead of secondary deviance the label encourages socially acceptable behavior. Labeling theory, it should be kept in mind, describes a process in which labels can be changed or replaced, provided that the societal reaction and internalization actually happen as expected.

The television show *Criminal Minds* routinely depicts steps 3 and 4 of this process. The Behavioral Analysis Unit's sole purpose is to look at an act of primary deviance and use the characteristics of that act to create a profile, or label, of the perpetrator (the "unsub"). When an unsub is caught, the label can be applied and steps 5 through 7 may be shown, depending on the plotline.

While the show as a whole lends itself very nicely to labeling theory, there are two episodes in particular that illustrate the steps of the labeling process. In the episode "Identity" (S3E7), an unsub wants to take on the identity of his mentor, a prolific serial killer who committed suicide. In this case, the unsub deliberately seeks to acquire the negative label, which is the opposite of what would be expected. Alternatively, in the episode "Profiler, Profiled" (S2E12), the tables are turned when the label is given to a member of the BAU. This episode gives an inside look at what happens when a label is given to the wrong person and/or the wrong label is applied to someone.

Labeling theory, as explained above, is usually used to explain how someone gets a label that they do not want. At the beginning of "Identity," in which the focus is on someone purposefully chasing after a negative label, serial killer Francis Goehring commits suicide after being caught by police. It does not take long for the BAU to realize that Francis had a partner, who is later identified as Henry Frost. The BAU determines that Frost was the submissive one in the relationship but now that Goehring is dead, Frost is attempting to take on Goehring's persona and label of serial killer.

Toward the end of the episode, agents Hotchner and Rossi, trying to figure out what is happening in the mind of Frost, have the following exchange:

ROSSI: OK, you're Goehring. Sadistic bastard. I'm Frost, a submissive, troubled gay man. I need you to dominate me because it gives me direction and a purpose in life.

HOTCHNER: And life is good. And then one day, I pull the pin on a grenade.

ROSSI: You die. And when I lose you, I begin to lose my identity because my sense of self was tied to you.

HOTCHNER: You're showing classic signs of depersonalization disorder precipitated by the stressor of losing a loved one.

ROSSI: Now all that's left is me.

HOTCHNER: And you hate yourself.

ROSSI: I do. Why?

HOTCHNER: Because I brainwashed you with all my rules, I've told you over and over how weak you are, how you're nothing without me.

ROSSI: Right. So I go back to my home and annihilate everything I own, every reminder of who I am. I erase myself and become you.

HOTCHNER: 'Cause it's the only way that you can survive. The only way that you can hold onto me.

ROSSI: Frost transforms himself into Goehring and goes back to abducting women because that's what Goehring would do.

HOTCHNER: We need to stop thinking like Frost and start thinking like Goehring, 'cause he's still calling the shots.

As moments in the episode show, Frost did take on the label of submissive in his relationship with Goehring. However, he cannot keep that label once Goehring dies. Confused, Frost no longer knows what his label is and begins to internalize the label of serial killer, the label

"Goehring." This internalization then turns to action when Frost dyes his hair the same color as Goehring's, gives himself a facial scar in the same place Goehring had one, dresses like Goehring, and finally abducts a woman to kill just as Goehring did.

The internalization process is shown when Frost is driving with the abducted woman in the trunk of a car. Music is playing in the background, the same music that was playing when Goehring committed suicide. Looking in the rearview mirror, Frost sees Goehring sitting in the backseat. The specter of Goehring says, "If you act like a nobody, you'll be treated like a nobody." Frost smirks and replies, "I'm not a nobody. I'm you." Frost has clearly accepted the label of Goehring and everything that goes along with it.

In the final scene, Frost acts like Goehring and is treated like Goehring by the BAU. The woman Frost abducted tells him her name is Becky in an attempt to convince him to let her go. Becky asks, "What's your name?" Frost smiles and yells, "What's my name? My name is Francis Goehring!" When the BAU arrives on the scene and attempts to negotiate with Frost, the negotiations are unsuccessful and a civilian sharpshooter kills Frost.

In the end, Frost accepted and acted in accordance with the label of Goehring. His final act of abduction and eventual death show how important the label was to Frost. Frost wanted the label, he wanted the societal reaction to the label of Goehring. Instead of shying away from the label of serial killer, Frost not only wanted the negative label but actively chased after it. This speaks to Tannenbaum's suggestion that an individual and a community can label actions in different ways, causing conflict.[29] In this situation it is not just the action that is labeled in different ways, but also the designation of a label as positive or negative that also matters.

In "Profiler, Profiled," the focus is on someone being given an incorrect label. BAU agent Derek Morgan, one of Criminal Minds' main characters, returns home to Chicago every year for his mother's birthday. On each trip, he always visits the grave of a young boy whose corpse—never identified—was found by Derek when he was younger. The opening scenes show Derek stopping by the Upward Youth Center after visiting the cemetery, where he talks to two boys after a football practice. One of the boys, Damien Walters, is found dead later that evening.

As it turns out, Derek was followed all day by law enforcement and is arrested for Damien's murder at his mother's home. The lead detective in the case, Stan Gordinski, reveals that Derek is suspected of Damien's murder, along with another unsolved homicide and the killing of the young boy whose grave Derek visits. When the BAU arrives to help with the investigation, they find out that Stan used a profile written by Gideon—the BAU's top profiler—to support his case against Derek. As the investigation amps up, Gideon says, "I don't like them calling him a suspect," to which Hotchner replies, "Neither do I."

This exchange shows a societal reaction to Derek Morgan being given the label of suspect, implying that he is a serial killer. Stan is convinced that Derek deserves that label and treats Morgan in accordance with it. The BAU agents, on the other hand, are taking their perceptions of Derek into account in rejecting the label. In the tug-of-war over the label, there is a source of legitimate authority attempting to attach a label to Morgan,[30] while the nature of the individual involved (Derek Morgan) is being used by others (the BAU) to reject the label.[31]

At one point, Gideon tells the rest of the BAU, "We should consider Morgan a victim." It seems as though Gideon is trying to replace the label of "suspect" with the label of "victim" with this statement. Stan is determined to attach a label to Derek, and Gideon seems to understand that. Gideon's societal reaction is not only to reject the label, but at the same time replace it with another one. This sends the process of labeling into two different directions, as the labels for Derek Morgan compete with one another.

Once it becomes clear that Derek has a juvenile record that he did not reveal to the members of the BAU, Hotchner appears distressed. Gideon tries to find out why Hotchner is so bothered by not knowing about Derek's expunged and sealed juvenile record. Hotchner asks, "Since when is the criminal history of a suspect not relevant?" Gideon gives Hotchner a strange look and says, "You just called him a suspect." Hotchner does not reply, but when he questions Derek about his record, he clearly treats Derek as a suspect. By using the undesired label unconsciously and then treating Derek in accordance with that label, it appears that Hotchner is beginning to accept the deviant label of Derek.

To help find the real killer, the BAU questions Derek's family about his past and juvenile record. Derek's sister Sara states that Stan Gordinski has "had it out" for Derek because he started spending time with a certain group of older kids in the neighborhood after their father passed away. According to Sara, these kids "were gangbangers, so people started looking at Derek like he was one of them." Derek was not part of a gang, he and his family insist, but because of his associations, Stan— representative of the police—assigned the label of gangbanger to Derek. Some 15 years later, Stan still treats Derek as though he has the label of gangbanger despite Derek's actions to the contrary. This supports Becker's suggestion that a deviant label can become a person's master status[32] and also supports Tannenbaum's view of gang formation.[33]

Over the course of the episode, it becomes clear that Derek is avoiding something from his past. As is finally revealed, Derek was avoiding a label: victim of child sexual abuse. He was almost willing to accept the label of serial killer over accepting the label of victim. Derek's abuser, Carl Buford, is in charge of the Upward Youth Center and turns out to be the killer. Once everything is out in the open, there are several nonverbal exchanges between Derek and Stan that appear to involve a form of apology on Stan's part. It looks as though Stan has finally rejected Derek's labels of gangbanger, suspect, and serial killer. On the other hand, there is also a nonverbal exchange between Derek, Hotchner, and Gideon. Derek looks down at the ground with a sad look on his face and closes his eyes, suggesting that he understands he will now have to accept the label of victim despite not wanting that label.

Conclusion

While the BAU labels unsubs on a regular basis, the two episodes described above show how the labeling process does not always go as expected. Labeling theory suggests that people do not want negative labels or labels that are not appropriate for them.[34] However, the process still works even if someone, like Henry Frost, wants a deviant label. As described above, Frost desperately wanted the label of serial killer because he saw himself as having no label once Goehring killed himself. Frost's previous label of submissive only works while Goehring is alive and giving Frost a reaction. Without the reaction, Frost is lost; he's labelless and decides to take on the label of Goehring/serial killer. Ultimately, Frost gets what he wants and suffers the same fate as Goehring. Here is a recap of how the labeling process went for Frost:

1. *An act of primary deviance is committed*—the abduction and murder of four women by Goehring and Frost.
2. *That act, assuming it is discovered, causes a societal reaction of some kind*—the fourth woman's abduction was witnessed and brought to the attention of law enforcement, prompting a search and eventual confrontation with Goehring.
3. *The severity of the act, the stature of the person committing the act, and the criminal history (or lack thereof) of the person all influence what type of reaction is given*—the acts are severe (murder) and the community wants the cases solved, especially when Goehring commits suicide and kills a police officer in the process.
4. *The person who committed the deviant act takes in the feedback from society*—Frost was getting feedback from Goehring, but does not know what to do when that feedback stops.
5. *If the feedback is accepted by the person, the label is internalized*—Frost most certainly accepted the feedback from Goehring and internalized it. Once he started trying to assign himself the label of Goehring, he internalized it very quickly as evidenced by his change in appearance and referring to himself as Francis Goehring.
6. *Secondary deviance can then occur, in accordance with the given label*—in this case, Frost abducts a fifth woman on his own and takes her to, presumably, rape and kill her in the same manner as Goehring.
7. *The label is then confirmed by societal reaction*—the label of Goehring is accepted by the BAU (as seen in the exchange between Hotchner and Rossi). They treat Frost the same way that they would have treated Goehring and Frost ends up dead, just like his mentor.

Becker also stated that labels can be applied inappropriately,[35] as was the case with Derek Morgan. While trying to avoid the assignment of the "victim" label, he almost ended up with the label of serial killer. When the case comes to a close, Derek appears to accept, albeit unhappily, the label of victim not just to clear his name, but to save other kids from being abused. Here is a recap of how the labeling process went for Morgan:

1. *An act of primary deviance is committed*—the murder of three young boys.
2. *That act, assuming it is discovered, causes a societal reaction of some kind*—the acts are discovered and prompt law enforcement to look for a suspect, using the profile created by Gideon.
3. *The severity of the act, the stature of the person committing the act, and the criminal history (or lack thereof) of the person all influence what type of reaction is given*—the act is severe (murder); Derek's stature is very good with the BAU, but not with Stan; and Derek has a juvenile record. These things in combination with his matching Gideon's profile lead to Derek being given the label of suspect.
4. *The person who committed the deviant act takes in the feedback from society*—Derek takes in this feedback from society (Stan) and pushes back by insisting he is not the perpetrator.
5. *If the feedback is accepted by the person, the label is internalized*—while Derek did not internalize the label, it appears that Hotchner briefly did.
6. *Secondary deviance can then occur, in accordance with the given label*—in this case, there was not an act of secondary deviance (another murder), but there was a confrontation with Carl and Derek about the abuse, resulting in Derek acting in accordance with the label of victim.
7. *The label is then confirmed by societal reaction*—the label of suspect is rejected for Derek, but the label of victim is confirmed.

Labeling theory has been written about for 80 years,[36] and it is clear that the theory is still relevant today. The show *Criminal Minds* relies on the use of labels not just to evoke emotions in viewers, but also to portray the consequences (intended and unintended) of those labels. This use of labels is something that many people can understand and identify with, making the show much more relevant to viewers.

Labels are used by everyone, every day. Labels are given to people, willingly or unwillingly, every day. But maybe we should be a little more careful about how we use them, and on whom.

13

Phrasing Deviance

ARCHER AND TECHNIQUES OF NEUTRALIZATION

Jonathan A. Grubb

Premiering in 2009 on the FX network, *Archer* is a comedic animated series that currently spans eleven seasons and 118 episodes. *Archer* is built on sarcastic and narcissistic one-liners and running gags framed around references that are both simplistic and straightforward as well as more esoteric. The show directly and indirectly pokes fun at the James Bond–esque exploits of staff at the International Secret Intelligence Service (ISIS) and then the Figgis Agency (after ISIS becomes defunct). The adventures that ISIS staff are involved in, most commonly missions to protect a target, retrieve an object, or assassinate a target, are diverse and take place in a range of exotic locations around the world. For example, in "Sea Tunt: Parts I and II" (S4E12 and S4E13), field agent Sterling Archer along with most of the ISIS staff are originally charged with retrieving a hydrogen bomb that went down with a B-52 bomber around Bermuda but end up being tasked with stopping the launch of a missile from an underwater sea lab once the original plan of securing the submerged bomb was exposed as a lie. The common thematic element across this mission and those in most episodes tends to be that whatever effort they are involved in goes off the rails and all hell breaks loose.

The Show

Mirroring the ridiculous missions and mischief that the staff of ISIS carry out are the unique and diverse lives of the staff themselves. Although most of the main characters are white (except Lana) and

American (except Dr. Krieger and Woodhouse), the show is relatively demographically diverse. For instance, there is an almost even split of males and females among the main characters, as well as an openly gay male (Ray), an elderly female and male (Malory, Woodhouse), and an upper-class female (Cheryl). Experientially, the personnel have different backgrounds as well: three are athletes (Archer—lacrosse, Pam—underground fighting, and Ray—giant slalom skiing), on is a military veteran (Woodhouse), two are musicians (Dr. Krieger, Cheryl), and one is an animal rights activist (Lane). Most of the staff also have a few things in common, including alcohol and drug use, sexual relationships with coworkers, and more generally ongoing dysfunctional relationships with one another.

The unique backgrounds and assignments that ISIS staff take on result in individuals committing crimes or deviant behavior, or being victimized, injured, or killed due either to direct conflict or negligence. Although Sterling and the rest of the staff express remorse once in a while for actions that negatively impact others, more regularly they utilize sarcastic and narcissistic banter to deflect any sense of responsibility. *Archer* thus showcases components of a longstanding framework in criminology, techniques of neutralization. Simply put, techniques of neutralization are psychological strategies used by an individual to deny or sidestep guilt or shame for an action perceived by the individual to be wrong. Prior to framing the different techniques of neutralization within *Archer*, an overview regarding the techniques and findings from extent research on them is provided.

Techniques of Neutralization

Our understanding of techniques of neutralization stem from the work of Gresham Sykes and David Matza.[1] Although aspects of neutralization theory are present in criminological work prior to their seminal 1957 article, it was the techniques of neutralization framed by Sykes and Matza that developed into one of the most well-known theoretical frameworks in criminology. Sykes and Matza argued that "delinquency is based on what is essentially an unrecognized extension of defenses to crimes, in the form of justifications for deviance that are seen as valid by the delinquent but not by the legal system or society at large."[2] More succinctly, delinquents use various rationalizations both before as well as after committing a delinquent act to justify their behavior. In total, five techniques of neutralizations were specified in their original work: (1) denial of responsibility, (2) denial of injury, (3) denial of the victim, (4) condemnation of the condemners, and (5) appeal to higher loyalties.

The first technique, denial of responsibility, posits that delinquents perceive themselves as not responsible or accountable for their actions based upon factors outside of their control. Literature has described a few of these factors, including poverty, substance use, and familial and other personal issues.[3] This technique commonly involves the individual claiming they were forced to commit an act or that they didn't have a choice to begin with. For example, a juvenile might rationalize stealing food from a grocery store because their family has no money and would otherwise starve. In this case, denial of responsibility is exemplified through lack of choice and is used to cognitively avert concerns related to the illegal activity of stealing food. Similarly, Shadd Maruna and Heith Copes describe how in certain contexts offenders deny responsibility on the basis that they were forced to participate in illegal actions to maintain their employment or ensure survival of their business.[4] Minor refers to this as possibly a separate technique from denial of responsibility, describing it as defense of necessity.[5]

The second technique, denial of injury, posits that delinquents nullify the impact of their actions by questioning whether anyone was hurt by what they did, especially when violence was not involved. This technique is especially relevant for victimless crimes, most notably drug use. Patrick Paretti-Watel suggests that in instances of drug use there is neither injury nor a victim and specifies that as it relates to injury, "denying a risk means denying a *potential* injury, not an *actual* one."[6] For instance, using the previous example of taking food from a store, an individual might suggest that no one was actually injured or harmed by the theft of the food.

The third technique, denial of the victim, has a two-pronged foundation. The first involves the delinquent suggesting that there actually is no victim, as the person perceived as a victim wronged them and, in turn, they are exacting revenge. The second revolves around a combination of relational and physical distance of the delinquent from the victim. More specifically, "Insofar as the victim is physically absent, unknown, or a vague abstraction (as is often the case in delinquent acts committed against property), the awareness of the victim's existence is weakened."[7] Research has found that while delinquents and non-delinquents had similar perspectives regarding denial of the victim when the victim was someone known to them, delinquents had a greater level of acceptance, relative to nondelinquents, when the victim was unknown to them or was an institution/organization.[8] This latter portion is backed up in work by Volkan Topalli that focuses on techniques of neutralization practiced by active criminals.[9] For example, he describes one drug dealer snitching on another, specifically denying the latter's status as a victim because the rival dealer was largely unknown to him.

The fourth technique, condemnation of the condemners, describes the delinquent as rejecting individuals who reject the delinquent's behavior, shifting attention from their own delinquency to individuals disapproving of the delinquent's actions. Joseph Rogers and M. D. Buffalo suggest that this technique is rooted in the delinquent's questioning the motives of those condemning them, whether they be teachers, criminal justice actors, parents, or individuals more generally.[10] One manner of achieving this involves the delinquent basically flipping the script and suggesting that the condemners have been involved in similar actions as the delinquent. For example, a juvenile caught shoplifting by a store owner might try to sidestep their actions by suggesting that the storeowner was involved in the same type of actions when they were a kid. Similar tactics have been found to be used by white-collar offenders. Scott Kieffer and John Sloan III relate that individuals involved in corporate fraud not only framed prosecutors as simply trying to climb ranks by taking down powerful individuals such as themselves, they also condemned laws and governmental regulations for limiting corporate power and free enterprise more generally.[11]

The final technique of neutralization, appeal to higher loyalties, is rooted in the notion that behaviors of the deviant adhere to norms of a specific group of individuals rather than to more expansive societal norms. Commonly, the individual will appeal to rules and behaviors adhered to by their friends or possibly a gang they belong to. An example would be a juvenile not snitching on their friends for a delinquent act or crime they had committed because loyalty to those friends overrides the norms of mainstream society. An important point regarding appeal to higher loyalties is that opting for one set of norms, those of society or those of a particular group, is not simply an all or nothing selection of one over the other. For instance, Rogers and Buffalo explain that individuals appealing to higher loyalties do not necessarily reject societal norms but rather accept the norms of persons or a group to which they have a higher loyalty than to societal norms.[12]

In addition to the original five techniques outlined by Sykes and Matza, a number of other techniques have also been proposed.[13] One is the metaphor of the ledger, whereby an individual tries to balance out their negative or illegal behavior with all of the positive acts that they have been involved in.[14] In essence, the individual might make a statement along the lines of "Sure I ended up getting a few DUIs and running over a mailbox, but I have done a lot of good in the community with my business and volunteering efforts." Alexander Alvarez suggests yet another technique, the denial of humanity, based on his investigation of the use of neutralization techniques by average Germans who participated in the Holocaust.[15] The denial-of-humanity perspective in this context underscores that the horrific acts that occurred during the Holocaust were facilitated by prior dehumanization of the Jewish population. Similarly, Emily Bryant, Emily Schimke, Hollie Brehm, and Chris Uggen describe two techniques of neutralization used by defendants charged with involvement in the Rwandan genocide.[16] The first was victimization, relating to their own victimization, the loss of family members and friends, or more generally the victimization of their ethnic group. The second was appeals to good character. While this technique has the same general foundation as the metaphor of the ledger, the difference is that "defendants stop short of admitting guilt when cataloging their virtuous acts."[17]

Aside from this array of specific techniques, a substantial body of research has emerged over the past 60 years more generally on techniques of neutralization. From a theoretical angle, this body of literature has questioned if neutralization operates similarly based upon race and sex,[18] examined the temporal ordering between involvement in delinquency and utilization of specific techniques,[19] proposed the reframing and expansion of the ways in which techniques are used,[20] and inquired into whether the techniques differ from various forms of cognitive distortions and disengagement strategies.[21] Aside from theoretical discourse, the techniques have also been used to investigate a variety of different offenses. Examples include violence in general,[22] sexual abuse,[23] substance use,[24] auto theft,[25] corporate crime,[26] genocide,[27] consumer fraud,[28] software and music piracy,[29] gambling,[30] street tagging,[31] and deer poaching.[32]

While analysis of the techniques originated out of efforts to explain delinquency, their analytical use has expanded beyond the boundaries of criminology to support investigations into a range of topics, including marketing ethics,[33] fair trade goods,[34] climate change,[35] prenatal nutrition,[36] abortion,[37] beauty pageants,[38] and animal rights activism.[39] Although there is now a substantial body of research on the techniques of neutralization, there has been minimal exploration of how the different techniques manifest in popular media, notably television shows. The purpose of the current chapter is to showcase techniques of neutralization in mainstream media, notably within the television show *Archer*.

Denial and Condemnation in *Archer*

Examples of the techniques of neutralization are numerous in *Archer* and individual chapters could be devoted to each. Rather than focusing on a single technique of neutralization, it is more advantageous to highlight each technique outlined by Sykes and Matza.[40] This also underscores another important consideration for examining the techniques within *Archer*, specifically which seasons of the show should be included and why. Although there are eleven, the current survey includes only the first seven seasons. The rationale for this is multifaceted. First, the first seven seasons occur in the real world in which Sterling and the ISIS staff live. Although season five (labeled *Archer Vice*) takes a turn from the previous four seasons, with ISIS operating not as a spy agency but as a criminal organization, it seemingly still occurs in the characters' real world. In contrast, events in seasons eight and nine occur in the subconscious of Sterling while he is in a coma after being shot during season seven. Second, season seven is the last in which all the main characters included in this analysis are alive. More specifically, the beginning of season eight opens with Woodhouse's funeral. The following examination of the techniques of neutralization in *Archer* thus includes only the first seven seasons.

Three additional points regarding the following sections are also warranted. First, they discuss a variety of different behaviors. Generally speaking, techniques of neutralization are used in situations involving criminal and delinquent acts. As *Archer* centers on secret agents and other intelligence agency staff members, the legality of their actions is not always a straightforward matter. Actions across a spectrum of legality and illegality are covered here to underscore how neutralization techniques can be applied in a variety of different situations and scenarios. Second, there is a heavy focus on the exploits of Sterling as he is the title character. Nevertheless, examples from other main characters working at ISIS are also integrated to underscore the diversity of techniques used throughout the show. Last, a heavy emphasis is placed on the specific dialogue between characters to illuminate the nuances of how the techniques manifest.

Denial of Responsibility

Of the five different techniques of neutralization described by Sykes and Matza[41] arguably none is more readily apparent in *Archer* than denial of responsibility. Although this technique is used by most characters, many examples are present in the actions and discourse of Sterling. For Sterling, denial of responsibility can take many different forms, however, a regularly observable element across a variety of examples where this technique is used involves him being drunk. This becomes evident barely three minutes into the pilot episode, "Mole Hunt" (S1E1). Heavily intoxicated and with a female companion, Sterling brings back the woman's pug to his apartment and becomes drunkenly excited when he thinks it starts barking "Puttin' on the Ritz." After he wakes up in the morning and realizes there is a dog in his apartment, he ends up blaming his valet, Woodhouse, for allowing him to violate his own rule of not allowing dogs into his apartment. Sterling quips, "It's a short list, Woodhouse. . . . Two things we don't allow in here—what are they?" Woodhouse responds, "Dogs and your mother. . . . Yes, but you were quite insistent . . . that an exception be made." Sterling, underscoring that Woodhouse should not listen to him, says, "I'm always insistent, Woodhouse. . . . But I'm not to be trusted, am I?" Woodhouse replies, "No, sir." In this example, Sterling tries to circumvent responsibility by arguing that Woodhouse should not have allowed him to bring the dog into the house to begin with, because he shouldn't be trusted when he is drunk.

Sterling has a unique knack for denying responsibility more generally. In arguably the most detrimental instances, he denies responsibility for multiple individuals being killed as a direct result of his actions. A prime example of this is in "Diversity Hire" (S1E3). In front of the staff, ISIS director (and Sterling's mother) Malory explains that "agent Hector Ruíz, who had infiltrated El Frente Rojo, was killed last night when his cover was blown." Agent Lana questions how this occurred, with a flashback showing a drunk Sterling at a bar calling Ruíz on a cell phone, excitedly asking, "Hey, man, talk to these chicks, all right? Tell them how we're really ISIS agents! They don't believe me." The following scene shows the individuals Ruíz was working with overhearing his true identity and raising their guns at him, alluding to the fact that they shot and killed him. Defensively, Sterling retorts, "Ruíz was a loose cannon. He played fast and he played loose. And in the end, he got burned." Shortly following this scene there are two additional flashbacks that show Sterling making similar phone calls to other undercover agents and blowing their identities, resulting in their deaths as well. Sterling again states, "Loose cannons!" Concerning all three of these untimely deaths, Sterling essentially denies responsibility for his actions and suggests that it was the fault of the other agents, due to their supposedly reckless lifestyles (which is, of course, more true of Sterling himself).

Aside from Sterling, several ISIS staffers deny responsibility for their actions through a variety of different justifications. A thematically reoccurring example of denial of responsibility appears in flashbacks and accounts pertaining to Malory's questionable parenting practices involving Sterling as a child. In "Job Offer" (S1E9), Malory gets hammered on absinthe and starts reminiscing about Sterling leaving ISIS to work for ODIN (the Organization of Democratic Intelligence Networks, which is depicted as a more elite and competent spy agency than ISIS), stating, "He'll be back, crying for his mommy! Just like that Christmas break when I moved and forgot to give my new address to his stupid boarding school. I mean, he rode the train into the city all by himself. He couldn't pick up a phone book? Nine years old, and bawling in that police station like a little girl! What's that tell you?" Cheryl, Malory's personal assistant, responds, "Kind of a lot, actually." In this case, Malory tries to shift responsibility and blame away from herself and onto Sterling for not finding their new home due to her negligence in not informing the school that she had moved.

Denial of Injury

While Sterling sustains a variety of different physical injuries across many episodes, it is also not uncommon for him to injure others. The most prominent examples include ODIN field agent Barry, whom he allows to be dropped from a roof multiple times; ISIS employee Brett, whom he ends up shooting both by accident and on purpose several times before Brett is killed by the FBI; and fellow ISIS agent Ray, who is paralyzed more than once in different ways by him. Sterling does not necessarily deny each injury that he has caused to these and other individuals outright, but rather jokes about it to each of them in subtle ways, suggesting that they are actually fine. A prime example of this involves Sterling continually shooting ISIS agent Cyril when he is wearing Kevlar. This comes to a head in "Palace Intrigue, Part II" (S5E11), which focuses on Sterling and the ISIS staff working to leave the island nation of San Marcos following their delivery of weapons to its president. Near the beginning of the episode, Sterling once again has shot Cyril in the chest to divert attention from the president's wife, who was about to disclose that she just had sex with Sterling. As ISIS human resources director Pam resuscitates Cyril, she exclaims, "Holy shit! That works," to which Sterling retorts, "Yeah, so does Kevlar." Sterling eventually emphasizes that he knew Cyril would be fine, declaring, "Cyril, you wear Kevlar every single time we go to Latin America." Cyril angrily responds, "Because every time, you shoot me!" Sterling quips, "Whoa, whoa, whoa. Not every time. Three out of four, tops. You big baby." In this case, Sterling suggests that he knew Cyril would be fine after being shot, because he suspected more likely than not that Cyril was wearing Kevlar and it would protect him from serious injury or death. Calling him out as a big baby cements that Sterling believes Cyril is overreacting and no lasting harm was actually done to him.

As touched on above, often it is Sterling who is on the receiving end of injury, responsibility for which someone else is trying to deny.

Near the end of the episode "Double Deuce" (S2E5), which centers on Woodhouse revealing he is one of the last surviving members of a World War I tontine, Sterling, thinking that Woodhouse is going to be killed by one of his wartime compatriots, kicks the individual off a roof to his death. Woodhouse begins to freak out and then instructs another veteran to strike Sterling with his gun, knocking him unconscious. The veteran states, "Damn shame he'll send you packing when he comes to," to which Woodhouse responds, "Oh, I'll just yank his pants off, splash a lot of scotch and women's underthings about then tell him he slipped and fell, chasing a terrified Asian prostitute out onto the patio. It's not the first time I bashed his head in and had to cover my tracks. Happens three, four times a year." Although Woodhouse does not directly deny that he might have caused injury, he suggests that, based upon the regularity with which he is required to knock out Sterling, this specific incident is likely no more harmful than the previous times he carried out the same type of act.

Another example of denying injury is in "Skytanic" (S1E7). While Sterling, Lana, and Malory were taking the newly constructed airship *Excelsior* from New York to London to uncover who made an anonymous bomb threat to the airship, Pam, Cheryl, and Cyril decided to secretly stow away on the airship. It is revealed that although Cyril and Lana were still in a relationship, Cheryl tries to make Sterling jealous by having sex with Cyril multiple times. During one of these sexual encounters, Cyril freaks out and runs off to confess what he has done to Lana, causing Cheryl to become hysterical, resulting in Pam trying to drown her in the tub. After Malory enters the room and discovers a seemingly dead Cheryl, Pam states, "Cyril got in over his head and . . . ." Malory, questioning Pam, asks, "Jesus God, did he kill her?!" Pam clarifies, "No. He ran from her, to go confess to Lana. But then this one starts freaking out and . . . I kinda had to drown her in the tub." Malory, still questioning Pam: "So you killed her?" Cheryl then starts coughing up water and passes out, revealing that she is not dead. Pam happily retorts, "Apparently not. So . . . good news." Although arguably more subtle than other examples, the last statement made by Pam could be interpreted as denying injury, specifically the assault on and near death of Cheryl, by emphasizing that she did not die, which she ties to neutralization by framing her apparent survival as "good news."

Denial of the Victim

Denial of the victim in *Archer* manifests in multiple ways, perhaps the most common involving revenge. A central example comes in "Placebo Effect" (S2E9), which centers around Sterling going on a rampage and killing a number of people following the discovery by ISIS's Dr. Krieger that medication for Sterling's breast cancer is essentially Zima and sucrose. Shortly after finding this out, Sterling is talking with Malory and Lana about his revenge plan. Questioning Sterling's intentions, Malory asks, "What're you, Sterling, no, you're not well! What are you going to do?" Sterling declaims, "Cry havoc, and let slip the hogs of war." Lana corrects him: "Dogs of war." He retorts, "Whatever farm animal of war, Lana, shut up." Sterling finds out from a pharmacist that the Irish mob was behind switching out the cancer drugs with placebos at a warehouse. Once Sterling and Lana arrive at the warehouse, they tie up three of the mobsters (two of whom he kills) as well as three janitors and find the location of a poker game the mob boss is supposed to be at. Showing up at the poker game, they shoot and kill most of the mobsters, with the exception of one who tells them where the boss is following the insertion into his anus of what they believe to be a smoke grenade (which they discover is not actually a smoke grenade after he blows up). Sterling and Lana finally encounter the old, handicapped mob boss at his house, and Sterling shoots him, concluding his rampage. In this context, Sterling is denying certain individuals, specifically those associated with Irish mob, qualify as victim, since they originally scammed him with the counterfeit drugs and thus his revenge rampage was warranted.

Another example of denial of the victim that incorporates an element of revenge involves Malory's killing of the prime minister of Italy. In "Lo Scandalo" (S3E5), Malory reveals that she has been having a decades-long relationship with the Italian premier since they worked together during World War II. In the most recent encounter between Malory and the prime minister it is revealed first to Sterling and Lana, and eventually to the rest of the staff at ISIS, that the prime minister was shot to death. Malory explains that a group of individuals broke in, killed the prime minister, and shot her on the way out. Eventually, Dr. Krieger dismembers the body while a detective shows up at Malory's house following a tip that the prime minister might have been killed in her apartment. After the detective finds no evidence of the killing and leaves, ISIS staffers take packages of the dismembered minister's body to dispose of around the city. During a flashback at the end of the episode, it is revealed that Malory killed the prime minister in an act of revenge. More specifically, while the prime minister is tied to a seat, Malory discloses that she has planned to kill him, stating, "And I figured, eh, what's the hurry? But then you started getting weird." The prime minister asks, "But why you make *la vendetta*?" Malory says, "Because one night, all those years ago in Rome, you and your fascist thugs gunned down a young man in the street. A beautiful man. Blue eyes, full lips, black thick wavy hair." The prime minister continues to question her: "*Perché?* What was his crime?" Malory responds, "Well, I wouldn't call speaking out against the rebirth of fascism a crime. More of a mistake. By a beautiful, idealistic young man. Who may have been my son's father." After some additional heated discussion between Malory and the prime minister in Italian she fires several shots into his chest, killing him. Similar to Sterling in the previous example, Malory employs a revenge-based justification for denying the prime minister the status of victim since he and his men killed Sterling's possible father.

Condemnation of Condemners

Sterling often condemns individuals who condemn his deviant behaviors. A common example of this occurs on the multiple occasions where he runs away from home to far-off locations to drink uncontrollably and have anonymous sex. For example, in "The Holdout" (S6E1), Sterling is found to have run away from home following the revelation at the end of season five that Lana's baby, A.J., is his child. Calling Sterling to try to figure out what he is doing, Malory states, "Once again you're off on one of your usual self-pitying benders." Sterling, annoyed, responds, "It's not a usual one, mother. In case you forgot, I was forced into becoming a parent against my will." Malory, not amused: "Join the club. But for God's sake, six weeks is long enough." After further conversation between Sterling and Malory, Lana asks him over the phone, "So, why'd you run away when you were so excited about being a father when A.J. was born? Did reality set in?" Sterling, confused, declares, "I—wait, was that rhetorical? Because the next time you use somebody's sperm to impregnate yourself, then maybe that decision should include that other somebody." In this example, both Malory and Lana condemn Sterling's running away when he finds out he is father to A.J. In response, he essentially suggests that Lana was also deviant in that she did not involve him in the decision-making process of having a child.

Lana provides an additional example of condemnation of condemners. Early in the show, there are multiple flashbacks and present-set scenes revealing that Lana has a passion for social and environmental activism, notably when it comes to animal rights. It also develops that Lana is not afraid of advocating or even perpetrating significant violence, even when it goes against principles she holds close. This comes to a head when she and Sterling are trying to thwart an ecoterrorist named Josh, a former lover of Lana's, from blowing up an oil pipeline in the episode "Pipeline Fever" (S2E4). After Lana and Sterling are almost killed by an alligator, Josh shows up in a boat and a discussion ensues among the three of them regarding how Lana knows him. During this discussion, Josh states, "That's when I realized I had to lead the fight against the systematic rape of Mother Nature." Lana points out, "But back then you just organized peaceful protests." Josh, with a reminiscent tone, says, "Like that day at the fur store where you disappeared without a trace," to which Lana responds, "I guess I kinda found my calling." Josh, annoyed, fires back: "What, as a hired gun for the military-industrial complex? A traitor to the cause of environmental protection?" Lana, now upset: "Me?! What about you?!—Always running around, blowing shit up, but Josh, seriously, do you really think the ends justify such violent means?" Josh, increasingly ecstatic, cries, "Yes! Because this is a war! And victory will only come when Americans will stop destroying the Earth just so they can drive bigger cars, build bigger houses, and eat bigger food." In this example, Josh condemns Lana's decision to join ISIS, essentially as a hired gun, and basically abandon a cause she believed in, protection of the environment and animals. Lana's retort to Josh, that he is involved in violence and property destruction to protect the environment, condemns her condemner by asserting that what he is doing is just as bad if not worse and that he is a hypocrite since he is trying to use violence to achieve his goals similar to what she is required to do in her job with ISIS.

Appeal to Higher Loyalties

Sterling regularly appeals to higher loyalties to justify his actions. One example, involving Sterling and a band of pirates, spans three episodes titled "Heart of Archness" (S3E1–S3E3). After running away following the murder of his fiancée by Barry, Sterling is eventually found on a French Polynesian island by a former ISIS agent named Rip. Flying back to ISIS headquarters, their plane crashes and they are captured by pirates. Upon returning to the island, which is the pirates' home base, and discovering that Sterling has essentially been crowned their new leader because he unwittingly killed the previous one, Rip states, "Once they're good and drunk we'll turn this tub around and head home." Sterling happily replies, "Home? Riley I am home." Rip, surprised, declares, "Wh—?! Over my dead body are you running away to be a pirate!" Excitedly, Sterling corrects him: "Of course, I'm not gonna be a pirate, I'm gonna be a pirate king." Sterling is unsuccessful in maintaining his role as pirate king, and is imprisoned along with Lana, Ray, and Rip. They finally break free and fly away on a helicopter, but Sterling again shows his loyalty to the pirates. The pirates start shooting at the helicopter and Lana fires back, killing a few who have been playing lacrosse. Upset, Sterling chews out Lana for killing one he was grooming to be a professional lacrosse player. Sterling appeals here to higher loyalties, specifically to the pirates, both when he becomes king as well as when trying to escape, over ISIS and its staff. Based upon the activities he is involved in with the pirates (e.g., drinking, having sex, playing lacrosse), his apparent appeal to them is that he is able to maintain significant power and participate in his favorite activities while doing little work, especially compared to what is required of him at ISIS.

Sterling provides another example of appeal to higher loyalties, one involving his friend and ex-colleague Lucas Troy, a former ISIS secret agent who left the agency to work for ODIN and then went rogue. In "The Wind Cries Mary" (S4E2), Mallory informs the ISIS staff that Lucas was killed in a plane crash after stealing uranium as part of his duties for ODIN, but Sterling believes that he is still alive. Sterling receives a phone call that Lana eventually deduces was from Lucas, after she finds out that he was taking a significant number of weapons and goods from the ISIS armory. Sterling is then shown driving fast down a road, on the phone with Lucas, stating, "Dude, I knew you faked your death because a mole framed you for stealing that uranium!" Lucas, happy that Sterling understands, says, "Dude, that is such a relief, I was worried they turned you against me." Sterling excitedly replies, "Are you kidding? Dude, bros before apparent threats to national security." They meet up, and Sterling discovers that Lucas has been in love with him, before Lucas drugs him. Lana and Cyril track Sterling down and kill Lucas by dropping a tree on him. In this example, Sterling appeals to his higher loyalty to Lucas to justify undermining ISIS and national security (due to the nature of what he stole) to help a rogue ODIN agent.

A final example of appeal to higher loyalties is provided by Ray in the episode "Bloody Ferlin" (S3E9). Ray reveals that his brother, Randy, has informed him that the sheriff in their West Virginia hometown has been trying to take over his marijuana farm. To rectify the situation, Ray, Sterling, and Cheryl (posing as Ray's wife) head to West Virginia. When the sheriff arrives at the farm and tries to get Randy to come out of his house, Ray believes that he is there to kill his brother and proclaims, "Randy, you may be a racist, homophobic, wife-swapping drug dealer, but nobody murders my brother." A firefight ensues between the brothers and the sheriff and his deputies. However, unbeknownst to Ray, the entire story about the sheriff taking over the farm was a lie told by Randy so that he could continue to illegally grow and sell marijuana. This becomes evident during the firefight when Ray screams at the sheriff, "You're gonna murder him so you can take over his dope farm." The sheriff, confused, responds, "What?! Cease fire! Hold your fire! Why in the world would you think that I, a peace officer sworn to uphold the law, would wanna murder your brother to get his marijuana farm?" Ray, now equally confused, says, "I—because that's what Randy said." The sheriff asserts, "Randy's a drug dealer! And I tried to get him to quit. I come to him as a friend, I come to him as an elder of the church, but he wouldn't give it up. And so now I gotta come to him as the law." Once Ray realizes what is going on, he knocks Randy unconscious and turns him over to the sheriff. In this example, Ray originally appeals to a higher loyalty, specifically to his family member, offering him protection from law enforcement even though he is illegally involved in marijuana production. His use of firearms against law enforcement officers is likewise justified on the basis of ensuring that his brother is not murdered by them. Once Ray finds out the truth about the situation, this appeal to higher loyalty ceases.

Conclusion

The original formulation of the techniques of neutralization by Sykes and Matza represents one of the most well-known frameworks in criminology.[42] Although neutralization theory has not substantially evolved since its initial formulation,[43] the original five techniques, as well as more recently proposed ones, have been used explore a range of different criminal behaviors as well as deviance more broadly. From this perspective, *Archer* and the substance-abusing, sarcastic, narcissistic, and sex-addicted employees of ISIS provide a unique context for investigating techniques of neutralization. The examples discussed above underscore the diversity of ways in which transgressive behaviors are neutralized. Similarly, although the series primarily centers on Sterling, we can observe his fellow ISIS employees and other major characters also employing most of the techniques. As a whole, characters throughout the show, most notably Sterling, incorporate a diverse array of techniques of neutralization within *Archer* to justify their behaviors.

14

Fighting the (Invisible) Hand

CONFLICT THEORY AND MARVEL'S *THE DEFENDERS*

Brian P. Schaefer

Conflict theory has a rich criminological history and argues that society's definitions of crime and reactions to crime represent the values and norms of the powerful.[1] Conflict theory is rooted in the work of Karl Marx. While Marx did not discuss crime explicitly, he did argue the law would be used as a means to protect the interests of the capitalist and ruling class. Subsequently, scholars contend that conflict emerges when the bourgeoisie (the ruling class) invokes the law to maintain favorable conditions while controlling the proletariat (the working class).[2] Conflict theory thus emerged to focus on how the behavior of law and criminal behavior develops from conflicts between competing interests, including cultural and group conflicts.

The conflict theory tradition does not have a single explanation of lawmaking or law breaking; examination of the theory therefore requires looking at multiple frameworks. To illuminate the breadth of conflict theory, we turn to Marvel's *The Defenders*, a one-season show on Netflix that brings together four superheroes—Luke Cage, Iron Fist, Daredevil, and Jessica Jones—to protect New York City from the evil group the Hand. Comic books have long influenced readers' sense of crime and justice and this influence has extended to movies and television.[3] Superhero shows have framed notions of good versus evil and order versus chaos and, at their core, center on everyday conflicts around issues of power, authority, and identity, but these underlying issues are often lost amid the wielding of the protagonists' extraordinary powers.[4] Putting aside the heroes' superpowers, the conflicts can emerge more clearly and inform our understandings of crime and criminality and our reactions to law breakers. In *The Defenders*, we can understand how the different heroes and their embodiment of different disenfranchised populations struggle to confront powerful group and cultural interests.

Conflict Theory

Unlike other criminological theories, conflict theory is not a single theory but a collection of theories that explain both the behavior of law and how group and cultural conflict lead to criminal behavior. Conflict theories argue criminal behavior is the result of conflict between social and economic interest groups resulting from cultural conflict or group conflict. Cultural conflict emerges when normative behaviors are in conflict with the dominant group who makes the laws, whereas group conflict occurs when groups compete over scarce resources.[5] The competition can result in criminal activity as a means of acquiring resources or political action designed to get a group more power.[6] In the latter instance, conflict theory focuses on how the behavior of law and the criminal justice system is affected by conflicts between groups and how these groups exercise their power. While the conflict perspective acknowledges that consensus does exist,[7] the powerful ultimately create the law, which Richard Quinney describes as "the formulation of criminal definitions."[8] Further, the powerful are in the position to enforce the law and determine sanctions, which is referred to as "the application of criminal definitions."[9] Conflict theorists diverge in their interpretation of who the powerful group or groups are and how they use their power. Pluralistic conflict theorists argue that societies have multiple power groups with some control over definitions, and that conflict ultimately leads to some consensus over laws.[10] Other conflict theorists, particularly Marxist criminologists, focus on how the powerful elite create and enforce laws that are in their interest.[11] The rest of this section provides a brief overview of prominent conflict theories.

Thorsten Sellin created one of the earliest conflict theories of crime, known as culture conflict theory.[12] Sellin argues that homogeneous societies have less crime because more of their norms and values are shared, resulting in a consensus model of law. Heterogeneous societies are characterized by a conflict model of law. In heterogeneous societies, there are fewer shared norms and values, increasing the likelihood that groups will come into conflict with each other. Sellin argues that crime emerges as a result of these conflicting conduct norms. Describing how culture conflict emerges, Sellin argues that the process involves primary and secondary forms of culture conflict. Primary cultural conflict occurs between two distinct cultures that may come into contact via colonization, at border areas between cultures, or as a result of migration. The disagreement over behavioral conduct results in law creation and enforcement of those laws by the dominant group. Secondary cultural conflict emerges in similar ways, but occurs between subcultures or between the dominant culture and one or more subcultures.

George Vold was the next to develop a conflict theory, focusing on group conflicts rather than cultural conflicts.[13] Vold argues that group conflicts occur due to competing interests and a power struggle over whose interests will be given primacy. Groups are formed by individuals with similar interests and a mutual recognition that their interests are best served by forming a collective. As groups form, they evolve and even disappear over time, but the process of creating and working within a group creates group loyalty and a desire to advance the group's interest. Thus, when two groups have competing interests they come into conflict. The interactions that emerge in the creation of a group and the confrontation between groups can create both checks and balances between group interests, but can also lead to power imbalances where some groups have greater ability to advance their interests, often at the expense of other groups' interests. Vold argues that groups with power can create laws or commit crime to advance their interests.

Richard Quinney proposed a different understanding of conflict theory, arguing that crime itself is socially constructed and powerful groups ultimately determine what behaviors are defined as crime.[14] Often the criminal definitions describe behaviors that are in conflict with the interests of the people creating laws and determining public policy. Similarly, existing laws are applied by the people who shape policy on the administration and enforcement of law. Behavior patterns are thus related to criminal definitions and persons in less powerful groups are more likely to engage in behavior that is criminalized, whereas dangerous behavior by the powerful is not criminalized and goes undetected. Quinney goes on to argue that the powerful groups disseminate their views on appropriate behavior via the application of criminal definitions, the development of behavior related to the criminal definitions, and conceptions of the people who commit these crimes. In this process, the less powerful groups are labeled as criminals and their behaviors monitored and controlled. The harmful actions of the powerful, meanwhile, are not conceptualized as criminal and therefore those behaviors are not disseminated as criminal, and persons committing those offenses are not viewed as criminals. Crimes of the powerful thus go undetected.

Austin Turk's conflict theory focuses on the role of authorities in resolving conflict.[15] Turk argued that social order occurs when authorities are able to balance consensus and coercion. Turk proposes that conflict can emerge in societies that are too coercive or too egalitarian. To explain this dynamic, Turk considers cultural and social norms. Cultural norms are the written laws and how they are enforced. Conflict occurs when authorities enforce laws (cultural norms) but the laws are in conflict with a particular group's social norms. This is particularly problematic when cultural norms are only enforced for certain groups. For instance, Turk argues that laws are unlikely to be enforced when they conflict with the powerful group's own values, whereas laws that reflect the authority group's norms and interests will result in enforcement. Yet Turk argues there are additional factors that determined whether or not norms are criminalized or enforced. The primary factor leading to criminalization is the attitude of the powerful group and the legal enforcers toward a prohibited behavior. Turk's theory, then, recognizes that criminalization of behavior is contingent on at least three groups' interests—the authority group, the legal enforcers, and the subordinate group. Turk argues that crimes are more likely to be enforced with the authority group when the enforcer group finds an act to be repulsive. Whereas, if the police find a behavior problematic but higher-level authorities do not, then the behaviors are less likely to be criminalized. Finally, social norms the subordinate group finds to be repulsive are likely to be ignored by the authority group and the enforcers.

William Chambliss and Robert Seidman expanded on the role of law enforcement has in cultural and social conflicts.[16] In particular, they focus on the organizational behaviors of the criminal justice system, analyzing the behavior of criminal justice organizations to determine if the state uses a consensus or conflict approach to resolving issues—in other words, whether the state uses its power to resolve conflict peacefully or if the state favors the powerful group's interests over those of the less powerful. Chambliss and Seidman argue that the state and, in particular, law enforcement agencies are rational bureaucratic organizations. As such, organizations and their members will replace official norms and values with their own to maximize their rewards, which creates goal substitution. The goal substitution, along with existing discretion, allows organizations and their members to enforce laws according to their worldview. Furthermore, Chambliss and Seidman recognize law enforcement agencies to be politically dependent, thus goal substitution can reflect political interests as a means of currying favor and acquiring more sources. One way to curry political favor is to avoid processing the politically powerful through the criminal justice system, which results in an overemphasis on crimes committed by the less powerful. Chambliss and Seidman propose that law enforcement organizations avoid conflict by ignoring the crimes of the powerful and in doing so increase their own power. Finally, law enforcement organizations will enforce laws against persons who threaten the power and interests of the politically powerful.

Conflict in *The Defenders*

The remainder of this chapter will examine the elements of conflict theory represented in *The Defenders*. In doing so, the chapter explores conflict theory's core concepts. In particular, the following sections show how crime and responses to crime occur via cultural and group conflicts. First, the chapter explores group conflicts between the Hand and the Defenders. Second, cultural conflict among the Defenders is explored.

The Invisible Hand of Power and State Control

The key antagonist in *The Defenders* is the Hand, a mythical group that seek immortality and the power that comes with it. The central conflict between the Hand and the Defenders arises from the former's efforts to increase their material possessions through their ongoing criminal and legitimate business enterprises, but also to achieve immortality by controling K'un-Lun, one of the seven capital cities of heaven. Throughout the show, we are exposed to how they are pulling the strings to further their power and control over society. Unlike many comic book villains portrayed as gangsters, thugs, or corrupt politicians, the Hand are not known to the wider population, remaining hidden. To understand how conflict emerges, we must understand the power and interests of each group. The Hand's power is displayed throughout the show, alluding to both their past and current operations. In one instance, the Hand's historical business activities are viewed through Jessica's investigation into a missing architect ("Mean Right Hook," S1E2). Jessica manages to swipe a case file from the NYPD that contains information about the Twin Oaks Shipping Company; in search of additional information about the Hand's business dealings, she quickly learns that it is one of many shell companies, but none of the files seem to provide information about what the companies do. She has an exchange with a city record keeper:

> JESSICA: Hi. I'm confused.
> EMPLOYEE: [sighs] Okay?
> JESSICA: I'm looking into this company, but they've been transferring assets from one corporation to the next.
> Like, they're changing their name, shell company stuff. Yet I have no idea what it is they actually do.
> EMPLOYEE: Oh, so what do you need from me? [sighs]
> JESSICA: The oldest record dates back to 1820, but as crazy as this sounds, I need to go back further than that. ("Mean Right Hook," S1E2)

The interaction allows the viewer to know the Hand has been working toward power for a long time and in the process influencing the economy and politics via shell companies. Up to this point, the Hand has been able to operate within the balance between consensus and coercion,[17] with their legal and illegal activities undetected. For instance, we learn the Hand is involved in illegal operations such as human and heroin trafficking around the world, but also has legitimate real estate businesses. These businesses have allowed the Hand to accumulate resources to support the pursuit of its primary goal, taking control over K'un-Lun and achieving immortality:

> ALEXANDRA: We have it.
> SOWANDE: How long have you waited for this? Too long. This will use the last of our resources. Are you sure it is a risk worth taking?

ALEXANDRA: I have never been more sure of anything. ("Worst Behavior," S1E3)

Conflict theorists argue that certain groups—most notably capitalists—have a monopoly or near monopoly on power.[18] These groups are cohesive and well organized such that group members agree on their interests and carefully develop strategies to pursue them. These strategies often generate conflicts that we can see throughout the show. When a group is down to their final resources, there is greater impetus to ensure their goals are met and crime is more likely to occur. Thus crime, from a conflict criminological perspective, results from overt group conflict and competition. This type of crime is a direct result of group competition for scarce resources. Individuals or groups may also commit deviant or criminal acts as a means of acquiring goods and resources to which they have unequal access. One of the first instances of direct conflict we see in the show is between the Hand and neighborhood kids from Harlem being used for cheap labor. The neighborhood kids, who are being used to help dig a hole under Midland Circle to access a hidden gate to K'un-Lun, are then being killed so the Hand's activities will not be discovered. Conflict theorists state that powerful groups use their power to enhance their advantage and that, in doing so, they commit acts that oppress members of less advantaged groups through legal and illegal means. The most common form of such exploitation is to pay for work in dangerous working conditions without protections. After Luke is released from prison for crimes committed in season 1 of *Luke Cage*, Detective Misty Knight is the first to visit him; during their conversation, Misty reveals the problems in the neighborhood.

LUKE: What happened here?

MISTY: Officially, 25-year-old male found deceased in a parked car. And unofficially? I think somebody's been using Harlem's youth for what can only be described as late-night duty.

LUKE: Couriers?

MISTY: Maybe. Might even be related to Mariah.

LUKE: You think it's something else.

MISTY: Seven in the last few months. Always the same story. Harlem 20-something moves his mom out of the projects into a nice home

in New Rochelle. Down payment in cash. What's the connection between them? Run their names, you talk to people. No guns, no drugs,
just a new job, off the books.

LUKE: Doing what?

MISTY: Nobody knows. ("The H Word," S1E1)

The conversation underscores the Hand's dedication to keeping their
activities largely hidden. Despite running a citywide police task force,
Misty has no real idea what criminal activity is occurring. We see that
conflict between two groups—in this case, the Hand and the police—
can emerge only if both groups are fully aware of what is occurring. One
outcome of conflict is that oppression can involve cultural practices that
serve to maintain the position of those in the disadvantaged group, so
they come to accept their disadvantage.[19] Such cultural practices may
also involve efforts to devalue or dehumanize those in the disadvantaged
group, such that their disadvantage and negative treatment are seen as
deserved or accidental. Dead bodies in Harlem are not new to the police
and sufficient resources are not being spent in response, so Misty has to
turn to Luke and his superpowers to investigate what is going on.

In "Worst Behavior" (S1E3), we see the continuation of Luke's investigation as he tracks down a known criminal in the neighborhood, Turk.
During their exchange, Luke discovers the conflict is not with the usual
suspects, but with a new threat.

LUKE: We need to talk.

TURK: This is how you talk?

LUKE: I want answers, Turk. How I get 'em is up to you.

TURK: Cage, what part of this shit looks like it's up to me?

LUKE: Mariah and Shades [a Harlem crime boss and her right-hand
man]—I need to know what they're up to.

TURK: Far as I know, nothing. They ghosted right after you left. If they
got their hands in anything, it ain't stuff I've seen.

LUKE: Then who's recruiting kids out of Harlem and getting them
killed?

TURK: Kids? Man, do I look like the PTA?

LUKE: Late-night work. Pays well, ends bad. No one seems to know
what they're doing.

TURK: Look, I'd love to help, but I don't know shit. ("Worst Behavior,"
S1E3)

After the initial denial, Turk finally spills what he knows, pointing to
a location where some of the boys have been seen. In this, conversation we see that even the local neighborhood offenders are not aware
of who is committing the crimes or even recognize that there is a wider
criminal effort at play. Quinney argues the dissemination of knowledge
about crimes is important for shaping what people recognize as social
problems.[20] The hidden nature of the Hand's activities and the use of
labor that is largely recognized as disposable ensures that neither the
police nor the larger public are aware of all the dead bodies. Further,
Luke assumes the problem is driven by old enemies and not new threats.
In the process, we see how conflicts can oppress groups that do not have
power, as the kids from Harlem certainly do not have access to groups
that threaten the Hand's interests. Turk and Misty see the kids as rational
actors looking to make money, while their criminal actions also reinforce perceptions of the neighborhood and place them in conflict with
the larger norms of society, dictated by powerful elites that punish street
crime. The Hand is thus able to commit acts that are harmful but not
viewed as crimes.[21]

Not all forms of conflict result in physical violence or the expulsion
of disadvantaged groups. Oppression can also be less blatant and in
volve institutional arrangements that favor those in power. In our first
encounter with Alexandra, the leader of the Hand, we see her listening
to classical music in a private recital at the city orchestra, when an orchestra administrator approaches her:

ADMINISTRATOR: I'm told your donation to the Philharmonic should
just about cover the remodeling.
ALEXANDRA: A small price to pay in the larger scheme of things.
ADMINISTRATOR: You know, with the kind of support you've pro-
vided, we would love to host you at our next gala. ("Mean Right
Hook," S1E2)

If the possession of money almost automatically confers power in
Western societies,[22] then an unequal distribution of this crucial resource

should lead to outcomes preferred by the rich. Power is a relational concept involving comparative differences in resources. The more unequally economic resources are distributed, the greater the economic elites' capacity to achieve their aims. It follows that the more unequal the distribution of economic power and economic resources in a society, the more one can expect that the social control apparatus of the state will conform to the preferences of monied elites.

The investigation into the missing Harlem boys is what kicks off the Defenders coming together and when we start to see how conflict emerges between the Hand and the Defenders. The Defenders, in short, are attempting to improve their own position by eliminating the harm caused by the Hand in the neighborhood while also ensure the Hand's power is not expanded. How the Defenders detect the Hand's activities is informative to how group conflict emerges. In particular, we see that each of the Defenders has differential access to powerful groups, which corresponds to how quickly they become aware of the Hand and the way in which they discover how the Hand's activities lead to Midland Circle. In this instance, their superpowers and access to institutions of power must be considered as part of their group power. With Danny Rand, he is aware of the Hand's activities via his two sources of power, first as Iron Fist and second through the Rand Corporation's resources. Both put him in direct conflict with the Hand. As Iron Fist, Danny is the direct target of the Hand as he stands between the Hand and K'un-Lun as its sworn protector. The Hand targets Iron Fist to open the door to the mystical city. As Rand CEO, he has tried to clean up his company's involvement in illegal activity, which has included dealings with the Hand's shell companies. For instance, in "Worst Behavior" (S1E3), Danny tracks down the Hand's operations at Midland Circle via the Rand Corporation's business dealings. He discovers the Hand has shell companies in São Paulo, Berlin, Phnom Penh, Paris, Miami, and Moscow that have business dealings with Rand Corporation.

Matt Murdock experiences the conflicts of large corporations and power interests in a different way. Matt, as a lawyer, confronts companies whose pursuit of power and profit have harmed the public. In "The H Word" (S1E1), we see Matt winning an $11 million settlement for a boy who was paralyzed in a subway station constructed with hazardous materials, exemplifying how he uses his access to the law in order to fight power, which leads to conflict with business. As Daredevil, Matt uses vigilante justice to fight for those who are not protected. Matt thus works both sides of the law to bring justice to the disenfranchised. Jessica Jones also comes into conflict via her private investigator business and work with powerful law firms in the city. She comes into conflict with the Hand via searching for a missing architect who was forced to work for the Hand. Her investigation exposes her to legal trouble, in which Matt Murdoch serves as her lawyer ("Worst Behavior," S1E3). Jessica, while with Matt, finds architectural plans for Midland Circle drafted by her missing client, architect John Raymond. This discovery motivates Daredevil and Jessica Jones to continue their investigation at Midland Circle.

Luke has the least amount of access to legitimate institutions. He discovers the activities of the Hand via the disappearing boys in Harlem, and he uncovers evidence that leads him to Midland Circle via Cole's mother's house, where he finds a wad of cash with a Midland Circle receipt hidden in a box where Cole put the used lottery tickets he gave his mom ("Worst Behavior," S1E3). This investigation leads him to run into Danny Rand in "Mean Right Hook" (S1E2), when they fight, but also his appearance at Midland Circle in "Worst Behavior" (S1E3). Each Defender's conflict with the Hand emerges from different routes in relation to their ability to access power. When they do arrive at Midland Circle, Danny arrives first and asks to speak to the CEO while the other three sneak in.

Another element of the Defenders' power in relation to the Hand's and how conflict emerges can be seen with their respective interactions with the police. While each group operates largely outside of the law, only the Defenders are confronted by the police throughout the season. As a result, we can see how power influences the administration of the law.[23] Conflict theory argues laws are more rigorously enforced against the members of less powerful groups, particularly when such groups pose a threat. For example, laws may be more vigorously enforced against minority group members when they are large in size,[24] are making political gains,[25] or, as in the case of the Defenders, are usurping the existing power arrangements. Behaviors that are a threat to the existing social order are criminalized, thus robbery and homicide are treated as serious criminal offenses. In "Fish in the Jailhouse" (S1E7), Luke, Daredevil, and Jessica Jones are brought to the NYPD precinct in Harlem and questioned by Misty about the deaths of Sowande and Stick. The theme is seen throughout the season as the police respond to homicides but not the economic crimes committed by the hand. In "Mean Right Hook" (S1E2), Hogarth, a powerful corporate lawyer and recurring character in the Defenders' solo shows, confronts Jessica Jones to encourage her to drop her investigation:

> HOGARTH: After your rather explosive discovery last night, your client's husband has been placed on a federal watch list. It's now a matter of national security. Which means hundreds of law enforcement officers. All hands on deck. Every ego on display. All it takes is one overzealous agent who wants to save the world, and this man, John Raymond, and anyone suspected of aiding him will be shot on sight.
> JESSICA: There is nothing in this guy's profile that suggests he's a terrorist.
> HOGARTH: They just found enough C-4 in that motel room to level a city block. ("Mean Right Hook," S1E2)

Within this exchange there are two threats to power. First, Jessica has worked for Hogarth's law firm in the past and Hogarth does not want her firm's reputation to be affected by the investigation. Second, the police are quick to respond to a potential explosion, even if they are unaware of what is occurring. Critical theorists in criminology have focused on the manner in which powerful groups influence criminal justice policy. Such groups influence the definition of crime, working to criminalize acts that threaten their interests and maintain the legality of acts and advance their interests, even if such acts harm others.[26] The Hand's heroin trafficking, use of shell companies to move resources, and digging of a giant hole under a building in midtown New York thus went undetected by the police.

> [over the radio]
> REPORTER: The mayor's office confirmed this morning, it was a 4.6 magnitude earthquake. A shallow one, actually, centered in Hell's Kitchen. I'm told seismologists are looking at a fault line on the Hudson to see if it could be the source of the problem. ("Mean Right Hook," S1E2)

The police, as a whole, are unable to find the missing children of Harlem or identify the source and cause of the "earthquake," even as they are capable of identifying and reacting to vigilantes who are threatening their power. As Chambliss and Seidman argue, the day-to-day functioning of criminal justice agencies reflects conflicting norms and expectations.[27] The presentation of the police and their lack of knowledge of the broader structural forces embodied by the Hand convey that the criminal justice system is not a meaningful avenue of social change, as reforms do little to address fundamental structural inequalities.[28] Yet, as Midland Circle implodes, the police are shown in action clearing the area and protecting the public.

> CAPTAIN: Our task force has been tracking a mysterious crime syndicate for months. They move fast and cover their tracks and often with the blood of innocent people.
> MISTY: People are in danger.
> MATT: Captain, my clients are exhausted and under emotional distress. I'm sure you understand they need to go home.
> CAPTAIN: And, see, I'm not sure you understand the severity of the situation. Everyone who's come in contact with these assholes turns up dead. Now, either you help us or I start clearing out a couple of jail cells.
> LUKE: They call themselves the Hand. They're real. They're murderers. And they took Danny Rand.
> CAPTAIN: But what do they want with him?
> LUKE: I don't know. They've been after him for a while now. Who knows what they'll do next.
> CAPTAIN: Look, when criminals feel like they're winning, they get sloppy. This could be good for us.
> LUKE: No, not these criminals. They don't get sloppy. They just get more dangerous. ("Fish in the Jailhouse," S1E7)

By the time the police department catches up to speed, the Hand have almost completed their mission while the authorities still underestimate the threat they pose. The police reassert their control over the law and thus reinforce the power structures the Hand use to complete their mission. Eventually, Luke, Matt, and Jessica break out of the station to confront the Hand, prompting the police to chase after the fugitives. In the final episode, the police's ineptness in recognizing the Hand is complete and is reflected in their efforts to appear in control. False official narratives of what occurred are heard on the radio program *Trish Talk*—such as the mayor's explanation that "unpermitted construction surrounding Midland Circle caused the earthquakes and sinking, but everything is stable now" ("The Defenders," S1E8)—and the police decide not to file a report on the Defenders or their sidekicks.

Defending What? Cultural Conflicts within the Defenders

The first section of this chapter focused on the group conflicts that emerge as a result of the Hand's activities, whereas this section focuses on the cultural conflicts that emerge between the Defenders. While we can understand the Defenders as a group in the interest sense—that is, topping the Hand—their varying approaches and character backgrounds give insight into the conflicts that emerge between them. Conflicts don't exist just at the structural level of control and between competing groups. Conflict also emerges within groups that share disenfranchisement.

Luke Cage is unwavering in pursuit of truth, justice, and doing it the right way. Daredevil uses violence and secrecy to accomplish his ends via street justice and overcome the inequalities he witnesses in the courtroom every day. Jessica Jones embodies women's struggle to display strength in a man's world; she is viewed as hysterical and crazy while she attempts to bring closure to those ignored by powerful institutions. Iron Fist displays the entitlement of elite actors as billionaire co-CEO Danny Rand enjoys his status as protector of K'un-Lun. We see Iron Fist's sense of entitlement in how the Defenders respond to criminal activity. Jessica, Matt, and Luke all fight for people who lack means or access to power. Luke is fighting for lost boys in Harlem, Jessica is helping a wife look for her husband when the police will not do it, and Matt is working a pro bono legal case for a kid hurt via corporate negligence. It is these conditions that separate them from the fourth Defender, Danny Rand, exemplified when Luke Cage confronts Danny about his privilege in "Worst Behavior" (S1E3).

The representations of each Defender set the stage for the cultural conflicts that emerge. The Defenders grind their way through various cultural adjustments as they determine the best course of action to confront the Hand and their illicit activities. In "Worst Behavior" (S1E3), Danny and Luke argue over the how to deal with the Harlem boys working for the Hand.

> LUKE: You call that helping? You were gonna beat that kid within an inch of his life.
>
> DANNY: [scoffs] Come on. I wasn't gonna kill him.
>
> LUKE: It sure looked like it.
>
> DANNY: The Hand is dangerous. They murdered my parents. Invaded the city I was sworn to protect.
>
> LUKE: That kid's got nothing to do with all that.
>
> DANNY: Of course he does. He works for them.
>
> LUKE: He needed a job.
>
> DANNY: That's not an excuse. You never fought someone to protect someone else?
>
> LUKE: Of course I have.
>
> DANNY: Okay, so what's the difference?
>
> LUKE: The difference is I live on their block. The difference is I'm not some billionaire white boy who takes justice into his own hands and slams a black kid against the wall because of his personal vendetta. Claire told me about you on the way over here. Not all the mystical parts, but everything else.
>
> DANNY: The money? That doesn't define me.
>
> LUKE: Maybe not, but that kid is sitting in a jail cell tonight and you're not.
>
> DANNY: Neither are you.
>
> LUKE: Not this time. But I've seen my share of injustice. The guy in the white hat, he's just the beginning. You're not thinking about the bigger picture. You're not thinking about anything but yourself.
>
> DANNY: Hey! You know nothing about me.
>
> LUKE: I know enough. And I know privilege when I see it. You may think you earned your strength, but you had power the day you were born. Before the dragons. Before the chi. You have the ability to

change the world without getting anybody hurt. These people won't be stopped that way. You're taking the war to the ones at the bottom, is that it? If I were in your shoes, I'd think twice about using that thing on people who are trying to feed their families.

DANNY: This isn't gonna work out, it's obvious.

In this interaction, Luke gives Danny a reality check on his privileges and conflict emerges over who the enemy is. Danny sees anyone associated with the Hand as the enemy, whereas Luke sees the Harlem boy's misdeeds as a byproduct of the Hand's oppression. Danny is forced to reckon with his privileges as a rich white male and how he is not in a jail cell for his illegal activity. The interaction relates back to several lines of inquiry in the conflict tradition. Luke as a poor black male has a certain understanding of crime and criminality, recognizing the lack of opportunities for offenders, whereas privileged Danny frames the boy's behavior in the context of choice.

Thus we see the social order among the Defenders is based not in consensus, but rather a series of uneasy adjustments born from the varying strengths and interests of the group's members. We further see the cultural conflicts following the fight at Midland Circle in "Worst Behavior" (S1E3). Despite fighting off the Hand together, the Defenders lack trust in each other and disagree on how to proceed or what their responsibility is. In "Royal Dragon" (S1E4), these tensions play out. Danny has no issue telling everyone he is the immortal Iron Fist and that the Hand must be destroyed. Matt keeps his mask on as he doesn't trust the other Defenders with his identity, but he will share his knowledge of the Hand with them. Luke and Jessica consider the Hand to be fanatical terrorists and do not believe they should be involved. They differ on whether they need to work together, and Jessica eventually gives up on the conversation and leaves to pursue her investigation. It is at the end of this episode that the Defenders recognize the need to work together, but a new conflict emerges between the group—the extent to which they should operate within the law.

Throughout the show the Defenders see the law as favoring the rich and powerful and leading to a multitude of injustices. As a result, they reject official definitions of the law and take it upon themselves to bring justice to those who do harm. While each of the Defenders seeks to protect the people of New York City, they regularly reject legal avenues, such as calling the police, for doing so. The Defenders also each have their own moral code for how far they are willing to go. As discussed in the previous section, Danny Rand is willing to harm anyone working with the Hand whereas Luke sees the laborers as caught in a bad system. We subsequently witness a debate on who can legitimately get hurt in the process of rescuing Danny from the Hand.

> JESSICA: Let's just get this shit over with. We'll all sleep easier once they're gone. We can all just [sigh] get on with our lives.
> LUKE: If we do this, no one but those Hand monsters gets hurt. Okay? Not one single innocent person. Can we all agree to that?
> DAREDEVIL: Yep.
> LUKE: Okay, then. ("The Defenders," S1E8)

In this discussion, we can see play out an example of Vold's group conflict theory,[29] which suggests society is built upon competing groups that maintain a balance of opposing interests and behaviors. Each of the Defenders has shown the willingness to use violence to get information or bring people to justice, yet in this instance Luke's unwillingness to use violence against innocents brings momentary tension to the group. The interaction raises questions about the presence of value-consensus positions in law. As Chambliss argues, those who control resources are able to exert more influence over what does and does not become law and which laws are enforced.[30] As the Defenders recognize they need everyone to confront the Hand, each of the characters has considerable resources to exert control and Luke uses his position to gain concessions.

We see a similar process play out in "Ashes, Ashes" (S1E6), when the Defenders are deciding what to do with Danny after discovering the Hand's plan to kidnap him. Danny prefers to attack whereas the rest of the Defenders want to hide him. Rather than solving the conflict through discussion, Danny attempts to use his power to subject the other Defenders to his will. This results in a fight primarily between Iron Fist and Daredevil, before Jessica steps in and helps Daredevil. This fight is an example of how powerful interests are defeated. Danny's dual privilege of wealth and superpowers has been a driving force in defeating the Hand, but the collective action of Daredevil and Jessica Jones is able to defeat his interests. By the end of the show, we see this process play out on a grander scale where it takes the collective action of the Defenders, multiple superheroes with considerable resources, to defeat the Hand. However, despite the Defenders' victory over the Hand, the conditions that allowed the Hand to rise in power are still present, bringing forth an important element of critical theory and change. Namely, critical theorists argue that the outcomes of conflicts involving justice have limited impact on broader societal changes and if meaningful change is to occur then the fundamental economic inequalities in society must be eliminated.[31]

Conclusion

Conflict theory argues that criminal behavior reflects the conflicts between social, economic, and political interest groups as a result of cultural or group conflict. Yet, as Quinney argues, all crime is socially constructed and what is identified and communicated as criminal reflects powerful group interests that can result in crime and enforcement disparities.[32] It is argued here that in *The Defenders* the viewer can see how group and cultural conflicts emerge. These conflicts manifest as the Hand uses its longstanding power to stay hidden from the primary legal system and operate with impunity. Without the intervention of four superheroes the Hand's plan would have succeeded. Yet we see within *The Defenders* that their different cultural understandings of crime, criminals, and the police created conflict within the group over how to confront the Hand. Each of the Defenders embodies different group interests at conflict with each other, but also with the dominant capitalist interests of the Hand. Ultimately, the show reveals how crime is the result of mismatched norms and rules of social behavior, as well as the result of overt group conflict and competition.[33]

Masculinity and *It's Always Sunny in Philadelphia*

Kevin F. Steinmetz and Don L. Kurtz

It's Always Sunny in Philadelphia (*Always Sunny*) is a sardonic show about a "gang" of "selfish assholes"—Mac, Dee, Charlie, Dennis, and Frank—who run a failing bar, drink in excess, and scheme. Deviating from the standard situational comedy or "sitcom" formula, the show is distinguished by a distinct lack of moral lessons and character growth. It's an "anti-sitcom" like *Seinfeld* and *Curb Your Enthusiasm*, where there is, to quote the godfather of the genre, Larry David, "no hugging, no learning."[1] As the creator of *Always Sunny*, Rob McElhenney (who also plays the character Mac), explains, the show tries to "do what's not being done on television, . . . literally deconstructing the sitcom. So, where most sitcoms try to make the characters as lovable and likeable, and as far as I'm concerned, as fake as possible, we try to go the opposite, which is to make them as deplorable as possible, just to see if we can get away with it."[2] In this quest for deplorability, the show plumbs the depths of human awfulness. The character narratives and humor, however, provide an allegorical vehicle to expose deep inconsistencies and contradictions within American society.

Always Sunny provides a glimpse into our collective id. In a 2015 interview, Glenn Howerton (who writes, coproduces, and plays the role of Dennis) explains:

> Sure, we do gross things and the characters are despicable, but it's a social commentary—our characters really are supposed to be the worst versions of you. The worst impulses that you all have, that we all have as people, that you're getting to see these characters act out, there's a wish fulfillment to it. If the show was just awful people being crass all the time I don't think it would have lasted. I don't think it would be funny. I think it's funny because you understand the reasons behind it. Even

though you wouldn't behave that way, you can relate to it in some deep, dark, awful level.[3]

In this capacity, the gang and their motley crew of supporting characters flay our contemporary sensibilities and, through humor, expose our collective moral composition across an assortment of issues including homophobia, racism, sexism, celebrity obsession, homelessness, sexual aggression, drug abuse, and mental illness. As Kenneth Ladenburg explains, "the situational humor performed in *Always Sunny* and the strategic use of tension employed by its cast members critiques the border between socially sanctioned and socially unacceptable."[4]

The social commentary of *Always Sunny* frequently deals with issues of crime, deviance, and immorality. The show thus offers a kind of "popular criminology" or pop-culture explanation of criminal behavior.[5] Of particular concern for this chapter, we explore *Always Sunny* through the perspective of feminist criminology because of the show's often perverse and over-the-top treatment of sexism, masculinity, sexual assault, harassment, and sexual degradation.[6] In particular, this chapter draws from feminist criminological theorizing on the connections between masculinity, deviance, and crime.[7] To summarize, such work argues that disparities between men and women's offending as well as the character of men's deviance can be explained through gendered norms surrounding masculinity. We argue that each member of the gang represents an archetypal form of masculinity evident in American culture, often in the extreme. Further, the show reveals how each form is conducive to different sorts of crime and deviance. These archetypes are described here as the *masculinity of unrequited love*, the *masculinity of bodily excess, badass masculinity, Casanova masculinity,* and *"just one of the guys" masculinity* (a kind of masculinity made use of by women in hypermasculine environments).[8] Before describing the manifestations of masculinity throughout *Always Sunny*, however, this chapter will first provide a brief overview of feminist criminology, with attention given to theorizing on gender as structured action and hegemonic masculinity.

Feminist Criminology

Feminist criminology is not a distinct theory of crime and crime control per se. Instead, it constitutes a "diverse set of perspectives"[9] that "concentrates on inclusiveness by examining male and female criminality (among other justice-related issues) and investigates gender as a variable that influences criminal perpetration, victimization, and treatment in the criminal justice system."[10] The orientation emerged amid the political turmoil and upheaval of the 1960s. Feminist criminologists of the period, in part, reacted to the relative absence of women in criminological research and theorizing up to that point. Women were mostly missing or, if present, often relegated to the odd footnote or throwaway paragraph. Across these works, the experience of boys and men were largely assumed to be generalizable to women. For many of the criminologists of the time (mostly men), gender was not a concern worthy of criminological explanation. Feminist criminologists, however, pointed out that gender may be one of *the* most important factors to consider as both crime and victimization are often heavily stratified by gender. In fact, with the exception of crimes like prostitution,[11] men commit most offenses. Further, they pointed out that the experiences of crime and victimization often vary by gender. For example, though men are more likely to be violently victimized in general, women are significantly more likely to be raped and sexually assaulted.[12] Further, women are more likely to be violently victimized by intimates and familiars than men.[13] In other words, gender is not something criminology can afford to relegate to afterthoughts and footnotes; it should be *central* to the criminological enterprise.

Feminist criminology thus asks us to address multiple problems with our theories of crime and deviance. One is the issue of "generalizability" or "whether the same theoretical constructs can explain both male and female offending."[14] Another is the "gender-ratio" problem, the fact that offending rates often vary significantly between genders.[15] Multiple theories and concepts have been advanced by feminist criminologists over the years to address these issues (so many that a comprehensive overview is beyond the scope of this chapter).

For many feminists, gender is not considered to be innate but *performed*. People "do" gender.[16] These gendered performances, however, are not conducted in a vacuum. The language, mannerisms, styles, and behaviors that compose performances of gender are learned through direct modeling and the culture at large. Drawing from Anthony Gidden's structuration theory,[17] James Messerschmidt adds that social structure often constrains and guides actors along gendered lines—individuals act out their gender roles but not under circumstances of their choosing.[18] He identifies three key social structural influences that regulate and constrain relations between men and women: "the gender division of labor, gender relations of power, and sexuality."[19] The rules established by these structures preexist any given performance of gender. Messerschmidt, however, explains that "social structures do not exist autonomously from humans; rather, they arise and endure through social practice."[20] Therefore, gendered social structures shape performances of gender *and* gendered performances give life to gendered social structures. From this perspective, gender constitutes "*situated action* or *situated accomplishment*" where "women and men 'do gender' in response to situated normative beliefs about masculinity and femininity."[21]

Raewyn Connell argues that one of the collective reservoirs of knowledge that informs gendered performances and social structures is *hegemonic masculinity*,[22] a normative, idealized type of masculinity that requires "all other men to position themselves in relation to it" and provides "models of relations with women and solutions to problems of gender relations."[23] The concept is considered "hegemonic" because it provides men the mental and relational resources to assert dominance and stabilize gendered hierarchies.[24] Importantly, performances of masculinity do not uniformly approximate hegemonic masculinity. Instead, they may vary significantly based on one's position within the social structure.[25] A factory worker may perform gender differently than a Wall Street executive. There thus exists a constellation of masculinities that may differ aesthetically and performatively, but all draw from similar ideas about manhood and masculinity. Important for criminology, different approximations of hegemonic masculinity may result in different forms of crime. For instance, while white-collar crime and violence are qualitatively different types of crime, both may be performances driven by efforts to achieve an idealized form of manhood through risk-taking and control-seeking.[26]

Turning to *Always Sunny*, this chapter argues that each member of the gang performs a different archetype of masculinity. Each archetype is connected to different forms of crime and deviance. All of these masculine performances are unified in that they invoke some form of control, aggression, and self-indulgence. As such, the archetypes described in this chapter can be thought of as different manifestations of hegemonic masculinity as they all reinforce men's power and dominance. Through the vehicle of humor, the show reveals the absurdities in such gendered performances and critiques contemporary masculinities in a way that draws attention to often taken-for-granted gender relations.

Perverse Masculinity

Guys, guys, guys. Your true power comes not from outside sources but from the delusional stories that you all convince yourselves of. And no one—no one—can take that away from you.
—Dennis, "The Gang Group Dates" (S10E2)

Each member of the gang is delusional—completely and blissfully unaware of their shortcomings (physical, mental, emotional, moral, and economic). As Daniel Leonard explains, "the false title of the show gets at something fundamental about its main characters: they're all masters of self-deception."[27] While there are many delusional stories the gang spin for themselves, there are many that hinge on peculiar relationships to certain forms of masculinity. The remainder of this chapter will chart the gang's relationships with masculinity linked with aggression, violence, crime, and deviance. Though each form of masculinity may manifest differently, they all can be viewed as shades of hegemonic masculinity.[28] It should be noted that the examples given in this chapter are only a representative sample—nary a single episode does not humorously skewer masculinity in some capacity. In addition, the reader should bear in mind that *Always Sunny* clearly makes the perpetrators of sexism and hypermasculinity the real objects of derision, not their victims.

Charlie Kelly and the Masculinity of Unrequited Love

Charlie Kelly is dirty, illiterate, naive, and prone to fits of savant-like musicality. He lives in a squalid apartment, eats strange (and "found") food, and does "Charlie work"—the undesirable tasks around Paddy's Pub, like killing rats with a baseball bat. One of his most defining characteristics is his obsessive adoration of the Waitress, an alcoholic and perennially underemployed woman he stalks throughout the show (she is only known as the Waitress, a running gag perhaps reflective of a gendered failure to see women as complete persons). *Unrequited love* is a common trope in television that usually involves a person—typically a man—who maintains a long-sustained romantic interest in a single character. Their feelings often go unrecognized or unreciprocated. In some cases, such unrequited love can manifest in on-and-off-again or "will they/won't they?" relationships (cf. Ross and Rachel in *Friends*). These relationships help generate a dramatic tension over the course of the show and are often envisioned as a kind of idealized form of love—enduring and seemingly fated. Male characters, in particular, try to garner the attention of their unrequited love and attempt to earn their affection, often by attempting to provide, protect, or otherwise "be there" for the person.

Charlie lampoons this kind of romantic masculinity in his relentless pursuit of the Waitress. Taken to the extreme, unrequited love can result in feelings of ownership over the subject of affection, as well as behaviors intended to control or protect the person that may be unwanted—sliding into harassment and stalking. In the early episodes, Charlie frequents the Waitress's place of work and repeatedly asks her out on dates. While in other shows this behavior might be viewed as adorable, *Always Sunny* makes clear that it is not admirable. Further, his stalking and harassment intensifies throughout the show. In "Dennis Reynolds: An Erotic Life" (S4E9), it is revealed that Charlie pays a private investigator to spy on the Waitress. That same season, in "The Nightman Cometh" (S4E13), Charlie writes and directs an elaborate musical for the express purpose of proposing marriage to the Waitress (predictably, she declines). By season eight, Charlie is breaking into the Waitress's apartment in misguided attempts to protect and provide for her ("Charlie and Dee Find Love," S8E4).

Throughout the show, Charlie actively attempts to curate a deceptive presentation of self to garner the favorable attention of the Waitress. For example, in "Charlie Has Cancer" (S1E4), he pretends to have cancer to elicit her sympathy. He tells this lie to Dennis in the hope that it will work its way back to the Waitress. When confronted by Dennis about the deception, Charlie explains that "she wears a Lance Armstrong bracelet, okay? So I tell you that I have cancer, right? Then you're gonna tell her, she's gonna feel sorry for me, we're gonna start dating, and that's the way that life works!" Dennis tells him "that is a horrible thing to do!" Charlie, sarcastically replies, "Well, I'm a bad guy then!" Lying and scheming is thus considered acceptable in romantic conquest or, in Charlie's words, "sometimes you gotta crack a few eggs to make an omelet."

This enduring harassment also results in Charlie being overcome with jealousy. Any potential suitors are adversaries to be driven off, no matter how ridiculous the situation. In one instance, the gang has to compete in a dancing competition to keep their bar (which Charlie mistakenly put up for grabs in a radio contest) ("The Gang Dances Their Asses Off," S3E15). The Waitress shows up, wanting to win the bar in an attempt to hurt the gang, who have caused her considerable grief. During a couple's dance event, Mac "dances" with the Waitress by performing pseudo-martial arts moves in her proximity and making "whoosh" noises. Dee tells Charlie that Mac is going to "bang" the Waitress, which immediately sends Charlie into a jealous panic. They conspire to get Mac out of the dance competition and thus out of the competition for her affection.

Charlie's stalking also entails repeated attempts to be a masculine provider and protector. In the previously mentioned episode where Charlie reveals that he has been breaking into the Waitress's apartment ("Charlie and Dee Find Love," S8E4), he explains to her, "Look, do you have any idea what a mess your life would be if I wasn't always helping you out? I keep a list. I keep a list of things that I do, okay? I watch your bike so it doesn't get stolen, okay? I put, uh, I put vitamins in your shampoo so your hair doesn't fall out. I test your food so it doesn't get poisoned." For Charlie, these are paternalistic and caring gestures. From her point of view, these are insane acts of harassment and privacy violation (later in the episode, Frank tries to perform these chores for Charlie and botches them, resulting in the Waitress being hospitalized and convinced that Charlie must have been doing something right. She begrudgingly welcomes Charlie's stalking back into her life).

Frank Reynolds and the Masculinity of Excess

American media tends to celebrate characters that slam drinks, pursue sex, stay up late, and expel bodily fluids at impressive distances. These men may not be the smartest, but they are certainly a presence in any scene. One of the most notorious movies featuring this sort of masculine excess is *The Hangover*, a story of three men who must find their missing friend while retracing their steps through a wildly hedonistic night in Las Vegas they cannot remember. These characters live out a kind of male fantasy in which they pursue absolute decadence while lamenting how relationships and social conventions rein in their desires. Movies like *The Hangover* series, *Animal House*, and *Old School* capture a kind of masculinity that uses up the body, disregards the consequences, and lives for the moment outside the demands of women and basic civility.

Frank Reynolds represents this cheap-beer-flavored masculinity, showing the ugly and often disgusting side of hedonistic excess mired in drugs, booze, sex, and bodily functions. Frank, introduced in the second season as the father of Dennis and Dee, quickly transforms from straitlaced business mogul into unhinged hedonist. With a seemingly endless supply of money, Frank frequently funds the antics and schemes of the gang while living a life of absolute filth and debauchery. Alongside Charlie, he sleeps on a grimy foldout couch, cleans his toenails with a "toe knife," cooks food on a hot plate, and consumes cat food to induce an uneasy yet effective state of drowsiness that allows him to cope with the wails of nearby alley cats. Frank is both dissolute and shameless or, in his words, "I don't know how many years on this Earth I got left. I'm gonna get *real* weird with it" ("The Gang Gives Frank an Intervention," S5E4). The particular kind of masculinity Frank represents is about the here and now; the body is sacrificed for immediate gratification.

The masculinity of excess also has a particular relationship to women and women's bodies. They are reduced to their capacity to be consumed or marketed for bodily satisfaction. For example, women are ascribed value based on the services they provide Frank (mostly sexual in nature). In one episode, Frank reveals that he has had a long-standing relationship (of sorts) with a foul-mouthed, crass sex worker, Roxy, and intends to marry her ("Frank's Pretty Woman," S7E1). It is unclear what qualities Frank loves about her beyond the sexual gratification she provides. At the end of the episode, he proposes and insists that he will keep paying her for her services, but he wants her to service him exclusively. A combination of the shock of the proposal and constant crack cocaine consumption stops her heart. With her lifeless body cooling on the floor,

Frank insists on a quick eulogy that distills Roxy down to her sexual abilities: "Roxy, God bless you. You were a good whore. You serviced me like no other whore ever did. Not only my crank, but my heart. And I'm gonna miss ya. Amen." The gang then unceremoniously drags her body into the hall and walks away.

In addition to satiating his own hedonistic desires, Frank exploits the bodies of others, even his own children, for personal financial benefit. In two separate episodes, Frank suggests having Dee dress "like a whore" to sexually entice a city official to facilitate a bribe ("The Gang Runs for Office," S2E8; "The Gang Recycles Their Trash," S8E2). He also has sexually exploited his son Dennis, acting as his pimp and prostituting him out as a means to pay back the Philadelphia mob ("The Gang Gets Whacked (Part 1)," S3E12; "The Gang Gets Whacked (Part 2)," S3E13). In sum, Frank's form of masculinity involves the consumption of his own body and the bodies of others. *Always Sunny* directly implicates this masculinity of bodily excess in sexual exploitation, drug use, violence, gambling, and other pursuits of self-interested sensation-seeking.

Dennis: #MeToo Casanova

Dennis is a delusional, self-absorbed monster who is clearly the most deranged and sociopathic member of the gang. He prides himself on his alleged sex appeal and sexual conquest of woman while also harboring deep insecurities about his looks and sexual abilities. In many ways he embodies the most extreme characteristics of hegemonic masculinity as conveyed through his belief in "macho sexual prowess" expressed via sexual harassment and exploitation of woman.[29] His view of sex and women is underpinned by a "winners versus losers" worldview that measures success predominantly through sexual conquests and desirability. Sharon Bird argues that such competitiveness tends to coincide with the objectification of women within heterosexual male social groups (termed "male homosociality").[30] Several long-running themes of the show center on Dennis's perceptions of himself as a winner in this manner, which he often curates through various forms of coercion he utilizes to force sexual capitulation including psychological manipulation, summed up by his so-called D.E.N.N.I.S..System ("The D.E.N.N.I.S. System," S5E10). Relatedly, the show often implies that he might be a serial killer—a jab at the stereotype that serial killers are often charismatic, intelligent, narcissistic sexual deviants.

Dennis unmistakably expresses his winner versus loser worldview while pursuing an uninterested sexual target in "The Aluminum Monster vs. Fatty Magoo" (S4E9). In this episode, Dennis discovers that a former high school classmate, Ingrid, whom the gang cruelly referred to as Fatty Magoo in high school, has lost weight and become a successful clothing designer and shop owner in Philadelphia—in other words, a winner. In light of Ingrid's success, Dee prods Dennis's frail ego by declaring that he "peaked" in high school and is no longer the winner he envisions. Dennis believes that this former "nerd" will serve as an easy sexual conquest to demonstrate that he is, in fact, a winner. He approaches Ingrid in her shop, offers to design some new dresses for her clothing line, and propositions her for sex. Dennis is rebuffed by Ingrid, who describes the offer as "terrible." He responds, "Well, I'm not going to take no for an answer because I just refuse to do that because I'm a winner and winners . . . we don't listen to words like 'no' or 'don't' or 'stop!' Those words are just not in our vocabulary." When Dennis declares that he plans to return the next day, Ingrid pleads, "Please don't do that." Dennis quickly replies, "Save your breath, Ingrid. Those words have never worked on me." This exchange provides a glimpse of Dennis's beliefs about winners and losers and also hints at his sexual aggression and deviant beliefs of sexual consent.

While Dennis envisions himself as extremely charming and naturally attractive to women, the reality is that he uses psychological manipulation and even the threat of harm as his primary means to secure sexual intercourse. One particular technique utilized by Dennis to force sexual compliance is known as "the implication." While never fully employing the direct threat of violence, Dennis will place women in vulnerable situations where they may feel incapable of rejecting his sexual advances for fear of potential harm. Though elements appear earlier in the show, the idea of "the implication" is first fully articulated in "The Gang Buys a Boat" (S6E3). Here, Dennis explains the concept to Mac as a justification for boat ownership. In short, Dennis argues that a woman would be unable to refuse his sexual advances on a boat at sea because of "the implication" that "things might go wrong for her" if she declines to sleep with him. While Dennis insists that there is no "real" danger because "if the girl said 'no' then the answer obviously is 'no,'" Mac appears visibly uncomfortable with the idea because it implies a threat of sexual violence. He asks, "Are you gonna hurt women?" Dennis, in frustration, shouts, "I'm not gonna hurt these women! Why would I ever hurt these women? I feel like you're not getting this at all!"

Of course, the tables are eventually turned on Dennis and Mac. Later in the episode, they excitedly join a group of unsavory men preparing for an ocean voyage, expecting to find a boat packed with women. As they stand aboard the vessel, where no women can be seen, they begin to suspect that they may be the potential targets of sexual assault. Their fears are further stoked when one of the men on board, Ray, describes the open water as a lawless place and utters, "Anything can happen out there." This veiled threat smacks of "the implication" and both Mac and Dennis, feeling vulnerable, panic. In a self-reflective moment, Mac connects his distress to Dennis's description of "the implication" and ask him, "Is this how you wanted those women to feel?" Dennis quickly responds, "No. You know what? I don't enjoy having this conversation with you. I feel like you're lumping me in with them." Dennis is seemingly incapable of connecting the sexual violence he threatens through "the implication" to his own potential sexual victimization (also see: "The Gang Goes to Hell," S11E9).

His cavalier attitude toward sexual consent is further demonstrated by his willingness to take advantage of the obliviousness or even unconsciousness of his sexual partners. For instance, the series frequently references his penchant for secretly recording video tapes of his sexual encounters. In another example, he introduces the concept of the "frame bang" in "Paddy's Pub: Home of the Original Kitten Mittens" (S5E8) as a way to aid a local lawyer potentially entering into divorce proceedings with his wife. As Dennis explains, "Here's how that works: I slip into your house one night while your wife is sleeping . . . and I ease into her real nice. That way you're both cheating on each other and she can't clean you out." The lawyer is understandably horrified and after extended discussion pleads with Dennis "not to break into my home and rape my wife while she's sleeping." Dennis fails to connect his behavior with rape and quips back, "Bro, rape? I wasn't talking about raping your wife. I was talking about making love to her sweetly while she sleeps." As with "the implication," Dennis fails to recognize that this would constitute rape and sexual assault, demonstrating a clear lack of empathy for his victims, whether real or imagined.

The refusal to take no for answer, the acceptance of sexual assault of sleeping victims, and the "implications" detailed in many *Always Sunny* episodes reflect all-too-widely held views of women and sex in American culture. Those views are mired in myths and misconceptions about sex and sexual violence that "serve to deny and justify male sexual aggression against women,"[31] involving narrative and linguistic strategies that excuse various forms of sexual coercion and violence.[32] In this manner, the dark humor employed by *Always Sunny* engages in subversive rape humor that "has the potential to target rape culture by pointing out the absurdity of the sexual hierarchy and its continuity, or by making individuals who perpetrate rape culture the butt of the joke."[33] Perhaps, then, we can suggest that Dennis represents the poster-child villain in the "#MeToo" era, a caricature of contemporary masculine sensibilities about sexual consent and coercion.

Mac and Badass Masculinity

Now, I've always been very passionate about dominating other men. There's nothing like the feeling of another man submitting to your will. Now that's power. In a lot of ways, that's love.

—Mac, "Wolf Cola: A Public Relations Nightmare" (S12E4)

Mac's character seems a comical exaggeration of popular culture action-hero masculinity, represented by his love for 1980s "kick-ass" movies, weightlifting, professional wrestling, mixed martial arts, and other extreme sports. Like the other members of the gang, Mac is delusional, though his self-deceptions largely concern an overinflated sense of physical prowess, combat capability, and moral righteousness—a kind of hypermasculinity that focuses on an "exaggerated physicality."[34] In reality, Mac is cowardly, physically unexceptional, and morally flawed. He is a parody that reveals the underlying contradictions of what we call *badass masculinity*—that projections of rugged, peak masculinity often belie deeper insecurities about one's identity and place in the world.

Mac's self-image seems to be gleaned directly from pop culture masculinity with no grounding in his actual ability or even the physical world in many cases. A notable example of his elevated self-conception occurs in Mac's stunt videos for "Project Badass," a series of self-produced recordings of him doing supposedly "badass" things. In the first installment of the project, Mac jumps a bicycle over a (small) ramp while wearing a jacket lined with lit firecrackers as the 1980s hair band Whitesnake blares in the background ("Mac's Banging the Waitress," S4E4). Like all of Mac's attempts at being a "badass," the bike stunt is a failure as he slams into an old mattress and falls to the ground. Unfazed, Mac deludes himself into believing others are awed by his abilities. Mac's badass masculinity also hinges on his supposed combat capabilities, reflecting how violence is often a resource for performing masculinity.[35] While he constantly boasts about his threat-assessment skills (giving potential assailants "ocular pat-downs") and talent for karate (in which he has no formal training), he cowers or fails miserably when actual confrontations occur. For instance, in "The Gang Saves the Day" (S9E6), during the armed robbery of a convenience store, Mac imagines that he quickly subdues the robbers and fights off a team of ninjas before dying and going to heaven to assume a seat next to a bodybuilding version of God. In reality, however, Mac, along with other members of the gang, cowers and hides before looting items as they escape. In contrast, there is Mac's father, Luther, who is first introduced in "Dennis and Dee Get a New Dad" (S2E10) when Mac and Charlie visit him in prison. He is physically intimidating, covered in tattoos, and in many ways presents the actual badass masculine persona that Mac believes he projects—while also demonstrating the criminogenic qualities that link such masculinity to violence and drug dealing.[36] The show frequently hints that Mac's psychological and emotional insecurities stem from his failed connection to his father, consistent with literature that highlights the damage wrought by absentee fathers.[37] Thus while he fears his father, Mac craves his approval and affection, even engaging in criminal activities at his father's behest like smuggling heroin into the prison via his rectum, which Luther describes as a "father-son type of thing." The show also draws from the "have a catch" cultural trope entrenched in the mythology of American fathering—that tossing a baseball with one's kid is the defining behavior of a caring dad.[38] We learn that Mac longed to play catch with his father as a child and Luther apparently used the excuse of a shoulder injury to avoid such interactions ("Mac Kills His Dad," S10E7). Mac suspects Luther faked the injury, nodding toward a sense of parental rejection. In season three, however, it is revealed that Luther is planning take Mac to the Baseball Hall of Fame to make amends for his neglect ("Dennis Looks like a Registered Sex Offender," S3E11). Unfortunately, Mac errantly believes Luther is plotting his death instead. Fearful, Mac reports his suspicions about Luther to authorities in the hope that his parole will be revoked. Upon finding out about this betrayal, Luther threatens Mac for real. Appropriately enough, the aggression, callousness, fear, and insecurity endemic to their violent badass masculinities compromise their ability to have an authentic father-son relationship. *Always Sunny* also explores the underlying tension between homoeroticism and homophobia endemic in action-hero masculinity as well, particularly through the show-spanning running joke that Mac is a latent homosexual unable to come to terms with his sexual orientation as it conflicts with his "badass" self-image and Catholic upbringing. Perhaps this conflict is most intensely represented by his relationship with Carmen—a transgender character. Carmen is openly transitioning from male to female and engages in an on-and-off relationship with Mac throughout season three. Although Mac is obviously attracted to her, he becomes embarrassed because Carmen is in a preoperative state. He therefore hides their relationship from the rest of the gang. Paradoxically, the gang seems unoffended by his (repressed) sexual orientation and it is Mac's own religious convictions and narrow conception of masculinity that generate his sense of shame. Later seasons of *Always Sunny* involve Mac going in and out of the closet. For instance, he declares he is gay in "The Gang Goes to Hell" (S11E9) only to deny his homosexuality again in a subsequent episode. In "Hero or Hate Crime" (S12E6) Mac seems to more fully come to terms with his sexuality as he attempts to use his homosexuality as part of a ploy to win a lottery ticket in a legal case, which the gang protests—pointing out that he has stepped in and out of the closet before. Toward the end of the episode, however, he says, with seeming earnestness, "I dunno, maybe I'll stay out. I think I'm out now. Yeah, I'm gay. Actually feels pretty good." The gang responds with "finally" and "it's a relief, honestly." Mac's struggle to address his sexual identity and concern that being gay represents a challenge to his masculinity and religious beliefs appears to be a genuine internal struggle, of which his over-the-top masculine performances are external manifestations. The suggestion is that the embrace of violence, aggression, and domination is a façade to mask his insecurities about his identity.

Dee Reynolds, Just One of the Guys?

Masculinity and gender stereotypes comprise resources people can draw from to situationally perform gender. In her work on street gangs, Jody Miller argued that women in gangs utilize masculinity differentially depending on the situation.[39] On the one hand, these "gang girls" might draw from masculine tropes to create gendered performances that will allow them to be accepted as "one of the guys." On the other, these women "routinely articulated the position that male members tend to be 'harder' than females."[40] She explains that this apparent incongruence in how they relate to masculinity actually works for these young women:

> It meant accepting protection from male members of their gangs in recognizably dangerous environments; it furnished a justification for avoiding or limiting participation in those aspects of gang involvement that were dangerous or morally troubling; and lastly, it allowed young women to view the gang as less central to their long-term life plans and, instead, to define their gang involvement as a primarily adolescent commitment.[41]

In this context, women can differentially draw from gender stereotypes in a way that allows them to negotiate hypermasculine environments, like street gangs.

Though the guys of the *Always Sunny* gang are anything but street-hardened hustlers and dealers, they do provide a parodic masculine environment the women in their lives must navigate. Deandra "Dee" Reynolds is the consistent womanly presence in this group and, as a result, frequently weathers the male bravado of the others. At one point, Dee proclaims that she should not "be the butt of everybody's jokes anymore," and Mac responds, "You're always going to be the butt of our jokes" ("The Gang Spies Like U.S.," S10E5). This mocking, however, is just part of a broader constellation of abuse they inflict upon her. For instance, the gang once tricked a depressed Dee into believing she had become a rising star on the stand-up comedy scene, only to dash her dreams against the rocks by revealing it was all an elaborate ruse designed to break her spirit further ("The Gang Broke Dee," S8E1).

Yet while she is a constant punching bag within the group, Dee can often "hold her own" against the slings and arrows of the guys. To do this, Dee situationally adjusts her gendered performances to suit the context. For instance, she is more than willing to play into a subservient role to a man if it advances her agenda as demonstrated in "Charlie Rules the World" (S8E8), where she and Charlie cooperate in an online game. She endures Charlie's abuse so that he will help her gain in-game resources, which she uses to acquire status within the game and even material possessions like a mink coat. She is also willing to exploit other women if it will advance her agenda, like when she produces a pornographic film in hopes of getting famous ("Dee Made a Smut Film," S11E4).

She also garners a degree of respect from the guys for her promiscuity. In "Dee Gives Birth" (S6E12), Mac and Charlie throw a party comprising Dee's former lovers to find out which one is the father of her child. The results of their interrogations are inconclusive, and Mac declares, with a hint of jealousy and admiration, that "she is slammin' ass all over town. She is getting way more action than us." While her sexual escapades earn some begrudging respect, they also backfire on Dee, underscoring the different sexual standards set between men and women. In "The Gang Group Dates," Dee sleeps with a slew of men to show she is an empowered woman, similar to how men measure their masculinity by their sexual conquests. By episode's end, Dee finds out that all of the men she slept with, ditched, and gave low ratings to are fine with the arrangement and view Dee as a source of easy sexual gratification. It turns out that Dee's attempt to empower herself only opened her up for further exploitation by men.

Dee not only uses sex itself as a source of empowerment, she also engages in her own forms of sexual aggression and coercion. For instance, while sunning on a cruise ship, Dennis explains to Dee how he intends to sleep with a young woman by exploiting "the implication" and immediately insists that Dee would not "get it," predicting that she would find the coercive character of "the implication" despicable ("The Gang Goes to Hell," S11E9). To his surprise, Dee completely understands the idea and admits to doing something similar in her sexual encounters with men:

It's like when I'm alone with a guy and we're messing around and he gets all skittish about banging. So then I insinuate that it would be a shame if my account of what happened was different from his and then he ended up getting a call from the sheriff. You know what I mean? And then "boom," we plow.

Dee thus indicates that sexual coercion and aggression are not exclusively used by men.

In sum, Dee represents the tricky position in which women are placed. In some cases, masculinity and aggression can be avenues for acceptance and empowerment. In other cases, however, they can also expose women to greater abuse and exploitation. Dee thus demonstrates how masculinity provides a set of tools that can be used by women to navigate male-dominated environments, but playing this game may also yield negative consequences and further marginalization.[42]

Conclusion

As argued here, each member of the *Always Sunny* gang demonstrates the criminogenic consequences of various forms of masculinity viewed through the lens of feminist criminology. Charlie shows how the romantic masculinity of unrequited love can easily transform into obsessive stalking and harassment. The debased and debauched masculinity of bodily pleasure and excess performed by Frank is linked to a constellation of criminal, deviant, and unsavory behaviors like the solicitation of prostitutes and the exploitation of women. Mac and his father show that being a manly "badass" is associated with brutal violence and fear, but the concept is also lampooned through its linkages to latent insecurities. Dennis, perhaps the most unconscionable of the group, reveals the coercive sexual aggression often underpinning the pursuit of sexual conquests. Finally, the show demonstrates that women may also present masculine behaviors and traits as a reservoir for navigating male-dominated environments—to become "one of the guys"—though these efforts may create problems for women as well.[43] In sum, *Always Sunny* provides an often humorous—though vulgar and outrageous—glimpse at contemporary American masculinity at its most extreme and its potential consequences.

Viewed in toto, the masculine archetypes presented by *Always Sunny* indicate an awareness on the part of the showrunners and audience of the potential toxicity of masculinity, making the show ideal for a feminist criminological consideration of the link between masculinity, crime, and deviance. The situations presented here could only be considered funny if the audience is "in on the joke"—that these archetypal forms of masculinity are farcical and create more problems than they solve. In this manner, *Always Sunny* is a satire of contemporary forms of American masculinity. As satire, the show suggests that such forms of masculinity ultimately undermine themselves. Each of these gendered performances, for example, speaks to the desire of the respective characters for control over their bodies, identities, and circumstances as well as control over others. Comedy is derived from the fact that the characters often fail to meet their goals because of the boorish means through which they work—they are self-sabotaging. These failures, in turn, reveal the characters' flaws and insecurities. Their performances speak to a fear of being rendered powerless, of their "tough guise" slipping and their weaknesses being revealed.[44] Michael Kimmel describes this anxiety as endemic to American manhood:

> Manhood is less about the drive for domination and more about the fear of others dominating us, having power or control over us. Throughout American history, American men have been afraid that others will see us as less than manly, as weak, timid, frightened.[45]

James Messerschmidt cautions that such criminality may not always stem purely from insecurity but, instead, from challenges to one's perceived superior social status.[46] In either case, *Always Sunny* implies that sexual coercion, bodily excess, stalking, aggression, and other outcomes wrought by these masculinities stem from insecurities over what it means to be a man or challenges to one's perceived superior status as a man.

The women of *Always Sunny*, on the other hand, enact or pander to masculine expectations not out of a fear of failing manhood, but to negotiate and exploit the insecurities of the men around them. While Dee was the primary example used in this analysis, other women in the show also situationally negotiate masculinity as necessary, including the Waitress and Artemis, a friend of Dee's. It would be easy to conclude that the show simplistically depicts women as subordinated by men, particularly as women are frequently the targets of the protagonists' indignities or outright abuses. Yet the show portrays a (slightly) more complicated picture, showing how women can use their agency to situationally navigate a hostile environment, differentially drawing from masculinity and femininity as resources to become "one of the boys" or to be protected.[47] The ultimate conclusion reached by *Always Sunny* appears to be, however, that regardless of how women use their agency, at best they can only hope to reduce the collateral damage caused by men's pursuit of masculinity. Successfully challenging it or stopping it appears to be out of the question. We argue that this should not be interpreted as a call for women to give up challenging masculinity. Instead, *Always Sunny* highlights that the source of the problem lies with men and masculinity. In other words, the burden of responsibility to address the harms caused by masculine performances is on men, not women.

As previously noted, the primary foible of the characters in *Always Sunny* is that they are delusional.[48] While there are many delusions under which the characters operate, perhaps the most significant is that they can achieve or have achieved idealized visions of manhood—visions that are wholly incongruous with their actual personalities, behaviors, and circumstances. The tension between the ideal and the actual is a tremendous source of laughter for the show but it also reflects the potential consequences for both men and women caused by cultural demands to perform (or overperform) masculinity. Though the show purposefully tests the limits of decorum, this chapter demonstrates that it is a fruitful reservoir of insights concerning contemporary gender relations and performances.

Race, Crime, and Justice in *American Crime*

A CRIMINOLOGICAL ANALYSIS

Michael Rocque and Andrea Lasselle-Rocque

A heinous crime is committed; blame instantly falls on an African American male who objective evidence suggests may not be guilty, but the justice process appears anything but objective and fair. Such is a well-trod story in the United States, in which justice seems often to be reserved for certain groups to the exclusion of others. Mass media often portray this issue, in television, radio, and on the silver screen. The movie *Rosewood* told the tale of a woman in Florida who, seeking to deflect blame for bruises inflicted by her lover, tells the neighbors that a black man attacked her.[1] A white woman lying about an attack by a black man is also at the heart of *To Kill a Mockingbird*, the 1960 novel by Harper Lee[2] and subsequent movie directed by Robert Mulligan. Race and (in)justice are integral themes of both American life and mass media productions.

The media is an essential outlet for stories to be told in ways that they otherwise would not be and to audiences who otherwise might not have paid attention. When it comes to racial injustice, the media, from podcasters to film producers, can do a service to the truth and help promote equality. After the hit podcast *Serial* released its first season, chronicling the story of Adnan Syed, who was convicted of the murder of his ex-girlfriend, Syed's conviction was vacated and a new trial ordered. The podcast was instrumental in this decision, as Syed's lawyer noted: "'Serial' has also helped build this groundswell of support for us and for Adnan and for the case, and that has fueled these efforts and helped us to fight on as we have."[3]

The media can also present criminologically informed perspectives to non–criminologically oriented audiences. Theories are often found within movies and television series, though not necessarily neatly packaged as they are in theory textbooks. For example, a criminological classic, differential association theory (or its more modern version, social learning theory), posits that people learn criminal behavior through peer associations. In the film *The Town*, directed by Ben Affleck, the main character—Doug MacRay, played by Affleck—grew up enmeshed in crime; his father was a thief, his best friend is a thief.[4] As Roger Ebert describes the Boston neighborhood of Charlestown, where the movie takes place, "This square mile, we're told, contains more thieves and bank robbers than anyplace else in the country. It's a family trade, like cobbling or the law."[5] When, as an adult, Doug wants to get out of the game, to "desist" from crime in criminological parlance, his boyhood friend Jem tells him in no uncertain terms that he cannot. Doug owes him for taking the heat for an earlier crime. In the end, Affleck's character does stay and participates in the heist in which Jem is killed.

In some ways, entertainment media can provide insight into issues of crime and justice more effectively than other sources. Issues such as illegal immigration get condensed into slogans on other platforms, with all nuance, backstories, and humanity lost. One crime drama series, produced for the American Broadcasting Company, has focused on presenting stories of race, crime, and justice from multiple perspectives; from the victim's family to the wrongfully accused to justice system actors trying to close cases, the audience sees things from a variety of points of view. *American Crime* ran for three seasons, each covering a different topical issue related to race/ethnicity and criminal justice.

We know from a vast array of scholarly literature that racism has historically and continues to influence outcomes in the criminal justice system. In addition, the public often hold racist views related to issues of crime and justice. Because most people do not have contact with the criminal justice system, particularly beyond interactions with police, racial biases in these contexts may be largely unfamiliar. How can people become informed about these issues? The media provides an outlet for such education. In this chapter, we analyze how *American Crime* portrays prejudice related to race/ethnicity in the context of crime/justice. We had watched the three-season series before embarking on this project and subsequently rewatched each episode for the purposes of analysis. During the second viewing, one of us took notes on each episode, noting the framings of race, crime, and justice to allow for an investigation of how the show portrays racial and ethnic bias or discrimination in the justice system. We also relied on websites such as IMDB.com, abc.go.com, and vulture.com for specific episode or season details not in our notes. Our analysis follows that of Nicole Rafter and Michelle Brown, interrogating how criminological work is presented in media forums.[6] Rafter asked, "How do crime films relate to criminology?"[7] In this chapter, we ask, similarly, "How does *American Crime* relate to criminology and knowledge about race and crime?"

We begin by providing a brief overview of race and crime/justice in America and then use criminological and criminal justice research to assess *American Crime*'s contribution to the discourse around the topics it highlights. What issues does the show shed needed light on? How are race and ethnic biases portrayed in each season? What are the lessons that can be drawn from the show regarding race and ethnicity in the criminal justice system? Finally, how does criminological research relate to *American Crime*? In the concluding section, we analyze how the show speaks to criminological work within its three seasons.

Race, Crime, and (In)Justice in America

The history of America is replete with racial and ethnic injustices, from what amounted to near-genocidal actions toward native populations to African slavery, the nation has struggled with upholding its mantra of "equality for all." It should thus be no surprise that the history of race and justice in America is also one of racial injustice, some of which persists to the present day. In this section, we very briefly provide some context on race and justice in America, including current issues identified in scholarly research.[8]

Race, Crime, and Justice: Historical and Contemporary Perspectives

Michele Alexander's award-winning book *The New Jim Crow* makes the argument that mass incarceration replaced "Jim Crow" as a de facto form of racial social control.[9] Before that, slavery had operated to maintain racial hierarchies. According to her account, though, the criminal justice system stepped in to fill the void left by slavery prior to the era of mass incarceration (around the mid-1970s). For example, the convict lease system allowed "slavery" in the form of prisoners being sent to plantations as laborers.[10]

Racial disparities in criminal behavior have been documented for decades. In his *The Philadelphia Negro*, W. E. B. Du Bois noted that there was a "vast problem of crime" within the African American population.[11] When looking at incarceration statistics, he found that African Americans were overrepresented. Official statistics, of course, tell only part of the story with respect to criminal behavior and can sometimes say as much about the behavior of criminal justice actors. Self-report studies came to prominence in criminology during the mid-20th century. Early surveys did not show the same types of disparities that official records did, which prompted some to argue that official statistics were not helpful. However, later researchers claimed that when surveys included more serious behaviors (such as those likely to lead to incarceration stints), official records showed the same patterns as self-report surveys.[12]

There is no question that, in the not-so-distant past, blatant, intentional racism infected the US system of justice, from extralegal lynchings to denial of adequate defense for minority defendants to all-white juries. Cassia Spohn, however, argues that most overt racial bias "has been eliminated."[13] At the same time, and taking into consideration that African Americans tend to commit higher rates of more serious criminal behavior in the general population,[14] research has continued to find evidence of "inequities."[15] For example, research has indicated that bias exists with respect to arrest and police stops[16] and application of the death penalty,[17] and that racial bias is "cumulative" across different stages of the justice system.[18] In other words, it is clear that racial/ethnic inequality exists in the criminal justice system.

It should be noted that bias is not the same thing as disparity. Disparity, or overrepresentation of particular groups, is evident across nearly every sector of the criminal justice system. For example, while blacks represent 13.4% of the general population, they accounted for 37.4% of known murder offenders in 2017.[19] In addition, blacks represented 33.4% of those incarcerated in 2016.[20] Such disparities may be due to legitimate reasons (e.g., differences in illegal behavior across race) or illegitimate reasons (e.g., prejudicial behavior on the part of law enforcement). When disparities are not due to legitimate or legal reasons, they are manifestations of bias. There is evidence of both illegitimate and legitimate disparity in the US criminal justice system. For example, research indicates that blacks and whites use and sell drugs at similar rates, but blacks are arrested and prosecuted for drug offenses at much higher rates than whites.[21] However, much research has indicated that legitimate/legal factors account for a large share of disparities in the criminal justice system.[22] In addition, scholarly work on racial bias in the justice system is very controversial, with conflicting results often cluttering the scene.[23] Nonetheless, it is incontrovertible that race is a primary factor in crime and justice in the United States.

A final issue concerning race, crime, and justice that is relevant to the series we are analyzing involves immigration. The media is a forum that may at times present immigrants, especially illegal immigrants, as a threat to security.[24] President Donald Trump made headlines during his campaign and subsequent first term by discussing the dangers of illegal immigration and the need for a wall between the US and Mexico. It is, then, perhaps unsurprising that the public often assumes immigration represents a threat to security. One study found that how people think about immigrants affects their perception of immigrants as criminals.[25] What is interesting in all this is that immigrants, particularly first-generation immigrants, pose *less* of a threat to security than those born in the US.[26] What is more, macro-level research spanning 50 states and Washington, DC, has underscored that *illegal* immigration does not disproportionately lead to more violent crimes; if anything, the opposite is true.[27] With respect to the topic of immigration and crime, the findings are in, and they are conclusive. Immigrants do not engage in more criminal behavior or make us less safe—a conclusion that is not shared by most of the public.

Race, Crime, and Justice in the Media

Public perceptions of race, crime, and justice are linked to the media. Research has indicated that the media, particularly news and entertainment media, has an effect on people's understandings of crime and justice.[28] Media presentations of crime focus disproportionately on violent and sensationalized incidents.[29] It may be no surprise, therefore, that fear of crime is sometimes impacted by the amount of crime media that is consumed,[30] though the research in this is mixed.

There is some research suggesting that race matters with respect to the effect of media on fear of crime.[31] In an interesting study, Sarah Eschholz and her colleagues found that those who thought they lived in an area with more black residents were more influenced by the media.[32] Whereas research has shown that blacks and Hispanics are depicted as more "threatening" than whites in the media,[33] the race of the viewer may also matter in terms of media effects. Eschholz found that, for blacks, the amount of time spent consuming media predicted fear of crime but, for whites, what really mattered was the amount of media with black offenders.[34]

The media has a significant role in the public's beliefs about crime. Indeed, the media tends to be the only means by which most people learn about crime and justice.[35] The danger, though, is that the media does not present the most unbiased or objective portrayal of crime. For example, the types of stories that titillate us, and are likely to get high ratings, are often those that are statistically the rarest.[36]

Research has indicated that news and reality media often portray criminals as nonwhite.[37] Two crime and media myths discussed by Rebecca Hayes and Kate Luther in their book *#Crime* are that "immigrants, migrants, and refugees are criminals" and "young men of minority racial/ethnic groups are criminals." Such myths perpetuate the notion that these groups are not part of "us" but rather to be feared. According to Mary Beth Oliver, however, fiction shows do not distort the representation of minorities in terms of perpetrators or victims.[38] Thus, while the media is an important source of information on crime and justice and has the potential to distort the public's understanding, it does not necessarily follow that the media is an inaccurate source of information.

There are clear disparities related to race and ethnicity in the criminal justice system. Research also strongly suggests that bias plays a role in these disparities.[39] What does the public know about these disparities and bias in general? The General Social Survey has long asked Americans whether African Americans' poorer housing and income are "mainly" due to discrimination and routinely less than half answer yes.[40] As recently as 2006, only 36% answered yes. With respect to the justice system, an ACLU survey in 2018 found that 42% of respondents disagreed that people of color are imprisoned at higher rates because of "racism" in the justice system and 45% disagreed that incarceration disparities are due to "bias" in the system. However, 62% disagreed that black people are treated fairly by the justice system.[41] Pew Research has shed light on racial differences. For example, a survey found that most blacks felt that they were treated unfairly by the system relative to whites, but only 61% of whites felt the same. Another survey found that 79% of blacks felt the treatment of minorities by the criminal justice system is a "very big problem," compared to only 32% of whites.[42] Finally, recent polls have shown that a substantial share (up to half) of Americans think that immigrants make crime worse (despite the empirical evidence) in the US.[43]

Race, Crime, and Justice in *American Crime*

Clearly there are varying perceptions and misconceptions about the role of race and bias in the justice system. The media represents one venue by which individuals can be more informed about such issues. Do popular shows tackle race and bias in the justice system? If so, how? In the following, we discuss how race and racial/ethnic bias are portrayed in *American Crime* through its three seasons. Space limitations prevent us from discussing every relevant issue, and so we restrict our attention to those that seem most pertinent. Within each section, we analyze how the issue was presented and how it comports with the available related evidence from the literature. In the end, we discuss how *American Crime* presents issues of race, crime, and justice, focusing on bias within these topics. To the extent that the public is not informed regarding how race is central to the criminal justice system, media forms, even those meant for entertainment, may be essential for education purposes. What follows is a discussion of four themes found within *American Crime* related to race/ethnicity, bias, and criminal justice.

Racial and Ethnic Prejudice in the Context of Crime and Justice

Racial and ethnic prejudice are prevalent themes throughout *American Crime*. In the very first season, we meet Barb, who is convinced that an "illegal" killed her son Matt and that race had everything to do with it. Viewers know better; Matt was involved in drug use and sales, and that was what led to his murder. As an example of prejudice, in the first episode of the first season, Barb assumes that because a suspect is Hispanic he must be an "illegal." The assumption that particular physical markers indicate one's citizenship status is a prevalent theme throughout the first season and emerges in the ways Alonzo Gutierrez (a Hispanic mechanic and single father) derides those who look like they are in a gang or came to the US illegally.

In season 1, other examples of racial stereotypes and crime/justice emerge. Episode 4 involves a character named Aliyah Shadeed, a Muslim, who tries to convince her brother, Carter, who is under suspicion of murder, to think about his relationship with a young white woman. She tells him that the government will try to use a bail hearing "to parade their [the victim's family's] sad faces and make you look like the very definition of the fearsome black man." This implies she is aware of the media stereotype we discussed in the last section, which Katheryn Russell Brown has referred to as the myth of the "criminalblackman," and potentially enlightens viewers who may not be aware of this form of bias.[44] Another example of racial prejudice and use of stereotypes with respect to crime and justice occurs in episode 6 when Hector discusses his belief that "brothers" always play the victim but are not always innocent. He also refers to criminal justice system actors with a racial phrase ("their pale asses").

While season 1 is replete with individual displays of racism and prejudice, the most overtly racist character is clearly Barb. First, she is convinced that an illegal immigrant murdered her son, and then that the murderer is a black man (Carter Nix). She goes on a talk show called *Good Morning Stockton* to discuss her troubles. Her description is telling: "You read all the time about a . . . a black person who's actually a criminal. They get shot by the police. People lose their minds. A good white kid gets murdered in his home, well . . . that's okay because maybe he smoked a joint on the weekends." Barb, in the end, gets mixed up in a social movement (discussed in more detail below) led by white supremacists to counter a movement to exonerate the black male suspect in her son's death.

The second season of *American Crime* includes portrayals of racism as well, but here the focal issue is sexual assault and athletic culture in education. The mother of one of the main characters, Kevin, a high school basketball captain, demonstrates prejudice when she says she would like him to have a black girlfriend. Kevin's mother, who is

African American, displays the most prejudice of all the characters. She is eventually fired from her job after emails she wrote discussing her disdain for whites emerge. It is interesting that, in this season, the most openly racist character is an African American, which runs counter to the dominant focus in the literature, which examines racism on the part of whites.

Season 3, which revolves around human trafficking and illegal immigration, also depicts elements of individual racism. For example, there is some evidence of derision toward "white trash" on the part of farm workers who are, for the most part, Hispanic. In addition, one of the primary stories of the season, involving a white couple hiring a migrant nanny, demonstrates racism. In episode 5, the husband, Nicholas, complains about what he perceives as white disadvantage, that whites' hardships do not get much sympathy and no trending "hashtags," as is the case for minorities.

All three seasons of *American Crime* deal with racism and prejudice on the part of individuals in different ways. Yet the portrayals do not seem to stretch beyond what happens in the "real world" or has been documented in the literature. For example, immigration is linked to crime, even violent crime, in the minds of many Americans. We observed that the association between immigrants and crime is one of the primary "crime myths" perpetuated by the media. A 2017 Gallup poll found that 45% of those polled felt that immigrants make the "crime situation" in America worse.[45] As we wrote this chapter, a horrifying murder of a white, female college student occurred. It turned out that the perpetrator was an undocumented immigrant. This revelation led to an outcry on the part of those seeking to link immigrants with violent crime, pushing for stronger borders.[46] Barb's initial belief that an "illegal" killed her son thus seems consistent with the evidence.

Finally, Nicholas's complaint that whites have it tough may be associated with the notion of "white racial resentment" a feeling of hostility toward preferential treatment and policies associated with minorities.[47]

Race and Justice/Authority

Another topic or theme that was prevalent throughout the three seasons of *American Crime* involves issues of race and the law or authority. Here we are referring to instances not only in which individual characters illustrate racist or prejudiced beliefs but where race plays a role in how authority and the law operate. In the very first episode of the series, a store clerk calls the police on a character named Hector, a small-time hustler. He runs and is seen being shot in the leg from behind. This wound eventually places him in the hospital. Hector's shooting certainly calls to mind viral videos of young minority men being shot by police while unarmed, particularly the video showing Walter Scott, who was shot after being pulled over for a traffic violation. While it is lawful for officers to shoot suspects who are running away if they are considered a threat, in these cases (like Hector's), no threat was evident. This incident thus relates to what is known as the "fleeing felon rule." The US Supreme Court, in *Tennessee v. Garner*,[48] ruled that it is not legal to shoot a felon who is running simply to stop them; it is only acceptable if they represent a threat to the officer or the public.[49] Hector clearly seems to understand the injustice of what happened to him, asserting that he was shot because "they" (the law/government) do not care about him (a Hispanic male).

In season 1, race and law take center stage. As mentioned above, Barb is interested in pursuing "special circumstances" in the case of her son Matt's shooting death, which she is convinced is about race. When the suspect, Carter Nix, is found to have beaten a drug dealer while calling him a "white bitch," the district attorney's office decides to pursue the murder case as a racially motivated hate crime. Related to this development, Hector is trying to cut a deal by providing witness testimony on the murder. In discussions with Hector, prosecutors pressure him for evidence that the murder was racially motivated. Hector knows he will be deported if he does not cut a deal, which introduces another element of race/ethnicity into the criminal justice process.

In season 2, a fight breaks out at Marshall High School between a Hispanic and an African American boy. The principal, who is black, suspends only the Hispanic boy, Mateo (after seeing only Mateo hitting the other student), sparking outcry in the community. The principal scoffs at the idea that there was any racial injustice in his decision, noting that a suspension is not equivalent to a black kid being shot in the street.

Also in season 2, Becca, a white female student, sells drugs to a student involved in an alleged rape at the Leyland School. Becca is the daughter of a high-profile coach, who immediately tries to cover up for her. The student who bought drugs from her, Taylor, ends up shooting and killing one of his tormentors, upping the stakes of Becca's crime. Yet when the police do find out and question her, she is then released on her own recognizance (e.g., released without having to post bail, under the assumption that "local roots" to the community deter pre-trial flight)[50] even though she committed a felony. While this action is within the law,[51] the viewer may wonder whether the same treatment would have been given to a person of color in Becca's situation. In the adult system, research has found racial disparities with respect to bail decisions,[52] and there are well-evidenced disparities in the juvenile justice system.[53]

In season 3, the issue of drugs and race is mentioned, however briefly. In episode 2, one of the characters, Kimara, talks to a human rights activist about drug abuse. She remarks with sarcasm that drug use is now called a "crisis" because it involves white people. Heroin in the suburbs, she says, is a crisis, but crack in the streets was an "epidemic." Now it is "just a bad thing that happens to good people." This comment reflects the differential treatment of drug offenses by race that has marked the United States in the late 20th and early 21st centuries. Only recently did President Obama alter the infamous "100–1" rule in which the possession of crack cocaine (predominantly used and sold by minority individuals in urban areas) was punished 100 times more severely than possession of the same amount of powder cocaine (more likely to be used by middle-class whites).[54] The moral panic of the drug war, focusing on crack cocaine and its so-called "epidemic," is well researched.[55]

Immigration, Social Justice Movements, and the Law

A final set of topics or subjects that appeared throughout the three seasons of *American Crime* includes issues of immigration and law as well as social justice movements. Illegal immigration is the subject of much discussion in the first season, with Hector having crossed into the United States unlawfully and facing deportation after he is apprehended by the police. In addition, the specter of immigration and violence is present as Barb initially thinks an illegal immigrant killed her son. Alonzo also has disdain for "illegals," as he believes they cheated a system into which he worked hard to integrate. For his remarks he is castigated by members of his church.

Season 3 more clearly focuses on immigration, both legal and illegal. Two of the primary stories involve immigration and the hazards of being an immigrant worker, and the other follows a young white sex worker. The first immigration story centers on a man who crosses the US border from Mexico to find his son, who had traveled to North Carolina to work. Throughout his time as an undocumented worker, the viewer learns how being "undocumented" translates into a lack of legal protections. This is manifested not only in low wages (we learn some workers are paid one to two dollars *per day* and, after their "expenses," they actually end up owing money), but also in not being able to use the criminal justice system for security.

In episode 2 of season 3, we view a speech from a human rights worker who claims that, in North Carolina, 39% of the state's farm workers are trafficked or otherwise abused. One migrant worker, Luis, comments that the police "don't care about migrants," which facilitates the systemic abuses. In episode 3, a man mentions to Luis, who is looking for his son, "People [undocumented workers] go missing all the time and no one cares." Another person he asks about his son is a female worker who tells him of how the fields are called the "Green Motel" because the supervisors "can do whatever they want [to the women]. No one cares." Luis's son saw her being raped and he disappeared shortly thereafter, likely in response to his protests regarding the treatment of women on the farm.

In episode 5, one of the workers on the Carson farm mentions that "people die all the time on that farm. Nobody cares . . . women get raped, regular." These scenes suggest that the undocumented workers are aware that they lack protections from the criminal justice system. If they go to the authorities with a complaint, they are afraid they will be deported. This situation allows abuse and other crimes to be committed against relatively helpless victims.

Undocumented workers are not the only group portrayed as vulnerable in the series. In season 3, a Haitian woman named Gabrielle moves to the United States to assist a family with household and child care. She is soon abused verbally and physically by Clair, who hired her. Clair tells others who see signs of abuse that Gabrielle hurt herself. She then impedes Gabrielle's ability to leave the situation by locking her passport in a safe. This story line concludes with Gabrielle in the hospital and Clair incarcerated for her crimes.

Social movements related to justice are also depicted in the series, primarily in seasons 1 and 2. In season 1, Carter Nix's sister, who calls herself Aliyah, draws strength from her church to develop a social movement to free her brother. In episode 7 of season 1, Aliyah meets with reporters and tells them freeing Carter is going to be her cause. She is aware that some will see her, an African American woman leading a diverse group of activists, as "looking for a fight, looking for trouble." But she will not back down. The movement she organizes results in marches in the street with picket signs (e.g., "Justice for Carter Nix," "Free Carter Nix"). One protester has the words "hands up, don't shoot" written on both hands. This movement brings to mind the Black Lives Matter social movement that arose after the August 2014 shooting of Michael Brown in St. Louis. The "hands up, don't shoot" phrase is identical to that used to protest the report that Brown was shot by a police officer with his hands up.[56]

Also in season 1, Barb attempts to organize for her son, Mark. She wants to counter Aliyah's organizing and ensure that her son's killer is held accountable. She is upset to find out that those willing to help her are tied to white supremacist organizations, noting the "horrible things" they are saying. Yet even though the groups are clearly racist, Barb ultimately ends up taking their assistance. Reports about hate groups and demonstrations by organizations aligning themselves with Nazis have increased in the United States in recent years. In the summer of 2017, a well-publicized march by a white supremacist group led to the death of a protester opposing the march.[57]

In seasons 2 and 3, organizing and social movements are also relevant. In season 2, as mentioned above, there is a protest against Principal Dixon for suspending Mateo, a Hispanic student, but not the black student he was fighting. The protest clearly begins to affect Dixon's job and he meets with students involved in the incident who tell him that the black student was not innocent and was perhaps the instigator. In the end, the incident—and likely in no small part the protest as well—leads to the dismissal of Dixon from his post.

Finally, a more formal social justice movement is involved in season 3, which incorporates a story about a program called Project Open Road that seeks to help young trafficked individuals. One of the main characters, Kimara, works for the program; in episode 2, she attends a talk related to the link between human trafficking and farm work in North Carolina in an attempt to bring more awareness to the issue. In this episode, statistics about trafficking in the state and the need for intervention are presented.

Protests focusing on school-related issues are relatively common in the United States. In the last few years, protests related to school violence have ramped up, led by students from Parkland High School in Florida. In addition, there are organizations dedicated to helping children at risk for abuse and individuals involved in trafficking. For example, the Polaris Project appears to be similar to Project Open Road, in that it seeks to assist victims and those at risk to protect themselves from trafficking.[58] In that respect, then, *American Crime's* depictions of social movements surrounding issues of race/ethnicity and justice are informative.

Finding Criminology in American Crime

Race and ethnicity are intimately and historically tied to crime and justice in America. Yet there are varying perceptions and misconceptions about how race and bias influence criminal justice outcomes. Because nearly everyone gets their information about crime and justice from the media, it is important to analyze how popular television shows portray issues of race and justice. In this chapter, we closely examined one fictional series, *American Crime*, from a criminological perspective, focusing on race and justice. Did *American Crime* advance our understanding of race, crime, and justice, or did it feed into "crime myths" that the media often perpetuate?[59]

We highlighted numerous ways that *American Crime* portrayed race/ethnicity issues, from racism among Americans to how race and ethnicity intersect with justice systems. We identified four general topics that cut across the three seasons of the show: (1) racism and ethnic prejudice; (2) race/ethnicity and authority; (3) immigration and crime/justice; and (4) social movements, race, and justice.

In this final section, we analyze how *American Crime* relates to criminology. Can criminological work be identified within the four racial/

ethnic bias–related themes? First, important criminological scholarship can be identified within the episodes of *American Crime*. For example, researchers have examined the extent to which racial attitudes predict preferences for punitive punishment. Steven Barkan and Steven Cohn, in a classic study, found that racial prejudice on the part of whites is related to support for the death penalty, police use of force, and spending more to fight crime.[60] They argue that if racial prejudice is what underlies preferences for more punitive criminal justice responses, it is "undemocratic" to use those preferences to guide policy.[61] In season 1 of *American Crime*, preferences for punitive action (elevating the murder to the level of a hate crime, for example) are clearly related to racial prejudice.

In addition, with respect to the first topic (racism/prejudice), *American Crime* seemed to portray American attitudes toward minorities in ways consistent with recent scholarship. Barb and Alonzo's assumption that "illegals" are likely to be criminals fits with the American public's dominant perception, one that is sometimes perpetuated by the media.[62] As discussed above, immigration is associated with crime in the minds of the American public. However, the public's view is that immigrants are disproportionately involved in criminal behavior, which the empirical record clearly shows is not the case.[63] Aliyah's suggestion that her brother, Carter, is being made to represent the "fearsome black man" is also consistent with research suggesting crime has a black face.[64]

With respect to racial bias and authority (topic 2), some of the stories in the series related to this topic match events occurring in the real world (e.g., the shooting of unarmed minority males), but others—perhaps purposely—flipped the script, as it were. For example, much of the vast amount of scholarship on school discipline and race shows that African American boys have a higher disciplinary rate than other students.[65] Research on Hispanic students is a bit more equivocal. Some researchers have found Hispanics to have lower rates of suspension than African American students,[66] and some research has found Hispanics to be underrepresented in suspensions compared to their student body numbers.[67] Race is an important factor in school discipline; the *American Crime* portrayal of an African American student getting the benefit of the doubt is interesting for its juxtaposition with the literature.

With respect to immigration and crime/justice (topic 3), the vulnerability of illegal immigrants to abuse and to the threat of deportation fits with the literature on those subjects.[68] As Majorie Zatz and Hilary Smith note:

> Immigrants, and especially undocumented immigrants, are highly vulnerable to violence, abuse, and exploitation. Ironically, it appears that the laws and policies enacted in response to the faulty fears that immigrants are dangerous contribute to their victimization by making immigrants, and other members of their communities, afraid to call the police or otherwise draw attention to themselves. This lack of protection from the criminal justice system makes immigrants particularly attractive targets for victimization.[69]

In addition, the relative noncriminality of particular immigrants (e.g., Alonzo from season 1, Luis from season 3) is consistent with research on immigration and crime.[70]

Finally, social movements portrayed in the show also fit with current events and research surrounding the roots of social movements such as Black Lives Matter (e.g., perceived racial injustice by the legal system). The literature on Black Lives Matter also suggests that the genesis for its actions and goals was similar to that which provoked the movement to free Carter Nix in season 1. As Russell Rickford explains, "What *is* evident is that most Black Lives Matter adherents recognize the inherent shortcomings of appeals to politicians, the courts, and other "acceptable" channels of redress, and have wholeheartedly embraced the arena of the street."[71]

While *American Crime* portrayed numerous issues related to race, crime, and justice in some depth, certain topics were relatively unexplored. For example, while viewers did not witness much crime by immigrants, the message that immigrants actually have lower crime rates than natural-born citizens was not clear. The show also had an opportunity to speak to the overrepresentation of minorities under criminal justice supervision, but this was largely absent from each season. In addition, perhaps in a purposeful effort to add suspense, certain strands within the show were never reconciled. In season 1, we are not certain who actually killed Matt. In season 2, we are unsure what, exactly, occurred between Taylor and Eric. The show could have provided more criminologically informed material by wrapping some of the loose ends up while, we argue, not losing any intrigue. In the end, it is obviously not the primary role of entertainment media to be criminologically informed, but addressing issues of race and bias in the criminal justice system can do much to educate viewers who may otherwise not be aware of them.

ACKNOWLEDGMENTS

There are several people and places that have come together in various ways to influence this book and make it possible. First and foremost, all of the authors gave some of their time, effort, and intellect for this book and each deserves a huge thank you. Quite obviously, this project would not have been possible without each one. We'd also like to thank our spouses for giving us the TV when we needed to watch shows and do our writing. Few ideas emerge directly out of the ether and this is true of this project. The pioneering work of Nicole Rafter and Michelle Brown laid the foundation for this type of project and inspired us to include streaming shows to the repertoire of criminological analysis and pedagogy. Thank you, Michelle, and thank you, Nicky, for continuing to inspire us all even in your absence from our lives. Finally, we would like to acknowledge Gnats Landing in Statesboro, Georgia, for assisting us, with some libations, for coming up with this idea and bringing it to fruition. May there be similarly productive nights in the future.

NOTES

PREFACE

1 Anna Leszkiewicz, "Will Traditional TV Channels Become Irrelevant in 2019?," *New Statesman*, January 2, 2019, www.newstatesman.com.

2 Leszkiewicz, "Will Traditional TV Channels Become Irrelevant?"

3 Ian Leslie, "Watch It While It Lasts: Our Golden Age of Television," *Financial Times*, April 13, 2017, https://www.ft.com.

4 Ruth Penfold-Mounce, David Beer, and Roger Burrows, "The Wire as Social Science-Fiction?," *Sociology* 45, no. 1 (February 2011): 152–67, https://doi.org/10.1177/0038038510387199.

5 Nicole Rafter, "Crime, Film and Criminology: Recent Sex-Crime Movies," *Theoretical Criminology* 11, no. 3 (August 2007): 403–20, https://doi.org/10.1177/1362480607079584.

6 Philip Rawlings, "True Crime," in *The British Criminology Conferences: Selected Proceedings*, vol. 1 (British Criminology Conferences, Loughborough: British Society of Criminology, 1995), www.britsoccrim.org.

7 Rawlings, "True Crime," 2.

8 Rafter, "Crime, Film and Criminology," 415.

9 Nicole Hahn Rafter and Michelle Brown, *Criminology Goes to the Movies: Crime Theory and Popular Culture* (New York: New York University Press, 2011).

10 Rafter and Brown, *Criminology Goes to the Movies*.

11 Rafter, "Crime, Film and Criminology."

12 Rafter and Brown, *Criminology Goes to the Movies*, 2.

13 Leszkiewicz, "Will Traditional TV Channels Become Irrelevant?"

INTRODUCTION

1 Nielsen Company, "The Nielsen Total Audience Report: Q3 2018," March 19, 2019, www.nielsen.com.

2 Aaron Smith and Monica Anderson, "Social Media Use in 2018," Pew Research Center, March 1, 2018, www.pewresearch.org.

3 Nielsen Company, "The Nielsen Total Audience Report."

4 Nielsen Company, "The Nielsen Total Audience Report."

5 Sandvine, "2016—Global Internet Phenomena—Latin America & North America," June 21, 2016, 15.

6 Clearleap, "State of Streaming," n.d., www.bpl-business.com.

7 Matthew B. Robinson, *Media Coverage of Crime and Criminal Justice*, 3rd ed. (Durham, NC: Carolina Academic Press, 2018).

CHAPTER 1. "THE MAN WHO PASSES THE SENTENCE SHOULD SWING THE SWORD"

1 Nicole Rafter, "Crime, Film and Criminology: Recent Sex-Crime Movies," *Theoretical Criminology* 11, no. 3 (August 2007): 403–20, https://doi.org/10.1177/1362480607079584; Stephen Wakeman, "'No One Wins. One Side Just Loses More Slowly': The Wire and Drug Policy," *Theoretical Criminology* 18, no. 2 (May 2014): 224–40, https://doi.org/10.1177/1362480613512669.

2 Martin O'Brien et al., "'The Spectacle of Fearsome Acts': Crime in the Melting P(l)ot in Gangs of New York," *Critical Criminology* 13, no. 1 (January 2005): 17–35, https://doi.org/10.1007/s10612-004-6111-9; Rafter, "Crime, Film and Criminology"; Nicole Hahn Rafter and Michelle Brown, *Criminology Goes to the Movies: Crime Theory and Popular Culture* (New York: New York University Press, 2011); Thomas Raymen, "Living in the End Times through Popular Culture: An Ultrarealist Analysis of *The Walking Dead* as Popular Criminology," *Crime, Media, Culture: An International Journal* 14, no. 3 (December 2018): 429–47, https://doi.org/10.1177/1741659017721277; Wakeman, "'No One Wins'"; Stephen Wakeman, "The 'One Who Knocks' and the 'One Who Waits': Gendered Violence in *Breaking Bad*," *Crime, Media, Culture: An International Journal* 14, no. 2 (August 2018): 213–28, https://doi.org/10.1177/1741659016684897.

3 Wakeman, "'No One Wins,'" 226.

4 David Garland, *Punishment and Modern Society: A Study in Social Theory* (Oxford: Oxford University Press, 1990), 243.

5 Ian Loader, "For Penal Moderation: Notes towards a Public Philosophy of Punishment," *Theoretical Criminology* 14, no. 3 (August 2010): 349–67, https://doi.org/10.1177/1362480610370166.

6 Rafter, "Crime, Film and Criminology," 415.

7 Wakeman, "'No One Wins.'"

8 Stuart Hall, "Notes on Deconstructing 'the Popular,'" in *People's History and Socialist Theory*, ed. Raphael Samuel (London: Routledge & Kegan Paul, 1981), 228.

9 Wakeman, "The 'One Who Knocks.'"

10 Julian V. Roberts and Michael Hough, *Understanding Public Attitudes to Criminal Justice*. (Maidenhead: Open University Press, 2005); Jesper Ryberg and Julian V. Roberts, eds., *Popular Punishment: On the Normative Significance of Public Opinion*, Studies in Penal Theory and Philosophy (Oxford/New York: Oxford University Press, 2014).

11 Chris W. Surprenant, ed., *Rethinking Punishment in the Era of Mass Incarceration*, Routledge Studies in Contemporary Philosophy 93 (New York: Routledge, 2018).

12 Wing Hong Chui, "'Pains of Imprisonment': Narratives of the Women Partners and Children of the Incarcerated: Impact of Imprisonment," *Child & Family Social Work* 15, no. 2 (May 2010): 196–205, https://doi.org/10.1111/j.1365--

2206.2009.00659.x; Laura Piacentini and Judith Pallot, "'In Exile Imprisonment' in Russia," *British Journal of Criminology* 54, no. 1 (January 1, 2014): 20–37, https://doi.org/10.1093/bjc/azt062.

13 Stanley Cohen, *Visions of Social Control: Crime, Punishment, and Classification* (New York: Polity Press/Blackwell, 1985); Fergus McNeill, *Pervasive Punishment: Making Sense of Mass Supervision* (Bingley: Emerald, 2018).

14 David Boonin, *The Problem of Punishment* (Cambridge/New York: Cambridge University Press, 2008).

15 Boonin, *The Problem of Punishment*, 3.

16 Boonin, *The Problem of Punishment*, 274.

17 Jonathan Simon, *Governing through Crime* (Oxford: Oxford University Press, 2007); David Garland, *The Culture of Control* (Oxford: Oxford University Press, 2001).

18 Joe Sim, *Punishment and Prisons: Power and the Carceral State* (Thousand Oaks, CA: SAGE, 2009); David Gordon Scott, *Against Imprisonment: An Anthology of Abolitionist Essays* (Hook, Hampshire: Waterside Press, 2018).

19 Garland, *The Culture of Control*; Simon, *Governing through Crime*.

20 Sim, *Punishment and Prisons*.

21 Sim, *Punishment and Prisons*, 65–66.

22 Scott, *Against Imprisonment*, 228–29.

23 Loader, "For Penal Moderation."

24 Loader, "For Penal Moderation," 351.

25 Scott, *Against Imprisonment*.

26 Colin Sumner, ed., *Censure, Politics, and Criminal Justice*, New Directions in Criminology Series (Milton Keynes/Philadelphia: Open University Press, 1990); Andrew von Hirsch, *Censure and Sanctions* (Oxford: Clarendon Press, 1993); Andrew Von Hirsch and Andrew Ashworth, *Proportionate Sentencing: Exploring the Principles*, Oxford Monographs on Criminal Law and Justice (Oxford/New York: Oxford University Press, 2005).

27 David Garland and Richard Sparks, "Criminology, Social Theory and the Challenge of Our Times," *British Journal of Criminology* 40, no. 2 (March 1, 2000): 189–204, https://doi.org/10.1093/bjc/40.2.189.

CHAPTER 2. *13 REASONS WHY* AND THE IMPORTANCE OF SOCIAL BONDS

1 Michael R. Gottfredson, "The Empirical Status of Control Theory in Criminology," in *Taking Stock: The Status of Criminological Theory*, ed. Francis T. Cullen, John Paul Wright, and Kristie R. Blevins, vol. 15 (Piscataway, NJ: Transaction Publishers, 2009), 77–100, https://doi.org/10.4324/9781315130620-3; Michael R. Gottfredson and Travis Hirschi, *A General Theory of Crime* (Stanford, CA: Stanford University Press, 1990); Travis Hirschi, *Causes of Delinquency* (Berkeley: University of California Press, 1969); F. I. Nye, *Family Relationships and Delinquent Behavior* (New York: John Wiley, 1958); Walter Reckless, "A New Theory of

Delinquency and Crime," *Federal Probation* 25, no. 4 (1961): 42–46; Albert J. Reiss, "Delinquency as the Failure of Personal and Social Controls," *American Sociological Review* 16, no. 2 (April 1951): 196, https://doi.org/10.2307/2087693; Robert J. Sampson and John H. Laub, *Crime in the Making: Pathways and Turning Points through Life* (Cambridge, MA: Harvard University Press, 1993); Eric A. Stewart, "School Social Bonds, School Climate, and School Misbehavior: A Multilevel Analysis," *Justice Quarterly* 20, no. 3 (September 2003): 575–604, https://doi.org/10.1080/07418820300095621.

2 Hirschi, *Causes of Delinquency*.

3 Hirschi, *Causes of Delinquency*.

4 Ronald L. Akers and Christine Sharon Sellers, *Criminological Theories: Introduction, Evaluation, and Application*, 6th ed. (New York: Oxford University Press, 2013); Bruce J. Arneklev et al., "Low Self-Control and Imprudent Behavior," *Journal of Quantitative Criminology* 9, no. 3 (September 1993): 225–47, https://doi.org/10.1007/BF01064461; Kimberly Kempf, "The Empirical Status of Hirschi's Control Theory," in *New Directions in Criminological Theory: Advances in Criminological Theory*, ed. Freda Adler and William Laufer (New Brunswick, NJ: Transaction Publishers, 1993), 143–85.

5 Akers and Sellers, *Criminological Theories*.

6 Gottfredson, "Empirical Status of Control Theory"; Hirschi, *Causes of Delinquency*; Sampson and Laub, *Crime in the Making*.

7 Marvin D. Krohn et al., "Social Bonding Theory and Adolescent Cigarette Smoking: A Longitudinal Analysis," *Journal of Health and Social Behavior* 24, no. 4 (December 1983): 337, https://doi.org/10.2307/2136400;

8 Stephen J. Bahr et al., "Family, Religiosity, and the Risk of Adolescent Drug Use," *Journal of Marriage and the Family* 60, no. 4 (November 1998): 979, https://doi.org/10.2307/353639; Douglas Longshore et al., "Self-Control and Social Bonds: A Combined Control Perspective on Deviance," *Crime & Delinquency* 50, no. 4 (October 2004): 542–64, https://doi.org/10.1177/0011128703260684.

9 Jeffrey A. Bouffard and Melissa A. Petkovsek, "Testing Hirschi's Integration of Social Control and Rational Choice: Are Bonds Considered in Offender Decisions?," *Journal of Crime and Justice* 37, no. 3 (September 2, 2014): 285–308, https://doi.org/10.1080/0735648X.2013.814547; Tyler J. Vaughan, Jeffrey A. Bouffard, and Alex R. Piquero, "Testing an Integration of Control Theories: The Role of Bonds and Self-Control in Decision Making," *American Journal of Criminal Justice* 42, no. 1 (March 2017): 112–33, https://doi.org/10.1007/s12103-016-9340-z.

10 Robert Agnew, "Social Control Theory and Delinquency: A Longitudinal Test," *Criminology* 23, no. 1 (February 1985): 47–61, https://doi.org/10.1111/j.1745-9125.1985.tb00325.x; Robert Agnew, "A Longitudinal Test of Social Control Theory and Delinquency," *Journal of Research in Crime and Delinquency* 28, no. 2 (May 1991): 126–56, https://doi.org/10.1177/0022427891028002002; Velmer S. Burton et al., "The Impact of Parental Controls on Delinquency," *Journal of Criminal Justice* 23, no. 2 (January 1995): 111–26, https://doi.org/10.1016/0047-2352(95)00009-F;

Kempf, "Empirical Status of Hirschi's Control Theory"; Marvin D. Krohn and James L. Massey, "Social Control and Delinquent Behavior: An Examination of the Elements of the Social Bond," *Sociological Quarterly* 21, no. 4 (September 1980): 529–44, https://doi.org/10.1111/j.1533-8525.1980.tb00634.x; Douglas Longshore, Eunice Chang, and Nena Messina, "Self-Control and Social Bonds: A Combined Control Perspective on Juvenile Offending," *Journal of Quantitative Criminology* 21, no. 4 (December 2005): 419–37, https://doi.org/10.1007/s10940-005-7359-2.

11 Hirschi, *Causes of Delinquency.*

12 Travis Hirschi, "Causes and Prevention of Juvenile Delinquency," *Sociological Inquiry* 47, no. 3–4 (July 1977): 329, https://doi.org/10.1111/j.1475-682X.1977.tb00804.x.

13 Hirschi, *Causes of Delinquency.*

14 Hirschi, *Causes of Delinquency.*

15 Michael D. Wiatrowski, David B. Griswold, and Mary K. Roberts, "Social Control Theory and Delinquency," *American Sociological Review* 46, no. 5 (October 1981): 525, https://doi.org/10.2307/2094936.

16 Gottfredson and Hirschi, *A General Theory of Crime.*

17 Travis Hirschi, "Self-Control and Crime," in *Handbook of Self-Regulation: Research, Theories, and Applications*, ed. R. F. Baumeister and K. D. Vohs (New York: Guilford Press, 2004), 538–52.

18 J. Brezo, J. Paris, and G. Turecki, "Personality Traits as Correlates of Suicidal Ideation, Suicide Attempts, and Suicide Completions: A Systematic Review," *Acta Psychiatrica Scandinavica* 113, no. 3 (March 2006): 180–206, https://doi.org/10.1111/j.1600-0447.2005.00702.x; Cheryl A. King and Christopher R. Merchant, "Social and Interpersonal Factors Relating to Adolescent Suicidality: A Review of the Literature," *Archives of Suicide Research* 12, no. 3 (June 11, 2008): 181–96, https://doi.org/10.1080/13811110802101203.

19 K. M. Devries et al., "Childhood Sexual Abuse and Suicidal Behavior: A Meta-analysis," *Pediatrics* 133, no. 5 (May 1, 2014): e1331–44, https://doi.org/10.1542/peds.2013-2166; Joseph C. Franklin et al., "Risk Factors for Suicidal Thoughts and Behaviors: A Meta-analysis of 50 Years of Research.," *Psychological Bulletin* 143, no. 2 (2017): 187–232, https://doi.org/10.1037/bul0000084; M. K. Holt et al., "Bullying and Suicidal Ideation and Behaviors: A Meta-analysis," *Pediatrics* 135, no. 2 (February 1, 2015): e496–509, https://doi.org/10.1542/peds.2014-1864; A. Miranda-Mendizábal et al., "Sexual Orientation and Suicidal Behaviour in Adolescents and Young Adults: Systematic Review and Meta-analysis," *British Journal of Psychiatry* 211, no. 2 (August 2017): 77–87, https://doi.org/10.1192/bjp.bp.116.196345; Mitch van Geel, Paul Vedder, and Jenny Tanilon, "Relationship between Peer Victimization, Cyberbullying, and Suicide in Children and Adolescents: A Meta-analysis," *JAMA Pediatrics* 168, no. 5 (May 1, 2014): 435, https://doi.org/10.1001/jamapediatrics.2013.4143.

20 Peter S. Bearman and James Moody, "Suicide and Friendships among American Adolescents," *American Journal of Public Health* 94, no. 1 (January 2004): 89–95,

https://doi.org/10.2105/AJPH.94.1.89; Jocelyn Brown et al., "Childhood Abuse and Neglect: Specificity of Effects on Adolescent and Young Adult Depression and Suicidality," *Journal of the American Academy of Child & Adolescent Psychiatry* 38, no. 12 (December 1999): 1490–96, https://doi.org/10.1097/00004583-199912000-00009; M. N. Christoffersen, H. D. Poulsen, and A. Nielsen, "Attempted Suicide among Young People: Risk Factors in a Prospective Register Based Study of Danish Children Born in 1966," *Acta Psychiatrica Scandinavica* 108, no. 5 (November 2003): 350–58, https://doi.org/10.1034/j.1600--0447.2003.00165.x; Jennifer J. Connor and Martha A. Rueter, "Parent-Child Relationships as Systems of Support or Risk for Adolescent Suicidality.," *Journal of Family Psychology* 20, no. 1 (March 2006): 143–55, https://doi.org/10.1037/0893-3200.20.1.143; Devries et al., "Childhood Sexual Abuse and Suicidal Behavior"; D. M. Fergusson, L. J. Woodward, and L. J. Horwood, "Risk Factors and Life Processes Associated with the Onset of Suicidal Behaviour during Adolescence and Early Adulthood," *Psychological Medicine* 30, no. 1 (January 2000): 23–39, https://doi.org/10.1017/S003329179900135X; Jeffrey G. Johnson et al., "Childhood Adversities, Interpersonal Difficulties, and Risk for Suicide Attempts during Late Adolescence and Early Adulthood," *Archives of General Psychiatry* 59, no. 8 (August 1, 2002): 741, https://doi.org/10.1001/archpsyc.59.8.741; Peter M. Lewinsohn, Paul Rohde, and John R. Seeley, "Psychosocial Risk Factors for Future Adolescent Suicide Attempts," *Journal of Consulting and Clinical Psychology* 62, no. 2 (1994): 297–305, https://doi.org/10.1037/0022-006X.62.2.297; Peter M. Lewinsohn et al., "Gender Differences in Suicide Attempts from Adolescence to Young Adulthood," *Journal of the American Academy of Child & Adolescent Psychiatry* 40, no. 4 (April 2001): 427–34, https://doi.org/10.1097/00004583-200104000-00011; Lydia O'Donnell et al., "Adolescent Suicidality and Adult Support: The Reach for Health Study of Urban Youth," *American Journal of Health Behavior* 27, no. 6 (November 1, 2003): 633–44, https://doi.org/10.5993/AJHB.27.6.6; Sara M. Rabinovitch et al., "Suicidal Behavior Outcomes of Childhood Sexual Abuse: Longitudinal Study of Adjudicated Girls," *Suicide and Life-Threatening Behavior* 45, no. 4 (August 2015): 431–47, https://doi.org/10.1111/sltb.12141; Suzanne Salzinger et al., "Adolescent Suicidal Behavior: Associations with Preadolescent Physical Abuse and Selected Risk and Protective Factors," *Journal of the American Academy of Child & Adolescent Psychiatry* 46, no. 7 (July 2007): 859–66, https://doi.org/10.1097/chi.0b013e318054e702; Mette Ystgaard et al., "Is There a Specific Relationship between Childhood Sexual and Physical Abuse and Repeated Suicidal Behavior?," *Child Abuse & Neglect* 28, no. 8 (August 2004): 863–75, https://doi.org/10.1016/j.chiabu.2004.01.009.

21 P. Castellví et al., "Exposure to Violence, a Risk for Suicide in Youths and Young Adults. A Meta-analysis of Longitudinal Studies," *Acta Psychiatrica Scandinavica* 135, no. 3 (March 2017): 195–211, https://doi.org/10.1111/acps.12679.

22 Hirschi, *Causes of Delinquency.*

23 Hirschi, *Causes of Delinquency*; Nye, *Family Relationships and Delinquent Behavior*; Sampson and Laub, *Crime in the Making*.

24 S. Alexandra Burt et al., "Differential Parent-Child Relationships and Adolescent Externalizing Symptoms: Cross-Lagged Analyses within a Monozygotic Twin Differences Design.," *Developmental Psychology* 42, no. 6 (November 2006): 1289–98, https://doi.org/10.1037/0012-1649.42.6.1289; Machteld Hoeve et al., "The Relationship between Parenting and Delinquency: A Meta-analysis," *Journal of Abnormal Child Psychology* 37, no. 6 (August 2009): 749–75, https://doi.org/10.1007/s10802-009-9310-8; Machteld Hoeve et al., "A Meta-analysis of Attachment to Parents and Delinquency," *Journal of Abnormal Child Psychology* 40, no. 5 (July 2012): 771–85, https://doi.org/10.1007/s10802-011-9608-1; Ronald L. Simons et al., "Collective Efficacy, Authoritative Parenting and Delinquency: A Longitudinal Test of a Model Integrating Community- and Family-Level Processes," *Criminology* 43, no. 4 (November 2005): 989–1029, https://doi.org/10.1111/j.1745-9125.2005.00031.x.

25 Hirschi, *Causes of Delinquency*.

26 Nye, *Family Relationships and Delinquent Behavior*; Hirschi, *Causes of Delinquency*.

27 Hirschi, *Causes of Delinquency*.

28 Hirschi, *Causes of Delinquency*.

29 J. Robert Lilly, Francis T. Cullen, and Richard A. Ball, *Criminological Theory: Context and Consequences*, 6th ed. (Thousand Oaks, CA: SAGE, 2015), 120–21.

30 Robert Agnew and Timothy Brezina, *Juvenile Delinquency: Causes and Control*, 6th ed. (New York: Oxford University Press, 2018).

31 J. Mitchell Miller, Christopher J. Schreck, and Richard A. Tewksbury, *Criminological Theory: A Brief Introduction*, 4th ed. (Boston: Pearson, 2015).

32 Hirschi, *Causes of Delinquency*.

33 Krohn and Massey, "Social Control and Delinquent Behavior"; Hirschi, *Causes of Delinquency*.

34 Scott Briar and Irving Piliavin, "Delinquency, Situational Inducements, and Commitment to Conformity," *Social Problems* 13, no. 1 (July 1965): 35–45, https://doi.org/10.2307/799304.

35 Hirschi, *Causes of Delinquency*.

36 Agnew and Brezina, *Juvenile Delinquency*; Patricia H. Jenkins, "School Delinquency and School Commitment," *Sociology of Education* 68, no. 3 (July 1995): 221, https://doi.org/10.2307/2112686; Cheri Ostroff, "The Relationship between Satisfaction, Attitudes, and Performance: An Organizational Level Analysis.," *Journal of Applied Psychology* 77, no. 6 (1992): 963–74, https://doi.org/10.1037/0021-9010.77.6.963; Stewart, "School Social Bonds, School Climate."

37 Mitch van Geel, Paul Vedder, and Jenny Tanilon, "Relationship between Peer Victimization, Cyberbullying, and Suicide in Children and Adolescents: A Meta-analysis," *JAMA Pediatrics* 168, no. 5 (May 1, 2014): 435, https://doi.org/10.1001/jamapediatrics.2013.4143.

38 Hirschi, *Causes of Delinquency*.
39 Travis Hirschi, "A Control Theory of Delinquency," in *Criminological Theory: Readings and Retrospectives*, ed. Heith Copes and Volkan Topalli (Boston: McGraw-Hill, 2010), 262–72.
40 Bridget M. Reynolds and Rena L. Repetti, "Adolescent Girls' Health in the Context of Peer and Community Relationships," in *Handbook of Girls' and Women's Psychological Health: Gender and Well-Being across the Life Span*, ed. Judith Worell and Carol D. Goodheart (New York: Oxford University Press, 2006), 292–300.
41 Julie Paquette and Marion Underwood, "Gender Differences in Young Adolescents' Experiences of Peer Victimization: Social and Physical Aggression," *Merrill-Palmer Quarterly* 45, no. 2 (1999): 242–66.
42 Hirschi, *Causes of Delinquency*.
43 Robert Agnew and David M. Petersen, "Leisure and Delinquency," *Social Problems* 36, no. 4 (October 1989): 332–50, https://doi.org/10.2307/800819; D. Wayne Osgood, "Routine Activities and Individual Deviant Behavior," in *Encyclopedia of Criminological Theory*, ed. Francis Cullen and Pamela Wilcox (Thousand Oaks, CA: SAGE, 2010); D. Wayne Osgood et al., "Routine Activities and Individual Deviant Behavior," *American Sociological Review* 61, no. 4 (August 1996): 635, https://doi.org/10.2307/2096397.
44 Hirschi, *Causes of Delinquency*.
45 Hirschi, *Causes of Delinquency*, 198.
46 Agnew and Brezina, *Juvenile Delinquency*, 159.
47 Hirschi, *Causes of Delinquency*; Longshore, Chang, and Messina, "Self-Control and Social Bonds"; Stewart, "School Social Bonds, School Climate."
48 Miller, Schreck, and Tewksbury, *Criminological Theory*.
49 Reynolds and Repetti, "Adolescent Girls' Health."
50 Paquette and Underwood, "Gender Differences in Young Adolescents' Experiences."
51 Hirschi, "Self-Control and Crime"; Piquero and Bouffard, "Something Old, Something New."
52 Hirschi, "Self-Control and Crime."
53 Hirschi, *Causes of Delinquency*.
54 Sally C. Curtin et al., "Recent Increases in Injury Mortality among Children and Adolescents Aged 10–19 Years in the United States: 1999–2016," *National Vital Statistics Reports: From the Centers for Disease Control and Prevention, National Center for Health Statistics, National Vital Statistics System* 67, no. 4 (June 2018): 1–16.
55 Dana L. Haynie, Scott J. South, and Sunita Bose, "Residential Mobility and Attempted Suicide among Adolescents: An Individual-Level Analysis," *Sociological Quarterly* 47, no. 4 (September 2006): 693–721, https://doi.org/10.1111/j.1533--8525.2006.00063.x.
56 Bearman and Moody, "Suicide and Friendships"; Haynie, South, and Bose, "Residential Mobility and Attempted Suicide."

57 O'Donnell et al., "Adolescent Suicidality and Adult Support."

58 Allyson Chiu, "Netflix's '13 Reasons Why' Adds New Warning Video: 'This Series May Not Be Right for You,'" *Washington Post*, March 23, 2018, www.washingtonpost.com.

59 Hirschi, "Self-Control and Crime."

CHAPTER 3. BREAKING BAD

1 James Bowman, "Criminal Elements," *New Atlantis*, 2013, www.thenewatlantis. com; Mark A. Lewis, "From Victim to Victor: 'Breaking Bad' and the Dark Potential of the Terminally Empowered," *Culture, Medicine, and Psychiatry* 37, no. 4 (December 2013): 656–69, https://doi.org/10.1007/s11013-013-9341-z; Hazel Work, "'Sometimes Forbidden Fruit Tastes the Sweetest, Doesn't It?' Breaking Bad: The Transgressive Journey of Walter White," *American Studies Today* 23 (June 30, 2014): 19–27.

2 Amanda Knopf, "Going West in Breaking Bad: Ambiguous Morality, Violent Masculinity, and the Antihero's Role in the Evolution of the American Western," Center of the American West, May 2015, 26, www.centerwest.org.

3 Scott Bowles, "Breaking Bad Shows Man at His Worst in Season 4," Scott Bowles, July 13, 2011, www.scottbowles.info.

4 Knopf, "Going West in Breaking Bad."

5 James Poniewozik, "Breaking Bad: TV's Best Thriller," *Time*, June 21, 2010, http://content.time.com.

6 Robert K. Merton, "Social Structure and Anomie," *American Sociological Review* 3, no. 5 (1938): 672, https://doi.org/10.2307/2084686.

7 Robert Agnew, "Foundation for a General Strain Theory of Crime and Delinquency," *Criminology* 30, no. 1 (1992): 47–88, https://doi.org/10.1111/j.1745-9125.1992.tb01093.x.

8 Agnew, "Foundation for a General Strain Theory," 48.

9 Robert Agnew, "Building on the Foundation of General Strain Theory: Specifying the Types of Strain Most Likely to Lead to Crime and Delinquency," *Journal of Research in Crime and Delinquency* 38, no. 4 (November 2001): 319, https://doi.org/10.1177/0022427801038004001.

10 Agnew, "Foundation for a General Strain Theory."

11 Agnew, "Foundation for a General Strain Theory," 57–58.

12 Robert Agnew, "When Criminal Coping Is Likely: An Extension of General Strain Theory," *Deviant Behavior* 34, no. 8 (August 2013): 663, https://doi.org/10.1080/01639625.2013.766529.

13 Merton, "Social Structure and Anomie."

14 Richard A. Cloward and Lloyd E. Ohlin, *Delinquency and Opportunity: A Theory of Delinquent Gangs* (New York: Free Press, 1960); Albert K. Cohen, *Delinquent Boys; The Culture of the Gang* (New York: Free Press, 1955).

15 Robert Agnew, "An Overview of General Strain Theory," in *Explaining Criminals and Crime: Essays in Contemporary Criminological Theory*, ed. Raymond Paternoster and Ronet Bachman (Los Angeles: Roxbury, 2001), 161–74.

16 Agnew, "An Overview of General Strain Theory."

17 Lewis, "From Victim to Victor."

18 Agnew, "An Overview of General Strain Theory."

19 Lewis, "From Victim to Victor."

20 Agnew, "Building on the Foundation of General Strain Theory," 162

21 Nicole Hahn Rafter and Michelle Brown, *Criminology Goes to the Movies: Crime Theory and Popular Culture* (New York: New York University Press, 2011).

22 Rafter and Brown, *Criminology Goes to the Movies.*

23 Rafter and Brown, *Criminology Goes to the Movies.*

24 Robert Agnew, "When Criminal Coping Is Likely: An Extension of General Strain Theory," *Deviant Behavior* 34, no. 8 (August 2013): 666, https://doi.org/10.1080/01 639625.2013.766529.

25 Rafter and Brown, *Criminology Goes to the Movies.*

26 David Polizzi, "Agnew's General Strain Theory Reconsidered: A Phenomenological Perspective," *International Journal of Offender Therapy and Comparative Criminology* 55, no. 7 (October 2011): 1054, https://doi.org/10.1177/0306624X10380846.

27 Lewis, "From Victim to Victor."

28 Bowman, "Criminal Elements."

29 Bowman, "Criminal Elements," 166.

30 Megan McCluskey, "The 10 Biggest Turning Points in Walter White's Breaking Bad Transformation," *Time*, January 20, 2018, https://time.com.

31 Lewis, "From Victim to Victor," 665

32 Jonathan Holmes, "Every Person Walter White Murdered in Breaking Bad," *Radio Times*, October 15, 2015, www.radiotimes.com.

33 Agnew, "Building on the Foundation of General Strain Theory."

34 Agnew, "Foundation for a General Strain Theory."

35 Agnew, "Building on the Foundation of General Strain Theory."

36 Cloward and Ohlin, *Delinquency and Opportunity.*

37 Agnew, "Building on the Foundation of General Strain Theory."

38 Poniewozik, "Breaking Bad: TV's Best Thriller."

39 Scott Meslow, "The Big Secret of 'Breaking Bad': Walter White Was Always a Bad Guy," *Atlantic*, August 31, 2012, www.theatlantic.com.

40 Work, "'Sometimes Forbidden Fruit," 4.

41 Work, "'Sometimes Forbidden Fruit."

42 Poniewozik, "Breaking Bad: TV's Best Thriller."

CHAPTER 4. "INSANE VIOLENCE HAS MEANING"

1 Matt DeLisi et al., "The Hannibal Lecter Myth: Psychopathy and Verbal Intelligence in the MacArthur Violence Risk Assessment Study," *Journal of Psychopathology and Behavioral Assessment* 32, no. 2 (2010): 169–77, https://doi.org/10.1007/s10862-009-9147-z.

2 Christopher T. Barry et al., "The Importance of Callous–Unemotional Traits for Extending the Concept of Psychopathy to Children," *Journal of Abnormal Psychology* 109, no. 2 (2000): 335–40, https://doi.org/10.1037/0021-843X.109.2.335.

3   Michael H. Stone, *The Anatomy of Evil* (Amherst, NY: Prometheus Books, 2009).

4   Adrian Raine, *The Anatomy of Violence: The Biological Roots of Crime*, 2014.

5   Hervey Cleckley, *The Mask of Sanity: An Attempt to Clarify Some Issues about the So-Called Psychopathic Personality*, 1st ed. (London: Henry Kimpton, 1941).

6   Matt DeLisi, "Psychopathy Is the Unified Theory of Crime," *Youth Violence and Juvenile Justice* 7, no. 3 (July 2009): 256–73, https://doi.org/10.1177/1541204009333834.

7   Elliott Christian and Martin Sellbom, "Development and Validation of an Expanded Version of the Three-Factor Levenson Self-Report Psychopathy Scale," *Journal of Personality Assessment* 98, no. 2 (2016): 155–68, https://doi.org/10.1080/00223891.20 15.1068176; Scott O. Lilienfeld et al., "The Role of Fearless Dominance in Psychopathy: Confusions, Controversies, and Clarifications.," *Personality Disorders: Theory, Research, and Treatment* 3, no. 3 (2012): 327–40, https://doi.org/10.1037/a0026987.

8   Robert D. Hare and Craig S. Neumann, "The PCL-R Assessment of Psychopathy: Development, Structural Properties, and New Directions," in *Handbook of Psychopathy*, ed. Christopher J. Patrick (New York: Guilford Press, 2006), 58–88; Craig S. Neumann and Dustin Pardini, "Factor Structure and Construct Validity of the Self-Report Psychopathy (SRP) Scale and the Youth Psychopathic Traits Inventory (YPI) in Young Men," *Journal of Personality Disorders* 28, no. 3 (June 2014): 419–33, https://doi.org/10.1521/pedi_2012_26_063.

9   Katherine R. Kelsey, Richard Rogers, and Emily V. Robinson, "Self-Report Measures of Psychopathy: What Is Their Role in Forensic Assessments?," *Journal of Psychopathology and Behavioral Assessment* 37, no. 3 (September 2015): 380–91, https://doi.org/10.1007/s10862-014-9475-5.

10 Laura E. Drislane, Christopher J. Patrick, and Güler Arsal, "Clarifying the Content Coverage of Differing Psychopathy Inventories through Reference to the Triarchic Psychopathy Measure," *Psychological Assessment* 26, no. 2 (June 2014): 350–62, https://doi.org/10.1037/a0035152.

11 Drislane, Patrick, and Arsal, "Clarifying the Content Coverage."

12 Zina Lee and Randall T. Salekin, "Psychopathy in a Noninstitutional Sample: Differences in Primary and Secondary Subtypes.," *Personality Disorders: Theory, Research, and Treatment* 1, no. 3 (2010): 153–69, https://doi.org/10.1037/a0019269.

13 Matt DeLisi, *Psychopathy as Unified Theory of Crime*, Palgrave's Frontiers in Criminology Theory (New York: Palgrave Macmillan, 2016).

14 Catherine Tuvblad et al., "The Heritability of Psychopathic Personality in 14- to 15-Year-Old Twins: A Multirater, Multimeasure Approach," *Psychological Assessment* 26, no. 3 (September 2014): 704–16, https://doi.org/10.1037/a0036711.

15 DeLisi, *Psychopathy as Unified Theory of Crime*.

16 R.J.R. Blair, "The Amygdala and Ventromedial Prefrontal Cortex in Morality and Psychopathy," *Trends in Cognitive Sciences* 11, no. 9 (2007): 387–92, https://doi.org/10.1016/j.tics.2007.07.003; Raine, *The Anatomy of Violence*.

17 Raine, *The Anatomy of Violence*.

18 S. Lang, B. af Klinteberg, and P.-O. Alm, "Adult Psychopathy and Violent Behavior in Males with Early Neglect and Abuse," *Acta Psychiatrica Scandinavica* 106, no.

s412 (June 2002): 93–100, https://doi.org/10.1034/j.1600-0447.106.s412.20.x; Raine, *The Anatomy of Violence*.

19 Seth Meyers, "Sex and the Psychopath," *Psychology Today*, October 7, 2014, www.psychologytoday.com.

20 Gerard Gilbert, "Jamie Dornan Interview: 'I'd Like to Know Why I Was Cast as a Murdering Psychopath,'" *Independent*, September 22, 2016, www.independent.co.uk.

21 Zeba Blay, "Sexualizing Serial Killers Like Ted Bundy Has Its Consequences," *HuffPost*, February 4, 2019, https://www.huffpost.com/entry/sexualizing-serial-killer-ted-bundy_n_5c50e35be4b0d9f9be6a2c3c.

22 David P. Farrington, Simone Ullrich, and Randall T. Salekin, "Environmental Influences on Child and Adolescent Psychopathy," in *Handbook of Child and Adolescent Psychopathy*, ed. Randall T. Salekin and Donald R. Lynam (New York: Guilford Press, 2010), 202–30.

23 Katherine M. Auty, David P. Farrington, and Jeremy W. Coid, "Intergenerational Transmission of Psychopathy and Mediation via Psychosocial Risk Factors," *British Journal of Psychiatry: The Journal of Mental Science* 206, no. 1 (January 2015): 26–31, https://doi.org/10.1192/bjp.bp.114.151050.

24 Jill Portnoy et al., "Heart Rate and Antisocial Behavior: The Mediating Role of Impulsive Sensation Seeking," *Criminology* 52, no. 2 (May 2014): 292–311, https://doi.org/10.1111/1745-9125.12038.

25 Ben Beaumont-Thomas, "Jamie Dornan: I Stalked a Woman to Get into *The Fall* Role," *Guardian*, April 1, 2015, www.theguardian.com.

26 Andrew Moskowitz, "Dissociation and Violence: A Review of the Literature," *Trauma, Violence, & Abuse* 5, no. 1 (January 2004): 21–46, https://doi.org/10.1177/1524838003259321.

CHAPTER 5. "THESE VIOLENT DELIGHTS HAVE VIOLENT ENDS"

1 Nicholas Moll, "A Special Kind of Game: The Portrayal of Role-Play in Westworld," in *Westworld and Philosophy*, ed. James B. South and Kimberly S. Engels (Chichester: Wiley Blackwell, 2018), 15.

2 Janice Hocker Rushing and Thomas S. Frentz, *Projecting the Shadow: The Cyborg Hero in American Film*, New Practices of Inquiry (Chicago: University of Chicago Press, 1995).

3 Rushing and Frentz, *Projecting the Shadow*, 53.

4 Rushing and Frentz, *Projecting the Shadow*, 54.

5 Rushing and Frentz, *Projecting the Shadow*, 54.

6 Rushing and Frentz, *Projecting the Shadow*, 54.

7 Eamonn Carrabine et al., *Criminology: A Sociological Introduction*, 3rd ed. (Abingdon: Routledge, 2014), 318; Stanley Cohen, *Visions of Social Control: Crime, Punishment, and Classification* (Cambridge, UK/New York: Polity Press/Blackwell, 1985).

8 Carrabine et al., *Criminology*, 318.

9   Thomas Hobbes, *Leviathan* (London, 1651).

10 Hobbes, *Leviathan*, 62.

11 Juan Camilo Castillo, Daniel Mejia, and Pascual Restrepo, "Scarcity without Leviathan: The Violent Effects of Cocaine Supply Shortages in the Mexican Drug War (Working Paper 356)," Center for Global Development, February 26, 2014, 1, www.cgdev.org.

12 Jean-Jacques Rousseau, *The Essential Rousseau: The Social Contract, Discourse on the Origin of Inequality, Discourse on the Arts and Sciences, The Creed of a Savoyard Priest* (New York: New American Library, 1974).

13 Barbara Goodwin, *Using Political Ideas*, 4th ed. (Chichester: John Wiley, 2001), 38.

14 Goodwin, *Using Political Ideas*, 273.

15 Martha J. Smith, "Rational Choice," in *The Routledge Companion to Criminological Theory and Concepts*, ed. Avi Brisman, Eamonn Carrabine, and Nigel South (Oxon: Routledge, 2017), 87.

16 Herbert A. Simon, "A Behavioral Model of Rational Choice," *Quarterly Journal of Economics* 69, no. 1 (February 1955): 99, https://doi.org/10.2307/1884852.

17 Derek B. Cornish and Ronald V. Clarke, "Understanding Crime Displacement: An Application of Rational Choice Theory," *Criminology* 25, no. 4 (1987): 933–48.

18 Amelie Pedneault et al., "Myopic Decision Making: An Examination of Crime Decisions and Their Outcomes in Sexual Crimes," *Journal of Criminal Justice* 50 (May 2017): 1, https://doi.org/10.1016/j.jcrimjus.2017.03.001.

19 Pedneault et al., "Myopic Decision Making," 2.

20 Pedneault et al., "Myopic Decision Making," 2.

21 Travis Hirschi and Michael R. Gottfredson, "The Generality of Deviance," in *Criminological Perspectives: Essential Readings*, ed. Eugene McLaughlin and John Muncie, 3rd ed. (London: SAGE, 2013), 179–87.

22 Hirschi and Gottfredson, "The Generality of Deviance," 179.

23 Jack Katz, *Seductions of Crime: Moral and Sensual Attractions in Doing Evil* (New York: Basic Books, 1988), 230–231.

24 Katz, *Seductions of Crime*, 231.

25 Vicki Quade, "The Seductions of Crime Interview," *Human Rights* 16, no. 1 (1989): 27.

26 Quade, "The Seductions of Crime Interview," 25.

27 Katz, *Seductions of Crime*; Richard A Bogg, "Dostoevsky's Enigmas," *Aggression and Violent Behavior* 4, no. 4 (December 1999): 373, https://doi.org/10.1016/S1359-1789(98)00010-X.

28 Mónica Botelho and Rui Abrunhosa Gonçalves, "Why Do People Kill? A Critical Review of the Literature on Factors Associated with Homicide," *Aggression and Violent Behavior* 26 (January 2016): 13, https://doi.org/10.1016/j.avb.2015.11.001.

29 Larry Alan Busk, "Westworld: Ideology, Simulation, Spectacle," *Mediations* 30, no. 1 (2016): 30.

30 Patricia Trapero-Llobera, "The Observer(s) System and the Semiotics of Virtuality in *Westworld*'s Characters: Jonathan Nolan's Fictions as a Conceptual Unity," in

Westworld and Philosophy, ed. James B. South and Kimberly S. Engels (Chichester: Wiley Blackwell, 2018), 162–72, https://doi.org/10.1002/9781119437932.ch15.

31 Trapero-Llobera, "The Observer(s) System."

32 Busk, "Westworld: Ideology, Simulation, Spectacle," 30.

33 Moll, "A Special Kind of Game."

34 Moll, "A Special Kind of Game," 21.

35 Onni Hirvonen, "Westworld: From Androids to Persons," in *Westworld and Philosophy*, ed. James B. South and Kimberly S. Engels (Chichester: Wiley Blackwell, 2018), 62.

36 Rushing and Frentz, *Projecting the Shadow*.

37 Mary Wollstonecraft Shelley, *Frankenstein; or, The Modern Prometheus: The 1818 Text* (Oxford/New York: Oxford University Press, 1998).

38 Rushing and Frentz, *Projecting the Shadow*, 54.

39 Rushing and Frentz, *Projecting the Shadow*, 67.

40 Daniel Mider, "The Anatomy of Violence: A Study of the Literature," *Aggression and Violent Behavior* 18, no. 6 (November 2013): 702–8, https://doi.org/10.1016/j.avb.2013.07.021.

41 Mider, "The Anatomy of Violence."

42 Mider, "The Anatomy of Violence," 705.

43 Mider, "The Anatomy of Violence," 705.

44 Mider, "The Anatomy of Violence," 704.

45 Anthony Petros Spanakos, "Violent Births: Fanon, *Westworld*, and Humanity," in *Westworld and Philosophy*, ed. James B. South and Kimberly S. Engels (Chichester: John Wiley & Sons, Ltd, 2018), 230, https://doi.org/10.1002/9781119437932.ch21.

46 Spanakos, "Violent Births," 230.

47 Spanakos, "Violent Births," 230.

48 Dan Dinello, "The Wretched of *Westworld*: Scientific Totalitarianism and Revolutionary Violence," in *Westworld and Philosophy*, ed. James B. South and Kimberly S. Engels (Chichester: John Wiley & Sons, Ltd, 2018), 248, https://doi.org/10.1002/9781119437932.ch22.

49 Dinello, "The Wretched of *Westworld*," 248.

50 Mike Presdee, *Cultural Criminology and the Carnival of Crime* (London/New York: Routledge, 2000), 78.

51 Spanakos, "Violent Births," 231.

52 Presdee, *Cultural Criminology and the Carnival of Crime*, 70.

53 Presdee, *Cultural Criminology and the Carnival of Crime*, 32.

54 Presdee, *Cultural Criminology and the Carnival of Crime*, 32.

55 Presdee, *Cultural Criminology and the Carnival of Crime*, 73.

56 Yvonne Jewkes and Travis Linnemann, *Media and Crime in the U.S.* (Thousand Oaks, CA: SAGE, 2018).

57 Sophie Fiennes, *The Pervert's Guide to the Cinema* (P Guide Ltd., 2006).

58 Fiennes, *The Pervert's Guide to the Cinema*.

CHAPTER 6. UNDERSTANDING *THE HANDMAID'S TALE*

1 Nicole Hahn Rafter and Michelle Brown, *Criminology Goes to the Movies: Crime Theory and Popular Culture* (New York: New York University Press, 2011), 8.

2 Margaret Atwood, *The Handmaid's Tale* (Toronto: McClelland and Stewart, 1985).

3 Rafter and Brown, *Criminology Goes to the Movies*, 8.

4 Gail Dines, "'The Handmaid's Tale' Offers a Terrifying Warning, but the Hijacking of Feminism Is Just as Dangerous," *Feminist Current* (blog), May 1, 2017, www. feministcurrent.com.

5 Walter S. DeKeseredy and Marilyn Corsianos, *Violence against Women in Pornography*, 1st ed. (London: Routledge, 2016); John D. Foubert, *How Pornography Harms* (Bloomington, IN: LifeRich, 2017).

6 Claire M. Renzetti, "Feminist Perspectives," in *Routledge Handbook of Critical Criminology*, ed. Walter S. Dekeseredy and Molly Dragiewicz, 2nd ed. (London: Routledge, 2018), 74–82, https://doi.org/10.4324/9781315622040-7.

7 Walter S. DeKeseredy and Amanda Hall-Sanchez, "Adult Pornography and Violence against Women in the Heartland: Results from a Rural Southeast Ohio Study," *Violence against Women* 23, no. 7 (June 2017): 830–49, https://doi. org/10.1177/1077801216648795; Gail Dines, *Pornland: How Porn Has Hijacked Our Sexuality* (Boston: Beacon Press, 2010); Robert Jensen, *Getting off: Pornography and the End of Masculinity* (Cambridge, MA: South End Press, 2007).

8 Dines, "'The Handmaid's Tale' Offers a Terrifying Warning," 1.

9 Gwen Hunnicutt, "Varieties of Patriarchy and Violence against Women: Resurrecting 'Patriarchy' as a Theoretical Tool," *Violence against Women* 15, no. 5 (May 1, 2009): 554, https://doi.org/10.1177/1077801208331246.

10 Claire M. Renzetti, *Feminist Criminology*, Key Ideas in Criminology (Abingdon, Oxon: Routledge, 2013), 8.

11 Walter S. DeKeseredy, "New Directions in Feminist Understandings of Rural Crime," *Journal of Rural Studies* 39 (June 2015): 180–87, https://doi.org/10.1016/j. jrurstud.2014.11.002.

12 Jeanne Flavin and Lillian Artz, "Understanding Women, Gender, and Crime: Some Historical and International Developments," in *Routledge International Handbook of Crime and Gender Studies*, ed. Claire Renzetti, Susan L. Miller, and Angela Gover (London: Routledge, 2013), 11, https://doi. org/10.4324/9780203832516.ch1.

13 Molly Dragiewicz, "Why Sex and Gender Matter in Domestic Violence Research and Advocacy," in *Violence against Women in Families and Relationships, Vol. 3: Criminal Justice and Law*, ed. Evan Stark and Eve Buzawa (Santa Barbara, CA: Praeger, 2009), 201–5, http://ebookcentral.proquest.com.ezp01.library.qut.edu.au.

14 Kathleen Daly and Meda Chesney-Lind, "Feminism and Criminology," *Justice Quarterly* 5, no. 4 (December 1988): 538, https://doi. org/10.1080/07418828800089871.

15 Renzetti, "Feminist Perspectives."

16 Daly and Chesney-Lind, "Feminism and Criminology"; Walter S. DeKeseredy and Martin D. Schwartz, *Contemporary Criminology* (Belmont, CA: Wadsworth, 1996).

17 Jill Radford, "Policing Male Violence—Policing Women," in *Women, Violence and Social Control*, ed. Jalna Hanmer and Mary Maynard (London: Palgrave Macmillan UK, 1987), 30–45, https://doi.org/10.1007/978-1-349-18592-4_3.

18 Radford, "Policing Male Violence," 43.

19 Harold Garfinkel, "Conditions of Successful Degradation Ceremonies," *American Journal of Sociology* 61, no. 5 (1956): 420.

20 Liz Kelly, *Surviving Sexual Violence* (Minneapolis: University of Minnesota Press, 1988); Renzetti, "Feminist Perspectives."

21 Culture Reframed, "Links between 'The Handmaid's Tale' and So-Called Feminist Porn," *Culture Reframed* (blog), July 19, 2017, www.culturereframed.org.

22 Brian Vallée, *The War on Women: Elly Armour, Jane Hurshman, and Criminal Violence in Canadian Homes* (Toronto: Key Porter Books, 2007), 22.

23 Claudia Garcia-Moreno et al., "WHO Multi-country Study on Women's Health and Domestic Violence against Women" (Geneva: World Health Organization, 2005), www.who.int.

24 Holly Johnson, Natalia Ollus, and Sami Nevala, *Violence against Women: An International Perspective* (New York: Springer, 2008).

25 Emma Williamson, "The Handmaid's Tale," *Journal of Gender-Based Violence* 1, no. 2 (December 15, 2017): 267, https://doi.org/10.1332/096278917X15048755283779.

26 Victoria Collins, *State Crime, Women and Gender*, 1st ed., Routledge Studies in Crime and Society 18 (New York: Routledge, 2016), 64.

27 Renzetti, "Feminist Perspectives," 79.

28 Williamson, "The Handmaid's Tale."

29 Williamson, "The Handmaid's Tale."

30 Dines, "'The Handmaid's Tale' Offers a Terrifying Warning," 1.

31 Mary Daly, *Gyn/Ecology: The Metaethics of Radial Feminism* (Boston: Beacon Press, 1978); Dines, "'The Handmaid's Tale' Offers a Terrifying Warning."

32 Jackson Katz, *The Macho Paradox: Why Some Men Hurt Women and How All Men Can Help* (Naperville, IL: Sourcebooks, Inc, 2006).

33 Diana E. H. Russell, *Against Pornography: The Evidence of Harm*, 1st ed. (Berkeley, CA: Russell, 1993), 3.

34 Walter S. DeKeseredy and Amanda Hall-Sanchez, "Thinking Critically about Contemporary Adult Pornography and Woman Abuse," in *Routledge Handbook of Critical Criminology*, ed. Walter S. DeKeseredy and Molly Dragiewicz (London: Routledge, 2018); Dines, *Pornland*.

35 Walter S. DeKeseredy and Rus E. Funk, "The Role of Adult Pornography in Intimate Partner Sexual Violence Perpetrators' Offending," in *Perpetrators of Intimate Partner Sexual Violence: A Multidisciplinary Approach to Prevention, Recognition, and Intervention*, ed. Louise McOrmond-Plummer, Jennifer Y. Levy-Peck, and Patricia Easteal (London: Routledge, 2017), 134–42.

36 Dines, *Pornland*, xi.
37 Ana J. Bridges et al., "Aggression and Sexual Behavior in Best-Selling Pornography Videos: A Content Analysis Update," *Violence against Women* 16, no. 10 (October 2010): 1065–85, https://doi.org/10.1177/1077801210382866; DeKeseredy and Hall-Sanchez, "Adult Pornography and Violence against Women."
38 Jensen, *Getting Off*.
39 Rowland Atkinson and Thomas Rodgers, "Pleasure Zones and Murder Boxes: Online Pornography and Violent Video Games as Cultural Zones of Exception," *British Journal of Criminology* 56, no. 6 (November 2016): 1291–1307, https://doi.org/10.1093/bjc/azv113; DeKeseredy and Hall-Sanchez, "Thinking Critically."
40 Richard Abowitz, "Rob Black, Porn's Dirty Whistlebower, Spills Trade Secrets," *Daily Beast*, April 21, 2013, www.thedailybeast.com; DeKeseredy and Funk, "The Role of Adult Pornography"; Dines, *Pornland*.
41 Jensen, *Getting Off*, 70.
42 Atkinson and Rodgers, "Pleasure Zones and Murder Boxes."
43 DeKeseredy and Hall-Sanchez, "Thinking Critically."
44 Walter DeKeseredy, "Critical Criminological Understandings of Adult Pornography and Woman Abuse: New Progressive Directions in Research and Theory," *International Journal for Crime, Justice and Social Democracy* 4, no. 4 (December 1, 2015): 4–21, https://doi.org/10.5204/ijcjsd.v4i4.184.
45 Jensen, *Getting Off*, 66.
46 DeKeseredy and Hall-Sanchez, "Thinking Critically."
47 Walter S. DeKeseredy and Martin D. Schwartz, "Thinking Sociologically about Image-Based Sexual Abuse: The Contribution of Male Peer Support Theory," *Sexualization, Media, & Society* 2, no. 4 (October 20, 2016): 237462381668469, https://doi.org/10.1177/2374623816684692.
48 DeKeseredy and Corsianos, *Violence against Women in Pornography*; Dines, *Pornland*; Jensen, *Getting Off*.
49 Michael Kimmel, *Guyland: The Perilous Word Where Boys Become Men* (New York: Harper, 2008), 182.
50 Kimmel, *Guyland*, 188.
51 Natasha Vargas-Cooper, "Hard Core: The New World of Porn Is Revealing Eternal Truths about Men and Women," *Atlantic*, January 4, 2011, www.theatlantic.com.
52 DeKeseredy and Corsianos, *Violence against Women in Pornography*; Foubert, *How Pornography Harms*.
53 Feona Attwood, *Sex Media* (Cambridge, UK: Polity Press, 2018); Karen Ciclitira, "Researching Pornography and Sexual Bodies," *Psychologist* 15, no. 4 (2002): 191–94; Gert Martin Hald and Neil M. Malamuth, "Self-Perceived Effects of Pornography Consumption," *Archives of Sexual Behavior* 37, no. 4 (August 2008): 614–25, https://doi.org/10.1007/s10508-007-9212-1.
54 Dines, *Pornland*, 100.
55 Marit Ostberg, "Vi Behover Fler Kata Kvinnor I Offenligheten," Newsmill, August 27, 2009, www.newsmill.se.

56 Naomi Salaman, "Women's Art Practice/Man's Sex . . . and Now for Something Completely Different.," in *Pleasure Principles—Politics, Sexuality and Ethic*, ed. Victoria Harwood, David Oswell, and Kay Parkinson (London: Lawrence and Wishart, 1993), 160–71.

57 Foubert, *How Pornography Harms*.

58 DeKeseredy and Corsianos, *Violence against Women in Pornography*.

59 Dines, "'The Handmaid's Tale' Offers a Terrifying Warning."

60 Dines, "'The Handmaid's Tale' Offers a Terrifying Warning," 1.

61 Dines, "'The Handmaid's Tale' Offers a Terrifying Warning," 1.

62 Erving Goffman, *The Presentation of Self in Everyday Life* (Garden City, NY: Doubleday, 1959).

63 Dines, "'The Handmaid's Tale' Offers a Terrifying Warning," 1.

64 Daly, *Gyn/Ecology: The Metaethics of Radial Feminism*.

65 Williamson, "The Handmaid's Tale," 262.

66 Dines, "'The Handmaid's Tale' Offers a Terrifying Warning," 1.

67 Andrea A. Park, "Joseph Fiennes on How 'The Handmaid's Tale' Mirrors Real Life," CBS News, July 24, 2018, www.cbsnews.com.

68 Daniel White, "Donald Trump on Abortion: 'I'm Saying Women Punish Themselves,'" *Time*, May 18, 2016, https://time.com.

69 Meda Chesney-Lind, "Abortion Politics and the Persistence of Patriarchy," in *Progressive Justice in an Age of Repression*, ed. Walter S. DeKeseredy and Elliott Currie, 1st ed. (New York: Routledge, 2019), 134–52, https://doi.org/10.4324/9781351242059-10; Claire M. Renzetti, Daniel J. Curran, and Shana L. Maier, *Women, Men, and Society*, 6th ed. (Boston: Pearson, 2012).

70 Margo Wilson and Martin Daly, "Till Death Do Us Part," in *Femicide: The Politics of Women Killing*, ed. Jill Radford and Diana E. H. Russell (New York: Twayne, 1992), 85.

71 Walter S. DeKeseredy, Molly Dragiewicz, and Martin D. Schwartz, *Abusive Endings: Separation and Divorce Violence against Women*, Gender and Justice 4 (Oakland: University of California Press, 2017).

72 Raquel Bergen, *Wife Rape: Understanding the Response of Survivors and Service Providers* (Thousand Oaks, CA: SAGE, 1996), 20, https://doi.org/10.4135/9781483327624.

73 Walter S. DeKeseredy and Martin D. Schwartz, *Dangerous Exits: Escaping Abusive Relationships in Rural America*, Critical Issues in Crime and Society (New Brunswick, NJ: Rutgers University Press, 2009), 38.

74 Martin D. Schwartz, "The Spousal Exemption for Criminal Rape Prosecution Symposium: Family Violence in America—Part II," *Vermont Law Review* 7, no. 1 (1982): 33–58.

75 Susan Caringella, *Addressing Rape Reform in Law and Practice* (New York: Columbia University Press, 2008).

76 Wilson and Daly, "Till Death Do Us Part," 95.

77 DeKeseredy, Dragiewicz, and Schwartz, *Abusive Endings*.

78 Paolo Bacchetta and Margaret Power, eds., *Right-Wing Women: From Conservatives to Extremists around the World* (London: Routledge, 2002).

79 Bacchetta and Power, *Right-Wing Women*, 1.

80 Dana Bolger and Alexandra Brodsky, "Betsy DeVos's Title IX Interpretation Is an Attack on Sexual Assault Survivors," *Washington Post*, September 8, 2017, www.washingtonpost.com.

81 Carrie Lukas, "Nancy M. Pfotenhauer, Margot Hill Appointed to the VAWA Advisory Committee," Independent Women's Forum, December 3, 2002, www.iwf.org.

82 Rhonda Hammer, *Antifeminism and Family Terrorism: A Critical Feminist Perspective*, Culture and Politics Series (Lanham, MD: Rowman & Littlefield, 2002), 28.

83 Lukas, "Nancy M. Pfotenhauer, Margot Hill Appointed," 1.

84 Ben Armbruster, "Fox Pundit Says Women in the Military Should 'Expect' to Be Raped," Think Progress, February 13, 2012, https://archive.thinkprogress.org.

85 Lee Madigan and Nancy C. Gamble, *The Second Rape: Society's Continual Betrayal of the Victim* (New York: Lexington Books, 1991).

86 Hammer, *Antifeminism and Family Terrorism*, 43.

87 bell hooks, *Outlaw Culture: Resisting Representations* (New York: Routledge, 1994), 86.

88 Susan Faludi, *Backlash: The Undeclared War against American Women* (New York: Crown, 1991), xix.

89 Michael S. Kimmel, *Angry White Men: American Masculinity at the End of an Era* (New York: Nation Books, 2017), 18.

90 Angelica Jade Bastién, "In Its First Season, The Handmaid's Tale Greatest Failing Is How It Handles Race," *Vulture*, June 14, 2017, www.vulture.com.

91 Cornel West, *Race Matters* (New York: Vintage, 2001).

92 West, *Race Matters*, 4.

93 Bastién, "The Handmaid's Tale Greatest Failing," 1.

94 Bastién, "The Handmaid's Tale Greatest Failing," 1.

95 Peter Beaumont and Amanda Holpuch, "How *The Handmaid's Tale* Dressed Protests across the World," *Guardian*, August 3, 2018, www.theguardian.com.

96 Nick Bilton, "Is *The Handmaid's Tale* the Allegory of the Trump Era?," *Vanity Fair*, June 23, 2017, www.vanityfair.com.

97 Chesney-Lind, "Abortion Politics and the Persistence of Patriarchy."

98 Walter S. DeKeseredy, Amanda Hall-Sanchez, and James Nolan, "College Campus Sexual Assault: The Contribution of Peers' Proabuse Informational Support and Attachments to Abusive Peers," *Violence against Women* 24, no. 8 (June 2018): 922–35, https://doi.org/10.1177/1077801217724920.

99 DeKeseredy and Hall-Sanchez, "Thinking Critically."

100 Chesney-Lind, "Abortion Politics and the Persistence of Patriarchy"; National Academies of Sciences, Engineering, and Medicine (U.S.) et al., eds., *The Safety and Quality of Abortion Care in the United States*, Consensus Study Report (Washington, DC: National Academies Press, 2018).

CHAPTER 7. CULTURAL CRIMINOLOGY AND *HOMELAND*

1 Laura Durkay, "'Homeland' Is the Most Bigoted Show on Television," *Washington Post*, October 2, 2014, www.washingtonpost.com.

2 Jeff Ferrell and Clinton Sanders, eds., *Cultural Criminology* (Boston: Northeastern University Press, 1995).

3 Keith Hayward, "The Critical Terrorism Studies–Cultural Criminology Nexus: Some Thoughts on How to 'Toughen Up' the Critical Studies Approach," *Critical Studies on Terrorism* 4, no. 1 (March 25, 2011): 59, https://doi.org/10.1080/17539153. 2011.553387.

4 Alexandra Campbell, "Imagining the 'War on Terror': Fiction, Film and Framing," in *Framing Crime: Cultural Criminology and the Image*, ed. Keith Hayward and Mike Presdee (London: Routledge-Cavendish, 2010), 112. www.dawsonera.com.

5 Jeff Ferrell, Keith Hayward, and Michelle Brown, "Cultural Criminology," in *Oxford Research Encyclopedia of Criminology and Criminal Justice*, by Jeff Ferrell, Keith Hayward, and Michelle Brown (Oxford: Oxford University Press, 2017), https://doi.org/10.1093/acrefore/9780190264079.013.202.

6 Campbell, "Imagining the 'War on Terror,'" 98.

7 Ferrell, Hayward, and Brown, "Cultural Criminology."

8 Joshua D. Freilich and Gary LaFree, *Criminology Theory and Terrorism: New Applications and Approaches* (New York: Routledge, 2016).

9 Ihekwoaba D Onwudiwe, "The Place of Criminology in the Study of Terrorism: Implications for Homeland Security," *African Journal of Criminology & Justice Studies* 3, no. 1 (2007): 50–94; Jennifer C. Gibbs, "Looking at Terrorism through Left Realist Lenses," *Crime, Law and Social Change* 54, no. 2 (September 2010): 171–85, https://doi.org/10.1007/s10611-010-9252-7.

10 Joshua D. Freilich et al., "Investigating the Applicability of Macro-level Criminology Theory to Terrorism: A County-Level Analysis," *Journal of Quantitative Criminology* 31, no. 3 (September 1, 2015): 383–411, https://doi. org/10.1007/s10940-014-9239-0; Robert Agnew, "A General Strain Theory of Terrorism," *Theoretical Criminology* 14, no. 2 (May 1, 2010): 131–53, https://doi. org/10.1177/1362480609350163; Gibbs, "Looking at Terrorism."

11 Alexandra Campbell, "Framing Terrorism," in *Oxford Research Encyclopedia of Criminology and Criminal Justice*, by Alexandra Campbell (Oxford: Oxford University Press, 2017), https://doi.org/10.1093/acrefore/9780190264079.013.148.

12 Gabe Mythen and Sandra Walklate, "Criminology and Terrorism: Which Thesis? Risk Society or Governmentality?," *British Journal of Criminology* 46, no. 3 (2006): 382.

13 Freilich et al., "Applicability of Macro-Level Criminology Theory," 385.

14 Campbell, "Framing Terrorism"; Shamila Ahmed, "Constitutive Criminology and the 'War on Terror,'" *Critical Criminology* 22, no. 3 (September 1, 2014): 357–71, https://doi.org/10.1007/s10612-014-9235-6.

15 Austin T. Turk, "Sociology of Terrorism," *Annual Review of Sociology* 30, no. 1 (August 2004): 271–86, https://doi.org/10.1146/annurev.soc.30.012703.110510.

16 Jayne Mooney and Jock Young, "Imagining Terrorism: Terrorism and Anti-terrorism Terrorism, Two Ways of Doing Evil," *Social Justice* 32, no. 1 (99) (2005): 113–25.

17 Campbell, "Framing Terrorism."

18 Mythen and Walklate, "Criminology and Terrorism," 380.

19 Campbell, "Framing Terrorism."

20 Tina Huang, "Is Our Fear of Islamic Extremism Grounded in Evidence?," *Newsweek*, May 7, 2016, www.newsweek.com.

21 Dawn Rothe and Stephen L. Muzzatti, "Enemies Everywhere: Terrorism, Moral Panic, and US Civil Society," *Critical Criminology* 12, no. 3 (November 2004): 334, https://doi.org/10.1007/s10612-004-3879-6.

22 Scott A. Bonn, "How an Elite-Engineered Moral Panic Led to the U.S. War on Iraq," *Critical Criminology* 19, no. 3 (September 1, 2011): 227–49, https://doi.org/10.1007/s10612-010-9116-6; Jim Naureckas, "A Mass Murderer Becomes a 'Terrorist'—Based on Ethnicity, Not Evidence," *Fair* (blog), July 16, 2016, https://fair.org.

23 Josh R. Klein, "Toward a Cultural Criminology of War," *Social Justice* 38, no. 3 (125) (2012): 86–103.

24 Klein, "Toward a Cultural Criminology of War," 192.

25 Mooney and Young, "Imagining Terrorism," 115.

26 Edward W. Said, *Orientalism*, 1st ed. (New York: Pantheon Books, 1978).

27 Basia Spalek, "Islam and Criminal Justice," in *Student Handbook of Criminal Justice and Criminology*, ed. John Muncie and David Wilson (London: Routledge, 2004), 123.

28 Spalek, "Islam and Criminal Justice," 125.

29 Edward W. Said, *Covering Islam: How the Media and the Experts Determine How We See the Rest of the World*, rev. ed. (New York: Vintage Books, 1997).

30 Jack G. Shaheen, *Reel Bad Arabs: How Hollywood Vilifies a People* (New York: Olive Branch Press, 2001).

31 Campbell, "Imagining the 'War on Terror,'" 103.

32 Steven Rose, "'Death to the Infidels!' Why It's Time to Fix Hollywood's Problem with Muslims," *Guardian*, March 8, 2016, www.theguardian.com.

33 Saifuddin Ahmed and Jörg Matthes, "Media Representation of Muslims and Islam from 2000 to 2015: A Meta-Analysis," *International Communication Gazette* 79, no. 3 (April 1, 2017): 219–44, https://doi.org/10.1177/1748048516656305.

34 Ahmed and Matthes, "Media Representation," 231.

35 Said, *Covering Islam*.

36 Claudia Aradau and Rens van Munster, "Exceptionalism and the 'War on Terror': Criminology Meets International Relations," SSRN Scholarly Paper (Rochester, NY: Social Science Research Network, September 1, 2009), https://doi.org/10.1093/bjc/azp036.

37 Mooney and Young, "Imagining Terrorism," 114.

38 Shamila Ahmed, "Constitutive Criminology and the 'War on Terror,'" *Critical Criminology* 22, no. 3 (September 1, 2014): 357–71, https://doi.org/10.1007/s10612-014-9235-6.

39 Campbell, "Framing Terrorism."
40 Durkay, "'Homeland' Is the Most Bigoted Show."
41 Durkay, "'Homeland' Is the Most Bigoted Show."
42 Yair Rosenberg, "'Homeland' Is Anything but Islamophobic," *Atlantic*, December 18, 2012, www.theatlantic.com.
43 Rosenberg, "'Homeland' Is Anything but Islamophobic."
44 Arun Kundnani, *The Muslims Are Coming! Islamophobia, Extremism, and the Domestic War on Terror*, pbk. ed. (London/New York: Verso, 2014).
45 Jonny Burnett and David Whyte, "Embedded Expertise and the New Terrorism," *Journal for Crime, Conflict and the Media* 1, no. 4 (2005): 379.
46 Rothe and Muzzatti, "Enemies Everywhere," 335.
47 Ahmed, "Constitutive Criminology," 360.
48 Campbell, "Framing Terrorism."
49 Frank Füredi, *Invitation to Terror: The Expanding Empire of the Unknown* (London: Continuum, 2009).
50 Füredi, *Invitation to Terror*.
51 Rothe and Muzzatti, "Enemies Everywhere," 337–38.
52 Mythen and Walklate, "Criminology and Terrorism."
53 Mythen and Walklate, "Criminology and Terrorism."
54 Mythen and Walklate, "Criminology and Terrorism," 379.
55 James Banks, "Unmasking Deviance: The Visual Construction of Asylum Seekers and Refugees in English National Newspapers," *Critical Criminology* 20, no. 3 (September 1, 2012): 303, https://doi.org/10.1007/s10612-011-9144-x.
56 Klein, "Toward a Cultural Criminology of War."
57 Campbell, "Framing Terrorism."
58 Mooney and Young, "Imagining Terrorism," 120.
59 Richard Jackson, "Language, Policy and the Construction of a Torture Culture in the War on Terrorism," *Review of International Studies* 33, no. 3 (July 2007): 353–71, https://doi.org/10.1017/S0260210507007553.
60 Mythen and Walklate, "Criminology and Terrorism."
61 Claudia Aradau and Rens van Munster, "Exceptionalism and the 'War on Terror': Criminology Meets International Relations," SSRN Scholarly Paper (Rochester, NY: Social Science Research Network, September 1, 2009), https://doi.org/10.1093/bjc/azp036.
62 Editorial Board, "Fearmongering at Homeland Security," *New York Times*, April 21, 2017, www.nytimes.com.
63 Kate Feldman, "'Homeland' Will Do a Better Job of Portraying Muslims, Says Star Mandy Patinkin," *New York Daily News*, March 8, 2017, www.nydailynews.com.

CHAPTER 8. *FOLLOW THE MONEY*

1 David Whyte, "Studying the Crimes of the Powerful," in *Crimes of the Powerful: A Reader*, ed. David Whyte (Maidenhead: Open University Press, 2009), 1–4.
2 Whyte, "Studying the Crimes of the Powerful."

3 Nils Christie, *A Suitable Amount of Crime* (London/New York: Routledge, 2004).

4 Christie, *A Suitable Amount of Crime*, 3.

5 David Garland, "Criminological Knowledge and Its Relation to Power: Foucault's Genealogy and Criminology Today," *British Journal of Criminology* 32, no. 4 (1992): 403–22; Veronique Voruz, "Michel Foucault," in *Fifty Key Thinkers in Criminology*, ed. Keith J. Hayward, Shadd Maruna, and Jayne Mooney (Oxon: Routledge, 2010).

6 Stuart Hall, "Foucault: Power, Knowledge and Discourse," in *Discourse Theory and Practice*, ed. Margaret Wetherell, Stephanie Taylor, and Simeon J. Yates (London: SAGE, 2001), 72–81.

7 Steve Tombs and David Whyte, "Scrutinising the Powerful: Crime, Contemporary Political Economy and Critical Social Research," in *Unmasking the Crimes of the Powerful*, ed. Steve Tombs and David Whyte (New York: Peter Lang Publishing, 2003), 3–47.

8 Whyte, "Studying the Crimes of the Powerful."

9 Marshall B. Clinard and Peter C. Yeager, "Corporate Crime Issues in Research," *Criminology* 16, no. 2 (August 1978): 255–72, https://doi.org/10.1111/j.1745-9125.1978.tb00091.x; Laureen Snider, "Researching Corporate Crime," in *Unmasking the Crimes of the Powerful*, ed. Steve Tombs and David Whyte (New York: Peter Lang Publishing, 2003), 49–68.

10 Tombs and Whyte, "Scrutinising the Powerful," 8.

11 Edwin H. Sutherland, "White-Collar Criminality," *American Sociological Review* 5, no. 1 (February 1940): 1, https://doi.org/10.2307/2083937; Edwin Sutherland, *White Collar Crime* (New York: Holt, Rinehart and Winston, 1949).

12 Sutherland, "White-Collar Criminality."

13 Sutherland, "White-Collar Criminality."

14 Sutherland, *White Collar Crime*, 9.

15 Susan P. Shapiro, "Collaring the Crime, Not the Criminal: Reconsidering the Concept of White-Collar Crime," *American Sociological Review* 55, no. 3 (1990): 346–65, https://doi.org/10.2307/2095761.

16 Steve Tombs and David Whyte, "White-Collar Crime," in *The SAGE Dictionary of Criminology*, ed. Eugene McLaughlin and John Muncie (London: SAGE, 2013), 492.

17 Alex Simpson, "Establishing a Disciplining Financial Disposition in the City of London: Resilience, Speed and Intelligence," *Sociology* 53, no. 6 (December 2019): 1061–76, https://doi.org/10.1177/0038038519860402; Sylvia Walby, *Crisis* (Cambridge, UK: Polity Press, 2015).

18 Shapiro, "Collaring the Crime, Not the Criminal."

19 David Nelken, "White-Collar and Corporate Crime," in *The Oxford Handbook of Criminology*, ed. Mike Maguire, Rodney Morgan, and Robert Reiner (Oxford: Oxford University Press, 2012).

20 Tombs and Whyte, "White-Collar Crime." 81.

21 Snider, "Researching Corporate Crime," 52.

22 Bethany McLean and Peter Elkind, *The Smartest Guys in the Room: The Amazing Rise and Scandalous Fall of Enron* (New York: Portfolio, 2004).

23 Tombs and Whyte, "Scrutinising the Powerful."

24 Michael L. Benson and Sally S. Simpson, *White-Collar Crime: An Opportunity Perspective*, Criminology and Justice Studies Series (New York: Routledge, 2009).

25 Kitty Calavita and Henry N. Pontell, "The State and White-Collar Crime: Saving the Savings and Loans," *Law & Society Review* 28, no. 2 (1994): 297, https://doi.org/10.2307/3054148.

26 Harold C. Barnett, "The Production of Corporate Crime in Corporate Capitalism," in *White-Collar and Economic Crime*, ed. Peter Wickman and Timothy Dailey (Lexington, MA: Lexington Books, 1982); Nelken, "White-Collar and Corporate Crime."

27 Gregg Barak, *Theft of a Nation: Wall Street Looting and Federal Regulatory Colluding*, Issues in Crime and Justice (Lanham, MD: Rowman & Littlefield, 2012).

28 Steven Box, *Power, Crime and Mystification* (London: Routledge, 1983); Gary Slapper and Steve Tombs, *Corporate Crime*, Longman Criminology Series (Harlow: Longman, 1999).

29 Paddy Hillyard et al., eds., *Beyond Criminology: Taking Harm Seriously* (London: Pluto Press, 2004), https://doi.org/10.2307/j.ctt18fscmm.

30 John Muncie, "Social Harm," in *The SAGE Dictionary of Criminology*, ed. Eugene McLaughlin and John Muncie (London: SAGE, 2013), 430.

31 Steve Tombs and Paddy Hillyard, "Towards a Political Economy of Harm: States, Corporations and the Production of Inequality," in *Beyond Criminology: Taking Harm Seriously*, ed. Paddy Hillyard et al. (London: Pluto Press, 2004), 30–54, https://doi.org/10.2307/j.ctt18fscmm.

32 Friedrich Engels, *The Condition of the Working Class in England*, Penguin Classics (London: Penguin Books, 1987), 127.

33 Steve Tombs, "Workplace Harm and the Illusions of Law," in *Criminal Obsessions: Why Harm Matters More than Crime*, ed. Danny Dorling et al. (London: Crime and Society Foundation, 2008), 39.

34 Howard Davis, "Taking Crime Seriously? Disaster, Victimisation and Justice," in *Expanding the Criminological Imagination: Critical Readings in Criminology*, ed. Alana Barton et al. (Cullompton: Willan, 2007), 160.

35 Tombs, "Workplace Harm and the Illusions of Law."

36 Vickie Cooper and David Whyte, eds., *The Violence of Austerity* (London: Pluto Press, 2017).

37 Tombs and Hillyard, "Towards a Political Economy of Harm."

38 Gary Fooks, "In the Valley of the Blind the One-Eyed Man Is King," in *Unmasking the Crimes of the Powerful*, ed. Steve Tombs and David Whyte (New York: Peter Lang Publishing, 2003).

39 Simpson, "Establishing a Disciplining Financial Disposition."

CHAPTER 9. "LET'S MAKE THIS SHOW HAPPEN, PEOPLE"

1 Charlie Brooker, "The Dark Side of Our Gadget Addiction," *Guardian*, December 1, 2011, www.theguardian.com.

2 Brooker, "The Dark Side of Our Gadget Addiction."

3 Anthony Bottoms, "The Philosophy and Politics of Punishment and Sentencing," in *The Politics of Sentencing Reform*, ed. Chris Clarkson and Rod Morgan (Oxford: Clarendon Press, 1995).

4 John Pratt, *Penal Populism: Key Ideas in Criminology*, Key Ideas in Criminology (London/New York: Routledge, 2007).

5 John Pratt, ed., *The New Punitiveness: Trends, Theories, Perspectives* (Cullompton, Devon/Portland, OR: Willan, 2005).

6 Michel Foucault, *Discipline and Punish: The Birth of the Prison*, 1st American ed. (New York: Pantheon Books, 1977); David Garland, *Punishment and Welfare: A History of Penal Strategies* (Aldershot: Gower, 1985).

7 Prison Reform Trust, "Prison: The Facts: Bromley Briefings Summer 2018," Prison Reform Trust, 2018, www.prisonreformtrust.org.uk.

8 Sentencing Project, "Trends in U.S. Corrections: U.S. State and Federal Prison Population, 1925–2017," Sentencing Project, 2019, https://sentencingproject.org.

9 Pratt, *The New Punitiveness*, xxi.

10 Pratt, *Penal Populism*.

11 Eric Schlosser, "The Prison-Industrial Complex," *Atlantic*, December 1, 1998, www.theatlantic.com.

12 Pratt, *Penal Populism*. 96.

13 Terry Thomas, *Sex Crime: Sex Offending and Society*, 2nd ed., Crime and Society Series (Cullompton, Devon/Portland, OR: Willan, 2005), 1.

14 Gordon Burn, *Sex & Violence, Death & Silence: Encounters with Recent Art* (London: Faber & Faber, 2009), 395.

15 Foucault, *Discipline and Punish*, 104.

16 John Braithwaite, *Crime, Shame, and Reintegration* (Cambridge, UK/New York: Cambridge University Press, 1989).

17 Thomas, *Sex Crime*.

18 Jon Silverman and David Wilson, *Innocence Betrayed: Paedophilia, the Media, and Society* (Cambridge, UK/Malden, MA: Polity, 2002).

19 Martin Innes, *Signal Crimes: Social Reactions to Crime, Disorder, and Control* (Oxford: Oxford University Press, 2014).

20 Ray Surette, *Media, Crime, and Criminal Justice: Images and Realities*, 2nd ed., Contemporary Issues in Crime and Justice Series (Belmont, CA: Wadsworth Pub, 1998).

21 Keith Hayward, "Pantomime Justice: A Cultural Criminological Analysis of 'Life Stage Dissolution,'" *Crime, Media, Culture: An International Journal* 8, no. 2 (August 2012): 213, https://doi.org/10.1177/1741659012444443.

22 Foucault, *Discipline and Punish*.

23 Michelle Brown, *The Culture of Punishment: Prison, Society, and Spectacle*, Alternative Criminology Series (New York: New York University Press, 2009); Pratt, *The New Punitiveness*.

24 J. John Lennon and Malcolm Foley, *Dark Tourism: The Attraction of Death and Disaster* (London/New York: Continuum, 2000).

25 Albert Camus, "Reflections on the Guillotine," in *Resistance, Rebellion and Death: Essays* (New York: Vintage, 1995), 175.

26 Susan Sontag, *On Photography* (New York: Farrar, Straus & Giroux, 1977).

27 Brown, *The Culture of Punishment*.

28 Stanley Cohen, *States of Denial: Knowing about Atrocities and Suffering* (Cambridge, UK/Malden, MA: Polity, 2001); Brown, *The Culture of Punishment*.

29 Phil Carney, "Foucault's Punitive Society: Visual Tactics of Marking as a History of the Present: Fig. 1," *British Journal of Criminology* 55, no. 2 (March 2015): 231–47, https://doi.org/10.1093/bjc/azu105.

30 Pratt, *Penal Populism*.

31 Emma Bell, *Criminal Justice and Neoliberalism*. (Basingstoke: Palgrave Macmillan, 2011), http://www.myilibrary.com?id=299951.

32 Loic Wacquant, "The Great Penal Leap Backward: Incarceration in America from Nixon to Clinton," in *The New Punitiveness: Trends, Theories, Perspectives*, ed. John Pratt et al. (Cullompton, Devon/Portland, OR: Willan, 2005), 3.

33 Nicole Hahn Rafter and Michelle Brown, *Criminology Goes to the Movies: Crime Theory and Popular Culture* (New York: New York University Press, 2011), 2.

34 Nicole Hahn Rafter, *Shots in the Mirror: Crime Films and Society* (Oxford/New York: Oxford University Press, 2000), 130, http://site.ebrary.com.

35 David Wilson and Sean O'Sullivan, *Images of Incarceration: Representations of Prison in Film and Television Drama* (Winchester, UK: Waterside Press, 2004).

36 Jamie Bennett, "Repression and Revolution: Representations of Criminal Justice and Prisons in Recent Documentaries," *Prison Service Journal*, no. 214 (2014): 33–38.

37 Camus, "Reflections on the Guillotine."

38 Eamonn Carrabine, "Telling Prison Stories: The Spectacle of Punishment and the Criminological Imagination," in *The Arts of Imprisonment: Control, Resistance and Empowerment*, ed. Leonidas Cheliotis (Farnham: Ashgate, 2012), 47–72; Michelle Brown, "Social Documentary in Prison: The Art of Catching the State in the Act of Punishment," in *The Arts of Imprisonment: Control, Resistance and Empowerment*, ed. Leonidas Cheliotis (Farnham: Ashgate, 2012), 101–17.

39 Anthony Burgess, *A Clockwork Orange* (London: Heinemann, 1962).

40 Gene Siskel, "Kubrick's Creative Concern," in *Stanley Kubrick: Interviews*, ed. Stanley Kubrick and Gene D. Phillips (Jackson: University Press of Mississippi, 2001), 116–25.

CHAPTER 10. *THE WALKING DEAD* AND CRIMINOLOGICAL THEORY

1 Majid Yar, *Crime and the Imaginary of Disaster: Post-apocalyptic Fictions and the Crisis of Social Order*, Palgrave Pivot (Basingstoke/New York: Palgrave Macmillan, 2015), 3.

2 Thomas Raymen, "Living in the End Times through Popular Culture: An Ultra-realist Analysis of *The Walking Dead* as Popular Criminology," *Crime, Media, Culture*, July 26, 2017, https://doi.org/10.1177/1741659017721277.

3 Nicole Hahn Rafter and Michelle Brown, *Criminology Goes to the Movies: Crime Theory and Popular Culture* (New York: New York University Press, 2011).

4 Raymen, "Living in the End Times," 2.

5 Robert Agnew, "Dire Forecast: A Theoretical Model of the Impact of Climate Change on Crime," *Theoretical Criminology* 16, no. 1 (February 2012): 21–42, https://doi.org/10.1177/1362480611416843.

6 United Nations International Strategy for Disaster Reduction, "2009 UNISDR Terminology on Disaster Risk Reduction" (United Nations, 2009), https://relief-web.int/sites/reliefweb.int/files/resources/Full_Report_2010.pdf, 9.

7 Sandra Banholzer, James Kossin, and Simon Donner, "The Impact of Climate Change on Natural Disasters," in *Reducing Disaster: Early Warning Systems for Climate Change*, ed. Ashbindu Singh and Zinta Zommers (Dordrecht: Springer Netherlands, 2014), 39, https://doi.org/10.1007/978-94-017-8598-3_2.

8 Agnew, "Dire Forecast," 23.

9 David L. Brunsma, ed., *The Sociology of Katrina: Perspectives on a Modern Catastrophe* (Lanham, MD: Rowman & Littlefield, 2007); Paul Cromwell et al., "Routine Activities and Social Control in the Aftermath of a Natural Catastrophe," *European Journal on Criminal Policy and Research* 3, no. 3 (September 1995): 56–69, https://doi.org/10.1007/BF02242928; Kelly Frailing, Dee Wood Harper, and Ronal Serpas, "Changes and Challenges in Crime and Criminal Justice after Disaster," *American Behavioral Scientist* 59, no. 10 (September 2015): 1278–91, https://doi.org/10.1177/0002764215591184; Michael Leitner and Marco Helbich, "The Impact of Hurricanes on Crime: A Spatio-temporal Analysis in the City of Houston, Texas," *Cartography and Geographic Information Science* 38, no. 2 (January 1, 2011): 213–21, https://doi.org/10.1559/15230406382213; "The Katrina Impact on Crime and the Criminal Justice System in New Orleans," April 10, 2007, https://www.govinfo.gov/content/pkg/CHRG-110hhrg34527/html/CHRG-110hhrg34527.htm; Sean P. Varano et al., "A Tale of Three Cities: Crime and Displacement after Hurricane Katrina," *Journal of Criminal Justice* 38, no. 1 (January 1, 2010): 42–50, https://doi.org/10.1016/j.jcrimjus.2009.11.006; R. D. White, ed., *Climate Change from a Criminological Perspective* (New York: Springer, 2012).

10 Agnew, "Dire Forecast," 26.

11 Agnew, "Dire Forecast," 22.

12 Robert Agnew, "Foundation for a General Strain Theory of Crime and Delinquency," *Criminology* 30, no. 1 (February 1992): 47–88, https://doi.

org/10.1111/j.1745-9125.1992.tb01093.x; Robert Agnew, "Building on the Foundation of General Strain Theory: Specifying the Types of Strain Most Likely to Lead to Crime and Delinquency," *Journal of Research in Crime and Delinquency* 38, no. 4 (November 2001): 319–61, https://doi.org/10.1177/0022427801038004001; Robert Agnew, *Pressured into Crime: An Overview of General Strain Theory* (New York: Oxford University Press, 2006); Robert Agnew and Helene Raskin White, "An Empirical Test of General Strain Theory," *Criminology* 30, no. 4 (November 1992): 475–500, https://doi.org/10.1111/j.1745-9125.1992.tb01113.x.

13 Robert Agnew, *Why Do Criminals Offend? A General Theory of Crime and Delinquency* (Los Angeles: Roxbury, 2005); Robert Agnew, *Toward a Unified Criminology: Integrating Assumptions about Crime, People and Society*, New Perspectives in Crime, Deviance, and Law Series (New York: New York University Press, 2011).

14 Agnew, "Dire Forecast."

15 Agnew, "Dire Forecast."

16 Agnew, "Dire Forecast," 28.

17 Agnew, "Dire Forecast."

18 Agnew, "Dire Forecast," 29.

19 Agnew, "Foundation for a General Strain Theory"; Agnew, *Pressured into Crime*.

20 Agnew, "Dire Forecast."

21 Agnew, "Dire Forecast."

22 Frailing, Harper, and Serpas, "Changes and Challenges"; Naomi Klein, *The Shock Doctrine: The Rise of Disaster Capitalism* (New York: Picador/H. Holt and Co., 2008); "The Katrina Impact on Crime."

23 Klein, *The Shock Doctrine*.

24 Klein, *The Shock Doctrine*.

25 Tammy S. Garland, Nickie Phillips, and Scott Vollum, "Gender Politics and *The Walking Dead*: Gendered Violence and the Reestablishment of Patriarchy," *Feminist Criminology* 13, no. 1 (January 2018): 59–86, https://doi.org/10.1177/1557085116635269.

26 Agnew, "Dire Forecast."

27 Agnew, "Dire Forecast."

28 Agnew, "Dire Forecast."

29 Agnew, "Dire Forecast," 32.

30 Cromwell et al., "Routine Activities and Social Control"; Sean P. Varano et al., "A Tale of Three Cities: Crime and Displacement after Hurricane Katrina," *Journal of Criminal Justice* 38, no. 1 (January 1, 2010): 42–50, https://doi.org/10.1016/j.jcrimjus.2009.11.006.

31 "The Katrina Impact on Crime."

32 Agnew, "Dire Forecast"; Robert J. Sampson and W. Byron Groves, "Community Structure and Crime: Testing Social-Disorganization Theory," *American Journal of Sociology* 94, no. 4 (1989): 774–802; Robert J. Sampson, Stephen W. Raudenbush, and Felton Earls, "Neighborhoods and Violent Crime: A Multilevel Study of Collective Efficacy," *Science* 277, no. 5328 (August 15, 1997): 918–24, https://

doi.org/10.1126/science.277.5328.918; Jackson Toby, "Social Disorganization and Stake in Conformity: Complementary Factors in the Predatory Behavior of Hoodlums," *Journal of Criminal Law & Criminology* 48 (1957): 12–17, https://doi.org/10.2307/1140161.

33 "The Katrina Impact on Crime."

34 Agnew, "Dire Forecast."

35 Marcus Felson, *Crime and Everyday Life*, 3rd ed. (Thousand Oaks, CA: SAGE, 2002).

36 Agnew, "Dire Forecast," 34.

37 Leitner and Helbich, "The Impact of Hurricanes on Crime."

38 Cromwell et al., "Routine Activities and Social Control."

39 Cromwell et al., "Routine Activities and Social Control," 62.

40 Agnew, "Dire Forecast."

41 Agnew, "Dire Forecast," 33.

42 Albert Bandura, "Selective Activation and Disengagement of Moral Control," *Journal of Social Issues* 46, no. 1 (April 1990): 27–46, https://doi.org/10.1111/j.1540-4560.1990.tb00270.x; Albert Bandura, "Moral Disengagement in the Perpetration of Inhumanities," *Personality and Social Psychology Review* 3, no. 3 (August 1999): 193–209, https://doi.org/10.1207/s15327957pspr0303_3; Albert Bandura, *Moral Disengagement: How People Do Harm and Live with Themselves* (New York: Worth Publishers, 2016).

43 Robert Agnew, "The Causes of Animal Abuse: A Social-Psychological Analysis," *Theoretical Criminology* 2, no. 2 (May 1998): 177–209, https://doi.org/10.1177/1362480698002002003; Agnew, *Toward a Unified Criminology*.

44 Bandura, "Selective Activation"; Bandura, "Moral Disengagement."

45 Agnew, "Dire Forecast," 33.

46 Agnew, "Dire Forecast," 33.

47 Agnew, "Dire Forecast," 38.

48 Per Sandin and Misse Wester, "The Moral Black Hole," *Ethical Theory and Moral Practice* 12, no. 3 (June 1, 2009): 291–301, https://doi.org/10.1007/s10677-009-9152-z.

49 Betsy Hartmann, *The America Syndrome: Apocalypse, War and Our Call to Greatness* (New York: Seven Stories Press, 2017); Mohsen Rezaeian, "The Association between Natural Disasters and Violence: A Systematic Review of the Literature and a Call for More Epidemiological Studies," *Journal of Research in Medical Sciences: The Official Journal of Isfahan University of Medical Sciences* 18, no. 12 (December 2013): 1103–7; Sandin and Wester, "The Moral Black Hole"; Rebecca Solnit, *A Paradise Built in Hell: The Extraordinary Communities That Arise in Disaster* (New York: Penguin Books, 2010).

50 Hartmann, *The America Syndrome*, 223.

51 Solnit, *A Paradise Built in Hell*, 2.

52 Hartmann, *The America Syndrome*.

53 Klein, *The Shock Doctrine*.

54 Hartmann, *The America Syndrome*; Solnit, *A Paradise Built in Hell*.
55 Yar, *Crime and the Imaginary of Disaster*, 14.

CHAPTER 11. *MR. ROBOT* AND RADICAL CRIMINOLOGY
1 Matthew Giles, "The Unusually Accurate Portrait of Hacking on USA's Mr. Robot," *Vulture*, July 23, 2015, www.vulture.com; Kim Zetter, "How the Real Hackers behind Mr. Robot Get It So Right," *Wired*, July 15, 2016, www.wired.com.
2 Gabriella Coleman, *Hacker, Hoaxer, Whistleblower, Spy: The Many Faces of Anonymous* (London: Bloomsbury, 2015).
3 Nicole Rafter, "Crime, Film and Criminology: Recent Sex-Crime Movies," *Theoretical Criminology* 11, no. 3 (August 2007): 403–20, https://doi.org/10.1177/1362480607079584; Nicole Hahn Rafter and Michelle Brown, *Criminology Goes to the Movies: Crime Theory and Popular Culture* (New York: New York University Press, 2011).
4 Thomas J. Bernard et al., *Vold's Theoretical Criminology*, 7th ed. (New York: Oxford University Press, 2016), 267.
5 Bernard et al., *Vold's Theoretical Criminology*, 267.
6 Valeria Vegh Weis, *Marxism and Criminology: A History of Criminal Selectivity* (Chicago: Haymarket Books, 2018). 11–15.
7 Friedrich Engels, *Condition of the Working Class in England* (New York: Macmillan, 1958).
8 Engels, *Condition of the Working Class in England*, 104.
9 Engels, *Condition of the Working Class in England*, 106–7.
10 Willem A. Bonger, *Criminality and Economic Conditions* (Boston: Little, Brown and Company, 1916).
11 Rick Matthews, "Marxist Criminology," in *Controversies in Critical Criminology*, ed. Martin Schwartz and Susanne E. Hatty (New York: Routledge, 2015), 1–14.
12 Evgeny Pashukanis, "General Theory of Law and Marxism (1924)," Marxists Internet Archive, 1924, www.marxists.org; Georg Rusche, "Labor Market and Penal Sanction: Thoughts on the Sociology of Criminal Justice," *Social Justice*, no. 10 (1978 1933): 2–8; Georg Rusche, "Prison Revolts or Social Policy Lessons from America," *Social Justice*, no. 13 (1980 1933): 41–44; Georg Rusche and Otto Kirchheimer, *Punishment and Social Structure* (New York: Columbia University Press, 1939); Vegh Weis, *Marxism and Criminology*, 10–11.
13 George Pavlich, "Critical Genres and Radical Criminology in Britain," *British Journal of Criminology* 41, no. 1 (2001): 150–67; Herman Schwendinger and Julia R Schwendinger, *Who Killed the Berkeley School?: Struggles over Radical Criminology* (Brooklyn: Thought Crimes, 2014); David Stein, "A Spectre Is Haunting Law and Society: Revisiting Radical Criminology at UC Berkeley," *Social Justice* 40, no. 1/2 (131–132) (2014): 72–84.
14 Vegh Weis, *Marxism and Criminology*.
15 Frank Pearce, *Crimes of the Powerful: Marxism, Crime & Deviance* (Chicago: Pluto Press, 1976).

16 Jeffrey H. Reiman and Paul Leighton, *The Rich Get Richer and the Poor Get Prison: Ideology, Class, and Criminal Justice*, 10th ed. (Boston: Pearson, 2013), 71.

17 Richard Quinney, *Class, State, and Crime* (New York: Longman, 1977), 127.

18 Gregg Barak, *Theft of a Nation: Wall Street Looting and Federal Regulatory Colluding*, Issues in Crime and Justice (Lanham, MD: Rowman & Littlefield, 2012).

19 Paul Stretesky, Michael A. Long, and Michael J. Lynch, *The Treadmill of Crime: Political Economy and Green Criminology*, New Directions in Critical Criminology (Abingdon, Oxon: Routledge, 2014).

20 Donna Selman and Paul Leighton, *Punishment for Sale: Private Prisons, Big Business, and the Incarceration Binge*, Issues in Crime & Justice (Lanham, MD: Rowman & Littlefield, 2010).

21 Stuart Hall et al., eds., *Policing the Crisis: Mugging, the State, and Law and Order*, Critical Social Studies (London: Macmillan, 1978); Sidney L. Harring, *Policing a Class Society: The Experience of American Cities, 1865–1915*, Crime, Law, and Deviance Series (New Brunswick, NJ: Rutgers University Press, 1983); Tony Platt et al., *The Iron Fist and the Velvet Glove: An Analysis of the U.S. Police* (San Francisco: Crime and Social Justice Associates, 1977).

22 Nils Christie, *Crime Control as Industry: Towards Gulags, Western Style*, 3rd ed. (London/New York: Routledge, 2000).

23 Majid Yar, "Computer Crime Control as Industry: Virtual Insecurity and the Market for Private Policing," in *Technologies of InSecurity: The Surveillance of Everyday Life*, ed. Katja Aas, Helene O. Gundhus, and Heidi M. Lomell (New York: Routledge, 2008), 193.

24 Yar, "Computer Crime Control as Industry," 195.

25 Yar, "Computer Crime Control as Industry."

26 James Banks, "Radical Criminology and the Techno-Security-Capitalist Complex," in *Technocrime and Criminological Theory*, ed. Kevin F. Steinmetz and Matt R. Nobles (New York: Routledge, 2018), 102–15, https://doi.org/10.4324/9781315117249; Kevin F. Steinmetz, *Hacked: A Radical Approach to Hacker Culture and Crime*, Alternative Criminology Series (New York: New York University Press, 2016).

27 Banks, "Radical Criminology and the Techno-Security-Capitalist Complex," 112; Yar, "Computer Crime Control as Industry."

28 Steinmetz, *Hacked*.

29 Charles W. Mills, *The Power Elite* (New York: Oxford University Press, 1956).

30 Gregg Barak, *Unchecked Corporate Power: Why the Crimes of Multinational Corporations Are Routinized Away and What We Can Do about It*, 1st ed., Crimes of the Powerful 1 (New York: Routledge, 2017); Bonger, *Criminality and Economic Conditions*; John Hagan, *Who Are the Criminals?: The Politics of Crime Policy from the Age of Roosevelt to the Age of Reagan* (Princeton, NJ/Oxford: Princeton University Press, 2012); Edwin H. Sutherland, *White Collar Crime* (New York: Dryden Press, 1949).

31 Daniel Bell, *The Cultural Contradictions of Capitalism*, 20th anniversary ed. (New York: Basic Books, 1996); Daniel P. Moynihan, "The Negro Family: The Case for

National Action" (Washington, DC: US Department of Labor, 1965); Charles
A. Murray, *Losing Ground: American Social Policy, 1950–1980* (New York: Basic
Books, 1984); Max Weber, *The Protestant Ethic and the Spirit of Capitalism* (New
York: Scribner, 1958).

32 David Harvey, *Seventeen Contradictions and the End of Capitalism* (New York:
Oxford University Press, 2014).

33 Barak, *Unchecked Corporate Power.*

34 Barak, *Unchecked Corporate Power*, 92–99.

35 Barak, *Unchecked Corporate Power*, 95.

36 Barak, *Unchecked Corporate Power*, 6.

37 Barak, *Unchecked Corporate Power*, 11–12.

38 Dereck Cooper, "On the Concept of Alienation," *International Journal of Contemporary Sociology* 28 (1991): 7–26; Joachim Israel, *Alienation: From Marx to
Modern Sociology* (Boston: Allyn & Bacon, 1971); Karl Marx, "Estranged Labour,"
Economic and Philosophical Manuscripts of 1844, Marxists Internet Archive, 1844,
www.marxists.org; Tom Meisenhelder, "Toward a Marxist Analysis of Subjectivity," *Nature, Society, and Thought* 4, no. 1/2 (1991): 103–25.

39 Frantz Fanon, *The Wretched of the Earth* (New York: Grove Press, 1963).

40 Becky Tatum, "The Colonial Model as a Theoretical Explanation of Crime and
Delinquency," in *African American Perspectives on Crime Causation, Criminal
Justice Administration and Prevention*, ed. Anne T. Sulton (Englewood, NJ: Sulton
Books, 1994), 40.

41 E. J. Hobsbawm, *Bandits* (New York: New Press, 2000); John Lea, "Social Crime
Revisited," *Theoretical Criminology* 3, no. 3 (August 1, 1999): 307–25, https://doi.or
g/10.1177/1362480699003003003.

42 Hobsbawm, *Bandits.*

43 Hobsbawm, *Bandits*, 19–20.

44 LEA, "Social Crime Revisited."

45 Hobsbawm, *Bandits.*

46 Tatum, "The Colonial Model."

47 Jean Baudrillard, *The Consumer Society: Myths and Structures* (Thousand Oaks,
CA: SAGE, 1970); William E. B. Du Bois, "The African Roots of War," *Atlantic
Monthly*, 1915, www.theatlantic.com; Karl Marx, *Capital, Vol. 1* (New York: Inter-
national Publishers, 1867).

48 Coleman, *Hacker, Hoaxer, Whistleblower, Spy*; Alan Moore, *V for Vendetta* (New
York: DC Comics, 1988).

49 Robert R. Palmer, *Twelve Who Ruled: The Year of Terror in the French Revolution*
(Princeton, NJ: Princeton University Press, 1941); John Reed, *Ten Days That Shook
the World* (New York: International Publishers, 1919).

50 David Harvey, *The Enigma of Capital: And the Crises of Capitalism*, pbk. ed. (Ox-
ford/New York: Oxford University Press, 2011).

51 Karl Marx, "The Civil War in France," Marxists Internet Archive, 1871, www.
marxists.org.

52 Hall et al., *Policing the Crisis*; Harring, *Policing a Class Society*; Richard Quinney, *The Social Reality of Crime* (Piscataway, NJ: Transaction Publishers, 1970); Steven Spitzer, "Toward a Marxian Theory of Deviance," *Social Problems* 22, no. 5 (June 1975): 638–51, https://doi.org/10.2307/799696.

53 Austin T. Turk, "Law as a Weapon in Social Conflict," *Social Problems* 23, no. 3 (February 1976): 276–91, https://doi.org/10.2307/799774.

CHAPTER 12. WHAT'S IN A NAME?

1 Columbia Broadcasting System, "About Criminal Minds—TV Show Information," CBS.com, accessed May 25, 2020, www.cbs.com.

2 Paul J. Hirschfield, "The Declining Significance of Delinquent Labels in Disadvantaged Urban Communities," *Sociological Forum* 23, no. 3 (2008): 575–601; Malcolm W. Klein, "Labeling Theory and Delinquency Policy: An Experimental Test," *Criminal Justice and Behavior* 13, no. 1 (March 1986): 47–79, https://doi.org/1 0.1177/0093854886013001004; Lening Zhang and Steven F. Messner, "The Severity of Official Punishment for Delinquency and Change in Interpersonal Relations in Chinese Society," *Journal of Research in Crime and Delinquency* 31, no. 4 (November 1994): 416–33, https://doi.org/10.1177/0022427894031004004.

3 Jon Gunnar Bernburg and Marvin D. Krohn, "Labeling, Life Chances, and Adult Crime: The Direct and Indirect Effects of Official Intervention in Adolescence on Crime in Early Adulthood," *Criminology* 41, no. 4 (November 2003): 1287–318, https://doi.org/10.1111/j.1745-9125.2003.tb01020.x; Jón Gunnar Bernburg, Marvin D. Krohn, and Craig J. Rivera, "Official Labeling, Criminal Embeddedness, and Subsequent Delinquency: A Longitudinal Test of Labeling Theory," *Journal of Research in Crime and Delinquency* 43, no. 1 (February 2006): 67–88, https://doi.org/10.1177/0022427805280068; Raymond Paternoster and Leeann Iovanni, "The Labeling Perspective and Delinquency: An Elaboration of the Theory and an Assessment of the Evidence," *Justice Quarterly* 6, no. 3 (September 1, 1989): 359–94, https://doi.org/10.1080/07418828900090261.

4 Frank Tannenbaum, *Crime and the Community* (Oxford: Ginn, 1938), 8.

5 Tannenbaum, *Crime and the Community*.

6 Tannenbaum, *Crime and the Community*.

7 Tannenbaum, *Crime and the Community*, 17.

8 Tannenbaum, *Crime and the Community*.

9 J. Robert Lilly, Francis T. Cullen, and Richard A. Ball, *Criminological Theory: Context and Consequences*, 5th ed. (Thousand Oaks, CA: SAGE, 2011).

10 Tannenbaum, *Crime and the Community*, 19.

11 Tannenbaum, *Crime and the Community*.

12 Tannenbaum, *Crime and the Community*.

13 Edwin M. Lemert, *Social Pathology; A Systematic Approach to the Theory of Sociopathic Behavior* (New York: McGraw-Hill, 1951).

14 Edwin M. Lemert, "Beyond Mead: The Societal Reaction to Deviance," *Social Problems* 21, no. 4 (April 1974): 457–68, https://doi.org/10.2307/799985.

15 Lemert, *Social Pathology*.
16 Lemert, *Social Pathology*, 76.
17 Lemert, *Social Pathology*.
18 Lemert, *Social Pathology*.
19 Lilly, Cullen, and Ball, *Criminological Theory*.
20 Lemert, *Social Pathology*.
21 Lemert, *Social Pathology*, 34.
22 Howard S. Becker, *Outsiders: Studies in the Sociology of Deviance*, Outsiders: Studies in the Sociology of Deviance (Oxford: Free Press Glencoe, 1963).
23 Lilly, Cullen, and Ball, *Criminological Theory*.
24 Becker, *Outsiders*.
25 Becker, *Outsiders*.
26 Becker, *Outsiders*.
27 Lemert, *Social Pathology*.
28 Becker, *Outsiders*.
29 Tannenbaum, *Crime and the Community*.
30 Becker, *Outsiders*; Lemert, *Social Pathology*.
31 Lemert, *Social Pathology*.
32 Becker, *Outsiders*.
33 Tannenbaum, *Crime and the Community*.
34 Becker, *Outsiders*; Lemert, *Social Pathology*; Tannenbaum, *Crime and the Community*.
35 Becker, *Outsiders*.
36 Becker, *Outsiders*; Lemert, *Social Pathology*; Tannenbaum, *Crime and the Community*.

CHAPTER 13. PHRASING DEVIANCE

1 Gresham M. Sykes and David Matza, "Techniques of Neutralization: A Theory of Delinquency," *American Sociological Review* 22, no. 6 (1957): 664–70, https://doi.org/10.2307/2089195.
2 Sykes and Matza, "Techniques of Neutralization," 666.
3 W. William Minor, "Techniques of Neutralization: A Reconceptualization and Empirical Examination," *Journal of Research in Crime and Delinquency* 18, no. 2 (July 1, 1981): 295–318, https://doi.org/10.1177/002242788101800206.
4 Shadd Maruna and Heith Copes, "What Have We Learned from Five Decades of Neutralization Research?," *Crime and Justice* 32 (2005): 221–320.
5 Minor, "Techniques of Neutralization."
6 Patrick Peretti-Watel, "Neutralization Theory and the Denial of Risk: Some Evidence from Cannabis Use among French Adolescents," *British Journal of Sociology* 54, no. 1 (March 2003): 29, https://doi.org/10.1080/0007131032000045888.
7 Sykes and Matza, "Techniques of Neutralization," 668.
8 J. A. Landsheer, H. T. Hart, and W. Kox, "Delinquent Values and Victim Damage: Exploring the Limits of Neutralization Theory," *British Journal of Criminology* 34, no. 1 (January 1, 1994): 44–53, https://doi.org/10.1093/oxfordjournals.bjc.a048382.

9 Volkan Topalli, "When Being Good Is Bad: An Expansion of Neutralization Theory," *Criminology* 43, no. 3 (2005): 797–836, https://doi.org/10.1111/j.0011-- 1348.2005.00024.x.

10 Joseph W. Rogers and M. D. Buffalo, "Neutralization Techniques: Toward a Simplified Measurement Scale," *Pacific Sociological Review* 17, no. 3 (1974): 313–31, https://doi.org/10.2307/1388569.

11 Scott M, Kieffer and John J Sloan III, "Overcoming Moral Hurdles: Using Techniques of Neutralization by White-Collar Suspects as an Interrogation Tool," *Security Journal* 22, no. 4 (October 1, 2009): 317–30, https://doi.org/10.1057/palgrave. sj.8350087.

12 Rogers and Buffalo, "Neutralization Techniques."

13 Sykes and Matza, "Techniques of Neutralization."

14 Carl Klockars, *The Professional Fence* (New York: Free Press, 1974).

15 Alexander Alvarez, "Adjusting to Genocide: The Techniques of Neutralization and the Holocaust," *Social Science History* 21, no. 2 (1997): 139–78, https://doi. org/10.2307/1171272.

16 Emily Bryant et al., "Techniques of Neutralization and Identity Work among Accused Genocide Perpetrators," *Social Problems* 65, no. 4 (November 1, 2018): 584–602, https://doi.org/10.1093/socpro/spx026.

17 Bryant et al., "Techniques of Neutralization and Identity Work," 11.

18 Jim Mitchell, Richard A. Dodder, and Terry D. Norris, "Neutralization and Delinquency: A Comparison by Sex and Ethnicity," *Adolescence* 25, no. 98 (1990): 487–97.

19 Minor, "Techniques of Neutralization."

20 Topalli, "When Being Good Is Bad"; Thomas Ugelvik, "Prisoners and Their Victims: Techniques of Neutralization, Techniques of the Self," *Ethnography* 13, no. 3 (September 1, 2012): 259–77, https://doi.org/10.1177/1466138111435447.

21 Denis Ribeaud and Manuel Eisner, "Are Moral Disengagement, Neutralization Techniques, and Self-Serving Cognitive Distortions the Same? Developing a Unified Scale of Moral Neutralization of Aggression," *International Journal of Conflict and Violence (IJCV)* 4, no. 2 (October 11, 2010): 298–315, https://doi.org/10.4119/ ijcv-2833.

22 Robert Agnew, "The Techniques of Neutralization and Violence," *Criminology* 32, no. 4 (1994): 555–80, https://doi.org/10.1111/j.1745-9125.1994.tb01165.x.

23 Jason D. Spraitz and Kendra N. Bowen, "Techniques of Neutralization and Persistent Sexual Abuse by Clergy: A Content Analysis of Priest Personnel Files from the Archdiocese of Milwaukee," *Journal of Interpersonal Violence* 31, no. 15 (September 1, 2016): 2515–38, https://doi.org/10.1177/0886260515579509.

24 Thomas Brian Priest and John H. McGrath, "Techniques of Neutralization: Young Adult Marijuana Smokers," *Criminology* 8, no. 2 (1970): 185–94, https://doi. org/10.1111/j.1745-9125.1970.tb00739.x.

25 Heith Copes, "Societal Attachments, Offending Frequency, and Techniques of Neutralization," *Deviant Behavior* 24, no. 2 (March 1, 2003): 101–27, https://doi. org/10.1080/01639620390117200.

26 Nicole Leeper Piquero, Stephen G. Tibbetts, and Michael B. Blankenship, "Examining the Role of Differential Association and Techniques of Neutralization in Explaining Corporate Crime," *Deviant Behavior* 26, no. 2 (February 16, 2005): 159–88, https://doi.org/10.1080/01639620590881930.

27 Alvarez, "Adjusting to Genocide."

28 David Strutton, Scott J. Vitell, and Lou E. Pelton, "How Consumers May Justify Inappropriate Behavior in Market Settings: An Application on the Techniques of Neutralization," *Journal of Business Research* 30, no. 3 (July 1, 1994): 253–60, https://doi.org/10.1016/0148-2963(94)90055-8.

29 Sameer Hinduja, "Neutralization Theory and Online Software Piracy: An Empirical Analysis," *Ethics and Information Technology* 9, no. 3 (July 1, 2007): 187–204, https://doi.org/10.1007/s10676-007-9143-5; Jason R. Ingram and Sameer Hinduja, "Neutralizing Music Piracy: An Empirical Examination," *Deviant Behavior* 29, no. 4 (April 7, 2008): 334–66, https://doi.org/10.1080/01639620701588131.

30 Jascha Wagner et al., "Identity Work, Techniques of Neutralization, and Deviance: Exploring the Relationship among Older Adult Gamblers," *Symbolic Interaction* 40, no. 3 (2017): 352–77, https://doi.org/10.1002/symb.304.

31 Arthur Vasquez and Lynne M. Vieraitis, "'It's Just Paint': Street Taggers' Use of Neutralization Techniques," *Deviant Behavior* 37, no. 10 (October 2, 2016): 1179–95, https://doi.org/10.1080/01639625.2016.1169830.

32 Stephen L. Eliason and Richard A. Dodder, "Techniques of Neutralization Used by Deer Poachers in the Western United States: A Research Note," *Deviant Behavior* 20, no. 3 (June 1, 1999): 233–52, https://doi.org/10.1080/016396299266489.

33 Scott J. Vitell and Stephen J. Grove, "Marketing Ethics and the Techniques of Neutralization," *Journal of Business Ethics* 6, no. 6 (August 1, 1987): 433–38, https://doi.org/10.1007/BF00383285.

34 Thomas A. Brunner, "Applying Neutralization Theory to Fair Trade Buying Behaviour," *International Journal of Consumer Studies* 38, no. 2 (2014): 200–6, https://doi.org/10.1111/ijcs.12081.

35 Ruth E. McKie, "Climate Change Counter Movement Neutralization Techniques: A Typology to Examine the Climate Change Counter Movement," *Sociological Inquiry* 89, no. 2 (2019): 288–316, https://doi.org/10.1111/soin.12246.

36 Denise A. Copelton, "'You Are What You Eat': Nutritional Norms, Maternal Deviance, and Neutralization of Women's Prenatal Diets," *Deviant Behavior* 28, no. 5 (August 7, 2007): 467–94, https://doi.org/10.1080/01639620701252571.

37 William C. Brennan, "Abortion and the Techniques of Neutralization," *Journal of Health and Social Behavior* 15, no. 4 (1974): 358–65, https://doi.org/10.2307/2137096.

38 Martha Heltsley and Thomas C. Calhoun, "The Good Mother: Neutralization Techniques Used by Pageant Mothers," *Deviant Behavior* 24, no. 2 (March 1, 2003): 81–100, https://doi.org/10.1080/01639620390117202.

39 Don Liddick, "Techniques of Neutralization and Animal Rights Activists," *Deviant Behavior* 34, no. 8 (August 1, 2013): 618–34, https://doi.org/10.1080/01639625.2012.759048.

40 Sykes and Matza, "Techniques of Neutralization."
41 Sykes and Matza, "Techniques of Neutralization."
42 Sykes and Matza, "Techniques of Neutralization."
43 Shadd Maruna and Heith Copes, "What Have We Learned from Five Decades of Neutralization Research?," *Crime and Justice* 32 (2005): 221–320.

CHAPTER 14. FIGHTING THE (INVISIBLE) HAND

1 George B. Vold, *Theoretical Criminology.*, Theoretical Criminology. (Oxford: Oxford Univer. Press, 1958).
2 Steven Spitzer, "Toward a Marxian Theory of Deviance," *Social Problems* 22, no. 5 (June 1975): 638–51, https://doi.org/10.2307/799696.
3 Nickie D. Phillips and Staci Strobl, *Comic Book Crime: Truth, Justice, and the American Way*, Alternative Criminology Series (New York: New York University Press, 2013).
4 Scott Vollum and Cary D. Adkinson, "The Portrayal of Crime and Justice in the Comic Book Superhero Mythos," *Journal of Criminal Justice and Popular Culture* 10, no. 2 (2003): 96–108.
5 Thorsten Sellin, *Culture Conflict and Crime* (New York: Social Science Research Council, 1938); Vold, *Theoretical Criminology*.
6 Richard Quinney, *The Social Reality of Crime* (Boston: Little, Brown and Company, 1970).
7 Thomas J. Bernard, *The Consensus-Conflict Debate: Form and Content in Social Theories* (New York: Columbia University Press, 1983).
8 Quinney, *The Social Reality of Crime*, 16.
9 Quinney, *The Social Reality of Crime*, 16.
10 Vold, *Theoretical Criminology*.
11 Quinney, *The Social Reality of Crime*; Sellin, *Culture Conflict and Crime*; Vold, *Theoretical Criminology*.
12 Sellin, *Culture Conflict and Crime*.
13 Vold, *Theoretical Criminology*.
14 Quinney, *The Social Reality of Crime*.
15 Austin T. Turk, *Criminality and Legal Order* (Chicago: Rand McNally, 1969).
16 William J. Chambliss and Robert B. Seidman, *Law, Order, and Power* (Reading, MA: Addison-Wesley, 1971).
17 Turk, *Criminality and Legal Order*.
18 Raymond J. Michalowski and Edward W. Bohlander, "Repression and Criminal Justice in Capitalist America," *Sociological Inquiry* 46, no. 2 (April 1976): 95–106, https://doi.org/10.1111/j.1475-682X.1976.tb00754.x; Quinney, *The Social Reality of Crime*.
19 Rick Ruddell and Matthew O. Thomas, "Minority Threat and Police Strength: An Examination of the Golden State," *Police Practice and Research* 11, no. 3 (June 2010): 256–73, https://doi.org/10.1080/15614260902830096.
20 Quinney, *The Social Reality of Crime*.

21 Raymond Michalowski, *Order, Law, and Crime: An Introduction to Criminology* (New York: McGraw-Hill, 1985); Michalowski and Bohlander, "Repression and Criminal Justice"; Spitzer, "Toward a Marxian Theory of Deviance."

22 Hubert M. Blalock, *Toward a Theory of Minority-Group Relations* (New York: Wiley, 1967).

23 Turk, *Criminality and Legal Order.*

24 Ruddell and Thomas, "Minority Threat and Police Strength."

25 David Eitle, Stewart J. D'Alessio, and Lisa Stolzenberg, "Racial Threat and Social Control: A Test of the Political, Economic, and Threat of Black Crime Hypotheses," *Social Forces* 81, no. 2 (2002): 557–76.

26 Quinney, *The Social Reality of Crime.*

27 Chambliss and Seidman, *Law, Order, and Power.*

28 Ralf Dahrendorf, *Class and Class Conflict in Industrial Society* (Stanford, CA: Stanford University Press, 1959); Michael J. Lynch and W. Byron Groves, *A Primer in Radical Criminology*, A Special Edge Text (New York: Harrow and Heston, 1986).

29 Vold, *Theoretical Criminology.*

30 William J. Chambliss, "The State, the Law, and the Definition of Behavior as Criminal or Delinquent," in *Crime and Criminals: Contemporary and Classic Readings in Criminology* (Los Angeles: Roxbury, 1999), 18–24.

31 Lynch and Groves, *A Primer in Radical Criminology.*

32 Quinney, *The Social Reality of Crime.*

33 Turk, *Criminality and Legal Order*; Vold, *Theoretical Criminology.*

CHAPTER 15. MASCULINITY AND *IT'S ALWAYS SUNNY IN PHILADELPHIA*

1 Randall Colburn, "'No Hugging, No Learning': 20 Years on Seinfeld's Mantra Still Looms Large," *Guardian*, May 10, 2018, www.theguardian.com.

2 "Rob McElhenney: The Interview (It's Always Sunny in Philadelphia)," Shakefire. com, September 15, 2011, http://shakefire.com.

3 Daniel D. Wray, "Talking Ten Years of 'It's Always Sunny in Philadelphia' with Two of Its Stars," *Vice*, November 19, 2015, www.vice.com.

4 Kenneth Ladenburg, "Illuminating Whiteness and Racial Prejudice through Humor in *It's Always Sunny in Philadelphia's* 'The Gang Gets Racist,'" *Journal of Popular Culture* 48, no. 5 (2015): 860, https://doi.org/10.1111/jpcu.12332.

5 Nicole Rafter, "Crime, Film and Criminology: Recent Sex-Crime Movies," *Theoretical Criminology* 11, no. 3 (August 2007): 403–20, https://doi. org/10.1177/1362480607079584; Nicole Hahn Rafter and Michelle Brown, *Criminology Goes to the Movies: Crime Theory and Popular Culture* (New York: New York University Press, 2011).

6 Laura Johnson, "The Not So Sweet Dee: A Feminist Analysis of Deandra Reynolds in *It's Always Sunny in Philadelphia*" (SEWSA 2016 Intersectionality in the New Millennium: An Assessment of Culture, Power, and Society Conference, Rockhill, SC, April 2016).

7   Raewyn W. Connell and James W. Messerschmidt, "Hegemonic Masculin-
    ity: Rethinking the Concept," *Gender & Society*, June 29, 2016, https://doi.
    org/10.1177/0891243205278639; James W. Messerschmidt, *Masculinities and
    Crime: Critique and Reconceptualization of Theory* (Lanham, MD: Rowman &
    Littlefield, 1993); James W. Messerschmidt, "Men, Masculinities and Crime,"
    in *Handbook of Studies on Men and Masculinities*, ed. Michael Kimmel, Jeff
    Hearn, and Raewyn W. Connell (Thousand Oaks, CA: SAGE, 2005); Jody Miller,
    "Up It Up: Gender and the Accomplishment of Street Robbery," *Criminology*
    36, no. 1 (1998): 37–66, https://doi.org/10.1111/j.1745-9125.1998.tb01239.x; Jody
    Miller, "The Strengths and Limits of 'Doing Gender' for Understanding Street
    Crime," *Theoretical Criminology* 6, no. 4 (November 1, 2002): 433–60, https://doi.
    org/10.1177/136248060200600403.
8   Miller, "The Strengths and Limits of 'Doing Gender.'"
9   Jeanne Flavin, "Feminism for the Mainstream Criminologist: An Invitation," in
    The Criminal Justice System and Women: Offenders, Prisoners, Victims, & Workers,
    ed. Barbara R. Price and Natalie J. Sokoloff, 3rd ed. (New York: McGraw-Hill,
    2004), 32.
10 Alison J. Marganski, "Feminist Theory and Technocrime," in *Technocrime and
    Criminological Theory*, ed. Kevin F. Steinmetz and Matt R. Nobles (New York:
    Routledge, 2017), 12–13.
11 Thomas J. Bernard et al., *Vold's Theoretical Criminology*, 7th ed. (New York: Ox-
    ford University Press, 2016), 286.
12 Gregg Barak, Paul Leighton, and Jeanne Flavin, *Class, Race, Gender, and Crime:
    The Social Realities of Justice in America* (Lanham, MD: Rowman & Littlefield,
    2010), 176.
13 Barak, Leighton, and Flavin, *Class, Race, Gender, and Crime*, 176–177.
14 Candace Kruttschnitt, "The Politics, and Place, of Gender in Research on Crime,"
    Criminology 54, no. 1 (2016): 9, https://doi.org/10.1111/1745-9125.12096.
15 Jody Miller, "Feminist Criminology," in *Controversies in Critical Criminology*,
    ed. Martin D. Schwartz and Susanne E. Hatty (Cincinnati: Anderson Publishing,
    2003), 19.
16 Candace West and Don H. Zimmerman, "Doing Gender," *Gender and Society* 1,
    no. 2 (1987): 125–51.
17 Anthony Giddens, *The Constitution of Society* (Cambridge, MA: Polity, 1984).
18 Messerschmidt, *Masculinities and Crime*.
19 Messerschmidt, *Masculinities and Crime*, 64.
20 Messerschmidt, *Masculinities and Crime*, 94.
21 Miller, "The Strengths and Limits of 'Doing Gender,'" 434.
22 Raewyn W. Connell, *Gender and Power: Society, the Person, and Sexual Politics*
    (Stanford, CA: Stanford University Press, 1987).
23 Connell and Messerschmidt, "Hegemonic Masculinity," 832, 838.
24 Connell and Messerschmidt, "Hegemonic Masculinity," 840.
25 Messerschmidt, *Masculinities and Crime*, 87–88.

26 Raewyn W. Connell, "On Hegemonic Masculinity and Violence: Response to
   Jefferson and Hall," *Theoretical Criminology* 6, no. 1 (2016): 89–99, https://doi.
   org/10.1177/13624806020060104; Michael Levi, "Masculinities and White-Collar
   Crime," in *Just Boys Doing Business? Men, Masculinities and Crime,* ed. Tim Newburn
   and Elizabeth A. Stanko (New York: Routledge, 1994), 234–52; James W. Messerschmidt, *Capitalism, Patriarchy, and Crime: Toward a Socialist Feminist Criminology*
   (Totowa, NJ: Rowman & Littlefield, 1986); Messerschmidt, *Masculinities and Crime.*

27 Daniel Leonard, "Psychoanalyzing the Game of Games," in *Always Sunny and
   Philosophy: The Gang Gets Analyzed,* ed. Roger Hunt and Robert Arp (Chicago:
   Open Court, 2015), 55.

28 Connell, *Gender and Power.*

29 Messerschmidt, *Masculinities and Crime.*

30 Sharon R. Bird, "Welcome to the Men's Club: Homosociality and the Maintenance
   of Hegemonic Masculinity," *Gender and Society* 10, no. 2 (1996): 122–23.

31 Kimberly A. Lonsway and Louise F. Fitzgerald, "Rape Myths. In Review," *Psychology of Women Quarterly* 18, no. 2 (1994): 133–64, https://doi.org/10.1111/j.1471-
   6402.1994.tb00448.x.

32 Kathryn M. Ryan, "The Relationship between Rape Myths and Sexual Scripts: The
   Social Construction of Rape," *Sex Roles: A Journal of Research* 65, no. 11–12 (2011):
   774–82, https://doi.org/10.1007/s11199-011-0033-2.

33 Megan L. Strain, Amanda L. Martens, and Donald A. Saucier, "'Rape Is the New
   Black': Humor's Potential for Reinforcing and Subverting Rape Culture," *Translational Issues in Psychological Science* 2, no. 1 (2016): 89, https://doi.org/10.1037/
   tps0000057.

34 Kerry Carrington and John Scott, "Masculinity, Rurality and Violence," *British
   Journal of Criminology* 48, no. 5 (September 1, 2008): 660, https://doi.org/10.1093/
   bjc/azn031.

35 Miller, "Up It Up."

36 Miller, "Up It Up."

37 Dennis A. Balcom, "Absent Fathers: Effects on Abandoned Sons," *Journal of Men's
   Studies* 6, no. 3 (1998): 283–96.

38 Ralph LaRossa, "'Until the Ball Glows in the Twilight': Fatherhood, Baseball, and
   the Game of Playing Catch," in *Fathering through Sport and Leisure,* ed. Tess Kay
   (London/New York: Routledge, 2009), 39–55.

39 Miller, "Strengths and Limits of 'Doing Gender.'"

40 Miller, "Strengths and Limits of 'Doing Gender,'" 453.

41 Miller, "Strengths and Limits of 'Doing Gender,'" 453.

42 Miller, "Strengths and Limits of 'Doing Gender.'"

43 Miller, "Strengths and Limits of 'Doing Gender.'"

44 Sut Jhally, *Tough Guise: Violence, Media, and the Crisis in Masculinity* (Northampton, MA: Media Education Foundation, 1999).

45 Michael Kimmel, *Manhood in American* (New York: Oxford University Press,
   2018), 5.

46 Messerschmidt, "Men, Masculinities and Crime."

47 Miller, "Strengths and Limits of 'Doing Gender.'"

48 Leonard, "Psychoanalyzing the Game of Games."

CHAPTER 16. RACE, CRIME, AND JUSTICE IN *AMERICAN CRIME*

1 John Singleton, *Rosewood* (Warner Bros. Pictures, 1997).

2 Harper Lee, *To Kill a Mockingbird* (New York: J. B. Lippincott, 1960).

3 Liam Stack, "New Trial Upheld for Adnan Syed of 'Serial,'" *New York Times*, March 29, 2018, www.nytimes.com.

4 Ben Affleck, *The Town* (Warner Bros. Pictures, 2010).

5 Roger Ebert, "Robbing Banks Is the Neighborhood Business," RogerEbert.com, September 15, 2010, www.rogerebert.com.

6 Nicole Hahn Rafter and Michelle Brown, *Criminology Goes to the Movies: Crime Theory and Popular Culture* (New York: New York University Press, 2011).

7 Nicole Rafter, "Crime, Film and Criminology: Recent Sex-Crime Movies," *Theoretical Criminology* 11, no. 3 (August 2007): 403, https://doi.org/10.1177/1362480607079584.

8 Steven E. Barkan, *Race, Crime, and Justice: The Continuing American Dilemma*, 1st ed. (New York: Oxford University Press, 2018); Shaun L. Gabbidon and Helen Taylor Greene, eds., *Race, Crime, and Justice: A Reader* (New York: Routledge, 2013); Spohn, "Race, Crime, and Punishment."

9 Michelle Alexander, *The New Jim Crow: Mass Incarceration in the Age of Colorblindness* (New York: New Press, 2010).

10 Douglas A. Blackmon, *Slavery by Another Name: The Re-enslavement of Black People in America from the Civil War to World War II*, 1st ed. (New York: Doubleday, 2008).

11 W. E. B. Du Bois, *The Philadelphia Negro: A Social Study* (Boston: Ginn, 1899), 249.

12 Michael J. Hindelang, Travis Hirschi, and Joseph G. Weis, "Correlates of Delinquency: The Illusion of Discrepancy between Self-Report and Official Measures," *American Sociological Review* 44, no. 6 (December 1979): 995–1014, https://doi.org/10.2307/2094722.

13 Cassia Spohn, "Race, Crime, and Punishment in the Twentieth and Twenty-First Centuries," *Crime and Justice* 44, no. 1 (September 2015): 55, https://doi.org/10.1086/681550.

14 Delbert S. Elliott, "Serious Violent Offenders: Onset, Developmental Course, and Termination—The American Society of Criminology 1993 Presidential Address," *Criminology* 32, no. 1 (February 1994): 1–21, https://doi.org/10.1111/j.1745-9125.1994.tb01144.x; Robert J. Sampson, Jeffrey D. Morenoff, and Stephen Raudenbush, "Social Anatomy of Racial and Ethnic Disparities in Violence," *American Journal of Public Health* 95, no. 2 (February 2005): 224–32, https://doi.org/10.2105/AJPH.2004.037705.

15 Spohn, "Race, Crime, and Punishment," 52.

16 Tammy Rinehart Kochel, David B. Wilson, and Stephen D. Mastrofski, "Effect of Suspect Race on Officers' Arrest Decisions," *Criminology* 49, no. 2 (May 2011): 473–512, https://doi.org/10.1111/j.1745-9125.2011.00230.x; Patricia Warren et al., "Driving While Black: Bias Processes and Racial Disparity in Police Stops," *Criminology* 44, no. 3 (2006): 709–38, https://doi.org/10.1111/j.1745-9125.2006.00061.x.

17 Jacqueline Lee, Raymond Paternoster, and Michael Rocque, "Capital Case Processing in Georgia after *McCleskey*: More of the Same," in *Race and the Death Penalty: The Legacy of "McCleskey v. Kemp,"* ed. Rob. J. Maratea and David Keys (Boulder, CO: Lynne Rienner, 2016), 89–108; Raymond Paternoster and Robert Brame, "Reassessing Race Disparities in Maryland Capital Cases," *Criminology* 46, no. 4 (November 2008): 971–1008, https://doi.org/10.1111/j.1745-9125.2008.00132.x.

18 William Y Chin, "Racial Cumulative Disadvantage: The Cumulative Effects of Racial Bias at Multiple Decision Points in the Criminal Justice System," *Wake Forest Journal of Law & Policy* 6, no. 2 (2016): 441–58.

19 US Census Bureau, "QuickFacts: United States," United States Census Bureau, accessed May 27, 2020, www.census.gov; Criminal Justice Information Services Division, "Expanded Homicide Data Table 3: Murder Offenders by Age, Sex, Race, and Ethnicity, 2017," FBI, 2017, https://ucr.fbi.gov.

20 E. Ann Carson, "Prisoners in 2016" (Washington, DC: Bureau of Justice Statistics, 2018), www.bjs.gov.

21 Alexander, *The New Jim Crow: Mass Incarceration in the Age of Colorblindness*; Ojmarrh Mitchell and Michael S. Caudy, "Examining Racial Disparities in Drug Arrests," *Justice Quarterly* 32, no. 2 (March 4, 2015): 288–313, https://doi.org/10.1080/07418825.2012.761721; Spohn, "Race, Crime, and Punishment."

22 Allen J. Beck and Alfred Blumstein, "Racial Disproportionality in U.S. State Prisons: Accounting for the Effects of Racial and Ethnic Differences in Criminal Involvement, Arrests, Sentencing, and Time Served," *Journal of Quantitative Criminology* 34, no. 3 (September 1, 2018): 853–83, https://doi.org/10.1007/s10940-017-9357-6; Alfred Blumstein, "On the Racial Disproportionality of United States' Prison Populations," *Journal of Criminal Law and Criminology* 73, no. 3 (1982): 1259–81, https://doi.org/10.2307/1143193.

23 Lois James, David Klinger, and Bryan Vila, "Racial and Ethnic Bias in Decisions to Shoot Seen through a Stronger Lens: Experimental Results from High-Fidelity Laboratory Simulations," *Journal of Experimental Criminology* 10, no. 3 (September 2014): 323–40, https://doi.org/10.1007/s11292-014-9204-9; Samantha Moore-Berg, Andrew Karpinski, and E. Ashby Plant, "Quick to the Draw: How Suspect Race and Socioeconomic Status Influences Shooting Decisions," *Journal of Applied Social Psychology* 47, no. 9 (September 2017): 482–91, https://doi.org/10.1111/jasp.12454.

24 J. David Cisneros, "Contaminated Communities: The Metaphor of 'Immigrant as Pollutant' in Media Representations of Immigration," *Rhetoric & Public Affairs* 11, no. 4 (2008): 569–601, https://doi.org/10.1353/rap.0.0068; Victoria M. Esses, Stelian Medianu, and Andrea S. Lawson, "Uncertainty, Threat, and the Role

of the Media in Promoting the Dehumanization of Immigrants and Refugees: Dehumanization of Immigrants and Refugees," *Journal of Social Issues* 69, no. 3 (September 2013): 518–36, https://doi.org/10.1111/josi.12027.

25 Xia Wang, "Undocumented Immigrants as Perceived Criminal Threat: A Test of the Minority Threat Perspective," *Criminology* 50, no. 3 (August 2012): 743–76, https://doi.org/10.1111/j.1745-9125.2012.00278.x.

26 John Hagan and Alberto Palloni, "Sociological Criminology and the Mythology of Hispanic Immigration and Crime," *Social Problems* 46, no. 4 (November 1999): 617–32, https://doi.org/10.2307/3097078; Graham C. Ousey and Charis E. Kubrin, "Immigration and Crime: Assessing a Contentious Issue," *Annual Review of Criminology* 1, no. 1 (January 13, 2018): 63–84, https://doi.org/10.1146/annurev-criminol-032317-092026.

27 Michael T. Light and Ty Miller, "Does Undocumented Immigration Increase Violent Crime?: Undocumented Immigration and Violent Crime," *Criminology* 56, no. 2 (May 2018): 370–401, https://doi.org/10.1111/1745-9125.12175.

28 Gregg Barak, "Media and Crime," in *Routledge Handbook of Critical Criminology*, ed. Walter S. DeKeseredy and Molly Dragiewicz (New York: Routledge, 2011), 373–86; Kathleen M. Donovan and Charles F. Klahm, "The Role of Entertainment Media in Perceptions of Police Use of Force," *Criminal Justice and Behavior* 42, no. 12 (December 2015): 1261–81, https://doi.org/10.1177/0093854815604180; Lisa M. Graziano, "News Media and Perceptions of Police: A State-of-the-Art-Review," *Policing: An International Journal* 42, no. 2 (April 8, 2019): 209–25, https://doi.org/10.1108/PIJPSM-11-2017-0134; Nicola Mastrorocco and Luigi Minale, "News Media and Crime Perceptions: Evidence from a Natural Experiment" (Rochester, NY, 2018), https://papers.ssrn.com/abstract=3170280.

29 Steven M. Chermak, "Body Count News: How Crime Is Presented in the News Media," *Justice Quarterly* 11, no. 4 (December 1, 1994): 561–82, https://doi.org/10.1080/07418829400092431; Grant Duwe, "Body-Count Journalism: The Presentation of Mass Murder in the News Media," *Homicide Studies* 4, no. 4 (November 2000): 364–99, https://doi.org/10.1177/1088767900004004004.

30 Ted Chiricos, Sarah Eschholz, and Marc Gertz, "Crime, News and Fear of Crime: Toward an Identification of Audience Effects," *Social Problems* 44, no. 3 (August 1997): 342–57, https://doi.org/10.2307/3097181; Sarah Eschholz, "The Media and Fear of Crime: A Survey of the Research," *University of Florida Journal of Law and Public Policy* 9 (1997): 37–60.

31 Valerie J. Callanan, "Media Consumption, Perceptions of Crime Risk and Fear of Crime: Examining Race/Ethnic Differences," *Sociological Perspectives*, March 1, 2012, https://doi.org/10.1525/sop.2012.55.1.93; Chiricos, Eschholz, and Gertz, "Crime, News and Fear of Crime."

32 Sarah Eschholz, Ted Chiricos, and Marc Gertz, "Television and Fear of Crime: Program Types, Audience Traits, and the Mediating Effect of Perceived Neighborhood Racial Composition," *Social Problems* 50, no. 3 (August 1, 2003): 395–415, https://doi.org/10.1525/sp.2003.50.3.395.

33 Ted Chiricos and Sarah Eschholz, "The Racial and Ethnic Typification of Crime and the Criminal Typification of Race and Ethnicity in Local Television News," *Journal of Research in Crime and Delinquency* 39, no. 4 (November 2002): 400–20, https://doi.org/10.1177/002242702237286.

34 Sarah Eschholz, "Racial Composition of Television Offenders and Viewers' Fear of Crime," *Critical Criminology* 11, no. 1 (2002): 41–60, https://doi.org/10.1023/A:1021178201580.

35 Nancy E. Marion and Willard M. Oliver, *The Public Policy of Crime and Criminal Justice*, 2nd ed. (Upper Saddle River, NJ: Pearson Prentice Hall, 2012).

36 Rebecca M Hayes and Kate Luther, *#Crime: Social Media, Crime, and the Criminal Legal System* (New York: Springer, 2018), https://doi.org/10.1007/978-3-319-89444-7.

37 Travis L. Dixon, "Good Guys Are Still Always in White? Positive Change and Continued Misrepresentation of Race and Crime on Local Television News," *Communication Research* 44, no. 6 (August 2017): 775–92, https://doi.org/10.1177/0093650215579223; Franklin D. Gilliam et al., "Crime in Black and White: The Violent, Scary World of Local News," *Harvard International Journal of Press/Politics* 1, no. 3 (June 1996): 6–23, https://doi.org/10.1177/1081180X96001003003; Hayes and Luther, *#Crime*; Mary Beth Oliver, "Portrayals of Crime, Race, and Aggression in 'Reality-Based' Police Shows: A Content Analysis," *Journal of Broadcasting & Electronic Media* 38, no. 2 (1994): 179–92, https://doi.org/10.1080/08838159409364255; Mary Beth Oliver, "African American Men as 'Criminal and Dangerous': Implications of Media Portrayals of Crime on the 'Criminalization' of African American Men," *Journal of African American Studies* 7, no. 2 (2003): 3–18.

38 Oliver, "African American Men as 'Criminal and Dangerous.'"

39 Michael H Tonry, *Punishing Race: A Continuing American Dilemma (Studies in Crime and Public Policy)* (Oxford: Oxford University Press, 2011).

40 National Opinion Research Center, "Are Racial Differences Due to Discrimination (All Races since 1978)," GSS Data Explorer, accessed May 27, 2020, https://gssdataexplorer.norc.org.

41 Benenson Strategy Group, "Smart Justice Campaign Polling on Americans' Attitudes on Criminal Justice" (American Civil Liberties Union, 2017), www.aclu.org.

42 John Gramlich, "From Police to Parole, Black and White Americans Differ Widely in Their Views of Criminal Justice System," Pew Research Center, May 21, 2019, www.pewresearch.org.

43 Gallup Inc, "Immigration," Gallup.com, July 10, 2007, https://news.gallup.com.

44 Katheryn Russell-Brown, *The Color of Crime*, 2nd ed., Critical America (New York: New York University Press, 2009).

45 Justin McCarthy, "Americans More Positive about Effects of Immigration," Gallup.com, June 28, 2017, https://news.gallup.com.

46 Ann Klein and Mitch Smith, "Killing of Mollie Tibbetts in Iowa Inflames Immigration Debate," *New York Times*, August 22, 2018, www.nytimes.com.

47 Christopher M. Federico and Rafael Aguilera, "The Distinct Pattern of Relation-ships between the Big Five and Racial Resentment among White Americans," *Social Psychological and Personality Science* 10, no. 2 (March 2019): 274–84, https://doi.org/10.1177/1948550617752063; Stanley Feldman and Leonie Huddy, "Racial Resentment and White Opposition to Race-Conscious Programs: Principles or Prejudice?," *American Journal of Political Science* 49, no. 1 (January 2005): 168–83, https://doi.org/10.1111/j.0092-5853.2005.00117.x.

48 Tennessee v. Garner, 105 U.S. 1694 (1985).

49 John Simon, "Tennessee v. Garner: The Fleeing Felon Rule Note," *Saint Louis University Law Journal* 30, no. 4 (1986): 1259–78.

50 Tim S. Bynum, "Release on Recognizance: Substantive or Superficial Reform?," *Criminology* 20, no. 1 (1982): 67–82, https://doi.org/10.1111/j.1745-9125.1982.tb00448.x.

51 Gerard A Rainville and Steven K Smith, "Juvenile Felony Defendants in Criminal Courts," Special Report (Washington, DC: Bureau of Justice Statistics, 2003).

52 Cynthia E Jones, "'Give Us Free': Addressing Racial Disparities in Bail Determina-tions," *New York University Journal of Legislation and Public Policy* 16 (2013): 919–61.

53 Donna M. Bishop and Charles E. Frazier, "Race Effects in Juvenile Justice Decision-Making: Findings of a Statewide Analysis," *Journal of Criminal Law and Criminology (1973-)* 86, no. 2 (1996): 392, https://doi.org/10.2307/1144031.

54 Alexander, *The New Jim Crow*; Tonry, *Punishing Race*.

55 James E. Hawdon, "The Role of Presidential Rhetoric in the Creation of a Moral Panic: Reagan, Bush, and the War on Drugs," *Deviant Behavior* 22, no. 5 (Sep-tember 30, 2001): 419–45, https://doi.org/10.1080/01639620152472813; Craig Reinarman and Harry G. Levine, eds., *Crack in America: Demon Drugs and Social Justice*, Crack in America: Demon Drugs and Social Justice. (Berkeley: University of California Press, 1997).

56 Josh Hafner, "How Michael Brown's Death, Two Years Ago, Pushed #BlackLives-Matter into a Movement," *USA Today*, August 8, 2016, www.usatoday.com; Hayes and Luther, *#Crime*.

57 Joe Heim, "Recounting a Day of Rage, Hate, Violence and Death," *Washington Post*, August 14, 2017, www.washingtonpost.com.

58 "Our Work," Polaris Project, August 21, 2019, https://polarisproject.org.

59 Hayes and Luther, *#Crime*.

60 Steven E. Barkan and Steven F. Cohn, "Racial Prejudice and Support for the Death Penalty by Whites," *Journal of Research in Crime and Delinquency* 31, no. 2 (May 1994): 202–9, https://doi.org/10.1177/0022427894031002007; Steven E. Barkan and Steven F. Cohn, "Racial Prejudice and Support by Whites for Police Use of Force: A Research Note," *Justice Quarterly* 15, no. 4 (December 1, 1998): 743–53, https://doi.org/10.1080/07418829800093971; Steven E. Barkan and Steven F. Cohn, "On Reducing White Support for the Death Penalty: A Pessimistic Appraisal," *Criminology & Public Policy* 4, no. 1 (2005): 39–44, https://doi.org/10.1111/j.1745--9133.2005.00003.x.

61 Steven E. Barkan and Steven F. Cohn, "Why Whites Favor Spending More Money to Fight Crime: The Role of Racial Prejudice," *Social Problems* 52, no. 2 (May 1, 2005): 300–14, https://doi.org/10.1525/sp.2005.52.2.300.

62 Hayes and Luther, #*Crime*.

63 Ousey and Kubrin, "Immigration and Crime."

64 Eschholz, "Racial Composition of Television Offenders"; Vernetta Young, "Demythologizing the 'Criminalblackman': The Carnival Mirror," in *The Many Colors of Crime: Inequalities of Race, Ethnicity, and Crime in America*, ed. Ruth D. Peterson, Lauren J. Krivo, and John Hagan (New York: NYU Press, 2006), 54–66.

65 Yolanda Anyon et al., "The Persistent Effect of Race and the Promise of Alternatives to Suspension in School Discipline Outcomes," *Children and Youth Services Review* 44 (September 1, 2014): 379–86, https://doi.org/10.1016/j.childyouth.2014.06.025; Michael Rocque, "Office Discipline and Student Behavior: Does Race Matter?," *American Journal of Education* 116, no. 4 (2010): 557–81, https://doi.org/10.1086/653629; Russell J. Skiba et al., "The Color of Discipline: Sources of Racial and Gender Disproportionality in School Punishment," *Urban Review* 34, no. 4 (2002): 317–42, https://doi.org/10.1023/A:1021320817372.

66 Virginia Costenbader and Samia Markson, "School Suspension," *Journal of School Psychology* 36, no. 1 (March 1998): 59–82, https://doi.org/10.1016/S0022-4405(97)00050-2; Daniel J. Losen and Russell J. Skiba, "Suspended Education: Urban Middle Schools in Crisis," *Southern Poverty Law Center*, 2010, https://escholarship.org/uc/item/8fho55dv.

67 Anna C. McFadden et al., "A Study of Race and Gender Bias in the Punishment of School Children," *Education and Treatment of Children* 15, no. 2 (1992): 140–46; Russell J. Skiba et al., "Race Is Not Neutral: A National Investigation of African American and Latino Disproportionality in School Discipline," *School Psychology Review* 40, no. 1 (2011): 85–107.

68 Shannon Leigh Vivian, "Be Our Guest: A Review of the Legal and Regulatory History of U.S. Immigration Policy toward Mexico and Recommendations for Combating Employer Exploitation of Nonimmigrant and Undocumented Workers Note," *Seton Hall Legislative Journal* 30, no. 1 (2005): 189–216; Marjorie S. Zatz and Hilary Smith, "Immigration, Crime, and Victimization: Rhetoric and Reality," *Annual Review of Law and Social Science* 8, no. 1 (October 26, 2012): 141–59, https://doi.org/10.1146/annurev-lawsocsci-102811-173923.

69 Zatz and Smith, "Immigration, Crime, and Victimization," 146–47.

70 Ousey and Kubrin, "Immigration and Crime."

71 Russell Rickford, "Black Lives Matter: Toward a Modern Practice of Mass Struggle," *New Labor Forum* 25, no. 1 (January 2016): 36, https://doi.org/10.1177/1095796015620171.

BIBLIOGRAPHY

1. "THE MAN WHO PASSES THE SENTENCE SHOULD SWING
THE SWORD"
Boonin, David. *The Problem of Punishment*. Cambridge: Cambridge University Press, 2008.
Chui, Wing Hong. "'Pains of Imprisonment': Narratives of the Women Partners and Children of the Incarcerated." *Child & Family Social Work* 15 (2010): 196–205.
Cohen, Stan. *Visions of Social Control*. Cambridge: Polity, 1985.
Garland, David. *Punishment and Modern Social Theory: A Study in Social Theory*. Oxford: Oxford University Press, 1990.
Garland, David. *The Culture of Control*. Oxford: Oxford University Press, 2001.
Garland, David, and Richard Sparks. "Criminology, Social Theory and the Challenge of Our Times." *British Journal of Criminology* 40 no. 2 (2000): 189–204.
Hall, Stuart. "Notes on Deconstructing 'The Popular.'" In *People's History and Socialist Theory*, edited by Raphael Samuel, 227–240. London: Routledge & Kegan Paul, 1981.
Loader, Ian. "For Penal Moderation: Notes towards a Public Philosophy of Punishment." *Theoretical Criminology* 14 no. 3 (2010): 349–367.
McNeill, Fergus. *Pervasive Punishment: Making Sense of Mass Supervision*. Bingley: Emerald, 2018.
O'Brien, Martin, Rodanthi Tzanelli, Majid Yar, and Sue Penna S. "'The Spectacle of Fearsome Acts': Crime in the Melting P(l)ot in *Gangs of New York*." *Critical Criminology* 13 no. 1 (2005): 17–35.
Piacentini, Laura, and Judith Pallot. "'In Exile Imprisonment' in Russia." *British Journal of Criminology* 54 no. 1 (2014): 20–37.
Rafter, Nicole. "Crime, Film and Criminology: Recent Sex-Crime Movies." *Theoretical Criminology* 11 no. 3 (2007): 403–420.
Rafter, Nicole, and Michelle Brown. *Criminology Goes to the Movies: Crime Theory and Popular Culture*. New York: NYU Press, 2011.
Raymen, Thomas. "Living in the End Times through Popular Culture: An Ultra-realist Analysis of *The Walking Dead* as Popular Criminology." *Crime Media Culture* 14 no. 3 (2018): 429–447.
Roberts, Julian V., and Michael Hough. *Understanding Public Attitudes to Criminal Justice*. Maidenhead: Open University Press, 2005.
Ryberg, Jesper, and Julian V. Roberts. *Popular Punishment: The Normative Significance of Public Opinion for Sentencing Theory and Practice*. Oxford: Oxford University Press, 2014.

Scott, David. *Against Imprisonment: An Anthology of Abolitionist Essays.* Sherfield on Loddon: Waterside Press, 2018.

Sim, Joe. *Punishment and Prisons: Power and the Carceral State.* London: SAGE, 2009.

Simon, Jonathan. *Governing through Crime.* Oxford: Oxford University Press, 2007.

Sumner, Colin. *Censure, Politics and Criminal Justice.* Maidenhead: Open University Press, 1990.

Suprenant, Chris W. *Rethinking Punishment in the Era of Mass Incarceration.* Abingdon: Routledge, 2018.

von Hirsch, Andrew. *Censure and Sanctions.* Oxford: Clarendon Press, 1993.

von Hirsch, Andrew, and Andrew Ashworth. *Proportionate Sentencing: Exploring the Principles.* Oxford: Oxford University Press, 2005.

Wakeman, Stephen. "'No One Wins. One Side Just Loses More Slowly': *The Wire* and Drug Policy." *Theoretical Criminology* 18 no. 2 (2014): 224–240.

Wakeman, Stephen. "The One Who Knocks and the One Who Waits: Gendered Violence in *Breaking Bad*." *Crime Media Culture* 14 no. 2 (2018): 213–228.

2. *13 REASONS WHY* AND THE IMPORTANCE OF SOCIAL BONDS

Agnew, Robert. "Social Control Theory and Delinquency: A Longitudinal Test." *Criminology* 23, no. 1 (1985): 47–61.

Agnew, Robert. "A Longitudinal Test of Social Control Theory and Delinquency." *Journal of Research in Crime and Delinquency* 28, no. 2 (1991): 126–156.

Agnew, Robert, and Timothy Brezina. *Juvenile Delinquency: Causes and Control,* 6th edition (2017). Oxford: Oxford University Press.

Agnew, Robert, and David M. Petersen. "Leisure and Delinquency." *Social Problems* 36, no. 4 (1989): 332–350.

Akers, Ronald L., and Christine Sharon Sellers. *Criminological Theories: Introduction, Evaluation, and Application* (2012). Oxford: Oxford University Press.

Arneklev, Bruce J., Harold G. Grasmick, Charles R. Tittle, and Robert J. Bursik. "Low Self-Control and Imprudent Behavior." *Journal of Quantitative Criminology* 9, no. 3 (1993): 225–247.

Bahr, Stephen J., Suzanne L. Maughan, Anastasios C. Marcos, and Bingdao Li. "Family, Religiosity, and the Risk of Adolescent Drug Use." *Journal of Marriage and the Family* (1998): 979–992.

Bearman, Peter S., and James Moody. "Suicide and Friendships among American Adolescents." *American Journal of Public Health* 94, no. 1 (2004): 89–95.

Bouffard, Jeffrey A., and Melissa A. Petkovsek. "Testing Hirschi's Integration of Social Control and Rational Choice: Are Bonds Considered in Offender Decisions?" *Journal of Crime and Justice* 37, no. 3 (2014): 285–308.

Brezo, Jelena, Joel Paris, and Gustavo Turecki. "Personality Traits as Correlates of Suicidal Ideation, Suicide Attempts, and Suicide Completions: A Systematic Review." *Acta Psychiatrica Scandinavica* 113, no. 3 (2006): 180–206.

Briar, Scott, and Irving Piliavin. "Delinquency, Situational Inducements, and Commitment to Conformity." *Social Problems* 13 (1965): 35.

Brown, Jocelyn, Patricia Cohen, Jeffrey G. Johnson, and Elizabeth M. Smailes. "Childhood Abuse and Neglect: Specificity of Effects on Adolescent and Young Adult Depression and Suicidality." *Journal of the American Academy of Child & Adolescent Psychiatry* 38, no. 12 (1999): 1490–1496.

Burt, S. Alexandra, Matt McGue, William G. Iacono, and Robert F. Krueger. "Differential Parent-Child Relationships and Adolescent Externalizing Symptoms: Cross-Lagged Analyses within a Monozygotic Twin Differences Design." *Developmental Psychology* 42, no. 6 (2006): 1289.

Burton, Velmer S., Jr., T. David Evans, Sesha R. Kethineni, Francis T. Cullen, R. Gregory Dunaway, and Gary L. Payne. "The Impact of Parental Controls on Delinquency." *Journal of Criminal Justice* 23, no. 2 (1995): 111–126.

Castellví, P., A. Miranda-Mendizábal, O. Parés-Badell, J. Almenara, I. Alonso, M. J. Blasco, A. Cebrià, et al. "Exposure to Violence, a Risk for Suicide in Youths and Young Adults. A Meta-analysis of Longitudinal Studies." *Acta Psychiatrica Scandinavica* 135, no. 3 (2017): 195–211.

Christoffersen, Mogens Nygaard, Henrik Day Poulsen, and Anne Nielsen. "Attempted Suicide among Young People: Risk Factors in a Prospective Register Based Study of Danish Children Born in 1966." *Acta Psychiatrica Scandinavica* 108, no. 5 (2003): 350–358.

Chui, Allyson. "Netflix's '13 Reasons Why' Adds New Warning Video: 'This Series May Not Be Right for You.'" *Washington Post*, March 23, 2018.

Connor, Jennifer J., and Martha A. Rueter. "Parent-Child Relationships as Systems of Support or Risk for Adolescent Suicidality." *Journal of Family Psychology* 20, no. 1 (2006): 143.

Curtin, Sally C., Melonie Heron, Arialdi M. Minino, and Margaret Warner. "Recent Increase in Injury Mortality among Children and Adolescents Aged 10–19 Years in the United States: 1999–2016." *National Vital Statistics Reports* 67, no 4 (2018): 1–16. Hyattsville, MD: National Center for Health Statistics. Retrieved from www.cdc.gov.

Devries, Karen M., Joelle Y. T. Mak, Jennifer C. Child, Gail Falder, Loraine J. Bacchus, Jill Astbury, and Charlotte H. Watts. "Childhood Sexual Abuse and Suicidal Behavior: A Meta-Analysis." *Pediatrics* 133, no. 5 (2014): 1331–1344.

Fergusson, David M., Lianne J. Woodward, and L. John Horwood. "Risk Factors and Life Processes Associated with the Onset of Suicidal Behaviour during Adolescence and Early Adulthood." *Psychological Medicine* 30, no. 1 (2000): 23–39.

Franklin, Joseph C., Jessica D. Ribeiro, Kathryn R. Fox, Kate H. Bentley, Evan M. Kleiman, Xieyining Huang, Katherine M. Musacchio, Adam C. Jaroszewski, Bernard P. Chang, and Matthew K. Nock. "Risk Factors for Suicidal Thoughts and Behaviors: A Meta-analysis of 50 Years of Research." *Psychological Bulletin* 143, no. 2 (2017): 187.

Gottfredson, Michael R. "The Empirical Status of Control Theory in Criminology." In *Taking Stock: The Status of Criminological Theory—Volume 15*, edited by Francis T. Cullen, John Wright, and Kristie Blevins, 77–100 (2009). Piscataway, NJ: Transaction Publishers.

Gottfredson, Michael R., and Travis Hirschi. *A General Theory of Crime* (1990). Redwood City, CA: Stanford University Press.

Haynie, Dana L., Scott J. South, and Sunita Bose. "Residential Mobility and Attempted Suicide among Adolescents: An Individual-Level Analysis." *Sociological Quarterly* 47, no. 4 (2006): 693–721.

Hirschi, Travis. *Causes of Delinquency* (1969). Berkeley: University of California Press.

Hirschi, Travis. "Causes and Prevention of Juvenile Delinquency." *Sociological Inquiry* 47, no. 3–4 (1977): 322–341.

Hirschi, Travis, "Self-Control and Crime." In *Handbook of Self-Regulation: Research, Theories, and Applications*, edited by R. F. Baumeister and K. D. Vohs, 537–552 (2004). New York: Guilford Press.

Hirschi, Travis. "A Control Theory of Delinquency." In *Criminological Theory: Readings and Retrospectives*, edited by H. Copes and V. Topalli, 262–272 (2010). New York: McGraw-Hill.

Hoeve, Machteld, Judith Semon Dubas, Veroni I. Eichelsheim, Peter H. van der Laan, Wilma Smeenk, and Jan R. M. Gerris. "The Relationship between Parenting and Delinquency: A Meta-Analysis." *Journal of Abnormal Child Psychology* 37, no. 6 (2009): 749–775.

Hoeve, Machteld, Geert Jan J. M. Stams, Claudia E. van der Put, Judith Semon Dubas, Peter H. van der Laan, and Jan R. M. Gerris. "A Meta-analysis of Attachment to Parents and Delinquency." *Journal of Abnormal Child Psychology* 40, no. 5 (2012): 771–785.

Holt, Melissa K., Alana M. Vivolo-Kantor, Joshua R. Polanin, Kristin M. Holland, Sarah DeGue, Jennifer L. Matjasko, Misty Wolfe, and Gerald Reid. "Bullying and Suicidal Ideation and Behaviors: A Meta-analysis." *Pediatrics* 135, no. 2 (2015): 496–509.

Jenkins, Patricia H. "School Delinquency and School Commitment." *Sociology of Education* (1995): 221–239.

Johnson, J. G., P. Cohen, and M. S. Gould. "Childhood Adversities, Interpersonal Difficulties, and Risk for Suicide Attempts during Late Adolescence and Early Adulthood." *Year Book of Psychiatry & Applied Mental Health* 2004, no. 1 (2004): 73–74.

Kempf, Kimberly L. "The Empirical Status of Hirschi's Control Theory." In *New Directions in Criminological Theory: Advances in Criminological Theory*, edited by F. Adler, and W. Laufer, vol. 4, 143–185 (1993). New Brunswick, NJ: Transaction Publishers.

King, Cheryl A., and Christopher R. Merchant. "Social and Interpersonal Factors Relating to Adolescent Suicidality: A Review of the Literature." *Archives of Suicide Research* 12, no. 3 (2008): 181–196.

Krohn, Marvin D., and James L. Massey. "Social Control and Delinquent Behavior: An Examination of the Elements of the Social Bond." *Sociological Quarterly* 21, no. 4 (1980): 529–544.

Krohn, Marvin D., James L. Massey, William F. Skinner, and Ronald M. Lauer. "Social Bonding Theory and Adolescent Cigarette Smoking: A Longitudinal Analysis." *Journal of Health and Social Behavior* (1983): 337–349.

Lewinsohn, Peter M., Paul Rohde, and John R. Seeley. "Psychosocial Risk Factors for Future Adolescent Suicide Attempts." *Journal of Consulting and Clinical Psychology* 62, no. 2 (1994): 297.

Lewinsohn, Peter M., Paul Rohde, John R. Seeley, and Carol L. Baldwin. "Gender Differences in Suicide Attempts from Adolescence to Young Adulthood." *Journal of the American Academy of Child & Adolescent Psychiatry* 40, no. 4 (2001): 427–434.

Lilly, J. Robert, Francis T. Cullen, and Richard A. Ball. *Criminological Theory: Context and Consequences* (2015). Thousand Oaks, CA: SAGE.

Longshore, Douglas, Eunice Chang, Shih-chao Hsieh, and Nena Messina. "Self-Control and Social Bonds: A Combined Control Perspective on Deviance." *Crime & Delinquency* 50, no. 4 (2004): 542–564.

Longshore, Douglas, Eunice Chang, and Nena Messina. "Self-Control and Social Bonds: A Combined Control Perspective on Juvenile Offending." *Journal of Quantitative Criminology* 21, no. 4 (2005): 419–437.

Marshall, Alex. "Netflix Deletes '13 Reasons Why' Suicide Scene." *New York Times*, July 16, 2019.

Miller, J. M., C. J. Schreck, R. Tewksbury, and J. C. Barnes. *Criminological Theory: A Brief Introduction*, 4th edition (2015). New York: Pearson Publishing.

Miranda-Mendizábal, A., P. Castellví, O. Parés-Badell, J. Almenara, I. Alonso, M. J. Blasco, A. Cebrià, et al. "Sexual Orientation and Suicidal Behaviour in Adolescents and Young Adults: Systematic Review and Meta-analysis." *British Journal of Psychiatry* 211, no. 2 (2017): 77–87.

Nye, F. Ivan. *Family Relationships and Delinquent Behavior.* (1958). New York: John Wiley and Sons, Inc.

O'Donnell, Lydia, Ann Stueve, Dana Wardlaw, and Carl O'Donnell. "Adolescent Suicidality and Adult Support: The Reach for Health Study of Urban Youth." *American Journal of Health Behavior* 27, no. 6 (2003): 633–644.

Osgood, D. Wayne. "Routine Activities and Individual Deviant Behavior." In *Encyclopedia of Criminological Theory*, edited by Francis T. Cullen and Pamela Wilcox, 675–679 (2010). Thousand Oaks, CA: SAGE.

Osgood, D. Wayne, Janet K. Wilson, Patrick M. O'Malley, Jerald G. Bachman, and Lloyd D. Johnston. "Routine Activities and Individual Deviant Behavior." *American Sociological Review* (1996): 635–655.

Ostroff, Cheri. "The Relationship between Satisfaction, Attitudes, and Performance: An Organizational Level Analysis." *Journal of Applied Psychology* 77, no. 6 (1992): 963.

Paquette, Julie A., and Marion K. Underwood. "Gender Differences in Young Adolescents' Experiences of Peer Victimization: Social and Physical Aggression." *Merrill-Palmer Quarterly* 45, no. 2 (1999): 242–266.

Picquero, Alex R., and Jeff A. Bouffard. "Something Old, Something New: A Preliminary Investigation of Hirschi's Redefined Self-Control." *Justice Quarterly* 24, no. 1 (2007): 1–27.

Rabinovitch, Sara M., David C. R. Kerr, Leslie D. Leve, and Patricia Chamberlain. "Suicidal Behavior Outcomes of Childhood Sexual Abuse: Longitudinal Study of Adjudicated Girls." *Suicide and Life-Threatening Behavior* 45, no. 4 (2015): 431–447.

Reckless, Walter C. "A New Theory of Delinquency and Crime." *Federal Probation* 25 (1961): 42.

Reiss, Albert J. "Delinquency as the Failure of Personal and Social Controls." *American Sociological Review* 16, no. 2 (1951): 196–207.

Reynolds, Bridget M., and Rena L. Repetti. "Adolescent Girls' Health in the Context of Peer and Community Relationships." In *Handbook of Girls' and Women's Psychological Health: Gender and Well-Being across the Life Span*, edited by Judith Worell and Carol D. Goodheart, 292–300 (2006). New York: Oxford University Press.

Salzinger, Suzanne, Margaret Rosario, Richard S. Feldman, and Daisy S. Ng-Mak. "Adolescent Suicidal Behavior: Associations with Preadolescent Physical Abuse and Selected Risk and Protective Factors." *Journal of the American Academy of Child & Adolescent Psychiatry* 46, no. 7 (2007): 859–866.

Sampson, Robert J., and John H. Laub. *Crime in the Making: Pathways and Turning Points through Life* (1993). Cambridge, MA: Harvard University Press.

Simons, Ronald L., Leslie Gordon Simons, Callie Harbin Burt, Gene H. Brody, and Carolyn Cutrona. "Collective Efficacy, Authoritative Parenting and Delinquency: A Longitudinal Test of a Model Integrating Community- and Family-Level Processes." *Criminology* 43, no. 4 (2005): 989–1029.

Stewart, Eric A. "School Social Bonds, School Climate, and School Misbehavior: A Multilevel Analysis." *Justice Quarterly* 20, no. 3 (2003): 575–604.

Van Geel, Mitch, Paul Vedder, and Jenny Tanilon. "Relationship between Peer Victimization, Cyberbullying, and Suicide in Children and Adolescents: A Meta-analysis." *JAMA Pediatrics* 168, no. 5 (2014): 435–442.

Vaughan, Tyler J., Jeffrey A. Bouffard, and Alex R. Piquero. "Testing an Integration of Control Theories: The Role of Bonds and Self-Control in Decision-Making." *American Journal of Criminal Justice* 42, no. 1 (2017): 112–133.

Wiatrowski, Michael D., David B. Griswold, and Mary K. Roberts. "Social Control Theory and Delinquency." *American Sociological Review* 46, no. 5 (1981): 525–541.

Ystgaard, Mette, Ingebjørg Hestetun, Mitchell Loeb, and Lars Mehlum. "Is There a Specific Relationship between Childhood Sexual and Physical Abuse and Repeated Suicidal Behavior?" *Child Abuse & Neglect* 28, no. 8 (2004): 863–875.

3. BREAKING BAD

Agnew, Robert. "Building on the Foundation of General Strain Theory Specifying the Types of Strain Most Likely to Lead to Crime and Delinquency." *Journal of Research on Crime and Delinquency*, 38 no. 4 (2001): 319–361. DOI: 10.1177/0022427801038004001.

Agnew, Robert. "An Overview of General Strain Theory." In *Explaining Criminals and Crime: Essays in Contemporary Criminological Theory*, edited by Raymond Paternoster and Ronet Bachman, 161–174. Los Angeles: Roxbury, 2001.

Agnew, Robert. "When Criminal Coping Is Likely: An Extension of General Strain Theory." *Deviant Behavior*, 34 no. 8 (2013): 653–670. DOI: 10.1080/01639625.2013.766529.

Bowles, Scott. "Breaking Bad Shows Man at His Worst in Season 4," last modified July 13, 2011. www.webcitation.org.

Bowman, James. "Criminal Elements." *New Atlantis: A Journal of Technology and Society*, Winter/Spring (2013): 163–173. www.thenewatlantis.com.

Cloward, Richard A., and Lloyd E. Ohlin. *Delinquency and Opportunity: A Study of Delinquent Gangs*. New York: Free Press. 1960.

Gilligan, Vince, cr. Breaking Bad. Culver City, CA: Sony Pictures Television. 2008. Television broadcast.

Holmes, Jonathan. "Every Person Walter White Murdered in Breaking Bad," last modified October 15, 2015. www.radiotimes.com.

Hudson, Laura. "Breaking Bad Recap: Walter White Is an Abuser," last modified August 26, 2013. www.wired.com.

Knopf, Amanda. "Going West in Breaking Bad: Ambiguous Morality, Violent Masculinity, and the Antihero's Role in the American Western," May 2015. www.centerwest.org.

Lewis, Mark A. "From Victim to Victor: 'Breaking Bad' and the Dark Potential of the Terminally Empowered." *Culture, Medicine, and Psychiatry*, 37 no. 4 (2013): 656–669. DOI: 10.1007/s11013-013-9341-z.

McCluskey, Megan. "Say My Name: The 10 Biggest Turning Points in Walter White's Breaking Bad Transformation," last modified January 20, 2018. http://time.com.

Meslow, Scott. "The Big Secret of 'Breaking Bad': Walter White Was Always a Bad Guy," last modified August 31, 2012. www.theatlantic.com.

Polizzi, David. "Agnew's General Strain Theory Reconsidered: A Phenomenological Perspective." *International Journal of Offender Therapy and Comparative Criminology*, 55 no. 7 (2011): 1051–1071. DOI: 10.1177/0306624X10380846.

Poniewozik, James. "Breaking Bad: TV's Best Thriller," last modified June 21, 2010. http://content.time.com.

Rafter, Nicole, and Michelle Brown. *Criminology Goes to the Movies: Crime Theory and Popular Culture*. New York: New York University Press. 2011.

Work, Hazel. "'Sometimes Forbidden Fruit Tastes the Sweetest, Doesn't It?': Breaking Bad: The Transgressive Journey of Walter White." *American Studies Today*, 23 (2014): 19–27. www.americansc.org.uk.

4. "INSANE VIOLENCE HAS MEANING"
Auty, K. M., Farrington, D. P., & Coid, J. W. (2015). Intergenerational transmission of psychopathy and mediation via psychosocial risk factors. *British Journal of Psychiatry, 206*, 26–31.

Barry, C. T., Frick, P. J., DeShazo, T. M., McCoy, M., Ellis, M., & Loney, B. R. (2000). The importance of callous–unemotional traits for extending the concept of psychopathy to children. *Journal of Abnormal Psychology, 109*(2), 335–340.

Beaumont-Thomas, B. (2015). Jamie Dornan: I stalked a woman to get into *The Fall* role. *Guardian.* www.theguardian.com.

Blagov, P. S., Patrick, C. J., Oost, K. M., Goodman, J. A., & Pugh, A. T. (2016). Triarchic psychopathy measure: validity in relation to normal-range traits, personality pathology, and psychological adjustment. *Journal of Personality Disorders, 30*(1), 71–81.

Blair, R. J. R. (2007). The amygdala and ventromedial prefrontal cortex in morality and psychopathy. *Trends in Cognitive Sciences, 11*(9), 387–392.

Blay, Zeba. (2019). Sexualizing serial killers like Ted Bundy has its consequences. *HuffPost.* www.huffpost.com.

Christian, E., & Sellbom, M. (2015). Development and validation of an expanded version of the three-factor Levenson Self-Report Psychopathy Scale. *Journal of Personality Assessment, 98*(2), 155–168.

Cleckley, H. M. (1941). *The Mask of Sanity: An Attempt to Clarify Some Issues about the So-Called Psychopathic Personality.* New York: Penguin.

DeLisi, M. (2009). Psychopathy is the unified theory of crime. *Youth Violence and Juvenile Justice, 7*(3), 256–273.

DeLisi M. (2016). *Psychopathy as Unified Theory of Crime.* New York: Palgrave Macmillan.

DeLisi, M., Vaughn, M. G., Beaver, K. M., & Wright, J. P. (2010). The Hannibal Lecter myth: Psychopathy and verbal intelligence in the MacArthur violence risk assessment study. *Journal of Psychopathology and Behavioral Assessment, 32*(2), 169–177.

Drislane, L. E., Patrick, C. J., & Arsal, G. (2014). Clarifying the content coverage of differing psychopathy inventories through reference to the Triarchic Psychopathy Measure. *Psychological Assessment, 26*(2), 350–362.

Farrington, D. P., Ullrich, S., & Salekin, R. T. (2010). Environmental influences on child and adolescent psychopathy. In Salekin, R. T., & Lynam, D. R. (eds.) *Handbook of Child and Adolescent Psychopathy* (pp. 202–230). New York: Guilford Press.

Gilbert, G. (2016). I'd like to know why I was cast as a murdering psychopath. *Independent.* www.independent.co.uk.

Hare, R. D., & Neumann, C. N. (2006). The PCL-R assessment of psychopathy: Development, structural properties, and new directions. In C. Patrick (Ed.), *Handbook of Psychopathy* (pp. 58–88). New York: Guilford Press.

Kelsey, K. R., Rogers, R., & Robinson, E. V. (2014). Self-report measures of psychopathy: What is their role in forensic assessments? *Journal of Psychopathology and Behavioral Assessment, 37*(3), 380–391.

Lang, S., Af Klinteberg, B., & Alm, P. O. (2002). Adult psychopathy and violent behavior in males with early neglect and abuse. *Acta Psychiatrica Scandinavica, 106,* 93–100.

Lee, Z., & Salekin, R. T. (2010). Psychopathy in a noninstitutional sample: Differences in primary and secondary subtypes. *Personality Disorders: Theory, Research, and Treatment, 1*(3), 153–169.

Lilienfeld, S. O., Patrick, C. J., Benning, S. D., Berg, J., Sellbom, M., & Edens, J. F. (2012). The role of fearless dominance in psychopathy: Confusions, controversies, and clarifications. *Personality Disorders: Theory, Research, and Treatment*, 3(3), 327–340.

Meyers, S. (2014). Sex and the psychopath. *Psychology Today*. www.psychologytoday. com.

Moskowitz, A. (2004). Dissociation and violence: A review of the literature. *Trauma, Violence, & Abuse*, 5(1), 21–46.

Neumann, C. S., & Pardini, D. (2014). Factor structure and construct validity of the Self-Report Psychopathy (SRP) Scale and the Youth Psychopathic Traits Inventory (YPI) in young men. *Journal of Personality Disorders*, 28(3), 419–433.

Portnoy, J., Raine, A., Chen, F. R., Pardini, D., Loeber, R., & Jennings, J. R. (2014). Heart rate and antisocial behavior: The mediating role of impulsive sensation seeking. *Criminology*, 52(2), 292–311.

Raine, A. (2014). *The Anatomy of Violence: The Biological Roots of Crime*. New York: Vintage Books.

Stone, M. H. (2009). *The Anatomy of Evil*. Amherst, NY: Prometheus Books.

Tuvblad, C., Bezdjian, S., Raine, A., & Baker, L. A. (2014). The heritability of psychopathic personality in 14-to 15-year-old twins: A multirater, multimeasure approach. *Psychological Assessment*, 26(3), 704–716.

5. "THESE VIOLENT DELIGHTS HAVE VIOLENT ENDS"

Bogg, Richard, A. "Dostoevsky's Enigmas: An Analysis of Violent Men." *Aggression and Violent Behavior* 4, no. 4 (Winter 1999): 371–386.

Botelho, Mónica, and Rui Abrunhosa Gonçalves. "Why Do People Kill? A Critical Review of the Literature on Factors Associated with Homicide." *Aggression and Violent Behavior* 26 (2016): 9–15.

Busk, Larry Alan. "Westworld: Ideology, Simulation, Spectacle." *Mediations* 30, no.1 (Fall 2016): 25–38.

Carrabine, Eamonn, Pamela Cox, Pete Fussey, Dick Hobbs, Nigel South, Darren Thiel, and Jackie Turton. *Criminology: A Sociological Introduction* (3rd ed.). Abingdon: Routledge, 2014.

Castillo, Juan Camilo, Daniel Mejía, and Pascual Restrepo. "Scarcity without Leviathan: The Violent Effects of Cocaine Supply Shortages in the Mexican Drug War." Center for Global Development, February 26, 2014. Accessed 9 July 2018. www. cgdev.org.

Cornish, Derek B., and Ronald V. Clarke. "Understanding Crime Displacement: An Application of Rational Choice Theory." *Criminology* 25 (1987): 933–947.

Dinello, Dan. "The Wretched of *Westworld*: Scientific Totalitarianism and Revolutionary Violence." In *Westworld and Philosophy*, edited by James B. South and Kimberly S. Engels, 239–251. Chichester: Wiley Blackwell, 2018.

Goodwin, Barbara. *Using Political Ideas* (4th ed.). Chichester: John Wiley, 2001.

Hirschi, Travis, and Michael R. Gottfredson. "The Generality of Deviance." In *Criminological Perspectives: Essential Readings* (3rd ed.), edited by Eugene McLaughlin and John Muncie, 179–187. London: SAGE, 2013.

Hirvonen, Onni. "*Westworld*: from Androids to Persons." In *Westworld and Philoso-phy*, edited by James B. South and Kimberly S. Engels, 61–70. Chichester: Wiley Blackwell, 2018.

Hobbes, Thomas. *Leviathan*. London, 1651.

Jewkes, Yvonne, and Travis Linnemann. *Media and Crime in the U.S.* Thousand Oaks, CA: SAGE, 2018.

Katz, Jack. *Seductions of Crime: Moral and Sensual Attractions in Doing Evil*. New York: Basic Books, 1988.

Mider, Daniel. "The Anatomy of Violence: A Study of the Literature." *Aggression and Violent Behavior* 18 (2013): 702–708.

Moll, Nicholas. "A Special Kind of Game: The Portrayal of Role-Play in *Westworld*." In *Westworld and Philosophy*, edited by James B. South and Kimberly S. Engels, 15–25. Chichester: Wiley Blackwell, 2018.

Pedneault, Amelie, Eric Beauregard, Danielle A. Harris, and Raymond A. Knight. "My-opic Decision Making: An Examination of Crime Decisions and Their Outcomes in Sexual Crimes." *Journal of Criminal Justice* 50 (2017): 1–11.

Presdee, Mike. *Cultural Criminology and the Carnival of Crime*. London: Routledge, 2000.

Quade, Vicki. "The Seductions of Crime (Interview with Jack Katz)." *Human Rights* 16 (1989): 25–27 and 50–51.

Rousseau, Jean-Jacques. *The Essential Rousseau: The Social Contract, Discourse on the Origin of Inequality, Discourse on the Arts and Sciences, The Creed of a Savoyard Priest*. New York: New American Library, 1974.

Rushing, Janice Hocker, and Thomas S. Frentz. *Projecting the Shadow: The Cyborg Hero in American Film*. London: University of Chicago Press, 1995.

Shelley, Mary Wollstonecraft. *Frankenstein; or, The Modern Prometheus: The 1818 Text*. Oxford/New York: Oxford University Press, 1998.

Simon, Hebert A. "A Behavioral Model of Rational Choice." *Quarterly Journal of Eco-nomics* 69, no. 1 (1955): 99–118.

Spanakos, Anthony Pertros. "Violent Births: Fanon, *Westworld*, and Humanity." In *Westworld and Philosophy*, edited by James B. South and Kimberly S. Engels, 229–238. Chichester: Wiley Blackwell, 2018.

Trapero-Llobera, Patricia. "The Observer(s) System and the Semiotics of Virtuality in *Westworld*'s Characters: Jonathan Nolan's Fictions as a Conceptual Unity." In *Westworld and Philosophy*, edited by James B. South and Kimberly S. Engels, 162–172. Chichester: Wiley Blackwell, 2018.

6. UNDERSTANDING *THE HANDMAID'S TALE*

Abowitz, Richard. "Rob Black, Porn's Dirty Whistleblower Spills Trade Secrets." *Daily Beast*, April 21, 2013. Accessed July 16, 2018. www.dailybeast.com.

Armbruster, Ben. "Fox Pundit Says Women in the Military Should 'Expect' to Be Raped." *Think Progress.Org*, February 13, 2012. Accessed February 23, 2012. https://thinkprogress.org.

Atkinson, Roland, and Thomas Rodgers. "Pleasure Zones and Murder Boxes: Online Pornography and Violent Video Games as Cultural Zones of Exception." *British Journal of Criminology* 56 no. 6 (2016): 1291–1307.

Attwood, Feona. *Sex Media*. Cambridge, UK: Polity, 2018.

Atwood, Margaret. *The Handmaid's Tale*. Toronto: McClelland & Stewart, 1985.

Bacchetta, Paola, and Margaret Power. *Right-Wing Women: From Conservatives to Extremists around the World*. London: Routledge, 2002.

Bastién, Angelica Jade. "In Its First Season, *The Handmaid's Tale* Greatest Failing Is How It Handles Race." *Vulture*, June 14, 2017. Accessed September 23, 2018. www.vulture.com.

Beaumont, Peter, and Amanda Holpuch. "How *The Handmaid's Tale* Dressed Protests across the World." *Guardian*, August 3, 2018. Accessed September 12, 2018. www.theguardian.com.

Bergen, Raquel K. *Wife Rape: Understanding the Response of Survivors and Service Providers*. Thousand Oaks, CA: SAGE , 1996.

Bilton, Nick. "Is *The Handmaid's Tale* the Allegory of the Trump Era?" *Vanity Fair*, June 23, 2017. Accessed September 12, 2018. www.vanityfair.com.

Bolger, Dana, and Alexandra Brodsky. "Betsy DeVos' Title IX Interpretation Is an Attack on Sexual Assault Survivors." *Washington Post*, September 8, 2017. Accessed September 9, 2018. www.washingtonpost.com.

Bridges, Anna J., Erica Scharer, Chyng Sun, and Rachel Liberman. "Aggression and Sexual Behavior in Best-Selling Pornography Videos: A Content Analysis Update." *Violence against Women* 16 no. 10 (2010): 1065–1085.

Caringella, Susan. *Addressing Rape Reform in Law and Practice*. New York: Columbia University Press, 2008.

Chesney-Lind, Meda. "Abortion and the Persistence of Patriarchy." In *Progressive Justice in an Age of Repression: Strategies for Challenging the Rise of the Right*, edited by Walter S. DeKeseredy and Elliott Currie. London: Routledge, in press.

Cicilitaria, Karen. "Researching Pornography and Sexual Bodies." *Psychologist* 15 no. 4 (2002): 191–194.

Collins, Victoria. *State Crime, Women and Gender*. New York: Routledge, 2016.

Culture Reframed. "Feminist Porn." *Culture Reframed*, July 19, 2017. Accessed June 20, 2018. www.culturereframed.org.

Daly, Kathleen, and Meda Chesney-Lind. "Feminism and Criminology." *Justice Quarterly* 5 no. 4 (1988): 497–538.

Daly, Mary. *Gyn/Ecology: The Metaethics of Radial Feminism*. Boston: Beacon Press, 1978.

DeKeseredy, Walter S. "New Directions in Feminist Understandings of Rural Crime." *Rural Studies* 39 (2015a): 180–187.

DeKeseredy, Walter S. "Critical Criminological Understandings of Adult Pornography and Woman Abuse: New Progressive Directions in Research and Theory." *International Journal for Crime, Justice and Social Democracy* 4 no. 4 (2015b): 4–21.

DeKeseredy, Walter S., and Marilyn Corsianos. *Violence against Women in Pornography*. London: Routledge, 2016.

DeKeseredy, Walter S., Molly Dragiewicz, and Martin D. Schwartz. *Abusive Endings: Separation and Divorce Violence against Women*. Oakland: University of California Press, 2017.

DeKeseredy, Walter S., and Rus E. Funk. "The Role of Adult Pornography in Intimate Partner Sexual Violence Perpetrators' Offending." In *Perpetrators of Intimate Partner Sexual Violence: A Multidisciplinary Approach to Prevention, Recognition, and Intervention*, edited by Louise McOrmond-Plummer, Jennifer Y. Levy-Peck, and Patricia Easteal, 134–142. London: Routledge, 2017.

DeKeseredy, Walter S., and Amanda Hall-Sanchez. "Adult Pornography and Violence against Women in the Heartland: Results from a Rural Southeast Ohio Study." *Violence against Women* 23 no. 7 (2017): 830–849.

DeKeseredy, Walter S., and Amanda Hall-Sanchez. "Thinking Critically about Contemporary Adult Pornography and Woman Abuse." In *Routledge Handbook of Critical Criminology* (2nd ed.), edited by Walter S. DeKeseredy and Molly Dragiewicz, 280–294. London: Routledge, 2018.

DeKeseredy, Walter S., Amanda Hall-Sanchez, and James Nolan. "College Campus Sexual Assault: The Contribution of Peers' Proabuse Informational Support and Attachments to Abusive Peers." *Violence against Women* 24 no. 8 (2018): 922–935.

DeKeseredy, Walter S., and Martin D. Schwartz. *Contemporary Criminology*. Belmont, CA: Wadsworth, 1996.

DeKeseredy, Walter S., and Martin D. Schwartz. *Dangerous Exits: Escaping Abusive Relationships in Rural America*. New Brunswick, NJ: Rutgers University Press, 2009.

DeKeseredy, Walter S., and Martin D. Schwartz. "Thinking Sociologically about Image-Based Sexual Abuse: The Contribution of Male Peer Support Theory." *Sexualization, Media, & Society* 2 no. 4 (2016): https://doi.org/10.1177/2374623816684692.

Dines, Gail. *Pornland: How Porn Has Hijacked Our Sexuality*. Boston: Beacon Press, 2010.

Dines, Gail. "*The Handmaid's Tale* Offers a Terrifying Warning, but the Hijacking of Feminism Is Just as Dangerous." *Feminist Current*, May 1, 2017. Accessed September 12, 2018. www.feministcurrent.com.

Dragiewicz, Molly. "Why Does Sex and Gender Matter in Domestic Violence Research and Advocacy?" In *Violence against Women in Families and Relationships, Vol. 3: Criminal Justice and Law*, edited by Evan Stark and Eve S. Buzawa, 201–215. Santa Barbara, CA: Praeger, 2009.

Faludi, Susan. *Backlash: The Undeclared War against American Women*. New York: Crown, 1991.

Flavin, Jeanne, and Lillian Artz. "Understanding Women, Gender, and Crime: Some Historical and International Developments." In *Routledge International Handbook of Crime and Gender Studies*, edited by Claire M. Renzetti, Susan L. Miller, and Angela Gover, 9–35. London: Routledge, 2013.

Foubert, John D. *How Pornography Harms*. Bloomington, IN: LifeRich, 2017.

Garcia-Moreno, Claudia, Henrica Jansen, Charlotte Watts, Mary Ellsberg, and Lori Heise. *WHO Multi-country Study on Women's Health and Domestic Violence against Women*. Geneva: World Health Organization, 2005.

Garfinkle, Howard. "Conditions of Successful Degradation Ceremonies." *American Journal of Sociology* 61 no. 5 (1956): 420–424.

Goffman, Erving. *The Presentation of Self in Everyday Life*. Garden City, NY: Doubleday, 1959.

Hald, Gert, and Neil M. Malamuth. "Self-Perceived Effects of Pornography Consumption." *Archives of Sexual Behavior* 37 no. 4 (2008): 614–625.

Hammer, Rhonda. *Antifeminism and Family Terrorism: A Critical Feminist Perspective*. Lanham, MD: Rowman & Littlefield, 2002.

hooks, bell. *Outlaw Culture: Resisting Representations*. New York: Routledge, 1994.

Hunnicutt, Gwen. "Varieties of Patriarchy and Violence against Women: Resurrecting 'Patriarchy' as a Theoretical Tool." *Violence against Women* 15 no. 5 (2009): 555–573.

Jensen, Robert. *Getting Off: Pornography and the End of Masculinity*. Cambridge, MA: South End Press, 2007.

Johnson, Holly, Natalia Ollus, and Sarri Nevala. *Violence against Women: An International Perspective*. New York: Springer, 2008.

Katz, Jackson. *The Macho Paradox: Why Some Men Hurt Women and How All Men Can Help*. Naperville, IL: Sourcebooks, 2006.

Kelly, L. *Surviving Sexual Violence*. Minneapolis: University of Minnesota Press, 1988.

Kimmel, Michael. *Guyland: The Perilous Word Where Boys Become Men*. New York: Harper, 2008.

Kimmel, Michael. *Angry White Men: American Masculinity at the End of an Era*. New York: Nation Books, 2017.

Lukas, Carrie. "Nancy M. Pfotenhauer, Margot Hill Appointed to the VAWA Advisory Committee." Independent Women's Forum, 2002. Accessed March 10, 2007. www.iwf.org.

Madigan, Lee, and Nancy C. Gamble. *The Second Rape: Society's Continued Betrayal of the Victim*. New York: Lexington Books, 1989.

National Academies of Sciences, Engineering, and Medicine. *The Safety and Quality of Abortion Care in the United States*. National Academy of Science, March 16, 2018. Accessed September 13, 2018. www.nationalacademies.org.

Ostberg, Marit. "Vi Behover Fler Kata Kvinnor I Offenligheten." *Newsmill*, August 27, 2009. Accessed August 28, 2010. www.newsmill.se.

Park, Andrea A. "Joseph Fiennes on How *The Handmaid's Tale* Mirrors Real Life." *CBS News*, July 24, 2018. Accessed September 10, 2018. www.cbsnews.com.

Radford, Jill. "Policing Male Violence—Policing Women." In *Women, Violence and Social Control*, edited by Jalna Hanmer and Mary Maynard, 30–45. Atlantic Highlands, NJ: Humanities Press International, 1987.

Rafter, Nicole, and Michelle Brown. "Introduction: Taking Criminology to the Movies." In *Criminology Goes to the Movies: Crime Theory and Popular Culture*, edited by Nicole Rafter and Michelle Brown, 1–13. New York: New York University Press, 2011.

Renzetti, Claire M. "Feminist Perspectives." In *Routledge Handbook of Critical Criminology* (2nd ed.), edited by Walter S. DeKeseredy and Molly Dragiewicz, 74–82. London: Routledge, 2018.

Renzetti, Claire M., Daniel J. Curran, and Shana L. Maier. *Women, Men, and Society*. Boston: Pearson, 2012.

Russell, Diana E. H. *Against Pornography: The Evidence of Harm*. Berkeley, CA: Russell Publication, 1993.

Schwartz, Martin D. "The Spousal Exemption for Criminal Rape Prosecution." *Vermont Law Review* 7 (1982): 33–57.

Vallee, Brian. *The War on Women: Elly Armour, Jane Harshman, and Criminal Violence in Canadian Homes*. Toronto: Key Porter Books.

Vargas-Cooper, Natasha. "Hardcore: The New World of Porn Is Revealing Eternal Truths about Men and Women." *Atlantic*, January 4, 2011. Accessed May 22, 2014. www.theatlantic.com.

West, Cornell. *Race Matters*. New York: Vintage, 2001.

White, David. "Donald Trump on Abortion: 'I'm Saying Women Punish Themselves.'" *Time*, June 16, 2016. Accessed June 16, 2016. http://time.com.

Williamson, Emma. "*The Handmaid's Tale*." *Journal of Gender-Based Violence* 1 no. 2 (2017): 261–269.

Wilson, Margo, and Martin Daly. "Till Death Do Us Part." In *Femicide: The Politics of Women Killing*, edited by Jill Radford and Diana E. H. Russell, 83–98. New York: Twayne, 1992.

7. CULTURAL CRIMINOLOGY AND *HOMELAND*

Agnew, R. (2010). "A General Strain Theory of Terrorism" in *Theoretical Criminology* 14 (2): 131–153.

Ahmed, A. (2014). "Constitutive Criminology and the 'War on Terror'" in *Critical Criminology* 22: 357–371.

Ahmed, S., and Matthes, J. (2016). "Media Representation of Muslims and Islam from 2000 to 2015: A Meta-analysis" in *International Communication Gazette* 79 (3): 219–244.

Aradau, C., and van Munster, R. (2009). "Exceptionalism and the 'War on Terror': Criminology Meets International Relations" in *British Journal of Criminology* 49: 686–701.

Banks, J. (2011). "Unmasking Deviance: The Visual Construction of Asylum Seekers and Refugees in English National Newspapers" in *Critical Criminology* 20: 293–310.

Bonn, S. (2011). "How an Elite-Engineered Moral Panic Led to the US War on Iraq" in *Critical Criminology* 19: 227–249.

Burnett, J., and Whyte, D. (2005). "Embedded Expertise and the New Terrorism" in *Journal for Crime, Conflict and the Media* 1 (4): 1–18.

Campbell, A. (2010). "Imagining the 'War on Terror': Fiction, Film, and Framing" in *Framing Crime*, edited by Hayward, K., and Presdee, M., 98–114. Abingdon: Routledge.

Campbell, A. (2017). "Framing Terrorism" in *Oxford Research Encyclopedia of Criminology*, edited by Pontell, H. Oxford University Press [online].

Durkay, L. (2014). "Homeland Is the Most Bigoted Show on Television" in *Washington Post*, October 2, 2014, www.washingtonpost.com.

Editorial Board. (2017). "Fearmongering at Homeland Security" in *New York Times*, April 21, 2017, www.nytimes.com.

Feldman, K. (2017). "Homeland Will Do a Better Job of Portraying Muslims, Says Star Mandy Patinkin" in *New York Daily News*, March 8, 2017, www.nydailynews.com.

Ferrell, J., Hayward, K., and Brown, M. (2017). "Cultural Criminology" in *Oxford Research Encyclopedia of Criminology*, edited by Pontell, H. Oxford University Press [online].

Ferrell J., and Sanders, C. R. (1995). *Cultural Criminology*. Boston: Northeastern University Press.

Freilich, J. D. (2014). "Investigating the Applicability of Macro-level Criminology Theory to Terrorism" in *Journal of Quantitative Criminology* 31: 383–411.

Freilich, J. D., and LaFree, G. (2015). *Criminology Theory and Terrorism: New Applications and Approaches*. New York: Routledge.

Furedi, F. (2007). *Invitation to Terror: The Expanding Empire of the Unknown*. London: Continuum.

Gibbs, J. (2010). "Looking at Terrorism through Left Realist Lenses" in *Crime, Law, Social Change* 54: 171–185.

Hayward, K. (2011). "The Critical Terrorism Studies—Cultural Criminology Nexus: Some Thoughts on How to Toughen Up the Critical Studies Approach" in *Critical Studies on Terrorism* 4 (1): 57–73.

Huang, T. (2016). "Is Our Fear of Islamic Extremism Grounded in Evidence?" in *Newsweek*, May 7, 2016, www.newsweek.com.

Jackson, R. (2007). "Language, Policy and the Construction of a Torture Culture in the War on Terrorism" in *Review of International Studies* 33: 353–371.

Klein, J. (2012). "Toward a Cultural Criminology of War" in *Social Justice*, 38 (3): 86–103.

Kundnani, A. (2014). *The Muslims Are Coming! Islamaphobia, Extremism, and the Domestic War on Terror*. New York: Verso Books.

Mooney, J., and Young, J. (2005). "Imagining Terrorism: Terrorism and Anti-terrorism, Two Ways of Doing Evil" in *Social Justice* 32 (1): 113–125.

Mythen, G., and Walklate, S. (2006a). "Criminology and Terrorism: Which Thesis? Risk Society or Governmentality" in *British Journal of Criminology* 46: 379–398.

Mythen, G. and Walklate, S. (2006b). "Communicating the Terrorist Threat: Harnessing a Culture of Fear?" in *Media, Crime, Culture* 2 (2): 123–142.

Naureckas, J. (2016). "A Mass Murderer Becomes a 'Terrorist'—Based on Ethnicity, Not Evidence" in *Fair*, July 16, 2015, https://fair.org.

Onwudiwe, I. (2007). "The Place of Criminology in the Study of Terrorism: Implications for Homeland Security" in *African Journal of Criminology and Justice Studies* 3 (1): 50–94.

Platt, T. (2014). "Editor's Introduction: Legacies of Radical Criminology in the United States" in *Social Justice* 40: 1–5.

Rose, A. (2016). "'Death to the Infidels': Why It's Time to Fix Hollywood's Problem with Muslims" in *Guardian*, March 8, 2016, www.theguardian.com.

Rosenberg, Y. (2016). "Homeland Is Anything but Islamaphobic" in *Atlantic*, December 18, 2016, www.theatlantic.com.

Rothe, D., and Muzzatti, S. (2004). "Enemies Everywhere: Terrorism, Moral Panic, and US Civil Society" in *Critical Criminology* 12: 327–350.

Said, E. (1970). *Orientalism*. New York: Vintage Books.

Said, E. (1997). *Covering Islam: How the Media and the Experts Determine How We Should See the Rest of the World*. New York: Vintage Books.

Shaheen, J. (2001). *Reel Bad Arabs: How Hollywood Vilifies a People*. New York: Olive Branch Press.

Silverman, J., and Thomas, L. (2012). "I Feel Your Pain: Terrorism, the Media, and the Politics of Response" in *Crime, Media, Culture* 8 (3): 279–295.

Spalek, B. (2004). "Islam and Criminal Justice" *Student Handbook of Criminal Justice and Criminology*, edited by Muncie, J., and Wilson, D., 123–130. London: Routledge.

Turk, A. (2004). "Sociology of Terrorism" in *Annual Review of Sociology* 30: 271–286.

8. *FOLLOW THE MONEY*

Barak, G., 2012. *Theft of a Nation: Wall Street Looting and the Political Economy of Crime*. Lanham, MD: Rowman & Littlefield.

Barnett, H., 1982. The Production of Corporate Crime in Corporate Capitalism. In: P. Wickman & T. Dailey, eds. *White-Collar and Economic Crime*. Lexington, MA: Lexington Books.

Benson, M., & Simpson, S., 2009. *White-Collar Crime: An Opportunity Perspective*. London: Routledge.

Box, S., 1983. *Power, Crime and Mystification*. London: Tavistock.

Calavita, K., & Pontell, H., 1994. The State and White Collar Crime: Saving the Savings and Loans. *Law & Society Review*, 28(2), pp. 297–324.

Christie, N., 2004. *A Suitable Amount of Crime*. London: Routledge.

Clinard, M., & Yeager, P., 1978. Corporate Crime: Issues in Research. *Criminology*, 16(2), pp. 255–272.

Cooper, V., & Whyte, D., 2017. *The Violence of Austerity*. London: Pluto Press.

Davis, H., 2007. Taking Crime Seriously? Disaster, Victimisation and Justice. In: A. Barton, K. Corteen, D. Scott, & D. White., eds. *Expanding the Criminological Imagination: Critical Readings in Criminology*. Cullompton: Willan.

Engels, F., 1987 [1845]. *The Condition of the Working Class in England*. London: Penguin Classics.

Fooks, G., 2003. In the Valley of the Blind the One-Eyed Man Is King. In: S. Tombs & D. Whyte, eds. *Unmasking the Crimes of the Powerful*. New York: Peter Lang, pp. 105–227.

Garland, D., 1992. Criminological Knowledge and Its Relation to Power: Foucault's Genealogy and Criminology Today. *British Journal of Criminology*, 32(4), pp. 403–422.

Hall, S., 2001. Foucault: Power, Knowledge and Discourse. In: M. Wetherell, S. Taylor, & S. Yates, eds. *Discourse Theory and Practice*. London: SAGE, pp. 72–81.

Hillyard, P., Pantazis, C., Tombs, S., & Gordon, D., 2004. *Beyond Criminology: Taking Harm Seriously*. London: Pluto Press.

McLean, B., & Elkind, P., 2004. *The Smartest Guys in the Room: The Amazing Rise and Scandalous Fall of Enron*. New York: Portfolio.

Muncie, J., 2013. Social Harm. In: E. McLaughlin & J. Muncie, eds. *The SAGE Dictionary of Criminology*. London: SAGE, p. 430.

Nelken, D., 2012. White-Collar and Corporate Crime. In: M. Maguire, R. Morgan, & R. Reiner, eds. *The Oxford Handbook of Criminology*. 5th ed. Oxford: Oxford University Press, pp. 623–659.

Shapiro, S., 1990. Collaring the Crime, Not the Criminal: Reconsidering the Concept of White-Collar Crime. *American Sociological Review*, 55(3), pp. 346–365.

Simpson, A., 2019. Establishing a Disciplining Financial Disposition in the City of London: Resilience, Speed and Intelligence. *Sociology*, 53(6), pp. 1061–1076.

Slapper, G., & Tombs, S., 1999. *Corporate Crime*. Harlow: Longman.

Snider, L., 2003. Researching Corporate Crime. In: S. Tombs & D. Whyte, eds. *Unmasking the Crimes of the Powerful: Scrutinising States and Corporations*. New York: Peter Lang, pp. 49–68.

Sutherland, E., 1940. White-Collar Criminality. *American Sociological Review*, 5(1), pp. 1–12.

Sutherland, E., 1949. *White Collar Crime*. New York: Holt, Rinehart & Winston.

Tombs, S., 2008. Workplace Harm and the Illusions of Law. In: D. Dorling, D. Gordon, P. Hillyard, C. Pantazis, S. Pemberton, & S. Tombs, eds. *Criminal Obsessions: Why Harm Matters More than Crime*. London: Crime and Society Foundation, pp. 41–61.

Tombs, S., & Hillyard, P., 2004. Towards a Political Economy of Harm: States, Corporations and the Production of Inequality. In: P. Hillyard, C. Pantazis, S. Tombs, & D. Gordon, eds. *Beyond Criminology: Taking Harm Seriously*. London: Pluto Press, pp. 30–54.

Tombs, S., & Whyte, D., 2003. Scrutinising the Powerful: Crime, Contemporary Political Economy and Critical Social Research. In: S. Tombs & D. Whyte, eds. *Unmasking the Crimes of the Powerful: Scrutinising States and Corporations*. New York: Peter Lang, pp. 3–47.

Tombs, S., & Whyte, D., 2013. White-Collar Crime. In: E. McLaughlin & J. Muncie, eds. *The SAGE Dictionary of Criminology*. London: SAGE, p. 492.

Voruz, V., 2010. Michel Foucault. In: K. Hayward, S. Maruna, & J. Mooney, eds. *Fifty Key Thinkers in Criminology*. Oxon: Routledge, pp. 152–158.

Walby, S., 2015. *Crisis*. London: Polity.

Whyte, D., 2009. Studying the Crimes of the Powerful. In: *Crimes of the Powerful: A Reader*. Maidenhead: Open University Press, pp. 1–4.

9. "LET'S MAKE THIS SHOW HAPPEN, PEOPLE"

Bell, Emma. 2011. *Criminal Justice and Neoliberalism*. Basingstoke: Palgrave Macmillan.

Bennett, Jamie. 2014. "Repression and revolution: Representations of criminal justice and prisons in recent documentaries" in *Prison Service Journal*. No.214: pp. 33–38.

Bottoms, Anthony. 1995. "The philosophy and politics of punishment and sentencing" in Clarkson, Chris, and Morgan, Rod (Eds.), *The Politics of Sentencing Reform*. Oxford: Clarendon Press. pp. 17–50.

Braithwaite, John. 1989. *Crime, Shame and Reintegration*. Cambridge: Cambridge University Press.

Brooker, Charlie. 2011. "The dark side of our gadget addiction." *Guardian*, Dec. 1. Available at www.theguardian.com.

Brown, Michelle. 2009. *The Culture of Punishment: Prison, Society and Spectacle*. New York: New York University Press.

Brown, Michelle. 2012. "Social documentary in prison: The art of catching the state in the act of punishment" in Cheliotis, Leonidas (Ed.), *The Arts of Imprisonment: Control, Resistance and Empowerment*. Farnham: Ashgate. pp. 101–117.

Burgess, Anthony. 1962. *A Clockwork Orange*. London: William Heinemann.

Burns, Gordon. 2009. *Sex & Violence, Death & Silence: Encounters with Recent Art*. London: Faber & Faber.

Camus, Albert. 1995. "Reflections on the guillotine" in Camus, Albert, *Resistance, Rebellion and Death: Essays*. New York: Vintage. pp. 173–234.

Carney, Phil. 2015. "Foucault's punitive society: Visual tactics of marking as a history of the present" in *British Journal of Criminology*. Vol.55 No.2: pp. 231–247.

Carrabine, Eamonn. 2012. "Telling prison stories: The spectacle of punishment and the criminological imagination" in Cheliotis, Leonidas (Ed.), *The Arts of Imprisonment: Control, Resistance and Empowerment*. Farnham: Ashgate. pp. 47–72.

Cohen, Stanley. 2001. *States of Denial: Knowing about Atrocities and Suffering*. Cambridge: Polity Press.

Foucault, Michel. 1977. *Discipline and Punish: The Birth of the Prison*. London: Penguin.

Garland, David. 1985. *Punishment and Welfare: A History of Penal Strategies*. Aldershot: Gower.

Hayward, Keith. 2012. "Pantomime justice: A cultural, criminological analysis of 'life stage dissolution'" in *Crime Media Culture*. Vol.8 No.2: pp. 213–229.

Innes, Martin. 2014. *Signal Crimes: Social Reactions to Crime, Disorder and Control*. Oxford: Oxford University Press.

Lennon, John, and Foley, Malcolm. 2000. *Dark Tourism: The Attraction of Death and Disaster*. London: Continuum.

Pratt, John. 2007. *Penal Populism*. Abingdon: Routledge.

Pratt, John, Brown, David, Brown, Mark, Hallsworth, Simon, and Morrison, Wayne (Eds.). 2005. *The New Punitiveness: Trends, Theories, Perspectives*. Cullompton, UK: Willan.

Prison Reform Trust. 2018. *Prison: The Facts: Bromley Briefings Summer 2018*. London: Prison Reform Trust. Available at www.prisonreformtrust.org.uk.

Rafter, Nicole. 2000. *Shots in the Mirror: Crime Films and Society*. Oxford: Oxford University Press.

Rafter, Nicole, and Brown, Michelle. 2011. *Criminology Goes to the Movies: Crime Theory and Popular Culture*. New York: New York University Press.

Schlosser, Eric. 1998. "The prison-industrial complex" in *Atlantic*, Dec. Available at www.theatlantic.com.

Silverman, John, and Wilson, David. 2002. *Innocence Betrayed: Paedophilia, the Media and Society*. Cambridge: Polity Press.

Siskel, Gene. 2001. "Kubrick's creative concern" in Phillips, Gene (Ed.), *Stanley Kubrick Interviews*. Mississippi: University of Mississippi. pp. 116–125.

Sontag, Susan. 1977. *On Photography*. New York: Farrar, Straus & Giroux.

Surette, Ray. 1997. *Media, Crime, and Criminal Justice*, 2nd Edition. Belmont: West/ Wadsworth.

Thomas, Terry. 2005. *Sex Crime: Sex Offending and Society*, 2nd Edition. Cullompton: Willan.

Wacquant, Loic. 2005. "The great penal leap backward: incarceration in America from Nixon to Clinton" in Pratt, John, Brown, David, Brown, Mark, Hallsworth, Simon, and Morrison, Wayne (Eds.), *The New Punitiveness: Trends, Theories, Perspectives*. Cullompton: Willan. pp. 3–26.

Wilson, David, and O'Sullivan, Sean. 2004. *Images of Incarceration: Representations of Prison in Film and Television Drama*. Winchester: Waterside Press.

10. *THE WALKING DEAD* AND CRIMINOLOGICAL THEORY

Agnew, Robert. "Foundation for a General Strain Theory of Crime and Delinquency." *Criminology 30* (1992): 47–88.

Agnew, Robert. "The Causes of Animal Abuse." *Theoretical Criminology 2*, no. 2 (1998): 177–209.

Agnew, Robert. "Building on the Foundation of General Strain Theory: Specifying the Types of Strain Most Likely to Lead to Crime and Delinquency." *Journal of Research on Crime and Delinquency 38*, no. 4 (2001): 319–361.

Agnew, Robert. *Why Do Criminals Offend? A General Theory of Crime and Delinquency*. New York: Oxford University Press, 2005.

Agnew, Robert. *Pressured into Crime: An Overview of General Strain Theory*. New York: Oxford University Press, 2006.

Agnew, Robert. "Dire Forecast: A Theoretical Model of the Impact of Climate Change on Crime." *Theoretical Criminology 16*, no. 21 (2012a): 21–41.

Agnew, Robert. *Toward a Unified Criminology: Integrating Assumptions about Crime, People, and Society*. New York: New York University Press, 2012b.

Agnew, Robert, & White, Helene R. "An Empirical Test of General Strain Theory." *Criminology 30*, no. 4 (1992): 475–499.

Bandura, Albert. "Selective Activation and Disengagement of Moral Control." *Journal of Social Issues 46* (1990): 27–46.

Bandura, Albert. "Moral Disengagement in the Perpetration of Inhumanities." *Personality and Social Psychology Review 3* (1999): 193–209.

Bandura, Albert. *Moral Disengagement: How People Do Harm and Live with Themselves*. New York: Worth Publishers, 2016.

Banholzer, Sandra, Kossin, James, & Donner, Simon D. "The Impact of Climate Change on Natural Disasters." In A. Zommers and A. Singh (Eds.), *Reducing Disaster: Early Warning Systems for Climate Change* (pp. 21–49). New York: Springer, 2010.

Brunsma, David L., Overfelt, David, & Picou, Steven J. (Eds.). *The Sociology of Katrina: Perspectives on a Modern Catastrophe*. Lanham, MD: Rowman & Littlefield, 2007.

Cromwell, Paul, Dunham, Roger, Akers, Ronald, & Lanza-Kaduce, Lonn. "Routine Activities and Social Control in the Aftermath of a Natural Catastrophe." *European Journal on Criminal Policy and Research 3*, no. 3 (1995): 56–69.

Felson, Marcus. *Crime and Everyday Life*. Thousand Oaks, CA: Pine Forge Press, 1994.

Frailing, Kelly, Harper, Dee W., & Serpas, Ronal. "Changes and Challenges in Crime and Criminal Justice after Disaster." *American Behavioral Sciences 59*, no. 10 (2015): 1278–1291.

Garland, T., Phillips, N., & Vollum, S. "Gender Politics and *The Walking Dead*: Gendered Violence and the Reestablishment of Patriarchy." *Feminist Criminology 13*, no. 1 (2016). DOI: 10.1177/1557085116635269.

Harmann, B. *The America Syndrome: Apocalypse, War, and Our Call to Greatness*. New York: Seven Stories Press, 2017.

Klein, N. *The Shock Doctrine: The Rise of Disaster Capitalism*. New York: Picador, 2007.

Leitner, M., & Helbich, M. "The Impact of Hurricanes on Crime: A Spatio-temporal Analysis in the City of Houston, Texas." *Cartography and Geographic Information Science 38*, no. 2 (2011): 214–222.

Merton, Robert. "Social Structure and Anomie." *American Sociological Review 3* (1938): 672–682.

Rafter, Nicole, & Brown, Michelle. *Criminology Goes to the Movies: Crime Theory and Popular Culture*. New York: New York University Press, 2011.

Raymen, Thomas. "Living in the End Times through Popular Culture: An Ultra-realist Analysis of *The Walking Dead* as Popular Criminology." *Crime, Media, Culture: An International Journal 14*, no. 3 (2017). DOI: 10/1177/1741659017721277.

Rezaeian, M. "The Association between Natural Disasters and Violence: A Systematic Review of the Literature and a Call for More Epidemiological Studies." *Journal of Research in Medical Sciences: The Official Journal of Isfahan University of Medical Sciences 18*, no. 12 (2013): 1103–1107.

Sampson, Robert J., & Groves, W. Byron. "Community Structure and Crime: Testing Social Disorganization Theory." *American Journal of Sociology 94*, no. 4 (1989): 774–802.

Sampson, Robert J., Raudenbush, Stephen W., & Earls, Felton. "Neighborhoods and Violent Crime: A Multilevel Study of Collective Efficacy." *Science 277*, no. 5328 (1997): 918–924.

Sandin, Per, & Wester, Misse. "The Moral Black Hole." *Ethical Theory and Moral Practice 12*, no. 3 (2009): 291–301.

Solnit, Rebecca. *A Paradise Built in Hell*. New York: Penguin, 2009.

Toby, Jackson. "Social Disorganization and Stake in Conformity: Complementary Factors in the Predatory Behavior of Hoodlums." *Journal of Criminal Law and Criminology 48*, no. 1 (1957): 12–17.

United States House of Representatives. *The Katrina Impact on Crime and The Criminal Justice System in New Orleans*. Hearing before the Subcommittee on Crime,

Terrorism, and Homeland Security of the Committee on the Judiciary, April 10, 2007. Serial No. 110–55.

Varano, S. P., Schafer, J. A., Cancino, J. M., Decker, S. H., & Greene, J. R. "A Tale of Three Cities: Crime and Displacement after Hurricane Katrina." *Journal of Criminal Justice 38* (2010): 42–50.

White, Rob (Ed.). *Climate Change from a Criminological Perspective.* New York: Springer, 2012.

Yar, Majid. *Crime and the Imaginary of Disaster: Post-apocalyptic Fictions and the Crisis of Social Order.* New York: Palgrave Macmillan, 2015.

11. *MR. ROBOT* AND RADICAL CRIMINOLOGY

Banks, James. "Radical Criminology and the Techno-Security-Capitalist Complex." In *Technocrime and Criminological Theory*, edited by Kevin. F. Steinmetz and Matt R. Nobles, 102–115. New York: Routledge, 2018.

Barak, Gregg. *Theft of a Nation: Wall Street Looting and Federal Regulatory Colluding.* Lanham, MD: Rowman & Littlefield, 2012.

Barak, Gregg. *Unchecked Corporate Power: Why the Crimes of Multinational Corporations Are Routinized Away and What We Can Do about It.* New York: Routledge, 2017.

Baudrillard, Jean. *The Consumer Society: Myths and Structures.* Thousand Oaks, CA: SAGE, 1970.

Bell, Daniel. *The Cultural Contradictions of Capitalism: Twentieth Anniversary Edition.* New York: Basic Books, 1996.

Bernard, Thomas J., Jeffrey B. Snipes, and Alexander L. Gerould. *Vold's Theoretical Criminology.* New York: Oxford University Press, 2016.

Bonger, Willem A. *Criminality and Economic Conditions.* Boston: Little, Brown and Company, 1916.

Christie, Nils. *Crime Control as Industry: Towards Gulags, Western Style.* 3rd ed. New York: Routledge, 2000.

Cohen, Stanley. *Folk Devils and Moral Panics: The Creation of the Mods and Rockers.* London: McGibbon and Kee, 1972.

Coleman, Gabriella. *Hacker, Hoaxer, Whistleblower, Spy: The Many Faces of Anonymous.* London: Verso, 2014.

Cooper, Dereck. "On the Concept of Alienation." *International Journal of Contemporary Sociology 28* (1991): 7–26.

Du Bois, William E. B. "The African Roots of War." *Atlantic Monthly* 115 (1915): 707–714.

Engels, Friedrich. *Condition of the Working Class in England.* New York: Macmillan, 1958.

Fanon, Frantz. *The Wretched of the Earth.* New York: Grove Press, 1963.

Giles, Matthew. "The Unusually Accurate Portrait of Hacking on USA's *Mr. Robot*." *Vulture*, July 23, 2015. Accessed June 30, 2018. www.vulture.com.

Hagan, John L. *Who Are the Criminals? The Politics of Crime Policy from the Age of Roosevelt to the Age of Reagan.* Princeton, NJ: Princeton University Press, 2012.

Hall, Stuart, Chas Critcher, Tony Jefferson, John Clarke, and Brian Roberts. *Policing the Crisis: Mugging, the State, and Law and Order.* London: MacMillan Press, 1978.

Harring, Sidney L. *Policing a Class Society.* New Brunswick, NJ: Rutgers University Press, 1983.

Harvey, David. *The Enigma of Capital and the Crises of Capitalism.* New York: Oxford University Press, 2010.

Harvey, David. *Seventeen Contradictions and the End of Capitalism.* New York: Oxford University Press, 2014.

Hobsbawm, Eric. *Bandits.* New York: New Press, 2000.

Israel, Joachim. *Alienation: From Marx to Modern Sociology.* Boston: Allyn & Bacon, 1971.

Lea, John. "Social Crime Revisited." *Theoretical Criminology* 3 (1999): 307–325.

Marx, Karl. "Estranged Labour." In *Economic and Philosophical Manuscripts of 1844.* Marxists Internet Archive. Accessed September 15, 2018. www.marxists.org.

Marx, Karl. *Capital, Vol. 1.* 1867. New York: International Publishers Co., 1967.

Marx, Karl. "The Paris Commune." In *The Civil War in France.* 1871. Marxists Internet Archive. Accessed September 25, 2018. www.marxists.org.

Matthews, Rick. "Marxist Criminology." In *Controversies in Critical Criminology*, edited by Martin Schwartz and Susanne E. Hatty, 1–14. New York: Routledge, 2015.

Meisenhelder, Tom. "Toward a Marxist Analysis of Subjectivity." *Nature, Society, and Thought* 4 (1991): 103–125.

Mills, Charles W. *The Power Elite.* New York: Oxford University Press, 1956.

Moore, Alan. *V for Vendetta.* New York: DC Comics, 1988.

Moynihan, Daniel P. *The Negro Family: The Case for National Action.* Washington, DC: US Department of Labor, 1965.

Murray, Charles. *Losing Ground: American Social Policy, 1950–1980.* New York: Basic Books, 1984.

Palmer, Robert R. *Twelve Who Ruled: The Year of Terror in the French Revolution.* Princeton, NJ: Princeton University Press, 1941.

Pashukanis, Evgeny. *The General Theory of Law and Marxism.* 1924. Marxists Internet Archive. Accessed August 19, 2018. www.marxists.org.

Pavlich, George. "Critical Genres in Radical Criminology in Britain." *British Journal of Criminology* 41 (2001): 150–167.

Pearce, Frank. *Crimes of the Powerful: Marxism, Crime & Deviance.* Chicago: Pluto Press, 1976.

Platt, Tony, Jon Frappier, Gerda Ray, Richard Schauffler, Larry Trujillo, Lynn Cooper, Elliot Currie, and Sidney Harring. *The Iron Fist and the Velvet Glove: An Analysis of the U.S. Police.* 3rd ed. San Francisco: Crime and Social Justice Associates, 1977.

Quinney, Richard. *The Social Reality of Crime.* Piscataway, NJ: Transaction Publishers, 1970.

Quinney, Richard. *Class, State, and Crime.* New York: Longman, 1977.

Rafter, Nicole. "Crime, Film and Criminology: Recent Sex-Crime Movies." *Theoretical Criminology* 11, no. 3 (2007): 403–420.

Rafter, Nicole, and Michelle Brown. *Criminology Goes to the Movies: Crime Theory and Popular Culture*. New York: New York University Press, 2011.

Reed, John. *Ten Days That Shook the World*. New York: International Publishers, 1919.

Reiman, Jeffrey, and Paul Leighton. *The Rich Get Richer and the Poor Get Prison*. 10th ed. Boston: Pearson, 2012.

Rusche, Georg. "Prison Revolts or Social Policy: Lessons from America." 1930. *Social Justice* 13 (1980): 41–44.

Rusche, Georg. "Labor Market and Penal Sanction: Thoughts on the Sociology of Punishment." 1933. *Social Justice* 10 (1978): 2–8.

Rusche, Georg, and Otto Kirchheimer. *Punishment and Social Structure*. New York: Columbia University Press, 1939.

Schwendinger, Herman, and Julia Schwendinger. *Who Killed the Berkeley School? Struggles over Radical Criminology*. Brooklyn: Thought Crimes, 2014.

Selman, Donna, and Paul Leighton. *Punishment for Sale: Private Prisons, Big Business, and the Incarceration Binge*. Lanham, MD: Rowman & Littlefield, 2010.

Spitzer, Steven. "Toward a Marxian Theory of Deviance." *Social Problems* 22, no. 5 (1975): 638–651.

Stein, David. "A Spectre Is Haunting Law and Society: Revisiting Radical Criminology at UC Berkeley." *Social Justice* 40 (2014): 72–84.

Steinmetz, Kevin F. *Hacked: A Radical Approach to Hacker Culture and Crime*. New York: New York University Press, 2016.

Stretesky, Paul B, Michael A. Long, and Michael J. Lynch. *The Treadmill of Crime: Political Economy and Green Criminology*. New York: Routledge, 2013.

Sutherland, Edwin H. *White Collar Crime*. New York: Dryden Press, 1949.

Tatum, Becky. "The Colonial Model as a Theoretical Explanation of Crime and Delinquency." In *African American Perspectives on Crime Causation, Criminal Justice Administration and Prevention*, edited by Anne T. Sulton, 33–52. Englewood, NJ: Sulton Books, 1994.

Turk, Austin. "Law as a Weapon in Social Conflict." *Social Problems* 23, no. 3 (1976): 276–291.

Weber, Max. *The Protestant Ethic and the Spirit of Capitalism*. New York: Scribner, 1958.

Weis, Valeria V. *Marxism and Criminology: A History of Criminal Selectivity*. Chicago: Haymarket Books, 2017.

Yar, Majid. "Computer Crime Control as Industry: Virtual Insecurity and the Market for Private Policing." In *Technologies of InSecurity: The Surveillance of Everyday Life*, edited by Katja F. Aas, Helene O. Gundhus, and Heidi M. Lomell, 189–204. New York: Routledge, 2008.

Zetter, Kim. "How the Real Hackers behind *Mr. Robot* Get It So Right. *Wired*, July 15, 2016. Accessed June 30, 2018. www.wired.com.

12. WHAT'S IN A NAME?

Becker, Howard S. *Outsiders: Studies in the Sociology of Deviance*. New York: Free Press, 1963.

Bernburg, Jón Gunnar, and Marvin D. Krohn. "Labeling, Life Chances, and Adult Crime: The Direct and Indirect Effects of Official Intervention in Adolescence on Crime in Early Adulthood." *Criminology*, 41, no. 4 (2003): 1287–1318.

Bernburg, Jón Gunnar, Marvin D. Krohn, and Craig J. Rivera. "Official Labeling, Criminal Embeddedness, and Subsequent Delinquency: A Longitudinal Test of Labeling Theory." *Journal of Research in Crime and Delinquency*, 43, no. 1 (2006): 67–88.

Columbia Broadcasting System. "About Criminal Minds—TV Show Information." CBS.com. www.cbs.com (Accessed September 19, 2018).

Hirschfield, Paul J. "The Declining Significance of Delinquent Labels in Disadvantaged Urban Communities." *Sociological Forum*, 23, no. 3 (2008): 575–601.

Klein, Malcolm W. "Labeling Theory and Delinquency Policy: An Experimental Test." *Criminal Justice and Behavior*, 13, no. 1 (1986): 47–79.

Lemert, Edwin M. *Social Pathology: A Systematic Approach to the Theory of Sociopathic Behavior.* New York: McGraw-Hill, 1951.

Lemert, Edwin M. "Beyond Mead: The Societal Reaction to Deviance." *Social Problems*, 21, no. 4 (1973): 457–468.

Lilly, J. Robert, Frances T. Cullen, and Richard A. Ball. *Criminological Theory: Context and Consequences.* 5th ed. Thousand Oaks, CA: SAGE , 2011.

Paternoster, Raymond, and Leeann Iovanni. "The Labeling Perspective and Delinquency: An Elaboration of the Theory and an Assessment of the Evidence." *Justice Quarterly*, 6, no. 3 (1989): 359–394.

Tannenbaum, Frank. *Crime and the Community.* Boston: Ginn and Company, 1938.

Zhang, Lening, and Steven F. Messner. "The Severity of Official Punishment for Delinquency and Change in Interpersonal Relations in Chinese Society." *Journal of Research in Crime and Delinquency*, 31, no. 4 (1994): 416–433.

13. PHRASING DEVIANCE

Agnew, Robert, "The Techniques of Neutralization and Violence," *Criminology* 32 (1994): 555–580.

Alvarez, Alexander, "Adjusting to Genocide: The Techniques of Neutralization and the Holocaust," *Social Science History* 21 (1997): 139–178.

Brennan, William C., "Abortion and the Techniques of Neutralization," *Journal of Health and Social Behavior* 15 (1974): 358–365.

Brunner, Thomas A., "Applying Neutralization Theory to Fair Trade Buying Behavior," *International Journal of Consumer Studies* 38 (2014): 200–206.

Bryant, Emily, Emily Brooke Schimke, Hollie Nyseth Brehm, and Christoper Uggen, "Techniques of Neutralization and Identity Work among Accused Genocide Perpetrators," *Social Problems* 65, no.4 (2017): 584–602.

Copelton, Denise A., "'You Are What You Eat': Nutritional Norms, Maternal Deviance, and Neutralization of Women's Prenatal Diets," *Deviant Behavior* 28 (2007): 467–494.

Copes, Heith, "Societal Attachments, Offending Frequency, and Techniques of Neutralization" *Deviant Behavior* 24 (2003): 101–127.

Eliason, Stephen L., and Richard A. Dodder, "Techniques of Neutralization Used by Deer Poachers in the Western United States: A Research Note," *Deviant Behavior* 20 (1999): 233–252.

Heltsley, Martha, and Thomas C. Calhoun, "The Good Mother: Neutralization Techniques Used by Pageant Mothers," *Deviant Behavior* 24 (2003): 81–100.

Hinduja, Sameer, "Neutralization Theory and Online Software Piracy: An Empirical Analysis," *Ethics and Information Technology* 9 (2007): 187–204.

Ingram, Jason R., and Sameer Hinduja, "Neutralizing Music Piracy: An Empirical Examination," *Deviant Behavior* 29 (2008): 334–366.

Kieffer, Scott M., and John J. Sloan III, "Overcoming Moral Hurdles: Using Techniques of Neutralization by White-Collar Suspects as an Interrogation Tool," *Security Journal* 22, no.4 (2009): 317–330.

Klockars, Carl "The Professional Fence" (1974): New York: Free Press.

Landsheer, J. A., H. T. Hart, and W. Kox, "Delinquent Values and Victim Damage: Exploring the Limits of Neutralization Theory," *British Journal of Criminology* 34, no.1 (1994): 44–53.

Liddick, Don, "Techniques of Neutralization and Animal Rights Activists," *Deviant Behavior* 34 (2013): 618–634.

Maruna, Shadd, and Heith Copes, "What Have We Learned from Five Decades of Neutralization Research?," *Crime and Justice* 32 (2005): 221–320.

McKie, Ruth E., "Climate Change Counter Movement Neutralization Techniques: A Typology to Examine the Climate Change Counter Movement," *Sociological Inquiry* 89, no.2 (2018): 288–316.

Minor, W. William, "Techniques of Neutralization: A Reconceptualization and Empirical Examination," *Journal of Research in Crime and Delinquency* 18, no.2 (1981): 295–318.

Mitchell, Jim, Richard A. Dodder, and Terry D. Norris, "Neutralization and Delinquency: A Comparison by Sex and Ethnicity," *Adolescence* 25, no. 98 (1990): 487–497.

Peretti-Watel, Patrick, "Neutralization Theory and the Denial of Risk: Some Evidence from Cannabis Use among French Adolescents" *British Journal of Sociology* 54, no.1 (2003): 21–42.

Piquero, Nicole Leeper, Stephen G. Tibbetts, and Michael B. Blankenship, "Examining the Role of Differential Association and Techniques of Neutralization in Explaining Corporate Crime," *Deviant Behavior* 26 (2005): 159–188.

Priest, Thomas Brian, and John H. McGrath III, "Techniques of Neutralization: Young Adult Marijuana Smokers," *Criminology* 8 (1970): 185–194.

Ribeaud, Denis, and Manuel Eisner, "Are Moral Disengagement, Neutralization Techniques, and Self-Serving Cognitive Distortions the Same? Developing a Unified Scale of Moral Neutralization of Aggression," *International Journal of Conflict and Violence* 4 (2010): 298–315.

Rogers, Joseph W., and M. D. Buffalo, "Neutralization Techniques: Toward a Simplified Measurement Scale," *Pacific Sociological Review* 17, no.3 (1974): 313–331.

Spraitz, Jason D., and Kendra N. Bowen, "Techniques of Neutralization and Persistent Sexual Abuse by Clergy: A Content Analysis of Priest Personnel Files from the Archdiocese of Milwaukee," *Journal of Interpersonal Violence* 31 (2016): 2515–2538.

Strutton, David, Scott J. Vitell, and Lou E. Pelton, "How Consumers May Justify Inappropriate Behavior in Market Settings: An Application on the Techniques of Neutralization," *Journal of Business Research* 30 (1994): 253–260.

Sykes, Gresham M., and David Matza, "Techniques of Neutralization: A Theory of Delinquency," *American Sociological Review* 22, no.6 (1957): 664–670.

Topalli, Volkan, "When Being Good Is Bad: An Expansion of Neutralization Theory," *Criminology* 43 (2005): 797–836.

Ugelvik, Thomas, "Prisoners and Their Victims: Techniques of Neutralization, Techniques of the Self," *Ethnography* 13 (2012): 259–277.

Vasquez, Arthur, and Lynne M. Vieraitis, "'It's Just Paint': Street Taggers' Use of Neutralization Techniques," *Deviant Behavior* 37 (2016): 1179–1195.

Vitell, Scott J., and Stephen J. Grove, "Marketing Ethics and the Techniques of Neutralization," *Journal of Business Ethics* 6 (1987): 433–438.

Wagner, Jascha, D'Janna Hamilton, Tammy L. Anderson, and Veronica F. Rempusheski, "Identity Work, Techniques of Neutralization, and Deviance: Exploring the Relationship among Older Adult Gamblers," *Symbolic Interaction* 40 (2017): 352–377.

14. FIGHTING THE (INVISIBLE) HAND

Bernard, Thomas J. *The Consensus-Conflict Debate: Form and Content in Social Theories.* New York: Columbia University Press, 1983.

Blalock, Hubert. *Towards a Theory of Minority Group Relations.* New York: Capricorn Books, 1967.

Bobo, Lawrence, and Vincent L. Hutchings. "Perceptions of Racial Group Competition: Extending Blumer's Theory of Group Position to a Multiracial Social Context." *American Sociological Review* 61 no. 6 (1996): 951–972.

Chambliss, William J. "The State, the Law, and the Definition of Behavior as Criminal or Delinquent." In *Crime and Criminals: Contemporary and Classic Readings in Criminology,* edited by Frank R. Scarpitti and Amie L. Nielsen, 18–24. Los Angeles: Roxbury Publishing Company, 1999.

Chambliss, William J., and Robert B. Seidman. *Law, Order, and Power.* Reading, MA: Addison Welsey, 1971.

Chambliss, William J., and Marjorie S. Zatz. *Making Law: The State, the Law, and Structural Contradictions.* Bloomington: Indiana University Press, 1993.

Dahrendorf, Ralf. *Class and Class Conflict in Industrial Societies.* Stanford, CA: Stanford University Press, 1959.

Daly, Kathleen, and Meda Chesney-Lind. "Feminism and Criminology." *Justice Quarterly* 5 no. 4 (1988): 497–538.

Eitle, David, Stewart J. D'Alessio, and Lisa Stolzenberg. "Racial Threat and Social Control: A Test of the Political, Economic, and Threat of Black Crime Hypotheses." *Social Forces* 81 no. 2 (2002): 557–576.

Lynch, Michael J., and W. Byron Groves. *A Primer in Radical Criminology*. New York: Harrow and Heston, 1986.

Michalowski, Raymond J. *Order, Law and Crime*. New York: Random House, 1985.

Michalowski Raymond J., and Edward W. Bohlander. "Repression and Criminal Justice in Capitalist America." *Sociological Inquiry* 46 no. 2 (1976): 95–106.

Phillips, Nickie D., and Staci Strobl. *Comic Book Crime: Truth, Justice, and the American Way*. New York: New York University Press, 2013.

Quinney, Richard. *The Social Reality of Crime*. Boston: Little, Brown and Company, 1970.

Ruddell, Rick, and Matthew O. Thomas. "Minority Threat and Police Strength: An Examination of the Golden State." *Police Practice and Research* 11 (2010): 256–273.

Sellin, Thorsten. *Culture Conflict and Crime*. New York: Social Science Research Council, 1938.

Spitzer, Scott. "Toward a Marxian Theory of Deviance." *Social Problems* 22 (1975): 638–651.

Turk, Austin T. *Criminality and the Legal Order*. Chicago: Rand-McNally, 1969.

Vold, Georgmie B. *Theoretical Criminology*. New York: Oxford University Press, 1958.

Vollum, Scott, and Cary D. Adkinson. "The Portrayal of Crime and Justice in the Comic Book Superhero Mythos." *Journal of Criminal Justice and Popular Culture* 10 no. 2 (2003): 96–108.

15. MASCULINITY AND *IT'S ALWAYS SUNNY IN PHILADELPHIA*

Balcom, Dennis A. "Absent Fathers: Effects on Abandoned Sons." *Journal of Men's Studies* 6, no. 3 (1998): 283–296.

Barak, Gregg, Paul Leighton, and Jeanne Flavin. *Class, Race, Gender, & Crime* (3rd ed.). Lanham, MD: Rowman & Littlefield, 2010.

Bernard, Thomas J., Jeffrey B. Snipes, and Alexander L. Gerould. *Vold's Theoretical Criminology* (7th ed.). New York: Oxford University Press, 2016.

Bird, Sharon R. "Welcome to the Men's Club: Homosociality and the Maintenance of Hegemonic Masculinity." *Gender and Society* 10, no. 2 (1996): 120–132.

Carrington, Kerry, and John Scott. "Masculinity, Rurality and Violence." *British Journal of Criminology* 48 (2008): 641–666.

Colburn, Randall. "'No Hugging, No Learning': 20 Years on Seinfeld's Mantra Still Looms Large." *Guardian*, May 10, 2018. Accessed August 7, 2018. www.theguardian.com.

Connell, Raewyn W. *Gender and Power*. Stanford, CA: Stanford University Press, 1987.

Connell, Raewyn W. "On Hegemonic Masculinity and Violence: Response to Jefferson and Hall." *Theoretical Criminology* 6 no. 1 (2002): 89–99.

Connell, Raewyn W., and James W. Messerschmidt. "Hegemonic Masculinity: Rethinking the Concept." *Gender & Society* 19 no. 6 (2005): 829–859.

Flavin, Jeanne. "Feminism for the Mainstream Criminologist: An Invitation . . . ." In *The Criminal Justice System and Women: Offenders, Prisoners, Victims, & Workers* (3rd ed.), edited by Barbara R. Price and Natalie J. Sokoloff. New York: McGraw-Hill, 2004.

Giddens, Anthony. *The Constitution of Society*. Cambridge, MA: Polity, 1984.

Johnson, Laura. "The Not So Sweet Dee: A Feminist Analysis of Deandra Reynolds in *It's Always Sunny in Philadelphia*." Presented at the SEWSA 2016 Intersectionality in the New Millennium: An Assessment of Culture, Power, and Society conference, Rockhill, SC, April 2016.

Katz, Jackson, Jason Young, Jeremy Earp, and Sut Jhally. "Though Guise: Violence, Media & the Crisis in Masculinity" [documentary]. Northampton, MA: Media Education Foundation, 1999.

Kimmel, Michael. *Manhood in America*. New York: Oxford University Press, 2018.

Kruttschnit, Candance. "2015 Presidential Address to the American Society of Criminology." *Criminology* 54 no. 1 (2016): 8–29.

Ladenburg, Kenneth. "Illuminating Whiteness and Racial Prejudice through Humor in *It's Always Sunny in Philadelphia*'s 'The Gang Gets Racist.'" *Journal of Popular Culture* 48 no. 5 (2015): 859–877.

LaRossa, Ralph. "'Until the Ball Glows in the Twilight': Fatherhood, Baseball, and the Game of Playing Catch." In *Fathering through Sport and Leisure*, edited by Tess Kay, 39–55. London/New York: Routledge, 2009.

Leonard, Daniel. "Psychoanalyzing the Game of Games." In *Always Sunny and Philosophy: The Gang Gets Analyzed*, edited by Roger Hunt and Robert Arp, 55–64. Chicago: Open Court, 2015.

Levi, Michael. "Masculinities and White-Collar Crime." In *Just Boys Doing Business? Men, Masculinities and Crime*, edited by Tim Newburn and Elizabeth A. Stanko, 234–252. New York: Routledge, 1994.

Lonsway, Kimberly A., and Louise F. Fitzgerald. "Rape Myths: In Review." *Psychology of Women Quarterly* 18 no. 2 (1994): 133–164.

Marganski, Alison J. "Feminist Theory and Technocrime." In *Technocrime and Criminological Theory*, edited by Kevin F. Steinmetz and Matt R. Nobles, 11–34. New York: Routledge, 2015.

Messerschmidt, James W. *Capitalism, Patriarchy and Crime: Towards a Socialist Feminist Criminology*. Totowa, NJ: Rowman & Littlefield, 1986.

Messerschmidt, James W. *Masculinities and Crime: A Critique and Re-conceptualisation of Theory*. Lanham, MD: Rowman & Littlefield, 1993.

Messerschmidt, James W. "Men, Masculinities and Crime." In *Handbook of Studies on Men and Masculinities*, edited by Michael S. Kimmel, Jeff Hearn, and Raewyn W. Connell. Thousand Oaks, CA: SAGE, 2005.

Miller, Jody. "Up It Up: Gender and the Accomplishment of Street Robbery." *Criminology* 36 no. 1 (1998): 37–66.

Miller, Jody. "The Strengths and Limits of 'Doing Gender' for Understanding Street Crime." *Theoretical Criminology* 6 (2002): 433–460.

Miller, Jody. "Feminist Criminology." In *Controversies in Critical Criminology*, edited by Martin D. Schwartz and Susanne E. Hatty. Cincinnati: Anderson Publishing, 2003.

Rafter, Nicole. "Crime, Film and Criminology: Recent Sex-Crime Movies." *Theoretical Criminology* 11 no. 3 (2007): 403–420.

Rafter, Nicole, and Michelle Brown. *Criminology Goes to the Movies: Crime Theory and Popular Culture.* New York: NYU Press, 2011.

Ryan, Kathryn M. "The Relationship between Rape Myths and Sexual Scripts: The Social Construction of Rape." *Sex Roles* 65 no. 11–12 (2011): 774–782.

Shakefire.com. "Rob McElhenney (*It's Always Sunny in Philadelphia*)." September 15, 2011. Accessed July 20, 2017. http://shakefire.com.

Strain, Megan L., Amanda L. Martens, and Donald A. Saucier. "'Rape Is the New Black': Humor's Potential for Reinforcing and Subverting Rape Culture." *Translational Issues in Psychological Science* 2 no. 1 (2016): 86–95.

Wray, Daniel D. "Talking Ten Years of 'It's Always Sunny in Philadelphia' with Two of Its Stars." *Vice,* November 19, 2015. Accessed July 20, 2017. www.vice.com.

16. RACE, CRIME, AND JUSTICE IN *AMERICAN CRIME*

Alexander, M. (2010). *The New Jim Crow: Mass Incarceration in the Age of Colorblindness.* New York: Free Press.

Anyon, Y., Jenson, J. M., Altschul, I., Farrar, J., McQueen, J., Greer, E., Downing, B., & Simmons, J. (2014). The persistent effect of race and the promise of alternatives to suspension in school discipline outcomes. *Children and Youth Services Review, 44,* 379–386.

Barak, G. (2011). Media and crime. In DeKeseredy, W. S., & Dragiewicz, M. (eds.), *Routledge Handbook of Critical Criminology,* 373–386. New York: Routledge.

Barkan, S. E. (2018). *Race, Crime, and Justice: The Continuing American Dilemma.* New York: Oxford University Press.

Barkan, S. E., & Cohn, S. F. (1994). Racial prejudice and support for the death penalty by whites. *Journal of Research in Crime and Delinquency, 31*(2), 202–209.

Barkan, S. E., & Cohn, S. F. (1998). Racial prejudice and support by whites for police use of force: A research note. *Justice Quarterly, 15*(4), 743–753.

Barkan, S. E., & Cohn, S. F. (2005). On reducing white support for the death penalty: A pessimistic appraisal. *Criminology & Public Policy, 4*(1), 39–44.

Barkan, S. E., & Cohn, S. F. (2005). Why whites favor spending more money to fight crime: The role of racial prejudice. *Social Problems, 52*(2), 300–314.

Beck, A. J., & Blumstein, A. (2018). Racial disproportionality in US state prisons: Accounting for the effects of racial and ethnic differences in criminal involvement, arrests, sentencing, and time served. *Journal of Quantitative Criminology, 34*(3), 853–883.

Bishop, D. M., & Frazier, C. E. (1996). Race effects in juvenile justice decision-making: Findings of a statewide analysis. *Journal of Criminal Law and Criminology, 86,* 392–414.

Blumstein, A. (1982). On the racial disproportionality of United States' prison populations. *Journal of Criminal Law & Criminology, 73*(3), 1259–1281.

Brown, K. R. (2009). *The Color of Crime. 2nd Edition.* New York: New York University Press.

Bynum, T. S. (1982). Release on recognizance: Substantive or superficial reform? *Criminology, 20*(1), 67–82.

Callanan, V. J. (2012). Media consumption, perceptions of crime risk and fear of crime: Examining race/ethnic differences. *Sociological Perspectives, 55*(1), 93–115.

Carson, E. A. (2018). *Prisoners in 2016*. Washington, DC: US Dept. of Justice, Bureau of Justice Statistics.

Chermak, S. M. (1994). Body count news: How crime is presented in the news media. *Justice Quarterly, 11*(4), 561–582.

Chin, W. Y. (2016). Racial cumulative disadvantage: The cumulative effects of racial bias at multiple decision points in the criminal justice system. *Wake Forest Journal of Law & Policy, 6,* 441–458.

Chiricos, T., & Eschholz, S. (2002). The racial and ethnic typification of crime and the criminal typification of race and ethnicity in local television news. *Journal of Research in Crime and Delinquency, 39*(4), 400–420.

Chiricos, T., Eschholz, S., & Gertz, M. (1997). Crime, news and fear of crime: Toward an identification of audience effects. *Social Problems, 44*(3), 342–357.

Cisneros, J. D. (2008). Contaminated communities: The metaphor of "immigrant as pollutant" in media representations of immigration. *Rhetoric and Public Affairs,* 569–601.

Costenbader, V., & Markson, S. (1998). School suspension: A study with secondary school students. *Journal of School Psychology, 36*(1), 59–82.

Dixon, T. L. (2017). Good guys are still always in white? Positive change and continued misrepresentation of race and crime on local television news. *Communication Research, 44*(6), 775–792.

Donovan, K. M., & Klahm, C. F., IV (2015). The role of entertainment media in perceptions of police use of force. *Criminal Justice and Behavior, 42*(12), 1261–1281.

Du Bois, W. E. B. (1899). *The Philadelphia Negro: a social study*. Boston: Ginn and Company.

Duwe, G. (2000). Body-count journalism: The presentation of mass murder in the news media. *Homicide Studies, 4*(4), 364–399.

Ebert, R. (2010). Robbing banks is the neighborhood business. www.rogerebert.com.

Elliott, D. S. (1994). Serious violent offenders: Onset, developmental course, and termination—American Society of Criminology 1993 presidential address. *Criminology, 32*(1), 1–21.

Eschholz, S. (1997). The media and fear of crime: A survey of the research. *University of Florida Journal of Law and Public Policy, 9,* 37–60.

Eschholz, S. (2002). Racial composition of television offenders and viewers' fear of crime. *Critical Criminology, 11*(1), 41–60.

Eschholz, S., Chiricos, T., & Gertz, M. (2003). Television and fear of crime: Program types, audience traits, and the mediating effect of perceived neighborhood racial composition. *Social Problems, 50*(3), 395–415.

Esses, V. M., Medianu, S., & Lawson, A. S. (2013). Uncertainty, threat, and the role of the media in promoting the dehumanization of immigrants and refugees. *Journal of Social Issues, 69*(3), 518–536.

Federico, C. M., & Aguilera, R. (2018). The distinct pattern of relationships between the Big Five and racial resentment among White Americans. *Social Psychological and Personality Science*, *10*(2), 274–284.

Feldman, S., & Huddy, L. (2005). Racial resentment and white opposition to race-conscious programs: Principles or prejudice? *American Journal of Political Science*, *49*(1), 168–183.

Gabbidon, S. L., & Greene, H. T. (Eds.). (2013). *Race, Crime, and Justice: A Reader*. New York: Routledge.

Gilliam, F. D., Jr., Iyengar, S., Simon, A., & Wright, O. (1996). Crime in black and white: The violent, scary world of local news. *Harvard International Journal of Press/Politics*, *1*(3), 6–23.

Graziano, L. M. (2018). News media and perceptions of police: a state-of-the-art review. *Policing: An International Journal of Police Strategies & Management*, *42*(2), 209–225.

Hafner, J. (2016). How Michael Brown's death, two years ago, pushed #BlackLivesMatter into a movement. *USA Today*. www.usatoday.com.

Hagan, J., & Palloni, A. (1999). Sociological criminology and the mythology of Hispanic immigration and crime. *Social Problems*, *46*(4), 617–632.

Hawdon, J. E. (2001). The role of presidential rhetoric in the creation of a moral panic: Reagan, Bush, and the war on drugs. *Deviant Behavior*, *22*(5), 419–445.

Hayes, R. M. L., & Luther, K. (2018). *#Crime: Social Media, Crime and the Criminal Legal System*. New York: Springer.

Heim, J. (2017). Recounting a day of rage, hate, violence and death. *Washington Post*. www.washingtonpost.com.

Hindelang, M. J., Hirschi, T., & Weis, J. G. (1979). Correlates of delinquency: The illusion of discrepancy between self-report and official measures. *American Sociological Review*, *44*(6), 995–1014.

James, L., Klinger, D., & Vila, B. (2014). Racial and ethnic bias in decisions to shoot seen through a stronger lens: Experimental results from high-fidelity laboratory simulations. *Journal of Experimental Criminology*, *10*(3), 323–340.

Jones, C. E. (2013). Give us free: Addressing racial disparities in bail determinations. *New York University Journal of Legislation and Public Policy*, *16*, 919–961.

King, G., Iwanyk, B., & Affleck, B. (2010). *The Town*. USA. Warner Bros.

Klein, A., & Smith, M. (2018). Killing of Mollie Tibbetts in Iowa inflames immigration debate. *New York Times*. www.nytimes.com.

Kochel, T. R., Wilson, D. B., & Mastrofski, S. D. (2011). Effect of suspect race on officers' arrest decisions. *Criminology*, *49*(2), 473–512.

Lee, H. (1960). *To Kill a Mockingbird*. New York: J.B. Lippincott.

Lee, J. G., Paternoster, R., & Rocque, M. (2016). Capital case processing in Georgia after *McCleskey*: More of the same. In Keys, D. P., & Maratea, R. J. (eds.), *Race and the Death Penalty: The Legacy of "McCleskey v. Kemp"* (pp. 89–108). Boulder, CO: Lynne Rienner.

Light, M. T., & Miller, T. (2018). Does undocumented immigration increase violent crime? *Criminology, 56*(2), 370–401.

Losen, D. J., & Skiba, R. J. (2010). Suspended education: Urban middle schools in crisis. Civil Rights Project. https://escholarship.org/uc/item/8fh0s5dv.

Marion, N. E., & Oliver, W. M. (2012). *The Public Policy of Crime and Criminal Justice.* Upper Saddle River, NJ: Pearson.

Mastrorocco, N., & Minale, L. (2018). *News Media and Crime Perceptions: Evidence from a Natural Experiment.* IZA Discussion Paper No. 11491. https://ssrn.com/abstract=3170280.

McCarthy, J. (2017). Americans more positive about effects of immigration. Gallup. https://news.gallup.com.

McFadden, A. C., Marsh, G. E., Price, B. J., & Hwang, Y. (1992). A study of race and gender bias in the punishment of school children. *Education and Treatment of Children*, 140–146.

Mitchell, O., & Caudy, M. S. (2015). Examining racial disparities in drug arrests. *Justice Quarterly, 32*(2), 288–313.

Moore-Berg, S., Karpinski, A., & Plant, E. A. (2017). Quick to the draw: How suspect race and socioeconomic status influences shooting decisions. *Journal of Applied Social Psychology, 47*(9), 482–491.

Oliver, M. B. (1994). Portrayals of crime, race, and aggression in "reality-based" police shows: A content analysis. *Journal of Broadcasting & Electronic Media, 38*(2), 179–192.

Oliver, M. B. (2003). African American men as "criminal and dangerous": Implications of media portrayals of crime on the "criminalization" of African American men. *Journal of African American Studies, 7*(2), 3–18.

Ousey, G. C., & Kubrin, C. E. (2018). Immigration and crime: Assessing a contentious issue. *Annual Review of Criminology, 1*, 63–84.

Paternoster, R., & Brame, R. (2008). Reassessing race disparities in Maryland capital cases. *Criminology, 46*(4), 971–1008.

Peters, J., & Singleton, J. (1997). *Rosewood.* USA. Warner Bros.

Pfaff, J. (2017). *Locked In: The True Causes of Mass Incarceration—and How to Achieve Real Reform.* New York: Basic Books.

Rafter, N. (2007). Crime, film and criminology: Recent sex-crime movies. *Theoretical Criminology, 11*(3), 403–420.

Rafter, N. H., & Brown, M. (2011). *Criminology Goes to the Movies: Crime Theory and Popular Culture.* NYU Press.

Rainville, G. A., & Smith, S. K. (2003). *Juvenile Felony Defendants in Criminal Courts.* Washington, DC: US Dept of Justice, Bureau of Justice Statistics.

Reinarman, C., & Levine, H. G. (Eds.). (1997). *Crack in America: Demon Drugs and Social Justice.* Berkeley: University of California Press.

Rickford, R. (2016). Black lives matter: Toward a modern practice of mass struggle. *New Labor Forum, 25*(1), 34–42.

Rocque, M. (2010). Office discipline and student behavior: Does race matter? *American Journal of Education, 116*(4), 557–581.

Sampson, R. J., Morenoff, J. D., & Raudenbush, S. (2005). Social anatomy of racial and ethnic disparities in violence. *American Journal of Public Health, 95*(2), 224–232.

Simon, J. (1985). Tennessee v. Garner: The fleeing felon rule. *Saint Louis University Law Journal, 30,* 1259–1277.

Skiba, R. J., Horner, R. H., Chung, C. G., Rausch, M. K., May, S. L., & Tobin, T. (2011). Race is not neutral: A national investigation of African American and Latino disproportionality in school discipline. *School Psychology Review, 40*(1), 85–107.

Skiba, R. J., Michael, R. S., Nardo, A. C., & Peterson, R. L. (2002). The color of discipline: Sources of racial and gender disproportionality in school punishment. *Urban Review, 34*(4), 317–342.

Spohn, C. (2015). Race, crime, and punishment in the twentieth and twenty-first centuries. *Crime and Justice, 44*(1), 49–97.

Stark, L. (2018). New trial upheld for Adnan Syed of "Serial." *New York Times.* www.nytimes.com.

Tennessee v. Garner, 105 S. Ct. 1694 (1985).

Tonry, M. H. (2011). *Punishing Race: A Continuing American Dilemma.* New York: Oxford University Press.

Wang, X. (2012). Undocumented immigrants as perceived criminal threat: A test of the minority threat perspective. *Criminology, 50*(3), 743–776.

Warren, P., Tomaskovic-Devey, D., Smith, W., Zingraff, M., & Mason, M. (2006). Driving while black: Bias processes and racial disparity in police stops. *Criminology, 44*(3), 709–738.

Young, V. (2006). Demythologizing the "Criminalblackman": The carnival mirror. In Peterson, R. D., Krivo, L. J., & Hagan, J. (eds.), *The Many Colors of Crime: Inequalities of Race, Ethnicity, and Crime in America* (pp. 54–66). New York: NYU Press.

Zatz, M. S., & Smith, H. (2012). Immigration, crime, and victimization: Rhetoric and reality. *Annual Review of Law and Social Science, 8,* 141–159.

Jonathan A. Grubb is Assistant Professor in the Department of Criminal Justice and Criminology at Georgia Southern University. He received his PhD in criminal justice from Sam Houston State University in 2015, during which time he worked with the Crime Victims Institute to investigate victimization within Texas. He currently conducts research on the spatiotemporal clustering of crime, victimization of vulnerable populations, perceptions and attitudes of professionals working with victims of domestic violence as well as human trafficking, and arson within urban environments.

Chad Posick is Associate Professor of Criminal Justice and Criminology at Georgia Southern University. He teaches in the areas of victimology, statistics, and quantitative research methods. His research focuses on the causes and consequences of victimization and on violence prevention. He is a member of the Scholars Strategy Network and the Health Criminology Research Consortium.

ABOUT THE CONTRIBUTORS

JAMIE BENNETT is Deputy Director in HM Prisons and Probation Service in England and Wales, currently Head of Operational Security. Along with holding a number of other senior positions, he has been governor of four prisons, including Grendon, the only British prison to operate entirely as a series of psychotherapeutic communities, and Long Lartin, a high-security prison. Dr. Bennett is also a Research Associate at University of Oxford. He has been editor of the *Prison Service Journal* since 2004, published over 100 articles and reviews, and produced six books, including *The Working Lives of Prison Managers, Handbook on Prisons* (with Yvonne Jewkes and Ben Crewe), and *The Penal System: An Introduction* (with Michael Cavadino, James Dignan, and George Mair). He is currently completing his latest book, titled *Prisoners on Prison Films*, which will be published by Palgrave MacMillan.

PATRICK Q. BRADY is Assistant Professor in the Department of Criminology at the University of West Georgia. He received his PhD in Criminal Justice from Sam Houston State University in 2017. His research interests focus on reducing burnout among criminal justice professionals and improving institutional responses to intimate partner stalking and strangulation. He is the recipient of the 2018 Academy of Criminal Justice Science's New Scholar Award for the Victimology division. His recently published work on these topics has appeared in the *Journal of Criminal Justice, Criminal Justice and Behavior*, and *Police Quarterly*. You can follow him (legally) on Twitter @Patrickology_.

CHRISTOPHER BREWER is a doctoral student of sociology in the Department of Sociology, Anthropology and Social Work at Kansas State University. His main research and teaching interests include critical criminology, technocrime, policing, and research methods.

JOHN A. BROWNE is Assistant Professor of Criminal Justice in the Department of Social, Cultural, and Justice Studies at the University of Tennessee Chattanooga. He received an MSCJ in criminal justice and is currently a doctoral student in the UTC Learning and Leadership Program. His research interests include violent crime and modern policing issues. He has published in *Feminist Criminology* and *International Journal of Offender Therapy and Comparative Criminology*. As a former police officer, he attempts to link his professional experience with the academic world.

ALEXANDRA CAMPBELL is Associate Professor of Sociology in the Department of Society, Culture, and Languages at the University of New England.

ANGELA M. COLLINS is Assistant Professor at the University of Central Missouri. She received her PhD in criminal justice from Sam Houston State University in August of 2016. She received her BS in sociology and criminology and her MS in criminology from Missouri State University. Her primary research interests include juvenile justice, juvenile delinquency, criminology, theory testing, and longitudinal research.

ANDREA DEKESEREDY received her bachelor's in social work from Ryerson University in Toronto and her master's in social work from West Virginia University. She is currently running after a toddler in Edmonton, Alberta, but she hopes to return to school in the near future and complete a PhD. Her research interests include sexual inequality, social policy and social control, digital humanities, and popular culture.

PATRICIA DEKESEREDY is a Clinical Research Specialist at WVU Medicine, Morgantown. After many years of clinical work as a registered nurse, she received her Master of Science in Nursing from York University in Toronto. Her published work focuses on healthcare disparities and health policy in West Virginia. She specializes in qualitative methods, with a special interest in visual methods.

WALTER S. DEKESEREDY is Anna Deane Carlson Endowed Chair of Social Sciences, Director of the Research Center on Violence, and Professor of Sociology at West Virginia University. He has published 26 books, over 110 scientific journal articles, and 86 scholarly book chapters on violence against women and other social problems. In 2008, the Institute on Violence, Abuse and Trauma gave him the Linda Saltzman Memorial Intimate Partner Violence Researcher Award. He also jointly received the 2004 Distinguished Scholar Award from the American Society of Criminology's (ASC) Division on Women and Crime and the 2007 inaugural UOIT Research Excellence Award. In 1995, he received the Critical Criminologist of the Year Award from the ASC's Division on Critical Criminology (DCC), and, in 2008 the DCC gave him the Lifetime Achievement Award. In 2014, he received the Critical Criminal Justice Scholar Award from the Academy of Criminal Justice Sciences' (ACJS) Section on Critical Criminal Justice, and, in 2015, he received the Career Achievement Award from the ASC's Division on Victimology. In 2017, he received the Impact Award from the ACJS's section on Victimology and the Robert Jerrin Book Award from the ASC's Division on Victimology.

ASHLEY K. FANSHER is Assistant Professor of Criminal Justice and Criminology in the School of Social Sciences at Avila University. Her research interests focus broadly on victimology, including sexual assault among college students and child abuse and neglect, along with technology-facilitated victimization. Her work has been published in *Crime & Delinquency, Journal of Interpersonal Violence, Law Enforcement Executive Forum*, and *Deviant Behavior*.

MICHAEL FIDDLER is a Senior Lecturer in Criminology at the University of Greenwich. Michael's PhD thesis explored the production of space within and around prisons. His published research explores the ways in which space, architecture, and visual arts coalesce to inform understandings of crime and punishment. His current research project sees him explore a "ghost criminology" that is informed by Derrida's notion of hauntology.

TAMMY S. GARLAND is Professor of Criminal Justice in the Department of Social, Cultural, and Justice Studies at the University of Tennessee at Chattanooga. Her current research emphasis includes victimization of the homeless, women, and children; gender, crime, and popular culture; and drug policy issues. Her publications can be found in *American Journal of Criminal Justice, Criminal Justice Policy Review, Criminal Justice Studies, Feminist Criminology,* and *Journal of Aggression, Maltreatment, & Trauma.* She is the co-author of *A Unified Theory of Justice and Crime: Justice That Love Gives.*

JONATHON HALL is a law student in the Walter F. George School of Law at Mercer University. He also is an Adjunct Professor at Georgia Southern University, where he received a bachelor's of science degree in psychology and a master's of science degree in criminology. His research interests include forensic psychology, interrogation processes, cybercrime, and the interaction of psychology, criminology, and the justice system, specifically within the process of voir dire and eyewitness testimony.

DON L. KURTZ is Department Head and Professor of Social Work in the Department of Sociology, Anthropology, and Social Work at Kansas State University. His research interests include police stress, youth violence, police storytelling and narrative development. He has been published in *Crime and Delinquency, Deviant Behavior, Criminal Justice Review, Journal of Research in Crime and Delinquency, Feminist Criminology, Critical Criminology, Victims and Offender and Women,* and *Criminal Justice,* among others. Prior to pursuing an academic career, Dr. Kurtz was employed as a social worker in the juvenile justice system.

CANDACE G. MURPHY is a Lecturer of Criminal Justice in the Social, Cultural, and Justice Studies Department at the University of Tennessee at Chattanooga. Her research interests include perceptions of police use of force, depictions of law enforcement in pop culture, and overall views of police forces and their policies.

NICKIE D. PHILLIPS is a Professor in the Sociology and Criminal Justice Department at St. Francis College in Brooklyn, N.Y. She is author of *Beyond Blurred Lines: Rape Culture in Popular Media* and co-author of *Comic Book Crime: Truth, Justice, and the American Way.*

ANDREA LASSELLE-ROCQUE is Emergency Response Training Coordinator for the Bureau of Remediation and Waste Management at the

Maine Department of Environmental Protection. She holds a degree in geological sciences from the University of Maine.

MICHAEL ROCQUE is Associate Professor of Sociology at Bates College. His research interests include life-course criminology, race, crime, and justice, and crime prevention.

ALEX T. SIMPSON is a Senior Lecturer in the Department of Security Studies and Criminology at Macquarie University, Sydney. Prior to completing his PhD at the University of York in 2015, Dr. Simpson was awarded an ESRC studentship, which focused on questions of harm and deviance in the City of London's financial services industry. Following graduation, he spent three years as a Lecturer in Criminology at the University of Brighton. While at Brighton, Dr. Simpson was on the management board for the Centre for Spatial, Cultural and Environmental Politics and was heavily involved in the Centre for Transforming Gender and Sexuality. This involvement brought new questions of space and place making as well as gendered performativity and embodiment to his research. He currently investigates interrelated themes of class, gender, embodiment, and organizational practice to explore the embedded, and often hidden, cultures of finance. Through ethnographic research methods, Dr. Simpson's work develops an "on-the-ground" account of the everyday practices, thought processes, and common assumptions that both legitimize and neutralize the production of social harm connected to finance work. Alongside continuing and ongoing research interests in the cultures of finance, he has also been part of a British Academy–funded ethnographic study of class-based experiences of dirt and dirty work.

BRIAN P. SCHAEFER is Assistant Professor of Criminology and Criminal Justice at Indiana University Southeast. His research interests include criminological theory, deviance, and the role of police in society. To this end he has conducted research on body-worn cameras, procedural justice training, hot-spots and pulling-levers crime reduction strategies, and narcotics policing. His research has been published in *Justice Quarterly*, *Theoretical Criminology*, and the *British Journal of Criminology*, among others.

KEVIN F. STEINMETZ is Associate Professor in the Department of Sociology, Anthropology, and Social Work at Kansas State University. His areas of interest include technocrime, critical criminology, inequality and criminal justice, and popular culture. His work appears in peer-reviewed journals like *British Journal of Criminology*, *Theoretical Criminology*, *Critical Criminology*, and others. He has also authored or edited scholarly books including *Hacked: A Radical Approach to Hacker Culture and Crime*, *Cybercrime & Society* (3rd ed., co-authored with Majid Yar), and *Technocrime and Criminological Theory* (co-edited with Matt Nobles).

SCOTT VOLLUM is Associate Professor and Department Head of Anthropology, Sociology, & Criminology at the University of Minnesota Duluth. At this time, his primary areas of academic interest and research are violence, the death penalty, restorative justice, media and crime, and moral disengagement. He is currently working on a variety of research projects including an evaluation of a restorative justice program for domestic violence offenders and an examination of death penalty attitudes and the impact of wrongful convictions in capital cases. He is author of *Last Words and The Death Penalty: Voices of the Condemned and Their Co-Victims* and co-author of *The Death Penalty: Constitutional Issues, Commentaries and Case Briefs*. His previous research has been published in a variety of scholarly journals, his most recent ("Gender Politics and The Walking Dead: Gendered Violence and the Reestablishment of Patriarchy") in the journal *Feminist Criminology*, with the same co-authors as his chapter in this book. He lives in Duluth with his son, Kai, and their dogs, Milo and Cooper.

STEPHEN WAKEMAN is a Senior Lecturer in Criminology at Liverpool John Moores University. He is known as an ethnographer, but he retains a strong interest in the criminological significance of entertainment media—specifically, the ways in which popular cultural forms like TV shows, movies, games, and comics represent, redirect, and reshape ongoing criminological debates. He has published extensively in this area around shows such as *The Wire*, *Boardwalk Empire*, and, most recently, *Breaking Bad*. He tweets as @Steve_Wakeman.

INDEX

Page numbers in *italics* indicate Figures